WESTMAR COLLE

THE FOREIGN POWERS IN LATIN AMERICA

A Rand Corporation Research Study
A list of other Rand publications appears at the back of this book.

THE
FOREIGN POWERS
IN LATIN
AMERICA

HERBERT GOLDHAMER

PRINCETON UNIVERSITY PRESS
PRINCETON, NEW JERSEY

This book has been composed in Linotype Times Roman
Printed in the United States of America
by Princeton University Press

For Jody

Preface

THE attention given to United States relations with Latin América has led, especially in the United States, to some neglect of the important part played in Latin America in recent years by the non-hemispheric nations. Perhaps the present study will help redress the balance.

My aim has been to provide a compact account of the political, economic, and cultural activities of the foreign powers in Latin America in the postwar period, but more especially during the last decade. Because the study provides an opportunity to analyze how countries with different national interests, policies, and capabilities have acted in a single world region, it will, I hope, be of value to students of interstate behavior even though they have no special interest in Latin America. Indeed, the reader should understand that this is an examination of the interests and activities of the foreign powers in Latin America, not a study of the foreign policies of the Latin republics. These are touched on only to the degree necessary to make the principal subject intelligible.

It was hardly possible to write this book, dealing as it does with the relations of some fifteen countries with the more than twenty states of the Latin American and Caribbean region and covering a broad range of political, economic, and cultural phenomena, without leaving only too evident lacunae imposed both by the absence of specialistic studies in a number of fields as well as by "mi ignorancia casi enciclopédica" in various areas. I would not have undertaken so large a task had I not believed that the reader would find enough new points of interest to compensate for those omissions or lapses that may disappoint him. The reader may discover that the points of special interest to him are sometimes embedded in rather dense thickets of information. I felt, however, that a certain amount of fine detail was required to render an accurate account of the subject and to provide the background for more general assertions. Each reader can best decide for himself which details sharpen and which blur the contours of the subjects of greatest interest to him.

The study proceeds in the following manner.

Part I deals with the interests and objectives of the foreign nations in Latin America. When I say "nations," I mean of course their governments and relevant private groups. These I have often distinguished where the nature of the discussion required and the data permitted. But I have not hesitated to speak simply of "British," "French," "United States" objectives or achievements where it will be perfectly clear that I am speaking in some cases of the governments of these countries, in other cases of the governments and their business classes, or, in still others, of the latter alone or of other private groups.

Part II discusses the instrumentalities and resources that have been employed or that have unintentionally contributed, both positively and negatively, to the pursuit of these ends.

Part III evaluates the extent to which the foreign powers achieved their goals (Chapter 12). In Chapter 13 I have imposed on the reader some reflections in which I give special attention to the experience of the United States in Latin America during the decade of the Alliance for Progress. As often happens with reflections, they have sometimes taken me well beyond my data.

The apparently simple three-part scheme of this study occasioned some expositional difficulties. In the first place, the usual circularity of means and ends sometimes made the distinction between objectives and instrumentalities a little arbitrary. Some ends are means to ulterior ends, and some means acquire a value in themselves. In addition, the threefold division of interests, instrumentalities, and results often faced me with the necessity of dealing with the same set of events from three different standpoints. In order to avoid undue repetition, I have, on occasion, departed from a strict adherence to the scheme of presentation.

viii

I want to express my indebtedness to the Rand Corporation which provided Corporation funds to develop a Rand program in Latin American studies, of which this work is one product.

During the early stages of the study I benefited greatly from discussions with François Bourricaud, Fabio Luca Cavazza, Mario Einaudi, Joseph Hasson, Yoshinori Ohara, and Albrecht von Gleich. Naturally, they are not responsible for statements in the present study except where papers by them are specifically cited.

My colleagues Luigi Einaudi, Fred Iklé, Nathan Leites, Richard Maullin, David Ronfeldt, and Alfred Stepan gave me helpful comments on various sections of the manuscript. During the first stage of the study David N. Holmes, Jr., provided valuable assistance. Tables 9.1, 9.2, and 11.2 are largely his work. I am particularly indebted to Geraldine-Marie Petty for unearthing and checking elusive data and sources and also for her careful review of the entire manuscript. To Doris Corbin I am grateful for further editing of the manuscript. My wife, Joan, assembled much of the material for Chapter 9 on cultural programs. Both the reader and I are in her debt for her unremitting insistence on understanding everything in the manuscript. Alyce Brewer meticulously typed the final manuscript with a charitable tolerance for last-minute additions.

HERBERT GOLDHAMER

Santa Monica, California
August 1971

Contents

PREFACE   vii

LIST OF TABLES   xiii

PART I. INTERESTS

1. TERRITORIAL INTERESTS   3
    1. Territories   3
    2. Territorial Waters   12
    3. Antarctica   16

2. NATIONAL SECURITY INTERESTS   18
    1. The Cold War   18
    2. National Security and Military Relations   26
    3. The Treaty of Tlatelolco   29

3. ECONOMIC INTERESTS   32
    1. Trade   32
    2. Investment   40
    3. Construction   47

4. POLITICAL OBJECTIVES   51
    1. Solicitation   51
    2. Latin American Potential   57
    3. United States Preemption   62
    4. "We Are Far Away"   66
    5. "No Policy Is the Best Policy"   70
    6. Protection of Nationals   71

PART II. INSTRUMENTS

5. THE MIGRANT PRESENCE   79
   1. Numbers   79
   2. Economic Benefits   90
   3. Political Significance   97
6. AFFINITIES   104
7. ADVOCACY   119
8. MODELS   126
9. CULTURAL PROGRAMS   131
   1. France   131
   2. Germany   137
   3. United Kingdom   140
   4. Italy   143
   5. Spain   144
   6. The Soviet Union   146
   7. The Smaller Countries   147
   8. The United States   148
   9. Books, Movies, and the Press   151
  10. Summary   157
10. AID   159
   1. The Aid Relationship   159
   2. Aid: The Nonhemispheric Countries and the United
         States   162
   3. Types of Aid   165
         Grants   165
         Technical Assistance   167
         Volunteer Services   167
         Bilateral and Multilateral Loans   171
         Private and Public Disbursements   173
         Military Assistance   174
   4. Political Uses   176
   5. Patron–Client Relations   185
   6. Public Opinion   188
   7. Economic Uses   190
11. DIPLOMACY   195
   1. Visits   195
   2. Representation   199
   3. Style   204

PART III. RESULTS AND INTERPRETATIONS

12. RESULTS   223
   1. Japan   223
   2. Germany   226
   3. France   228
   4. United Kingdom   232
   5. Italy and Spain   235
   6. The Smaller Countries   237
   7. The Soviet Union   238
   8. The United States   242
13. INTERPRETATIONS   260
   1. Hubris   260
   2. The Managers   261
   3. Contradictions   263
   4. The Home Front   267
   5. Responses to Failure   272
   6. Leverage   275
   7. Economics and Politics   282
   8. Latin America   288
   9. Unpredictability   296
   10. Dilemmas   300

INDEX   303

List of Tables

1.1 Limits of the Territorial Sea and Exclusive Fishing Zones Claimed by Latin American and Caribbean States   14

3.1 Distribution of Latin America's Imports by Country of Origin, 1938–1968   33

3.2 Distribution of Latin America's Imports from and Exports to Specified Countries, 1968   34

3.3 United States Private Direct Investments in Latin America   41

3.4 Movement of Foreign Capital in Brazil   44

5.1 Percentage of Population Foreign Born and European Born, and Percentage of Foreign Nationals among Foreign Born

5.2 Place of Birth of the Foreign Born in Latin America   81

5.3 Number of Migrants to Latin America (to 1946)   83

5.4 Number of Migrants to Latin America (1946–1960)   88

9.1 Value of Imported Books, Periodicals, and Newspapers, Percent by Country of Origin, for Six Latin American Republics   88 152

9.2 Percent of All Translations Published from Specified Languages in Four Latin American Countries, 1960–1963   153

10.1 Official Development Assistance to Latin America, 1960–1965, by Type, by Donor Country   163

11.1 Number of Diplomatic Missions and Diplomats Received by Specified Countries, 1963–1964   200

11.2 Number of Diplomatic Personnel in Latin American Countries   201

Part I

INTERESTS

1. Territorial Interests

1. *Territories*

OF THE nonhemispheric powers Great Britain, France, and the Netherlands still retain today a territorial presence in the Latin American—largely the Caribbean—region. In a period in which vestiges of the colonial past have been viewed elsewhere with suspicion or hostility by Third World countries, the continued existence of British, French, and Dutch territories in Latin America has had no serious impact on the relations of these European nations with the Latin republics. Independent for a century and a half, the Latin American states have been less sensitive than the new states of Africa and Asia to these reminders of a past colonial epoch.[1] Britain, France, and the Netherlands had, to be sure, taken steps to decolonize their territories, which are, in any case, linguistically, ethnically, and geographically peripheral to much of Latin America. French Guiana, Martinique, and Guadeloupe became overseas departments of France in 1946 and constitutionally have the same status as the departments of the metropole. Dutch Surinam, on the South American mainland, and the Netherlands Antilles[2] are each provinces, self-governing in internal matters,

[1] A qualification of this is Mexico's sensitivity, not to those European powers that still have territories in the Western Hemisphere, but to Spain, the country from which it won its independence a century and a half ago. See Chapter 6.

[2] The six islands of Aruba, Bonaire, Curaçao, Saba, St. Maarten, and St. Eustatius.

3

of the Kingdom of the Netherlands, whose third part is the Netherlands itself.

Great Britain found no neat formula for its more dispersed and variegated territories. The Federation of the Indies, established in 1958, disbanded in 1962 owing to island particularism; and the successor East Caribbean Federation disintegrated in 1965. In July 1971, a conference to discuss once more the formation of a West Indies federation met in Grenada, but the absence of several important island heads did not auger well for the success of this new attempt. Later in the same year Guyana, Dominica, Grenada, St. Kitts-Nevis, St. Lucia, and St. Vincent declared their intention to form a new state by early 1973. Jamaica, Barbados, and Trinidad-Tabago, however, declined to join in this declaration. In the meantime, four of the British Caribbean territories have become independent states;[3] six are associated states[4] with Britain overseeing foreign relations, defense, and finances; and four have remained colonies—the Bahama Islands, British Honduras, Montserrat, and the British Virgin Islands. To this roster should be added, deep in the South Atlantic, the Falkland (Malvinas) Islands.

Great Britain can hardly be charged with attempting to maintain an imperial presence in the Western Hemisphere. On the contrary, it has been accused of showing an indecent haste to divest itself of some of its colonies, particularly British Guiana (now Guyana). In British Honduras and in the Falklands it has been accused of wanting to turn these colonies over to Guatemala and Argentina respectively.[5] When Anguilla tried in 1967 to break away from the newly founded tripartite island state of St. Kitts–Nevis–Anguilla and asked readmittance to colonial status, its plea was rejected.[6] Two years later it voted to cut ties with Britain and to become a republic.[7] Disturbances led Great Britain subsequently to send a few soldiers and police to the island and to appoint a commissioner, but this was less the result of a British interest in maintaining colonial

[3] Barbados, Guyana, Jamaica, Trinidad–Tobago.

[4] Antigua, Dominica, Grenada, St. Kitts–Nevis–Anguilla, St. Lucia, St. Vincent.

[5] *The Economist,* March 30, 1968, pp. 30 and 37.

[6] *Manchester Guardian Weekly,* December 28, 1967, p. 5. *The Economist* wryly comments in reviewing Britain's problems of decolonization that "Any fool can pick up an empire. Getting rid of it is the trouble." *The Economist,* December 3, 1966, p. 1017.

[7] *The New York Times,* February 8, 1969.

4

rule than it was of her original withdrawal from the island. Finally, Britain agreed, at the request of the Anguilla Council, to resume direct rule.[8]

Nonetheless, it is Great Britain, not France or the Netherlands, that has been in conflict with Latin American states over several of its territories. These conflicts have not arisen from Latin American sentiment that Britain is failing to grant independence or self-rule but rather from specific claims to the territories involved. Britain's grant of independence to Guyana was viewed by Venezuela as an attempt to evade its responsibility for a settlement of Venezuelan claims to 150,000 square kilometers of Guyana.[9] Venezuelan students have demonstrated before the British ambassador's residence with cries of "English, go home." The Venezuelan government, on the contrary, did not want the British to go home before their claim (laid before the United Nations in 1962) had been dealt with. Nonetheless, British Guiana became independent Guyana on May 26, 1966, and the Cooperative Republic of Guyana in February 1970. How little the Venezuelan–Guyana border conflict is associated with colonialist–imperialist interpretations is perhaps indicated by the fact that former President Leoni of Venezuela did not think it politically dangerous to remark to a British journalist that "Britain is historically but not politically linked to the days of imperialism."[10] In 1970 Venezuela and Guyana, with Britain's approval, signed an agreement to shelve border claims for twelve years. Guyana had no claims, but the agreement was made reciprocal. Britain is a signatory to the agreement because she was a party to the mixed border commission appointed in 1966.

[8] *The Times* (London), June 29, 1971.

[9] Venezuela's claim stems from its rejection of the 1899 ruling of an international court of arbitration. More than half of Guyana's territory is affected by the claim. The Venezuelan case is reviewed in *El Litigio de la Guyana*, Ministry of Defense, Caracas, n.d. Revelations in a posthumous letter of a United States lawyer for Venezuela in the case, published in the *American Journal of International Law* in 1949, reanimated Venezuelan interest in the disputed area. For a recent review of the history of the boundary dispute and its current status, see Leslie B. Rout, Jr., *Which Way Out? An Analysis of the Venezuelan–Guyana Boundary Dispute*, Monograph No. 4, Latin American Studies Center, Michigan State University, 1971. Dutch Surinam also claims some 5,000 square miles of Guyana. Surinam police and Guyanese soldiers clashed in this disputed border area in 1969.

[10] *Manchester Guardian*, July 29, 1965, p. 2.

5

Similarly, Great Britain's problems with respect to British Honduras center on Guatemala's claim to sovereignty over the colony, not on British reluctance to grant independence to British Honduras. Guatemala's claim is based on its successor rights to Spanish territory. Spain never recognized British claims to Belize (British Honduras). In 1963 Guatemala reduced relations with Britain to a consular level. A private United States attempt at mediation has led to proposals that after independence British Honduras consult with Guatemala on foreign affairs and defense, in effect a restriction in favor of Guatemala on British Honduras' sovereignty.[11]

Argentina's vigorously pressed claim to the Falkland (Malvinas) Islands [12] was assisted by a United Nations vote of November 1965 instructing Britain to negotiate Argentina's claim to sovereignty. Although agreeing to discussions, Great Britain has stated that she will not agree to a change of status not approved by the 2,000 islanders, most of whom are of British descent. Nonetheless, the latter's fear that they will be put under pressure to accede to a transfer to Argentinian sovereignty is understandable in the light of the foreign secretary's statement in the House of Commons that an "immediate transfer" is not envisaged and can only occur in a framework of guarantees. . . .[13] Subsequent British statements precipitated new fears and prompted Conservative pressure on the Labour government to reaffirm its regard for island preferences.[14] Yet it was a Conservative government that in 1970 was responsible, together with the Argentinian government, for arranging a visit of a small Falkland Islands group to Argentina, ostensibly for commercial purposes but apparently for political ends. London, it appears, is gently pushing the Falkland Islanders toward a not entirely welcome independence, which may mean in fact a dependence on

[11] Mexico also asserts a right to participate in discussions of British Honduras' status, but has said it will not reactivate its dormant claim to the northern part of British Honduras provided that a solution is based on the wishes of its people. *Britain and Latin America*, Central Office of Information, London, 1968, p. 43.

[12] The Malvinas Islands have successively passed from French to English to Spanish to Argentinian and back again in 1833 to English hands. See José Arce, *Las Malvinas*, Madrid, 1950. The legal issues are treated in Raúl S. Martínez Moreno, *La cuestión Malvinas*, Tucumán, 1965.

[13] *Primera Plana* (Buenos Aires), March 19, 1968, p. 17, and April 2, 1968, pp. 14–15.

[14] See *Economist para América Latina*, November 12, 1968, pp. 26–27, and *The Times* (London), December 2 and 5, 1968.

6

Argentina.[15] Explorations by Shell Oil of the Argentinian southern continental shelf and of the Malvinas Basin have reportedly indicated promising oil deposits ("a new Kuwait," "the Curaçao of Argentina"). Where oil is involved, speculation is rife. It is rumored that the British will turn over the Malvinas Islands to Argentina in return for the concession to exploit the coastal oil deposits.

Although the language of anticolonialism is sometimes used in the prosecution of these territorial claims against Great Britain, it is apparent that the issues involved have little to do with the maintenance of colonial rule and much more to do with its abandonment.[16] No general Latin American interest in the territorial claims of Venezuela and Guatemala exists, although an occasional rather detached expression of Latin American governmental solidarity has been elicited by the claimants. The British embargo of Argentinian beef and lamb in 1967 following the development of foot-and-mouth disease in Britain provoked a more serious crisis in British–Argentinian relations than has the long-standing Argentinian claim to the Falkland Islands.

The French government has no intention of relinquishing sovereignty or administrative control over what it took the trouble to incorporate in 1946 into its national territory. After Algerian independence French Guiana replaced the Sahara as the site of France's major nonmilitary rocket launching and space research base, a site suitable for equatorial as well as polar orbits. An initial trial launch occurred in April 1968, but this major base was not completed until 1970. French Guiana did not make representations to Paris for a changed political status as did the French Pacific territories of New Caledonia and French Polynesia in early 1968, but claims for greater freedom in internal administration have been made, reflecting an attitude shared by the recently arrived space center specialists who, only recently removed from the metropolitan environment, already find themselves at odds with a Paris bureaucracy that does not always understand local conditions.[17]

Guadeloupe and Martinique are presently a drain on French

[15] *Latin America* (London), December 4, 1970, p. 390.

[16] Black power politics in the English-speaking Caribbean, sensitive to issues of colonialism, and prominent in the independent states of Trinidad–Tobago and Jamaica, grew mostly after British withdrawal.

[17] Michel Legris, "La Guyane en proie à l'espace," *Le Monde,* August 2, 3, 4, 5, and 6, 1968.

funds. France's net official financial flow to its Western Hemisphere possessions was $122 million in 1965, making these territories the recipients of the world's largest per capita net official aid.[18] These costs do not seem to have weighed heavily, as similar costs did for Great Britain, with a government whose ambitions for France were not easily commensurable with cost considerations. Disorders in Pointe-à-Pitre in 1967 and the subsequent trial, in France, of nineteen Guadeloupians for attack on the territorial integrity of the state (that is, for promoting independence) indicated an intention not to remain passive in the face of separatist movements that claim the right, under Article 72 of the French Constitution, to autonomy and, through plebiscite, to independence. The trial ended in a major political and almost complete legal victory for the defendants.[19] Subsequent events suggest that the French government will be under increasing pressure from the French Antilles to grant greater autonomy in place of their present departmental status. The effect of this pressure was already observable in the government's plan to graft regional councils in each of the overseas departments on to the departmental structure,[20] a proposal not likely to satisfy political sentiment in the Antilles. This proposal was announced in advance of President de Gaulle's declaration concerning regional decentralization in metropolitan France. The defeat of the bill on regional reform in the referendum of April 1969, together with its Chapter VII containing special provisions for France's overseas departments, will presumably require that new steps be taken to meet dissatisfaction in the Antilles. The electoral success in March 1971 of M. Aimé Césaire, proponent of autonomy but not independence, suggests that constitutional reforms preserving a French affiliation will be acceptable to the Antilles departments.[21]

Surinam and the Dutch Antilles have not been quite as restless, politically, as the former and present British colonies or as the French Antilles. Nonetheless, when British Guiana became inde-

[18] OECD, *The Flow of Financial Resources to Less-Developed Countries,* Paris, 1967, p. 155. In 1971, exports covered only 32 percent of Antilles imports. *Le Monde,* May 14, 1971.

[19] Extensive reports of the trial and surrounding events can be found in *Le Monde* in the issues of February 1968.

[20] *Le Monde,* January 16, 1969.

[21] N. J. Bergeroux, "Les Antilles Françaises en Quête d'un Statut," *Le Monde,* May 7–8, 1971. See also *Le Monde,* August 18, 1971.

pendent in 1966, Minister-President Pengel of Surinam (Dutch Guiana) expressed an interest in following the lead of the British colony. Guyana's indication that it would be willing to negotiate its border conflict (see note 9 above) with an independent Surinam precipitated the independence issue anew. It appears that Minister-President Pengel was interested in having the Netherlands negotiate the dispute and only then take up the question of Surinam's independence. However, destruction and rioting by strikers in Willemstad, Curaçao, in 1969 and the need to fly in Dutch marines from the Netherlands brought about renewed demands for a new statute for the Antilles.

Internal agitation for autonomy or independence in the French Antilles and Dutch Surinam has not stirred responsive supporting agitation in the Latin American republics. Latin American governments and private groups were more concerned with France's nuclear tests in its distant Pacific territories than with events in the French or Dutch territories in the Caribbean. Even a left-wing Latin American journal such as *Marcha* (Montevideo) pays little attention to British, French, and Dutch colonialism. French and Dutch policies and diplomacy in Latin America have not, then, had to be oriented around the defense of their overseas territories against political or other attacks by the Latin American states. Nor, indeed, has this been the case for Great Britain either, except where specific territorial claims have been involved. When the United Nations Special Committee on Colonialism adopted a resolution in 1967 that Britain must continue to report to the United Nations on the Associated British Caribbean States as if they were not yet self-governing, this was more the result of action by the African and Asian than by the Latin American members.[22] This does not mean that the European nations are free from Latin American charges of neocolonialism, but these charges stem from the economic relations of the European countries with Latin America and are only marginally related to their territorial involvement in the region.

Both the French and Dutch possessions are associated overseas territories of the EEC (European Economic Community), and this status provides them with a European link that extends beyond,

[22] *The New York Times,* March 24, 1967.

but is contingent upon, their French and Dutch relations. The Netherlands Antilles and Surinam are distinguished by being associated with the EEC without having to provide in return reverse preferences for EEC exports.[23] The former British possessions, on the other hand, faced a possible future British membership in the EEC and a possible loss of Commonwealth preferences without any real confidence that they would be able, like the French and Dutch possessions, to acquire EEC associate status.[24] When Prime Minister Hugh Shearer of Jamaica returned from a European trip in late 1967, he found it useful, in a radio address, to transmit assurances from Prime Minister Wilson that Great Britain would not enter the EEC without adequate provision for Jamaica and the Caribbean; from West German Chancellor Kiesinger that Jamaica's interests would be kept in mind; from Dutch Premier de Jong that a solution would be found; and from General de Gaulle that he "understood our problem." That the outlook for an effective European linkage was viewed as uncertain was indicated both by the decision of Barbados, Trinidad–Tobago, and Jamaica to join the OAS (Organization of American States) and by Prime Minister Shearer's visit to Washington in 1970 to persuade President Nixon to take measures that would compensate the English-speaking Caribbean islands for the loss of British preferences, especially for their sugar, in the event of Britain's entry into the EEC.[25] In fact, Britain succeeded in obtaining French approval, in the event of her Common Market membership, for associate membership for Commonwealth developing countries and for Britain's continued preferential treatment of Commonwealth sugar until the expiration of the Commonwealth Sugar Agreement on January 1, 1975. This has not dissipated the uneasiness of Jamaica and the other twelve Commonwealth sugar-producing countries.[26] If in 1975 sugar or other tropical products of former and existing British dependencies are accorded privileges in the EEC, tensions between the EEC and several of the Latin American states—already sensitive to privileges

[23] Aaron Segal, *The Politics of Caribbean Economic Integration*, Institute of Caribbean Studies, University of Puerto Rico, 1968, pp. 81–88.

[24] Nigeria, nonetheless, had achieved associate status in the EEC without relinquishing its Commonwealth preferences.

[25] This approach to Washington was followed a week later by an invitation from London to the Caribbean Commonwealth members to meet in London to discuss Caribbean apprehensions.

[26] *Le Monde*, May 11, 1971; *The New York Times*, June 3, 1971.

from which they are excluded—will no doubt be exacerbated.[27] The effects of such new arrangements on Latin American trade in tropical products would probably not be very great, however, since more than 90 percent of the value of Caribbean agricultural exports is already exported under various external preferential arrangements.[28]

Latin American indifference to European possessions in the Caribbean is in marked contrast to the attention given from time to time to the United States presence in Panama, in Puerto Rico, and, to a lesser extent, in Cuba (Guantánamo). The United States presence in the Canal Zone is largely a military one. The headquarters of the United States Southern Command (SOUTHCOM) in the Canal Zone has relations, not just to Panama and the protection of the Canal, but through training programs and military missions to all of Central and South America. This military presence exacerbates emotions aroused especially in Panama but also throughout much of Latin America by issues revolving around ownership and control of the Canal and sovereignty of the Zone. However, not all Latin American sentiments and interests conflict with conservative United States positions on the Canal. The Canal toll rates, subsidized by the United States, enable Chilean copper, Peruvian fishmeal and copper, and Ecuadorian bananas to be more readily marketed in Europe, and these three countries (like Japan, Britain, and other major international traders) have not supported Panamanian claims to ownership of the Canal.[29]

Latin America has paid little attention to the two small Swan Islands, a little less than 100 miles northeast of Honduras, claimed by both the United States (in 1893) and Honduras. In 1966 Hon-

---

[27] EEC relations with Latin America are discussed more fully in Chapter 7, "Advocacy."

[28] Aaron Segal, "Economic Integration and Preferential Trade: The Caribbean Experience," *The World Today,* October 1969, p. 417.

[29] David Bronheim, "Relations Between the United States and Latin America," *International Affairs* (London), 46 (3), July 1970, p. 512. Shipping interests in Great Britain and Japan made known to the United States their opposition to "the proposed surrender at Panama." *Cuba and the Caribbean,* Hearings before the House Subcommittee on Inter-American Affairs, 91st Congress, 2d Session, 1970, p. 206. Because of reduced traffic the Panama Canal had a substantial deficit in fiscal 1970. *Los Angeles Times,* January 28, 1971.

duras threatened to enlist the United Nations on behalf of its claim.[30] Honduras, Colombia, and the United States have also had conflicting claims to the Quita Sueño Bank and Roncador Bay, and Colombia and the United States have had conflicting claims to the Serrana and Serranilla Banks. These and the two foregoing claims of Colombia were put in abeyance under a 1928 agreement between the United States and Colombia by which "the status quo [that is, United States control] . . . shall be maintained." [31]

The Bryan-Chamorro Treaty (1914) gave the United States exclusive and perpetual rights to the construction and operation of an interoceanic canal across Nicaragua. This irritant in United States–Nicaraguan relations was terminated on April 25, 1971, by a convention between the two countries. The new convention also canceled a United States 99-year lease to Great Corn Island and Little Corn Island and ended a United States option to build and maintain a naval base on the Nicaraguan shores of the Gulf of Fonseca.[32]

2. Territorial Waters

Sovereignty issues not related to past colonial ventures have arisen over Latin American territorial waters, largely in the context of fishing rights. The extension in 1952 by Peru, Chile, and Ecuador of jurisdiction over waters within 200 marine miles of their coasts has increased the occasions for conflict. On the east coast, Argentina in 1966 and Brazil in 1970 also extended jurisdiction to 200 miles. Table 1.1 summarizes the various jurisdictional and fishing zone claims of the Latin American and Caribbean republics.

Between 1955 and late March 1971 over 140 United States tuna boats were seized, mostly by Ecuador and Peru, with Ecuador accounting for a little more than 100 of the seizures. Fines amounting to over $1.3 million were paid for their release and reimbursed to the fishermen by the United States Treasury in accordance with the Fishermen's Protective Act.[33] The first seizure by Mexico occurred

[30] In a treaty signed on November 22, 1971, the United States ceded the Swan Islands to Honduras. *The New York Times*, November 23, 1971.

[31] David R. Robinson, "The Treaty of Tlatelolco and the United States," *American Journal of International Law*, 64 (2), April 1970, pp. 296–297.

[32] United States Department of State, Press Release No. 81, April 23, 1971.

[33] From statements released by Congressman Thomas M. Pelly and the American Tuna Boat Association. United States reimbursement to the fishermen for fines paid is based on United States government requests to the fishing fleet not to make any agreement with the West Coast Latin American states that might imply a United States recognition of the 200-mile limit.

in June 1970 when two United States boats were seized. That this incident was kept secret for two weeks indicated the sensitivity of both countries to the event.[34]

United States boats have not been the only ones involved. France's "Lobster War" of 1963 with Brazil was the continuation of a dispute of many years' standing arising from the operation of French lobster and shrimp boats inside Brazil's 12-mile fishing limit. Despite subsequent agreements by France to employ Brazilian fishermen on its boats, Brazil in 1966 seized 28 French fishermen ("fishing technicians") off Fortaleza.[35] Canadian, German, Spanish, Cuban, Japanese, and Soviet vessels have also been involved in disputes with one or several Latin American countries. The year 1968 was especially discomfiting for the Soviets. In May the Brazilian Navy held a Soviet vessel for ten days until the Soviet Embassy apologized. In June Venezuelan naval vessels seized another Soviet ship. In the same month Argentina apprehended two Soviet vessels; one escaped when being escorted to port, the other paid a $25,000 fine after being held for seventeen days.[36] Uruguay also protested a Soviet violation of its territorial waters.

These incidents led to a flurry of diplomatic activity, but it was the United States that first attempted to substitute a more general resolution of the issues for sporadic diplomatic reactions. This has so far been achieved only in the case of a five-year agreement (1967) with Mexico.[37] Following the renewed seizure of United States tuna boats by both Ecuador and Peru in 1968 and 1969, the United States imposed a ban on military credit sales to these countries in accordance with an amendment to the Military Sales Act that made the ban mandatory. After this ban was lifted, Chile, Peru, and Ecuador met with the United States to discuss fishing issues, but without any formal agreement being reached. The ban was reimposed on Ecuador following repeated seizures in January– March 1971. The State Department, on the other hand, has never invoked the Pelly Amendment to the Fishermen's Protective Act

[34] *The New York Times,* June 20, 1970. Another United States tuna boat was detained by Mexico in December 1970 for an alleged violation of the Inter-American Tropical Tuna Commission Treaty. *Los Angeles Times,* December 6, 1970.

[35] *Le Monde,* November 9, 1966.

[36] *The New York Times,* May 9 and 18, 1968; *Los Angeles Times,* June 18, 19, and 23, 1968, and July 11, 1968.

[37] See United States Department of State, *Bulletin,* March 18, 1968, p. 398.

TABLE 1.1

LIMITS OF THE TERRITORIAL SEA AND EXCLUSIVE FISHING ZONES CLAIMED BY
LATIN AMERICAN AND CARIBBEAN STATES

State	Territorial Sea [a]	Exclusive Fishing Zone [b]	Notes
Argentina	200 miles, 1966		(1) By a 1967 agreement nationals of Argentina and Brazil may fish in each other's territorial sea beyond the 6-mile limit. (2) Permits to fish in Argentine waters may be granted foreign vessels subject to conditions of Decree No. 8802, November 20, 1967.
Barbados	3 miles		(1) New legislation is under consideration.
Brazil	12 miles, 1969 200 miles, 1970		(1) See Note (1) under Argentina. (2) President Emílio G. Médici issued decree extending territorial waters to 200 miles. *New York Times,* March 26, 1970.
Chile	50 kilometers, 1941 (200 miles, 1952)	200 miles, 1947	(1) Line 1 of Chile is national legislation. (2) Line 2 is based on the Declaration on the Maritime Zone of 1952 signed and ratified by Chile, Ecuador, and Peru which proclaims sole jurisdiction and sovereignty over the area of the sea, the subsoil and seabed adjacent to their coastlines and extending to a line parallel to, and not less than 200 nautical miles from, the said coastlines.
Colombia	3 miles, 1964	12 miles, 1923	(1) Colombia has talked of extending its fishing limit to 200 miles. *Latin America* (London), March 20, 1969, p. 103.
Costa Rica	"In accordance with international law," 1949. 3 miles, 1950. 200 miles, decree pending, January 1972.		(1) Adherence in 1955 to Declaration on Maritime Zone of 1952 was vetoed by President in 1966. *Sala de Casación* defined territorial sea as 3 miles in 1950. (2) Costa Rica's foreign minister announced January 22, 1972, a decree would shortly extend territorial sea to 200 miles.
Cuba	3 miles, 1942		
Dominican Republic	6 miles, 1967	12 miles, 1967	
Ecuador	200 miles, 1966 (200 miles, 1952)		(1) Line 1 is national legislation. For line 2 see Note (2) under Chile.

14

TABLE 1.1 (continued)

State	Territorial Sea [a]	Exclusive Fishing Zone [b]	Notes
El Salvador	200 miles, 1950		
Guatemala	12 miles, 1934		
Guyana	3 miles, 1878		(1) New legislation is under consideration.
Haiti	6 miles		
Honduras	12 miles, 1965		
Jamaica	3 miles, 1878		(1) New legislation is under consideration.
Mexico	12 miles, 1969	12 miles, 1966	(1) The Mexico/U.S. Fisheries agreement of October 27, 1967 provides for reciprocal fishing rights for U.S. and Mexican fisherman off each other's coasts in the 9 to 12 mile area for 5 years beginning January 1, 1968. (2) In 1969 Mexico's Congress amended the General Law of National Property and extended territorial waters from 9 to 12 miles. *Diario Official* (Mexico), December 26, 1969.
Nicaragua		200 miles, 1965	
Panama	200 miles, 1967		
Peru	(200 miles, 1952)	200 miles, 1947	(1) See Note (2) under Chile.
Trinidad–Tobago	3 miles, 1878		
Uruguay	12 miles, 1969	See Note (1)	(1) Exclusive fishing zone: Maritime Zone between the outer limit of the territorial sea and the outer limit of the continental shelf.
Venezuela	12 miles, 1965		

[a] Territorial Sea: Numbers not in parentheses are territorial sea limits as defined by national legislation. Numbers in parentheses are territorial sea limits defined by bilateral or multilateral agreements.

[b] Exclusive Fishing Zone: Zones reserved for nationals, regardless of whether fishing by nonnationals is permitted subject to certain conditions. Where no number is cited, it can be assumed not to be less than the limits of the territorial sea, except where special inter-nation agreements are noted.

SOURCES: Food and Agricultural Organization of the United Nations, *Limits and Status of the Territorial Sea, Exclusive Fishing Zones, Fishery Conservation Zones and the Continental Shelf,* FAO Legislative Series No. 8, Rome, 1969; and other sources as indicated in Notes.

by which economic aid in the amount of fines paid is to be withheld from states seizing United States boats in international waters unless they reimburse the United States within 120 days of presentation of a United States claim.

15

When Brazil extended its territorial waters to 200 miles by presidential decree in 1970, French, Soviet, and United States boats continued fishing for shrimp, which together with other shell fish Brazil reserved for its own fishermen. The Japanese ambassador in Brazil, on the other hand, indicated that Japan was willing to allow its fishermen to negotiate an agreement; and France is also said now to be seeking an accord. Since such actions might constitute an indirect recognition of Brazil's 200-mile territorial waters claim,[38] the United States State Department advised United States fishermen that they might fish in waters claimed by Brazil without buying licenses. However, in late 1971, after several other countries negotiated fishing arrangements with Brazil, the United States opened discussions, while emphasizing that these did not imply any intent to recognize Brazil's 200-mile territorial limit. The United States still adheres to the 3-mile limit, but it is clear that her policy now is to gain support for a new international treaty to extend territorial waters to 12 miles.[39] Latin American interest in retaining the 200-mile limit has, however, been intensified by increasing technical possibilities of recovering minerals from coastal waters.

3. *Antarctica*

An additional issue involving sovereignty problems, not in Latin America itself but in an area of Argentinian and Chilean interest, exists in Antarctica. Most of Antarctica is claimed by Argentina, Chile, Great Britain, Norway, France, Australia, and New Zealand. A sector fanning out from the Pole between west longitude 90° and 150° was unclaimed until 1967 when Ecuador's Assembly entered a claim to that part of Antarctica between 84° 30' and 95° 30' west longitude.[40] The claims of Great Britain, Argentina, and Chile con-

---

[38] *The Times* (London), April 2, 1971; *Latin America* (London), February 5, 1971, p. 43, and May 14, 1971, p. 160; *Los Angeles Times,* April 4, 1971, and June 3, 1971.

[39] *The New York Times,* February 22, 1970. In accordance with a United Nations General Assembly resolution of December 1970 an international conference on the law of the sea is to be held in Geneva in 1973. In the meantime Ecuador rejected a United States offer to submit their difference to the World Court of Justice. Preparatory discussions for the Geneva conference suggest that the countries claiming territorial waters of 200 miles may be willing to abandon this claim provided they maintain exclusive rights to and control over all resources, living and mineral, within the 200-mile zone. *Latin America* (London), August 20, 1971, p. 272.

[40] *Visión,* January 31, 1969, p. 4.

16

flict, each with those of the other two. The non-Latin American states recognize each other's claims. The United States and the Soviet Union make no claims, reserve the right to do so, and do not recognize any existing claims.

In 1944 and 1947 Argentina and Chile established bases in Antarctica in support of their claims. This was an irritant in their relations with Great Britain until the International Geophysical Year (1957–1958) and the Antarctica Treaty signed in Washington in 1959 put claims to Antarctic territory in abeyance while safeguarding them in Article IV of the treaty. There is no evident governmental concern over the uncertain status of the area. Chile, Argentina, and Great Britain, which have directly conflicting claims, amicably arranged for their Antarctic study parties to be located close to each other in case of mutual need.[41]

[41] Central Office of Information, *Britain and Latin America,* London, 1968, p. 37; and Richard O'Mara, "Antarctica: Where Rivals Work Together," *The Christian Science Monitor,* October 26, 1966. See also Finn Sollie, "The Political Experiment in Antarctica," *Science and Public Affairs,* December 1970, pp. 18–19.

2. National Security Interests

1. *The Cold War*

UNLIKE the United States, the nonhemispheric governments do not view Latin America as a region closely related to their national security concerns. This simple fact goes a long way to explain some of the differences between their relations with the Latin republics and those of the United States.

In the years before, and during, World War II, a strong German presence in Latin America and the existence of political forces sympathetic to Nazi Germany and Fascist Italy had brought Latin America into the orbit of European as well as United States security interests. A struggle ensued between Germany and the Allies to secure the adherence of the region, politically, economically, and in some cases, militarily, to their respective causes, or at least to preclude the enemy from obtaining such benefits for himself. In the postwar conflict with the Soviet Union, on the contrary, Latin American attachment to Western security objectives appeared initially to be ensured by the region's association with the United States in the OAS, by its conservative and often military governments, by its close economic ties with the West, by its Catholic culture, and finally, by United States readiness to intervene, as in Guatemala in 1954. In the United Nations during the fifties, on cold war issues that brought the United States and the Soviet Union into sharp opposition, the votes of the Latin American republics went very largely in support of the United States and against the Soviet position.[1]

[1] William G. Cornelius, "The 'Latin American Bloc' in the United

18

In the fifties, the significance of Latin America for Western, especially European, security interests [2] was diminished by the stress on cataclysmic nuclear wars of short duration. This discouraged in strategic analysis the type of geopolitical calculations dealing with lines of communication, access to vital supplies, and to population reserves so common in Europe before and during World War II.[3] In a world in which war was envisaged in terms of weeks or even days, Latin America seemed to have more relevance as an area from which devastated nuclear powers might be able to draw resources for postwar recuperation than as an area relevant to the deterrence or prosecution of nuclear war. The Soviet Union, however, viewed the matter differently. The Cuban missile crisis of 1962 brought the nuclear concerns of the Atlantic Alliance into sudden and close relation to Latin America. But United States action, especially its unilateral character, served further to emphasize that the affairs of the Atlantic Alliance in the Latin American region were largely in its hands.

This, however, did not preclude European beliefs that the United States was not the best spokesman for the Western powers in Latin America, lacking as it did affinities and sensitivities that derive from European historical, cultural, and linguistic ties with the subcontinent. But it was only Italy, among the NATO powers, that took the trouble, in the political rhetoric of the Saragat–Fanfani

---

Nations," *Journal of Inter-American Studies,* III (3), July 1961, pp. 420–421. See also Gastón de Prat Gay, *Política Internacional del Grupo Latino-americano,* Buenos Aires, 1967, p. 64.

[2] For a compact account of security affairs viewed from the standpoint of Latin American policy, see Fred Parkinson, "Latin American Foreign Policies" in Claudio Véliz (ed.), *Latin America and the Caribbean,* New York, 1968, especially pp. 417–422.

[3] The Korean War did not greatly alter the preoccupation with nuclear conflict. In any case, the fact that only one Latin American country, Colombia, sent troops to Korea no doubt reinforced the view that Latin America remained on the margin of Western security affairs. Latin American participation in Vietnam has been less than in Korea. According to a 1965 statement of Colombian Foreign Minister Fernando Gómez Martínez, several Latin American governments rejected a United States invitation to send symbolic missions to Saigon. However, in March 1966, Argentinian Foreign Minister Miguel Angel Zabala Ortiz visited Saigon and expressed the solidarity of his government with South Vietnam; and in May 1968, an Argentinian mission of five military officers arrived in Saigon as observers. Rogelio García Lupo, "Argentinos en Saigon," *Marcha* (Montevideo), May 24, 1968, p. 19; *Primera Plana* (Buenos Aires), May 28, 1968.

"triangular policy" of 1962–1965, to include Latin America together with Europe and the United States as one of three points in a proposed "triangular" set of alignments which would bring Latin America into closer association with Europe and, by compensating for stresses in United States–Latin American relations, ensure a greater degree of Western unity and security.[4] But this geometric image was not supported by a policy with sufficient specificity to alter anything in the political or military security arrangements of the Western powers.[5]

Germany and, to a lesser extent, Italy have, by the Latin American activities of their trade union and political party organizations (particularly those of the German and Italian Christian Democratic parties), shown some interest in participating with the United States in the ideological and political contest in Latin America.[6] Britain has been less active, although the British Labour party as a member of the Socialist Internationale has formal links with Latin America. The Conservative party, through its Conservative Overseas Bureau, has maintained some British contact with South American Christian Democracy.[7]

Although both belong to the World Union of Christian Democracies (WUCD), the relation between the European Union of Christian Democracies (EUCD) and the Organization of Latin American Christian Democratic Parties (ODCA) has been a difficult one. The European parties have been oriented toward a Communist threat, both internally and from the East. For the Christian Democrats of Latin America, however, the enemy has

[4] See Fabio Luca Cavazza, *Italy and Latin America,* The Rand Corporation, Santa Monica, RM-5400-RC, November 1967, pp. 33–36.

[5] See, however, Chapter 9.4 on the possible future relevance in this respect of the Instituto Italo-Latinoamericano in Rome.

President Frei, during his 1965 Italian visit, made favorable public reference to Italy's triangular policy (*Il Giorno* [Milan], July 6, 1965), but is said to have criticized it privately on the grounds that it represented a continuation of the cold war and an undesirable, because exclusive, focus for Latin America on the Atlantic community. Whether or not President Frei made such representations to his Italian hosts, they corresponded to a strong current in Latin American opinion.

[6] See Cavazza, *op. cit.,* pp. 67–82, and Albrecht von Gleich, *Germany and Latin America,* The Rand Corporation, Santa Monica, RM-5523-RC, June 1968, pp. 31–35.

[7] Joseph A. Hasson, *The British Role in Latin America,* Ms., 1967, pp. 132–136.

often been various center and right-wing economic and political sectors of their domestic élites. The Communists have been not so much their enemies as their competitors in promoting a revolution, peaceful or not, within their societies. Many left-wing Christian Democrats in Latin America are no less or are more radical than their Communist party competition and have little or no political rapport with a German Christian Democratic party that for years was dominated by the personality of Konrad Adenauer. German Christian Democracy has supported the free enterprise system and Italian Christian Democracy also guaranteed the rights of private property, although the party while in power retained the nationalized and seminationalized enterprises inherited from fascism.[8] In contrast, in 1971, the National Council of the Christian Democratic Party of Chile, faced with Salvador Allende's electoral success in 1970 and the restlessness of its left wing, redefined Christian Democracy "as a revolutionary movement . . . which will fight for the replacement of the capitalist regime and the creation of a new society of communitarian socialism, inspired by the permanent values of Christianity." [9]

Despite difficulties in the dialogue with Latin America, the International Solidarity Institute (ISI) established by the EUCD is estimated to have had, in the mid-sixties, a budget of about $800,000–$1,000,000, much of which supported the political training of Latin American Christian Democratic party and union cadres. Of this budget the Konrad Adenauer Foundation provided about 70 percent, the Italian Christian Democrats about 20 percent, and the other European parties the remaining 10 percent.[10] In addition, the Social Democrats of Germany through the Friedrich Ebert Foundation, and the German Free Democratic party through its Friedrich Naumann Foundation, pursue somewhat similar activities.

The intervention of European Communist parties in Latin America is more obscure, although it is known that the Italian Communist party has a special Latin American division which in-

[8] Margot Lyon, "Christian Democratic Parties and Politics," *Journal of Contemporary History,* 2 (4), October 1967, pp. 79–85.

[9] *Latin America* (London), May 14, 1971, p. 154.

[10] Cavazza, *op. cit.,* p. 73. It appears that ISI does not contribute, except in some exceptional cases, to the ordinary expenses of the Latin American Christian Democratic parties and does not provide funds for electoral campaigns.

21

cludes an agitprop center for Latin America. It was this Latin American division that was involved in the intercepted transmittal in 1965 of $330,000 to the Venezuelan Communist party.[11]

Great Britain has been almost exclusively concerned in Latin America with the liquidation of its colonial heritage and with the reestablishment of its trading position and avoids political involvements not related to these ends. Tensions between it and Argentina over the Falkland (Malvinas) Islands have certainly not been interpreted by the British government as requiring military precautions. Although the British have only one frigate on patrol in the South Atlantic, they have not hesitated to sell Argentina two guided missile frigates from British Vickers; and have offered to sell, in addition, three postwar destroyers.[12]

France, under de Gaulle, had little inclination to promote the ideology of Western liberalism or to view an East–West ideological contest in third areas as a significant aspect of its security interests,[13] especially in Latin America where political tendencies hostile to the United States were not unwelcome indications of a growing Latin independence from the United States. That France, however, is not indifferent to Communist influence in its own Caribbean territories is evident from the precaution it took, following the disorders of 1967–1968 in the French Antilles, to refuse visas to a Soviet delegation to a meeting of the Martinique Communist party,[14] and from its exclusion from French territories of the Cuban publication, *Tricontinental,* organ of the Afro-Asian and Latin American Solidarity Organization.[15] French military interests acquired a

[11] *Neue Zürcher Zeitung,* August 13, 1965.

[12] *Visão,* January 17, 1969, p. 23; *Latin America* (London), February 14, 1969, p. 51; *The New York Times,* December 27, 1968. In 1969, the Labour minister of defense, in defending government policy on the Falkland Islands, stated that the Falklands contributed nothing to British maritime strategy. This statement was attacked in Parliament without any significant consequences. *Revista de derecho internacional y ciencias diplomáticas* (Rosario), XVIII (35/36), 1969, pp. 155–156.

[13] Cf. Alfred Grosser, *French Foreign Policy Under de Gaulle,* Boston, 1967, for a discussion of de Gaulle's belief in nation-states confronting each other without reference to ideologies.

[14] *Le Monde,* April 14–15, 1968.

[15] *Latin America* (London), December 13, 1968, p. 400; and *Le Monde,* February 13, 1969; May 11–12, 1969; and June 8–9, 1969.

marginal Latin American dimension as a result of Latin, especially South American West Coast, opposition in 1966, 1968, and 1971 to France's Pacific nuclear tests (see Chapter 12.3); as a result of the Treaty for the Prohibition of Nuclear Weapons in Latin America; and from France's interest in South American uranium deposits.

Castro's willingness to permit or encourage Soviet use of Cuba for military purposes cooled Latin American pro-Castro sentiment but did nothing in the longer run to diminish anti-American feelings, nationally oriented revolutionary and radical activity, and the increasing desire of the governments of the Latin republics to extend their economic and political relations not only with Europe and Japan but also with the Communist bloc countries.[16]

This weakening of the United States position in Latin America could have been viewed by the Western powers as harmful to their own security interests, at least insofar as they regarded the United States as the principal guardian of Western security interests in the subcontinent. In fact, the Western powers have, for several reasons, been little apprehensive on this score. They (and Japan) were the most likely beneficiaries—more so than the Communist countries—of any loosening of Latin American ties with the United States. The economic gains that might result therefrom were more tangible and immediate than the hypothetical dangers that might ensue from increased communist or national–revolutionary influences.

In addition it was reasonable for the Western powers to suppose that specific military threats such as the Soviet missile venture would be repulsed or contained by the United States, while changes in Latin America of a more purely political character were likely to be of little immediate significance to the security of Western Europe from Soviet military threats.

Further, the developing East–West détente in the middle sixties, Soviet interest in establishing diplomatic and economic relations with the Latin republics while rejecting Castro's and Guevara's guerrilla strategy for Latin American revolution,[17] together with the

[16] The increased interest of Latin American governments in relations with the Communist countries was already apparent by 1964, the year of Frei's election, but developed much more rapidly in the closing years of the decade.

[17] On Soviet strategy in Latin America, see *Kommunist*, May 1968, reprinted in *Current Digest of the Soviet Press*, June 18–24, 1968, pp. 3–8;

failures of the latter, provided further justification for Europe's almost exclusive concern with investment and trade in Latin America and its tendency to find somewhat dated both United States preoccupation with security issues and its political posture in the region. In any event, the Saragat–Fanfani triangular policy and similar lines of thought in Europe and the United States viewed Soviet and Latin American national revolutionary influences as more likely to be blunted by a diversified Western influence than by an overly dominant and sensitive United States presence.

The Western nations, while observing a limited embargo on strategic materials to Cuba, did not share United States security concerns to the extent of cooperating in the 1964 OAS call for a policy of broader economic denial to Cuba.[18] Approximately 25 percent of Cuban trade in 1966 was with non-Communist (mostly Western European) countries. Since part of this trade was supported by government-guaranteed export credits, in effect government participation, and not simply private transactions, was involved. Ships of Western registry, especially British and Greek, continue to call at Cuban ports, although the number of such calls has substantially declined since 1963 and 1964,[19] in considerable measure because of Cuba's shortage of foreign currency.

Pravda, March 19 and November 29, 1968; W. Raymond Duncan (ed.), *Soviet Policy in Developing Countries,* Waltham (Mass.), 1970; and J. Gregory Oswald and Anthony J. Strover, *The Soviet Union and Latin America,* New York, 1970.

[18] Nor did all the OAS states vote in 1964 for more severe measures against Cuba. Mexico, Chile, Uruguay, and Bolivia dissented. The then Mexican foreign minister made clear that the 15–4 vote resulted from differing juridical interpretations of the Treaty of Rio de Janeiro and, with the authorization of the president of Mexico, expressed Mexico's willingness to take the issues of interpretation to The International Court of Justice and to abide by its decision. Letter of Dr. Silvio Zavala, ambassador of Mexico to France, to *Le Monde,* May 29, 1969.

[19] For trade and shipping statistics of non-Communist countries to Cuba, see *United States Congressional Record—House,* September 20, 1967, pp. 12232 and 12235. The number of Cuban calls by ships of non-Communist registry (but including Yugoslavia) from 1963 through 1970 was: 370, 394, 290, 224, 218, 204, 197, 285. The 181 trips in 1968 comprised the following: Greek and Cypriot, 68; British, 56; Lebanese, 13; Somali, 9; Italian, 8; Yugoslav, 8; Finnish, 7; Maltese, 7; French, 4; Japanese, 1. In 1970, 285 trips comprised the following: Cypriot, 199; British, 53; Italian, 13; Yugoslav, 7; French, 5; Somali, 4; Maltese, 2; Finnish, 1; Lebanese, 1. Department of Commerce, Maritime Administration, *Report No. 93,* December 27, 1968, p. 8, and *Report No. 113,* April 19, 1971, p. 7.

From the standpoint of the United States government, the Cuban embargo (and the intervention in 1965 in the Dominican Republic) were not simply acts of hemispheric significance but were in defense of the interests of the Western powers as a whole and consequently called for their comprehension. It is understandable that this was not forthcoming to the extent that the United States government hoped.[20] An alliance whose members perceive their risks to differ considerably in degree, kind, and geographical locus are disposed to evaluate alliance policy differently, especially when a discounting of those concerns of another partner—in any case viewed as overly sensitive to the dangers of communism—is accompanied by immediate gains of an economic or political character. To be sure, the rash of incidents in 1969 involving the use of troops in present and former European territories in the Caribbean—Anguilla, the French and Dutch portions of St. Martin, Curaçao, and the Guyana borders with Surinam and Venezuela—created minor problems for Great Britain, Holland, and France but were hardly of a nature to strengthen a common Western security interest in the Caribbean.[21] Nor did the election of Salvador Allende to the Chilean presidency in 1970 and the prospects of an increased Soviet presence in Latin America appear to raise security issues for the nonhemispheric countries so much as trade and investment questions. In this respect the reaction of nonhemispheric and United States private interests have not been too dissimilar. On the other hand, the nonhemispheric governments appear less concerned about long-term security im-

[20] However, Prime Minister Wilson and Foreign Minister Stewart reportedly told their visitor, President Frei of Chile, whose government was critical of United States action in the Dominican Republic, that Britain fully supported the United States. *Latin American Times,* July 16, 1965.

[21] Britain and the Netherlands flew small forces into the Caribbean to help deal with these incidents. In 1967 Britain had a company of infantry in British Honduras, a small frigate force with a Royal Marine detachment in the West Indies, and an ice patrol ship in the Falkland Islands and Antarctic during the southern summer. Two battalions previously based in British Guiana were withdrawn when Guyana became independent. The Netherlands maintained in 1967 an infantry battalion in Surinam and a naval unit with two companies of marines in the Netherlands Antilles. France in 1967 had a total service strength in the Caribbean of 2,500, organized in a joint service command. David Wood, *Armed Forces in Central and South America,* The Institute for Strategic Studies, London, Adelphi Papers No. 34, 1967, p. 19. In 1970, the USSR had a training group of about 1,000 officers and men in Cuba. John Erickson, *Soviet Military Power,* Royal United Services Institute for Defense Studies, London, 1971, p. 99.

plications than does the government of the United States, although the discretion of the former and the talkativeness of United States "spokesmen" render comparisons difficult.

2. *National Security and Military Relations*

Prior to World War II, the training of Latin American officers in European military academies and the stationing of European military missions in South America served national security purposes of the European powers since they provided opportunities to strengthen political and military relations that might become important in the event of war in Europe. During the war, the United States pressed successfully for the exclusion of the Italian and German military missions from Latin America. France, too, had maintained a long series of important military missions in Peru (1895–1940) and in Brazil (1907 and 1919–1939),[22] but her equivocal position after 1940 doomed her missions as well.

After World War II, the United States retained its monopoly on military missions in Latin America,[23] but the loss by the European nations of this military relationship had little national security significance for them given the shift in their security interests to the confrontation between the West and the Soviet Union.

The Western European states continued to receive, after World War II, some Latin American officers in their academies and military units, but this represented a declining influence compared with the period before World War II. In 1940, eight of Peru's nine army general officers had received training in France. In the 1960's, on the other hand, of those Peruvian general officers who studied abroad, only 30 percent studied in France and 10 percent in other European countries, mostly Italy, Britain, and Belgium. Some 75 percent studied in the United States.[24]

[22] For a review of French military missions in Peru and Brazil, see Jean-Paul Palewski, "Les relations franco-péruviennes," in *Revue Juridiques et Politique* (3), July–September 1964, p. 364; and "Le Brésil et la France," *ibid.,* pp. 413–414. See also Fritz T. Epstein, *European Military Influences in Latin America,* Library of Congress, Manuscript Division, 1941.

[23] United States conflicts with Peru and Ecuador led in 1969 and 1971 to demands by these countries for the recall of United States military missions. See Chapter 10.3.

[24] Luigi Einaudi, *Peruvian Military Relations with the United States,* The Rand Corporation, Santa Monica, P-4389, 1970, p. 37. The percentages in the text add to more than 100 percent because some officers studied in more than one foreign country.

26

The sale of military equipment to Latin American countries by the nonhemispheric powers (see Chapter 12), and subsequent opportunities afforded for contact between the military establishments of the countries involved are, from the standpoint of the nonhemispheric countries, largely of political and economic significance and are related to security interests only in cases, such as Sweden and perhaps France, where military sales are needed to support arms production for the country's own military requirements.[25]

Similarly, the naval exercises, primarily antisubmarine maneuvers that Italian, Japanese, Spanish, and South African naval units have engaged in with Argentina and Uruguay, are essentially politically motivated goodwill missions and do not involve mutual security arrangements.[26]

The limited military interests of the European powers in Latin America in the sixties contrasted with the substantial United States military presence in the Canal Zone and in Cuba (Guantánamo);[27] missions throughout Central and South America; military assistance in the form of credit sales, grant matériel, and training (see Chapter 10.3); assistance to governments fighting rural and urban insurgents; interventions in Guatemala, Cuba, and the Dominican Republic; and participation in the Inter-American Defense Board (1942), the Inter-American Treaty of Reciprocal Assistance (Rio Pact, 1947), and the Organization of American States (OAS, 1948), the world's oldest regional collective security system. These activities did not only reflect United States interests in hemispheric defense and a growing concern in the sixties for the internal security of the Latin American states against Communist and other left insurgencies. The important part that the Latin American military establishments and their officer corps play in the political life of most of the Central and South American states gave to the contacts of the United States military with their Latin colleagues a greater political importance than such contacts generally have in states with stronger civilian governmental traditions.

[25] On Sweden's internal conflict over the sale of matériel to Latin America, see *Latin America* (London), January 17, 1969, p. 22; October 8, 1971, p. 323. For French military sales to Latin America, see Chapter 12.3.

[26] See *Latin American Times*, August 31, 1965, and September 2, 1965; and *The Christian Science Monitor*, January 23, 1968.

[27] In 1967 the United States had the following forces in the Caribbean: Panama 12,000, Guantánamo 7,000, Puerto Rico 2,500, and about 1,500 in small radar and satellite tracking installations on Caribbean islands. David Wood, *op. cit.*, pp. 19–20.

The security problems of the smaller states bring them into a different relation with Latin America than do the security interests of the United States and the larger European powers. For the United States and Western Europe, Latin America has been in varying degrees an area of concern; it itself poses a security problem. For the smaller states that are involved in conflicts with their neighbors—Portugal, Israel, the UAR, Cyprus, Turkey, South Africa, Spain—Latin America is a potential ally. Their interests are readily aflected by political maneuvers in the United Nations and by Great Power pressure. The smaller states depend, therefore, on the goodwill and political assistance of the Latin republics and attach considerable importance to the pursuit of their support. Since, however, the conflicts that the smaller states are involved in scarcely affect Latin America's own security, they have provided little basis for common action and have not led to joint security arrangements.

South Africa, nonetheless, has reportedly been interested in promoting a South Atlantic Treaty Organization that would embrace several Latin American nations, presumably Argentina, Brazil, and Uruguay, and several Western powers, a move consistent with its diplomatic and economic offensives in Argentina and Brazil during the past several years.

Portugal, also faced with African problems, welcomed a Brazilian demonstration of solidarity in February 1967 when a Brazilian naval squadron with 2,800 marines aboard visited Angola. This provided an occasion for the commander of the Brazilian unit to express his shock at the "war . . . being waged against Portugal in her overseas territories . . .," and for the Portuguese Chief of Naval Staff to express his belief "that a powerful Lusitanian–Brazilian naval force would ensure for our countries an indisputable position in the central and south Atlantic Ocean, enabling us to call it Mare Nostrum." This Brazilian military demonstration in Portuguese Africa followed another Latin American military presence in Africa, namely, the Cuban military buildup of 1966 in Congo–Brazzaville.[28]

The visit of the Brazilian squadron to Angola and the vigorous

[28] *The New York Times,* October 23, 1966. By 1968, the Cuban military presence had been reduced to a mere handful and Cuban influence was declining. *Frankfurter Allgemeine Zeitung,* March 25, 1970. The Portuguese, however, continued to report some Cuban activity in West Africa including in late 1969 the capture of a Cuban army officer in Portuguese Guinea. *The New York Times,* November 22, 1969.

language of the Portuguese and Brazilian naval chiefs do not seem to portend a significant Portuguese–Brazilian military relation. The naval visit was presumably an expression of the interest of some Portuguese and Brazilian circles in a Luso-Brazilian Community and is related to Brazilian economic interests in Angola and Mozambique. Even before the Brazilian squadron sailed for Africa the diplomatic representatives of Algeria, Ghana, Senegal, Nigeria, and the UAR voiced their concern to the Brazilian government.[29] Although the Brazilian foreign minister rejected the protest of the five African states as an invasion of Brazilian affairs, Brazil's anti-colonial posture, its interests in non-Portuguese areas of Africa, together with domestic considerations, appear to exclude military cooperation with Portugal in favor of occasional cautious support of Portugal in the United Nations. Portugal, however, has continued to show an interest in military collaboration with Brazil, and the five-day state visit of Premier Marcello Caetano of Portugal to Brazil in 1969 was the occasion for the conservative press of Portugal to call for a common Portuguese–Brazilian defense force "to preserve common cultural values."[30]

3. *The Treaty of Tlatelolco*

The nuclear concerns of the Western states were given a Latin American dimension for a second time—but not in a cold war context—by the Treaty for the Prohibition of Nuclear Weapons in Latin America (Treaty of Tlatelolco, February 14, 1967). Protocol I of the treaty applies only to powers with territories in the treaty area and requires them to exclude nuclear weapons from these possessions. The Netherlands signed Protocol I in 1968, but of the three nuclear powers with territories in the Latin American region, only the United Kingdom has signed and ratified Protocol I. France has not agreed to forego the right to introduce nuclear weapons into its Western Hemisphere possessions[31] and the United

---

[29] *Le Monde,* January 8–9, 1967.

[30] *The New York Times,* July 9, 1969. Brazil, consistent with its participation in World War II, has in the postwar period taken part in several military activities outside its borders: the United Nations peace-keeping brigade at Suez; the United Nations air force in the Congo, whose first commander was a Brazilian; and the intervention in the Dominican Republic in 1965.

[31] In speculating on possible sites for a French "all points" IBM force, Alastair Buchan (*Interplay,* May 1968, p. 7) suggests that French-speaking

States has made similar reservations with respect to Puerto Rico and the Virgin Islands, but not with respect to the Panama Canal Zone.

The United States and the United Kingdom have signed Protocol II. This requires nuclear powers, irrespective of whether they have territories in the region, to respect its nonnuclear status, that is, not to use or threaten to use nuclear weapons against the contracting parties (the Latin republics) nor assist them in any way to violate the treaty.[32] France has limited itself to a declaration of good intentions and so far (1971) has not signed Protocol II.

Under Paragraph 1 of Article 28, the treaty cannot acquire full force until all Latin American countries subscribe to it and until all nuclear powers and all foreign powers with territories in Latin America subscribe to Protocols I and II. There is no prospect of this occurring in the foreseeable future. Cuba refused to participate in Latin American negotiations leading to the treaty and has refused to sign it. Communist China and the Soviet Union, while expressing a cautious appreciation of the initiative taken by the Latin American states, have withheld positive action. A United Nations resolution calling for a speedy accession of all potential signatories to the treaty was passed by 82 votes with none opposed, but with 28 abstentions (mostly the Communist states, Cuba, France, and a number of African countries).[33]

In order to prevent Paragraph 1 of Article 28 from keeping the treaty indefinitely nonoperational, signatories are permitted to waive

---

Africa, the French Pacific Islands, or even an "independent Quebec" may interest France. Oddly enough, he makes no reference to French Guiana, where France has a rocket launching base.

[32] United States Department of State, *Bulletin,* April 29, 1968, pp. 554–556.

[33] *External Affairs* (Ottawa), XX (2), February 1968, p. 115. For documents bearing on the treaty, see Alfonso García Robles, *El Tratado de Tlatelolco,* Mexico, 1967. For an analysis of the treaty, especially in relation to United States involvement, see David R. Robinson, "The Treaty of Tlatelolco and the United States," *American Journal of International Law,* 64 (2), April 1970, pp. 282–310; and Secretary Roger's report to President Nixon recommending that Protocol II be transmitted to the Senate for ratification, Department of State *Bulletin,* September 14, 1970, pp. 305–309. For brief accounts of negotiations leading to the 1967 treaty and the reservations of the various nuclear powers, see Peter Barnes, "Latin America: First Nuclear Treaty Zone?," *Bulletin of the Atomic Scientists,* December 1966, pp. 37–40; and Richard Hudson, "Latin Americans Sign Treaty to Prohibit Nuclear Weapons," *War/Peace Report,* April 1967, 7 (4), pp. 15–16.

it. When in April 1969 Barbados became the twelfth country to deposit its instrument of ratification and at the same time the eleventh to waive Paragraph 1 of Article 28, it was possible under the treaty for Mexico to convene a meeting (June 1969) to bring into existence the treaty's controlling agency OPANAL (Organismo para la proscripción de las armas nucleares en la América latina). The discrepancy between the twelve ratifications and the eleven waivers of Paragraph 1, Article 28, is important—Brazil is one of the ratifying powers but she did not waive Paragraph 1 and the treaty is not valid for her.[34]

Whether the Treaty of Tlatelolco will be viewed by all its Latin American signatories as proscribing the possession of nuclear explosives for peaceful uses is uncertain. The treaty defines a nuclear weapon as a device for the release of uncontrolled nuclear energy and that has characteristics that make it suitable for military purposes. In signing the Treaty of Tlatelolco, the United States emphasized that "the technology of making nuclear explosive devices is indistinguishable from the technology of making nuclear weapons . . . we understand the definition contained in Article 5 of the Treaty as necessarily encompassing all nuclear explosive devices."[35] Some Latin American, especially Brazilian, opposition developed to provisions of the United States–Soviet Union sponsored nonproliferation pact that would restrict their freedom to use nuclear energy for peaceful purposes.[36] Should one or more Latin American countries retain and exercise the right to produce or otherwise control the use of nuclear explosives for peaceful uses, a nuclear military capability would, in effect, exist in Latin America.

[34] The 12 ratifying powers as of June 1969 were: Mexico, Bolivia, Brazil, Dominican Republic, Ecuador, El Salvador, Uruguay, Honduras, Nicaragua, Paraguay, Peru, Barbados. All Latin American countries except Cuba and Guyana are signatories of the treaty.

[35] From Statement Accompanying Signature for the United States of America of Protocol II . . ., United States Department of State, *Bulletin,* April 29, 1968, p. 556.

[36] Although 13 Latin American countries signed the Nuclear Non-Proliferation Treaty in July 1968, all of the Latin American countries (with the exception of Cuba) abstained on June 12, 1968, from voting for the Assembly resolution commending the treaty. (Cuba voted against the resolution.) Brazil has also been sharply critical of the United States and Soviet positions on a proposed treaty to bar nuclear weapons on the ocean floor. For a reaction of the Soviet Union to Argentinian nuclear developments, see note 47, Chapter 3.

3. Economic Interests

1. *Trade* [1]

IN 1938, on the eve of World War II, three countries—the United States, the United Kingdom, and Germany—accounted for two-thirds of Latin American visible exports and imports (see Table 3.1). In 1968, although approximately 40 percent of Latin America's trade was with the United States, it took four additional non-Latin American countries to account for two-thirds of the region's trade (see Table 3.2). To the three major trading partners of 1938 have been added Japan and Italy. Canada and Spain also took on increased importance for Latin America after World War II. The Communist countries have emerged as more interested trading partners, although if Cuba is excluded less than 2 percent of Latin America's trade is with the Communist countries,[2] that is, about the same as with Sweden (see Table 3.2). Argentina and Brazil have accounted for about four-fifths of Latin American exports to the Communist bloc (if Cuba is excluded).[3]

[1] The trade data in this chapter deal primarily with the position of the foreign powers during the postwar period and especially the decade of the sixties. For the outcome of their trade drives and the current status of their trade with the region, see Chapter 12, "Results."

[2] International Monetary Fund, *Direction of Trade 1963–67*. With Cuba included, Eastern Europe took 6.4 percent of Latin America's exports (1966) and the centrally managed economies provided 7.6 percent of her imports. United Nations, *Economic Survey of Latin America 1967*, New York, 1969, pp. 61 and 66.

[3] It should be recalled that the East bloc is only now recovering from the

TABLE 3.1

DISTRIBUTION OF LATIN AMERICA'S [a] IMPORTS BY COUNTRY OF ORIGIN,
1938–1968 [b]

Country	1938	1948	1960	1968
United States	37	59	44	44
France	4	1	3	3
Germany	18	3 [c]	10	10
Italy	3	4	3	4
United Kingdom	14	9	6	5
Spain	—	1	1	2
Japan	2	1 [c]	4	6
Latin America [d]	8	11	9	9
All others	14	11	20	17
Total percent	100	100	100	100
Total in billions of U.S. dollars	1.3	5.4	7.8	10.6

[a] Cuba is included through 1960.
[b] The data are not entirely comparable over the thirty-year period, but sufficiently so to establish the principal trends.
[c] Data for 1950.
[d] Imports of Latin American republics from each other.
SOURCES: IMF, *Direction of Trade,* various annual issues. For 1968 see Table 3.2.

This diversification of Latin America's [4] trade relations with the outside world has been accompanied by a decline in the number of industrial countries having a substantial proportion of *their* trade with Latin America. In 1938, eight countries sent 5 percent or more of their exports to Latin America and eleven received 5 percent or more of their imports from the region. In 1965 the corresponding figures were reduced to three [5] and six [6] countries respectively. This, of course, is due to the disproportionate increase

decline in its share of Latin American trade that set in after 1960. However, even before this decline the trade of the entire bloc with Latin America was less than that of Italy.

[4] "Latin America," in an international trade context, largely means: Argentina, Brazil, Chile, Colombia, Mexico, Peru, and Venezuela. These seven countries accounted in 1966 and 1967 for 80–85 percent of Latin American exports and 80 percent of Latin American imports. International Monetary Fund, *Direction of Trade 1966.* Except where otherwise noted, post-1959 Latin American trade data exclude Cuba.

[5] United States, Spain, and Switzerland.

[6] United States, Japan, Spain, Italy, Germany, and Sweden.

TABLE 3.2

DISTRIBUTION OF LATIN AMERICA'S IMPORTS FROM AND EXPORTS
TO SPECIFIED COUNTRIES, 1968

Country	Latin America's Imports	Latin America's Exports
United States	44.3	38.3
Canada	3.1	4.4
Belgium–Luxembourg	1.4	2.5
France	3.1	2.8
Germany	9.9	8.9
Italy	3.9	4.9
The Netherlands	1.6	2.4
United Kingdom	4.9	6.1
Spain	1.8	2.3
Sweden	1.8	1.7
Switzerland	2.3	1.0
Soviet areas [a]	1.0	1.8
Japan	5.7	7.2
Latin America [b]	9.3	9.1
All others	5.9	6.6
Total percent	100.0	100.0
Total in billions of U.S. dollars	10.6	12.2

[a] Includes USSR, Eastern Europe, Mainland China, Cuba.
[b] Foreign trade of Latin American countries among themselves.
SOURCE: IMF, *Direction of Trade,* quarterly figures for 1968, regional summary, Part B.

in trade among the industrial countries. The United States and the nonhemispheric countries now have a smaller proportion of their total trade with Latin America than they had in some prior period— for some countries the period before World War II, for others the decade after the war.[7]

The decline in the relative importance of Latin America in the

[7] From 1960 to 1966 Italy, Austria, Portugal, the Soviet Union, and some of the other East European countries had a generally rising proportion of their imports coming from Latin America. Only Spain showed an appreciable trend toward an increasing proportion of exports going to Latin America. These trends mostly came to an end in 1967. In 1938, 23 percent of United States imports came from Latin America. This figure rose sharply as a result of World War II and in 1948 Latin America supplied one-third of United States imports. This figure has dropped steadily to about 12 percent. IMF, *Direction of Trade,* various years.

trade of the industrial nations [8] is more marked and more general with respect to its imports than to its exports. The greater role of Latin America as a supplier than as a customer is underlined by the negative trade balance of the industrial countries with Latin America. The principal exceptions are Switzerland, with a consistent positive trade balance, and the United States, whose Latin American exports and imports are in approximate balance.[9] The negative trade balances of most of the European countries, Canada, and Japan with Latin America [10] are only partially compensated for, and then only in some cases, by earnings in Latin America from transportation, insurance, investment, travel, and other services.[11]

The declining role of Latin America in world trade by no means signifies an indifference by the nonhemispheric countries to commercial relations with the region. The contrary is indeed the case as is evident from the intensive deployment of official visitors to Latin America, from the use of export incentives, from various diplomatic

[8] Latin America's share in world exports declined each year between 1962 and 1967: 6.6, 6.3, 6.1, 5.9, 5.7, 5.4 percent. United Nations, *Economic Survey of Latin America, 1965*, New York, 1967, p. 63. Brazil declined from a 2.41 percent share of world trade (non-Communist countries) in 1950 to 0.90 percent in 1968. *Visão,* January 31, 1969, p. 138. In 1948 Latin America had accounted for 12.5 percent of world exports. C. W. Baerresen *et al., Latin American Trade Patterns*, Washington, D.C., 1965, p. 74. Latin America's share finally took a small upturn in 1968 when it registered 5.5 percent. United Nations, *Economic Survey of Latin America 1969*, New York, 1970, p. 6.

[9] For a more exact statement of United States visible trade balances with Latin America, see Chapter 12.8.

[10] This has been true throughout most of the sixties. In the last years of the decade, however, German and French trade deficits with Latin America declined considerably. Negative balances do not, of course, preclude positive trade balances with individual Latin American countries. In 1966, Japan had positive balances with Bolivia, Colombia, and Venezuela; the United Kingdom with Colombia and Mexico; France and the Netherlands with Mexico; Italy with Venezuela; Spain with Colombia. IMF, *Direction of Trade 1962–1966*.

[11] This is indicated by the regional column in the IMF Balance-of-Payments Year Books, although an exact analysis is not possible from this source since Latin America is rarely completely distinguishable as a separate region in the accounts of the individual countries. Approximately 75 percent of the Latin American negative balance for services (including investment income) is accounted for by the United States.

35

and investment initiatives in Latin America motivated by trade considerations, from the intensive competition for large-scale construction contracts, and from the increased use of commercial fairs and trade centers.

There are several reasons for the great zeal displayed in the cultivation of the Latin American market despite the restraints on its import capabilities. The negative trade balances with Latin America of most of its trading partners provide a major incentive, and particularly so since a number of these countries have had in addition overall negative trade balances. Reports of trade and diplomatic discussions between the nonhemispheric countries and the Latin republics show an insistent reference by the former to the reduction of their Latin American negative trade balances. The mercantilist tendencies of government officials appear to be fortified by the belief that a negative trade balance provides, if not a moral justification, at least a form of bargaining leverage to induce greater consumption of their countries' products by those countries that enjoy a positive trade balance with them.

Longer-range motives enter into some of the nonhemispheric governmental export campaigns in Latin America. Countries such as Japan, but also more recently France, that combine *dirigiste* tendencies with limited raw material resources sometimes view their long-range programs for raw material acquisition [12] as requiring export campaigns to provide sources of payment in the areas from which the raw materials are to come. Another long-range motive is the somewhat vague but pervasive belief that Latin America has an enormous economic potential and that it is therefore important to establish oneself by both diplomatic and economic initiatives in the Latin American arena.[13]

These incentives and efforts to cultivate the Latin American market might appear of limited significance as long as Latin America's import capacity remains restricted. But this conclusion does not quite follow. There is an increasing interest in Latin America in further diversification of its trade relations, partly out of political considerations and partly to strengthen its hand in economic negotiations. The important role played by Latin American

[12] Jean-Paul Pigasse, "Le rôle des approvisionnements en matières premières industrielles dans la politique extérieure de la France," *Politique Etrangère,* 31 (5–6), 1966, p. 517.

[13] See Chapter 4.2.

governments in the economic affairs of their nations facilitates the conscious pursuit of such a policy, and may increasingly make relations more attractive with those countries that have *dirigiste* or centrally managed economies.[14] The turning of the Latin American republics toward the nations of Europe, toward Japan, and toward the Soviet bloc provides a favorable political environment for nonhemispheric economic aspirations and efforts in Latin America. The United States today provides Latin America with about 40 percent of its imports. Given the magnitude of United States exports to Latin America relative to that of the nonhemispheric countries, an ability of the latter to make inroads in the United States export position would throw open to them a very sizable market even were the total Latin American market to remain unchanged. More concretely, a reduction of the United States share of the Latin American market from 40 percent to 30 percent would leave a Latin American import gap equivalent to the combined exports to Latin America of the United Kingdom, Japan, Italy, and Spain. Or, expressed otherwise, the reduction from 40 to 30 percent of the United States share of the Latin American market would, if taken up by the nonhemispheric countries, eliminate the combined trade deficit with Latin America of all nonhemispheric countries.

Given the negative trade balances with Latin America of the nonhemispheric powers it is apparent that successful pressure by any one country to increase its share of the region's market could easily lead to a worse imbalance for some of the other nonhemispheric countries (were they to maintain their Latin American import levels) and consequently to increased pressure from them. One possible reaction to this dilemma, especially in those Latin American countries that have a negative trade balance with the United States, would be a reduction of their imports from the United States. That such a process may indeed set in is suggested by Argentinian reaction to strong pressures from Western and Communist commercial missions and especially to representations made by Italy, Spain, and Israel. In the spring of 1968 Spain decided to suspend purchases of Argentinian meat until Argentina increased

---

[14] A substantial part of Latin American economic activity is under government control. On this and on the possible relation between Latin American governmental intervention in economic life and Latin American preferences for certain types of investment and trade partners, see Chapter 13.7.

its purchases from Spain and brought trade more closely into equilibrium.[15] The Onganía government stated that "readjustments will be necessary" and that it was trying to switch some purchases from the United States (which in 1967 and 1968 had an annual trade surplus of over $100 million with Argentina) to other trade partners.[16] Of course the United States, which in 1968 took 38 percent of Latin America's exports (see Table 3.2), is also in a position to exercise pressure to prevent serious trade deficits with Latin America. But it is evident that some switches from the United States to other countries could occur that would make a substantial difference to the latter without, perhaps, being great enough in the context of the large United States trade with Latin America to lead to a sharp United States reaction.

Shortly after World War II Germany began to recover its prewar position in Latin America, and Japan won for itself an entirely new importance in the area. Consequently, in the period 1948–1962 the United States share of the market that had increased enormously as a result of the war dropped steadily from almost 60 percent to 40 percent. Between 1962 and the end of the decade, the United States retained about 40 percent of the Latin American market. But toward the end of the decade, and in the early years of the new decade, signs of a decline in the United States share were multiplying.[17]

Governmental campaigns to increase export trade with Latin America do not necessarily mean that the private sectors share their governments' sense of urgency. Private balance sheets impose a somewhat different perspective from that provided by government concerns with various national objectives. Many of the statements by government leaders and officials on Latin American trade directed toward their own producers sound like nothing so much as a football coach exhorting his lagging charges to a maximum effort. Expanding domestic markets combined with inadequate information and facilities for export trade sometimes discourage ventures abroad,

[15] *Primera Plana* (Buenos Aires), April 22, 1968, p. 23; *Le Monde,* April 14, 1968.

[16] *The Christian Science Monitor,* November 29, 1968.

[17] See Chapter 12 for a discussion of indications provided by current data. These seem to be affected not only by a redirection of trade motivated by trade imbalances, but also by additional shifts in trade patterns resulting from political and ideological factors.

and government measures to provide special tax incentives and credit and insurance facilities have been required to overcome the resistance of some parts of the private sectors.

Trade fairs, both national and international, play an important role in promoting trade. At the end of 1969, 23 international trade fairs were scheduled for the succeeding months in Latin America.[18] In 1970, the United States opened a permanent commercial center in Mexico to counter the inroads of Japanese and European manufacturers. As the first United States commercial center it reflected the importance that the government attributed both to coordinating the efforts of individual entrepreneurs and to cultivating its principal Latin America market, which is also its fifth largest foreign market. In 1970, too, France held in Buenos Aires its first commercial fair in Latin America since World War II;[19] this was closely followed by a major British trade fair in the same city. Japan has taken advantage of the maritime character of almost all of the Central and South American countries to institute a continuing industrial floating fair aboard her ship, the *Sakura Maru*. An Italian trade fair of 1971 in Havana attracted over 100 Italian firms. When, in 1955, Khrushchev and Bulganin launched their trade, aid, and political offensive in the Third World and the West, one of their initial steps was to invest over $4 million in trade fairs.[20]

Government assistance in financing sales is particularly important in working in Third World markets. In 1966 the French agency COFACE sought to improve the competitive position of French exporters by shifting from guaranteeing the credits extended by French manufacturers (*crédit-fournisseur*) to providing, in the case of sufficiently important contracts, French bank credit directly to foreign buyers (*crédit-acheteur*) who are thus able to pay French suppliers the entire sum due them. Similarly, a United States export credit insurance program supports the government's $50 billion export goal. Private banks supplement government facilities. The advantage of having banks in Latin America of one's own national origin and an indication that national loyalties may transcend bank-

---

[18] *International Commerce,* Semi-Annual Listing of Impending International Fairs, December 29, 1969, pp. 5–29.

[19] For an account of the Buenos Aires trade fair and French disappointments, see *Le Monde,* November 3, 1970.

[20] Karel Holbik, *The United States, the Soviet Union, and the Third World,* Hamburg, 1968, p. 50.

ing confidentiality is suggested by the fact that German businessmen operating in Latin America have complained that they were handicapped by their inability to discuss German trade secrets with foreign bankers.[21]

Trade is by far the single largest category of economic transactions between Latin America and the rest of the world. In 1965 commodity together with service exchanges (insurance, travel, freight, other transportation and services, but not including investment income)—commerce in the broadest sense—accounted for roughly three-quarters of the gross volume in money terms of all economic transactions between Latin America and the rest of the world.[22] The remainder is represented by financial flows between Latin America and other governments and between Latin American governments and international organizations (grants, loans, amortization and interest payments), but more largely by international private financial flows—essentially trade credit, investment income, and investment.

2. *Investment*

International investment data are notoriously inadequate and unreliable. The figures in the following pages on foreign investment in Latin America should be regarded with caution. They are estimates taken from a great variety of sources and vary considerably in completeness and definition. However, they do provide a useful picture of the relative role of different countries or regions in Latin American investment.

In 1914 total foreign investment in Latin America was about $8.5 billion. The European share of this was close to 80 percent, the United States share 20 percent.[23] The United Kingdom had a 44 percent share, France 14 percent, Germany 11 percent, and other countries about 10 percent.

Fifty years later, in 1965, the situation is reversed; the United States share of direct foreign investment in Latin America (book value, $11 billion, see Table 3.3) was about 70–75 percent. The

[21] *German International,* September 30, 1965, p. 20.

[22] Based on trade and service data in United Nations, *Economic Survey of Latin America, 1965,* p. 83, and financial flow data in OECD *Geographical Distribution of Financial Flows to Less-Developed Countries, 1965,* Paris, 1967, and IMF, *Balance-of-Payments Year Book,* Vol. 18.

[23] United Nations, Department of Economic and Social Affairs, *Foreign Capital in Latin America,* New York, 1955, p. 6.

TABLE 3.3

UNITED STATES PRIVATE DIRECT INVESTMENTS IN LATIN AMERICA [a]
(IN BILLIONS OF CURRENT DOLLARS)

Year	Book Value	Net Capital Outflows to Latin America	Earnings
1960	8.4	.149	1.0
1961	9.2	.219	1.1
1962	9.5	.029	1.2
1963	9.9	.235	1.1
1964	10.3	.113	.2
1965	10.9	.271	1.3
1966	11.5	.307	1.5
1967	12.0	.296	1.4
1968	13.1	.677	1.6
1969	13.8	.344	1.6
1970	14.7	.559	1.5

[a] Includes the Caribbean countries. The book value of U.S. direct investment in the 19 Latin American republics was $11.7 billion in 1969 as compared with $13.8 billion for the entire area.
SOURCE: U.S. Department of Commerce, *Survey of Current Business,* October 1970, p. 31, and October 1971, p. 28.

remainder is largely accounted for by European countries, Canada, and Japan.[24] A 1970 estimate gives United States investment as about 60 percent and non-United States investment 40 percent.[25]

During the decade 1950–1959, the United States share in the flow of direct investment to Latin America was about 78 percent and the European share most of the remaining 22 percent. However, in the last half of the decade the European share rose to 32 percent, and to 47 percent if Venezuela is excluded.[26] During the years 1960–1967 United States investments of $4.1 billion exceeded non-United States investments of probably $2.5 billion. Of the net investments made by countries other than the United States, those of Britain were greatest, with German investments following closely. Italy and Japan were next, with Sweden and France following.[27]

World War II necessitated the liquidation by Great Britain of

[24] Inter-American Development Bank, *Financiamiento europeo en América Latina,* Mexico, 1966, p. 76.

[25] Penelope Roper, *Investment in Latin America,* The Economist Intelligence Unit, London, 1970, pp. 7–8.

[26] United Nations, *Economic Survey of Latin America, 1963,* p. 248; Inter-American Development Bank, *op. cit.,* p. 77.

[27] Penelope Roper, *op. cit.,* pp. 7–8.

much of its Latin American assets. Despite this and despite post-war restrictions on the export of capital, Great Britain's holdings are second only to those of the United States and perhaps one-seventh as large. Direct investment is about £400 million including oil but exclusive of banking, insurance, and portfolio holdings which might bring the total to about £750 million. Net direct annual investment was about £18 million in 1964 and 1965.[28]

The European nations and Japan have relatively little of their direct investment in the Caribbean and Central American countries with the exception of Venezuela, where British and Dutch investments are about 20–30 percent of the total, and of Mexico, where the nonhemispheric share is about 15 percent.[29]

In South America the nonhemispheric foreign investment share is 27 percent in Chile, 20 percent in Colombia, and 15 percent in Peru.[30] However, in the two largest South American countries, Brazil and Argentina, the nonhemispheric share in direct investment is considerably larger than global Latin American figures might suggest. This is particularly significant since Argentina and Brazil accounted in 1960–1963 for 86 percent of Latin American net direct investment.[31]

In Argentina, as late as 1939, about three-quarters of direct foreign investments were still European. In 1961, Europe (48 percent) still exceeded the United States share (41 percent) although new investment flows in the period 1958–1962 showed a greater inflow of United States than of European investments.[32] Nonetheless, in 1967, among the 50 largest public and private enterprises in Argentina, 17 European corporations still outranked 13 United States corporations, the former with 344 billion pesos of business annually and the latter with 260 billion. Among the European

[28] Central Office of Information, *Britain and Latin America*, London, 1968 (revised), pp. 17 and 55–56; James C. Hunt, "Britain and Latin America," in Claudio Véliz (ed.), *Latin America and the Caribbean*, New York, 1968, p. 455; and *Economist para América Latina*, October 30, 1968, p. 38.

[29] Inter-American Development Bank, *op. cit.*, p. 78.

[30] *Ibid.*, pp. 363–365.

[31] United Nations, *Economic Survey of Latin America*, New York, 1966, p. 279.

[32] Stanford Research Institute, *Factors Affecting Foreign Investment in Argentina*, 1963; Inter-American Development Bank, *op. cit.*, pp. 353–355; and *Moniteur officiel de commerce international*, Paris, No. 339, May 6, 1964.

corporations Italian enterprises lead with those of the United Kingdom, France, the Netherlands, Germany, and Switzerland following, in that order.[33]

In Brazil, which accounts for about one-quarter of the book value of all foreign direct investment in Latin America, the European and Japanese share rose from about 32 percent in 1956 to 58 percent in 1967. The substantial increases in the German, French, Italian, and Japanese shares were not, on the surface, at the expense of the United States investment position which remained stable at about 35–37 percent. The only country whose share significantly declined was Canada. However, part of the Canadian investment in Brazil was composed of United States funds.[34] Table 3.4 shows the position on June 30, 1967, of the cumulative movement of foreign capital in Brazil.

Of particular interest is the leading position of France among the nonhemispheric countries, a position that is not evident when comparisons are made of investments exclusive of reinvested profits. However, if instead of taking the cumulative position as of mid-1967 we examine investment flows (including reinvestment of profits) only for the last two years available, 1965–1966 and 1966–1967, we find that France is surpassed by Switzerland, the United Kingdom, Japan, Germany, the Netherlands, and Belgium–Luxembourg, in that order. During these two years the United States position relative to that of European and Japanese investment remained unchanged.[35]

The share of the nonhemispheric countries in foreign direct investment in Latin America throws light on the weight of their

[33] Julian Delgado, "Industria: El Desafío a la Argentina," *Primera Plana* (Buenos Aires), September 3–9, 1968, p. 69ff.

[34] United States funds are not the only foreign funds involved in corporations classified as Canadian. Thirty-six percent of the equity capital of Brazilian Traction, Light and Power of Toronto is held in the United States as compared with only 25 percent in Canada. But European investors also hold about one-third of the equity in the form of share warrants. Judith Tendler, *Electric Power in Brazil: Entrepreneurship in the Public Sector,* Cambridge, Mass., 1968, p. 30.

[35] For Brazilian investment data, see Stanford Research Institute, *Brazil: Factors Affecting Foreign Investment,* 1958, p. 29; Inter-American Development Bank, *op. cit.,* p. 356; *The Christian Science Monitor,* December 7, 1967; Banco Central do Brasil, *Movimento de Capitais Estrangeiros no Brasil, Posição em 30 de Junho de 1967,* 1968, pp. 92–93, 95–97.

TABLE 3.4

Movement of Foreign Capital in Brazil
(percent distribution by country, as of june 30, 1967)

Country	New Transfers	Reinvestment of Profits	Total
Canada	3.3	3.5	3.4
United States	37.0	34.4	35.2
Belgium–Luxembourg	8.6	0.4	3.0
France	8.3	25.2	19.8
Germany	8.8	3.3	5.0
Italy	2.4	1.6	1.8
The Netherlands	4.3	2.0	2.8
Switzerland	6.8	7.3	7.2
United Kingdom	8.6	15.7	13.4
Japan	7.1	1.1	3.0
Other countries	4.8	5.5	5.4
Total percent	100.0	100.0	100.0
Total in millions of U.S. dollars	$1,108	$2,368	$3,476

Source: Banco Central do Brasil, *Movimento de Capitais Estrangeiros no Brasil, Posição em 30 de Junho de 1967*, 1968, pp. 92–93, 95–96.

investment presence relative to each other and to the United States. However, in order to judge the importance of Latin America to their overall foreign investment activity, we need to know how much of each country's total foreign investment goes to Latin America.

On this basis it is clear that Latin America is far more important to Germany, Japan, and Italy than it is to the other nonhemispheric countries or to the United States. From 1952 to 1965, Germany sent 20 percent of its direct investment funds to Latin America, approximately three-quarters of its investments in less-developed countries. Of its total net investments in 1963 and 1964 Latin America received 31 percent, and by 1969 one-fifth of all German investments abroad was in Latin America.[36]

[36] Albrecht von Gleich, *Germany and Latin America,* The Rand Corporation, RM-5523-RC, June 1968, p. 53; Inter-American Development Bank, *op. cit.,* p. 218; Pan-American Union, *Capital Flow,* 1963, p. 49; and *Economist para América Latina,* March 5, 1969, p. 38. Argentina, Mexico, and Brazil account for 76 percent of German manufacturing investment (as compared with 69 percent for the United States, which has also shown a preference for these three countries). T. Graydon Upton, address to International Conference on Latin American Investment Policy Models, Hamburg, October 13, 1971.

Between 1951 and 1967, 28 percent of Japanese gross postwar private investment had gone to Latin America, mostly to Brazil. Of the book value of Japanese foreign investment in 1963, 39 percent was estimated to be in Latin America. In 1968, 38 percent ($250 million) of Japanese overseas capital was reported to be in Brazil alone.[37]

Latin America's share of Italian gross foreign investment rose from 13 percent in 1960 to 24 percent in 1962 and to 29 percent in 1963. By 1969 it was estimated to have reached 40 percent,[38] with about 85 percent of this concentrated in Argentina and Brazil.

Whereas Germany, Japan, and Italy have been placing approximately 25–40 percent of their total direct investment in Latin America, no other nonhemispheric country sends more than about 10 percent of its direct investment to Latin America. The Netherlands, to be sure, sent 24 percent (1962) and 32 percent (1963) of her gross foreign investments to the Latin American region, but most of this went to Surinam and the Dutch Antilles and only about 7 percent in 1962 and 1963 to Latin American exclusive of the Dutch territories.[39]

Despite restrictions on the export of capital to nonsterling areas, the United Kingdom slowly increased the proportion of its total direct investment that went to Latin America. In 1958, about 3.6 percent of British investments went to that region, in 1962,

[37] Yoshinori Ohara, *Japan and Latin America,* The Rand Corporation, RM-5388-RC, November 1967, p. 50; Kiyoshi Kojima, "Japan's Foreign Aid Policy," *Hitotsubashi Journal of Economics,* 6 (2), February 1966, p. 48; *Visão,* July 19, 1968; p. 73; Japan Economic Research Center, "Experiencias y problemas de las inversiones del sector privado japonés an América latina," Table I-4, Paper for Sixth Annual Meeting of the Inter-American Social and Economic Council, Port-of-Spain, Trinidad, June 1969. *The New York Times,* June 21, 1971, reports a Japanese government estimate of Japanese investment in Latin America in 1969 as $420 million, or 21 percent of Japanese foreign investment. This percent is a very sharp drop from the figures cited in the text and if accurate could only be explained as the result of very great increases in Japanese investment in other parts of the world. The same report gives Japanese investment in Brazil as $213 million in 1969 and $361 million in 1970.

[38] Pan-American Union, *Capital Flow,* p. 52; Inter-American Development Bank, *op. cit.,* p. 312; *Economist para América Latina,* April 4, 1969, p. 48.

[39] Inter-American Development Bank, *Financiamiento europeo en América Latina,* Mexico, 1966, pp. 287–288.

5 percent, and by 1964, 7 percent (exclusive of sterling areas).[40] However, 1965 and 1966 saw an increasing share of British investment go to North America, West Europe, and other nonsterling areas with a corresponding decline in British investments in Latin America to about 5 percent of British placements abroad.

The Latin American and West Indies share of France's direct investments in 1965 to the Third World was about 10 percent.[41] A substantial proportion of this represents French Antilles investment. Between 1957 and 1963, new gross French investment in Latin America was only $51.5 million and net investment only $28.8 million,[42] although Brazilian data indicate substantial French investments in 1963–1965.

In contrast with the substantial and increasing investment interest in Latin America of several of the nonhemispheric countries is the decline in the share of United States private investment going to the region. In 1950, 38 percent (without Cuba, 32 percent) of the book value of United States foreign private investment was in Latin America. In 1966 this figure had dropped sharply to 18 percent. From 1960 to 1966 Latin America received only 9 percent of all United States net direct investment, one-third of such United States investment in less-developed countries.[43] By 1968, 30 percent of the value of United States direct investment abroad was in Canada as compared with only 17 percent for all of the Latin republics, although the latter investments had a higher rate of return. Even investments in mining, smelting, and petroleum were larger in Canada than in Latin America. The decline in the Latin American share

[40] United Kingdom published estimates exclude investments in petroleum and insurance. "Foreign Investment in Latin America: The Role of Private Capital," Bank of London and South America, *Quarterly Review,* July 1963; Inter-American Development Bank, *op. cit.,* pp. 338–341; *Board of Trade Journal* (London), 190 (3612), June 10, 1966, pp. 1307–1308; James C. Hunt, *op. cit.,* pp. 444–445.

[41] OECD, *Flow of Financial Resources to Less-Developed Countries,* Paris, 1967, p. 158; *Industries et Travaux d'outre-mer,* January 1969, pp. 19–20.

[42] Jean Meyriat, "France and Latin America," in Claudio Véliz (ed.), *op. cit.,* p. 438.

[43] Inter-American Development Bank, *op. cit.,* p. 80; United States Department of Commerce, *Survey of Current Business,* September 1967, p. 40; United States Congress—House, Subcommittee on Foreign Economic Policy, *The Involvement of U.S. Private Enterprise in Developing Countries,* March 1968, p. 37.

of United States direct foreign investments did not mean, of course, that United States investments in Latin America declined but only that investments in other countries and regions increased at a faster rate than investments in Latin America.

In summary we note: (1) The overall Latin American foreign investment picture tends to obscure the very large participation of nonhemispheric capital in Brazil and Argentina; in Brazil the proportion of nonhemispheric capital has substantially increased in the past decade. (2) Of the capital exporting countries, Germany, Japan, and Italy show the most pronounced investment interest in Latin America. These three countries are also distinguished, among the major capital exporting countries, by a substantial emigrant presence in Latin America (see Chapter 5.2). (3) Although the sheer magnitude of total United States foreign direct investment has virtually guaranteed a major role to United States investment in Latin America, the world distribution of United States investment altered in the sixties and the Latin American share declined sharply. Latin America was in 1965 and 1966 the only world region in which reinvested United States earnings was the major component of its private direct investment. By 1968, however, new United States funds once again exceeded reinvested profits.[44]

3. *Construction*

Construction projects for large-scale public works are an important and highly competitive form of foreign economic enterprise in Latin America. Since about 1960 Italy, France, and Germany especially, but also Japan, Sweden, and the United Kingdom have been increasingly active in this field and have pressed American contractors very hard.[45] The $230 million contract for the Mantaro

[44] United States Department of Commerce, *Survey of Current Business,* September 1967, pp. 42–43, and October 1969, pp. 28–29. For a discussion of current investment data and the effect of Latin American nationalism on United States investment behavior, see Chapter 12.8.

[45] For complaints on this score, see *The New York Times,* March 22, 1964, and *Los Angeles Times,* November 12, 1967. The engineering companies reputed to be the world's four largest are Hitachi and Mitsubishi of Japan, Mannesmann of Germany, and GKN of Great Britain. Italian success is partly related to the combination into ItalConsult of a number of major Italian industrial firms. For a review of North American problems in exporting engineering services to Central and South America, with some remarks on European and Japanese competition, see *International Commerce,* January 2, 1967, pp. 9–11.

hydroelectric complex in Peru, awarded to Impreglio of Italy in 1966, was approximately two-thirds the dollar value of Italy's annual exports to all of Latin America and about ten times the value of its annual exports to Peru. The award by Argentina to Siemens of Germany of a $75 million contract to construct Latin America's first nuclear power station involved an amount equal to about two-thirds of Germany's exports to Argentina in 1966. Of course, a substantial part of contract amounts are represented by local costs and subcontracting, but the foreign equipment and service portions nonetheless represent sizable contributions to visible and invisible trade balances. According to a Siemens statement, the participation of Argentine enterprises in the construction of and supplies for the Atucha atomic power plant will represent only one-third of the cost of the project.[46] The annual value of construction contracts completed abroad by Italy, although equivalent in dollar value to only about 2–3 percent of its total export trade, equals about 15 percent of the value of its export trade with less-developed countries.

Many of these projects are high-prestige undertaking and are sought after not only for their immediate economic benefits but because they open other opportunities in Latin America and the rest of the world. Since the bigger construction projects extend over several years and are government-sponsored, they permit prolonged contact of foreign industry with local business and technical people and with government planners. Thus the Argentine award to Siemens has been viewed in France as reinforcing the German industrial position in South America.[47] The Chilean contract for an experimental atomic reactor, won by a British engineering firm, although having a value of only £600,000, gave Britain an important opening in the field; it was followed by a £1.5 million contract with Brazil for a similar nuclear plant.[48] France's participa-

[46] *Primera Plana* (Buenos Aires), June 18–24, 1968, p. 65. The Atucha plant is not expected to be in service until 1973. *Ibid.*, September 7, 1971, p. 20.

[47] *Le Monde*, February 25–26, 1968. In the Soviet Union, on the other hand, the Siemens contract is viewed as having ugly impiications for German military–nuclear interests. *Pravda*, April 14, 1969, p. 5. At the 1969 Pugwash Conference, these Argentinian nuclear developments were attributed to Argentinian fears of a Brazilian revolution. *The New York Times*, October 27, 1969.

[48] *Economist para América Latina*, January 8, 1969; and *Latin America* (London), July 4, 1969, p. 211.

tion in the construction of the Montreal subway system (1962–1966) apparently played a role in France's later series of successes in connection with the Caracas, Mexico City, and Santiago de Chile metro contracts.[49]

Considering both the sums involved and the prestige component of major contracts, it is not surprising that they are eagerly pursued. United States, British, West German, Canadian, and Japanese enterprises sought the Mexico City metro contract and firms from ten countries went after the one in Santiago de Chile.[50] The Argentine Atucha nuclear plant was bid for by four United States and two German firms, and by firms from the United Kingdom, France, Canada, and Switzerland. Japan and other countries have expressed an interest in financing a new canal in Panama.[51] Bids to construct the Argentine satellite communications station (won by an Italian consortium) were submitted by Italian, Spanish, Japanese, German, and United States firms. (Mexico's satellite contract was won by Japan and Chile's by the United States.) The Colombian government contract to build and operate an auto assembly plant, awarded to Renault of France, was bid for by ten enterprises from seven different countries.[52] The great Mantaro Dam project began with technical surveys first by an American and then by a French consulting firm, developed into a contract with an Anglo-German consortium, and under circumstances that created a minor international scandal was finally awarded—after arbitration by a Swiss engineering firm—to an Italian enterprise.[53]

Two new factors are entering the construction field. Increasingly, foreign engineering firms find themselves in competition with Latin American firms, not only firms competing for contracts in their own country but also from Latin American firms that have crossed boundaries to compete in other Latin America countries.[54] In addition, some South American governments are exploring major con-

---

[49] *Le Monde,* March 30, 1966, and October 14, 1967; *Figaro* (Paris), September 20, 1966. The Mexican subway was opened in the summer of 1969. Its equipment costs were covered by a French loan of $130 million.

[50] *Le Monde,* March 30, 1966, and *Visión,* July 21, 1967, p. 50.

[51] *Latin America* (London), February 26, 1971. One would have to infer from several French actions in 1965 that General de Gaulle at that time may have been seriously interested in building a new Panama Canal.

[52] *The New York Times,* August 12, 1969.

[53] *The Economist,* February 6, 1966, p. 536.

[54] *Latin America* (London), December 27, 1968, p. 411, and January 3, 1969, p. 3.

struction contracts with Soviet bloc governments. Peru has announced plans for the construction of a tractor factory by Rumania,[55] and the USSR may build fishing ports for both Chile and Peru.[56]

[55] Penelope Roper, *op. cit.*, p. 12.

[56] *Le Monde*, January 21, 1971; and *The New York Times*, September 14, 1971.

4. Political Objectives

1. *Solicitation*

PRIOR to World War I Latin America was significant to the European powers largely because of interests—territorial, investment, trade—in the Latin American region itself. The foreign powers had little need to solicit or neutralize Latin American influence in connection with their concerns in other parts of the world. Latin America possessed neither the ability nor the inclination to mix into these matters. Although Germany and to some extent Italy had not been indifferent to the role South America might play in forwarding their national aspirations,[1] it required a conflict on the scale of World War I to make the major powers more sensitive to the importance for them of the political sympathies of the Latin states. The end of the war largely terminated this concern.

In the postwar years, the League of Nations provided a forum in which for the first time the Latin American republics had an opportunity to make their voices heard.[2] But the European powers experienced little need to cultivate Latin American support or to

[1] Albrecht von Gleich, *Germany and Latin America,* The Rand Corporation, RM-5523-RC, June 1968, pp. 3–10; Fabio Luca Cavazza, *Italy and Latin America,* The Rand Corporation, Santa Monica, RM-5400-RC, November 1967, pp. 4–11.

[2] Even Argentina, which before World War I was one of the ranking countries of the world, participated for the first time in an international conference with European powers in 1908. Calixto A. Armas Barea, *Curso Sobre Política Internacional en Naciones Unidas,* Rosario, 1965, p. 19.

51

discourage Latin American initiatives in the League in connection with matters that lay outside the subcontinent. Although forming a substantial bloc in the League of Nations, the Latin republics did not act in concert except on administrative and representational (electoral) matters.[3] They were never at any one time all members of the League and at its final meeting in 1945 only ten of them were members.[4] The instability of Latin membership, the frequent abstentions and withdrawals, reflected a primary concern with hemispheric affairs and the effect of the United States failure to join. So little were Latin American states involved in the issues that most preoccupied the major powers that Latin American representatives at the League were sought after to serve as rapporteurs, a function for which they seemed eminently suited by virtue of their neutrality on or indifference to the nonhemispheric issues before the League.[5]

World War II, and the period preceding it, underlined for the second time that political and military conflict on virtually a global scale was required to lend to Latin America a more substantial significance in the affairs of the great powers. But this time the end of the war did not mark, as did the end of World War I, a sharp contraction of foreign diplomacy in Latin America. This was due partly to the cold war and to the greatly increased role of the United States in world affairs, and partly to a new Latin interest in establishing itself on the world political stage. This interest was amply reciprocated. The Federal Republic of Germany had a major political objective in Latin America, as elsewhere, of ensuring the nonrecognition of the East German government and the restoration of a national image badly damaged by two world wars. France sought to establish its cultural prestige and preeminence and to further the process of Latin American reorientation toward Europe. Italy shared this latter interest, if less evidently so, and like Japan has had a continuing interest in its emigrant communities. Spain has had a major interest in emphasizing *hispanidad* over *latinité* and in ensuring Latin American support for its contest with Great Britain over Gibraltar. Great Britain has had political objectives

[3] Georges Scelle, *Les relations des états de l'Amérique latine avec la Société des Nations,* Paris, 1936, pp. 57–59.

[4] Norman A. Bailey, *Latin America and World Politics,* New York, 1967, p. 146.

[5] Warren H. Kelchner, *Latin American Relations with the League of Nations,* Boston, 1929, p. 140.

associated with the decolonization of its Western Hemisphere territories. And, in varying degrees, the Western-oriented countries shared political objectives in Latin America associated both with the containment of communism and the Soviet Union and with the pursuit of economic relations with the Latin republics.

The Soviet Union has had political interests in Latin American related to its conflict with the West generally and more particularly with the United States; to its conflict with Red China and deviant ideologies emanating from there and Cuba; to its involvement in Cuba; and more generally to its inclination to view all parts of the world as so many dioceses providing either political opportunities or presenting potential threats. Soviet interest in diplomatic and economic ties with Latin America raises a question as to whether increased Soviet trade with Latin America is primarily intended to serve political ends or is of genuine economic interest to the Soviet Union. It could, of course, equally serve both purposes. The tendency to give weight to a political interpretation perhaps underestimates Soviet interest in benefiting from the international division of labor, the rewards of which—despite the diffusion of technology, the increased use of synthetics, and the obvious advantages in resources and internal markets of countries like the United States and the Soviet Union—seem in no way to have diminished. In the Soviet view UNCTAD II (United Nations Conference on Trade and Development, New Delhi, 1968) achieved real progress over UNCTAD I because it devoted attention to improving economic relations among countries with different socio-political systems. Nonetheless, for the Soviets, the cold war is "without question, still hindering the broader entry of the countries of socialism into the arena of world trade." [6] In any case Soviet behavior in Latin America and its doctrine of revolutionary struggle for the region represent some shift toward pursuing political influence in Latin America where political power largely resides, that is, in the governments of the Latin American states.

The United Nations has provided a forum in which the Latin American republics have played a far greater role than in the

[6] Lev Stepanov, "One Percent: The Problem of Economic Aid," *The Annals of the American Academy of Political and Social Science,* Vol. 386, November 1969, p. 43. This paper originally appeared in *World Economy and International Relations* [in Russian], Moscow, No. 6, June 1968.

53

League of Nations. Although the United Nations is sometimes viewed as politically impotent and a mere debating society, it is nonetheless true that obtaining a favorable United Nations action or resolution is a matter of concern to most countries. Such action (whether in the Assembly, the various Assembly committees, the Security Council,[7] or the various United Nations specialized bodies and commissions) sometimes extends or restricts the field of political and even military maneuver of the countries involved. The growth of international economic and technical organizations and arrangements in the postwar world would in itself have increased the need of foreign powers to solicit the cooperation of the Latin American states. But there have been issues in the postwar international arena with respect to which Latin America would have been largely ignored by the powers concerned had it not been for United Nations potential or actual involvement in these issues and the voting strength of the Latin American states in it. The Latin republics possessed neither the economic nor military power to compel this regard for their views.

Although the cultivation of Latin American votes has by no means been unimportant on a number of occasions for the larger powers,[8] the pursuit of Latin political support in the United Nations has been of particular importance for some of the smaller nations with limited political and military resources.

Initially Spain was excluded from the United Nations on a motion of the Mexican representative, whose government still does not recognize the Franco regime. Nevertheless a number of the Latin republics resisted resolutions in favor of action against the Franco regime, and Spanish success in courting Latin America was established with her admission to the United Nations in 1955.[9] Since then Spain has increasingly succeeded in winning Latin American

---

[7] Of the 15 Security Council seats, 5 are permanent and 10 elective. Of these 10, 2 are reserved for Latin American countries. In the three years 1969–1971 Brazil, Paraguay, Colombia, Nicaragua, and Argentina held seats on the Council.

[8] The Soviet Union cannot be accused of being excessively impressed by the power of the United Nations General Assembly, but even its interest in Latin America has been interpreted as being in part due to Latin America's voting power in the United Nations. Stephen Clissold, "The Soviet Union and Latin America," in Claudio Véliz (ed.), *Latin America and the Caribbean,* New York, 1968, p. 448.

[9] Arthur Whitaker, *Spain and Defense of the West: Ally and Liability,* New York, 1961, pp. 344–346.

support on issues important to her. Her success in eliciting Latin American and other Third World support in the General Assembly in her conflict with Great Britain over Gibraltar led Spain to harden her attitude in dealing with the issue.[10] This support was in part Spain's anticipated reward from Third World countries for steps taken toward the decolonization of Spanish Guinea.[11]

Italy's conflict with Austria over Italian administration of the German-speaking population of the Alto Adige (South Tyrol) ceded to her in 1919, as well as her interest, after World War II, in the disposition of her former colonies, provided occasions in which Latin American support in the United Nations was important to her.[12] In addition the great majority of the Latin American group in the United Nations backed Foreign Minister Fanfani in 1965 to preside at the General Assembly.[13]

Both South Africa and Portugal have received help from Latin America against pressure in the United Nations from the Afro-Asian countries that in a 1969 Security Council resolution almost succeeded in getting sanctions against Rhodesia extended to them. In 1960–1962 under Quadros, and in 1962–1964 under Goulart, Brazil had on occasion voted against Portugal in the United Nations[14] but since then has provided cautious support both in and outside the United Nations.

The Arab–Israeli and the Cyprus–Greece–Turkey conflicts, al-

[10] "Les Conflits Internationaux," *Revue française de science politique,* 18 (2), April 1968, pp. 339–345. On the Assembly resolution of December 18, 1968, proposing that Great Britain decolonize Gibraltar before October 1, 1969, only the British Commonwealth members among the Latin American–Caribbean states abstained or voted against the resolution. The Arab and Latin American states gave Spain almost unanimous support.

[11] An increasing unwillingness to tolerate the use of United Nations platforms for intemperate speeches rather than work has led to withdrawals from the United Nations Special Committee on Colonialism (sometimes known as the Committee of 24) formed to assure implementation of a 1960 United Nations declaration on the granting of independence to colonial countries. Australia withdrew from the committee in 1969 and was followed by Britain and the United States in early 1971.

[12] John A. Houston, *Latin America in the United Nations,* New York, 1956, pp. 189–190.

[13] *Latin American Times,* September 17, 1965; and *Le Monde,* September 21, 1965.

[14] Aaron Segal, "African Studies in Brazil," *Africa Today,* 15 (4), August–September 1969, p. 10. Presidential policy did not, however, prevent circles in the Brazilian Congress from supporting the Portuguese position.

though involving military action and much political maneuvering outside the United Nations, required the parties to the conflict (and their political allies) to solicit support in the Security Council and the Assembly. The director of the Israeli aid program, a part of which has gone to Latin America, has candidly acknowledged that its principal aim was to secure votes in the United Nations in support of the Israeli position in the Middle East.[15] The Israeli government is mindful of past Latin American interventions in her behalf. The almost unanimous support of Latin America in 1947 for the division of Palestine was crucial for the United Nations action that gave birth to Israel. Nor did the lesser powers hesitate to open their embassies in Jerusalem at a time when some of the great powers contested the city's status as a capital.

The cultivation of Latin American goodwill for the sake of Latin American votes in the United Nations was particularly understandable in the early years of the organization. At the First Session of the United Nations, 20 Latin American states constituted 39 percent of the membership, and in 1959, 24 percent. By 1966, however, the 23 Latin American members held only 19 percent of the memberships. African membership is now approximately double that of the Latin states.[16] Although the relative voting strength of the Latin American countries has been sharply reduced, the new states, whose accession has diminished Latin relative voting strength, share on the whole similar views with Latin America on many issues of economic development and anticolonialism.[17] In addition, the growth of African membership appears to have led to some increase in Latin American voting solidarity both in the mid-fifties and (according to the president of the 23rd General Assembly, the late Emilio Aranales Catalán) again more recently.[18] The Latin

[15] *The New York Times,* August 28, 1968.

[16] Thomas Hovet, Jr., *Bloc Politics in the United Nations,* Cambridge, Mass., 1960, p. 65; and Foreign Policy Association, *Handbook on Latin America,* New York, 1966, p. 66.

[17] John A. Houston, *op. cit.,* p. 296.

[18] Thomas Hovet, Jr., *op. cit.,* p. 67; and *Economist para América Latina,* January 8, 1969, pp. 9–10. Both in the 15th Session (1960–1961) and in the 18th Session (1963) the Latin American regional group in the United Nations showed a higher agreement score on roll call votes than any of the other regional groups except the Communist bloc. See Robert Owen Keohane, *Political Influence in the General Assembly,* Carnegie Endowment for International Peace, New York, 1966, p. 10; Gastón de Prat Gay, *Política Exterior del Grupo Latinoamericano,* Buenos Aires, 1967; and

republics have not, however, exhibited quite the same energy and initiative as the Afro-Asian groups of nations. Nonetheless, in 1969 when the latter broke a gentlemen's agreement to permit regional groups to select their own representatives on various United Nations bodies—forcing the election of Cuba over the Latin American choice of Argentina for a place on the governing council of the United Nations Development Board—this produced at least a temporary further increase in Latin American solidarity within the United Nations.[19]

2. *Latin American Potential*

The cultivation by the foreign powers of Latin American relations is further stimulated by a vision of Latin America as a region with enormous political and economic potential. The exaggerations of public discourse no doubt enter here. Nevertheless, there appears to be a genuine, if vague, conviction that Latin America's future requires non-Latin powers to keep this future very much in mind.

"It is foreseeable," writes Sir George Bolton,[20] a not entirely unprejudiced witness, "that by the end of the century this comparatively unknown and neglected group of countries will have acquired a political weight and economic strength that Europe, apparently condemned to continuing fragmentation along ethnic lines, will come to envy."

President Saragat of Italy is equally convinced that South America is the continent "where Europe's future lies" [21] and that its "process of development . . . despite crises, mistaken directions and errors carries within itself the germs of a future on which depends . . . the destiny not only of the continent but also of the world." [22]

Jack E. Vincent, "An Analysis of Caucusing Group Activity at the United Nations," *Journal of Peace Research* (Oslo), 2, 1970, pp. 133–150.

[19] The Afro-Asian nations commanded by far the single largest bloc of votes. Cuba got 15 votes to Argentina's 14. Mexico just made it with 17 votes. The Latin American United Nations group sent a note of protest to the Arab group, which was largely responsible for the exclusion of Argentina, apparently because of positions deemed to favor Israel.

[20] Chairman of the Bank of London and South America, in his Annual Review. Cf. *The Economist*, March 15, 1969, p. 82.

[21] *Latin American Times*, September 28, 1965.

[22] President Guiseppe Saragat in a speech following his return from South America, *Corriere della Sera* (Milan), September 25, 1965, p. 1. President Saragat linked this view of South America's future to Italy's "triangular

General de Gaulle, speaking before the Mexican Congress, declared: "Here . . . is France, who, through instinct as well as through reason, tends to turn toward the vast potential . . . represented by Latin America." [23]

Paul Martin, former Canadian secretary of state for external affairs, wished to "frankly assert one of the main reasons for my conviction that Canada must develop increasingly close relations with Latin America. This is the prospect that, between now and the end of the century, Latin America will become one of the most influential regions of the world." [24]

United States spokesmen are not more reserved. Former Assistant Secretary for Inter-American Affairs Covey T. Oliver believes that "few important industries wish to overlook a market which, when it achieves its projected economic and physical integration, will exceed Europe and the United States in size." [25] Former presidential candidate Barry Goldwater states that "South America shortly will be the most important part of the world for us." [26] And former Secretary of Agriculture Orville L. Freeman has emphasized that Latin America is expected to have, by the turn of the century, a population of 600 million and a gross domestic product of $300 billion, "too large a market to ignore." [27]

Difficulties and setbacks in economic development have not discouraged in Latin America itself the sense of a Latin America destined to replace "a Europe that is old and saturated." [28]

---

policy" (see Chapter 2.1) by adding: "Consequently it is not utopian to predict a *partnership* [in English in the original] that will unite Europe and North America with the South American continent."

[23] Address to the Mexican Congress, March 17, 1964. Press and Information Service, Embassy of France, New York.

[24] *External Affairs* (Ottawa), XIX (7), July 1967, p. 266.

[25] United States Department of State, *Bulletin,* September 30, 1968, p. 341.

[26] *The New York Times,* November 30, 1968.

[27] Alliance for Progress *Weekly Newsletter,* May 31, 1971, p. 2.

[28] In remarks before the ministers of the four Río de la Plata countries in April 1969, the late President Costa e Silva of Brazil is reported to have said: "Latin America must urgently prepare itself . . . to exercise the important role of leadership that is reserved for it in a world context. . . . The young people of our countries will yet see Latin America giving orders to the world. . . . Today, with Europe saturated, the natural tendency will be for civilization to move towards the East or towards Latin America, depending on which offers better conditions. . . . We shall be ready to absorb the progress that is already leaving a Europe that is old and saturated." *Latin America* (London), May 2, 1969, pp. 142–143.

These various European and North American statements are not entirely plausible, but they suggest a politically significant myth and not simply banquet hall bonhomie. Brazil especially is a principal object and beneficiary of these views on Latin American political and economic development. Contemporary judgments thus repeat an evaluation of the future of Brazil already made in 1935 by Nazi officials concerned with shaping German strategy in Latin America.[29] Brazilian expectations of a population of 120 million by 1980 and a 200 million population by the year 2000 lead it to view itself and to be viewed by others today for what it will become or hopes to become in the future.[30] The importance of numbers to national self-esteem is also suggested by a Latin American reminder to a North American audience: "You must remember, and this is very important, that by the year 2000, 700 million Latin Americans will live south of the border, and your relations with Latin America should not be sustained on the basis of pressure. . . ."[31] This appreciation of numbers is echoed in the developed countries and hardly serves to encourage Latin American governmental interest in population control. Following his visit in 1970 to attend the installation of Luis Echeverría as president of Mexico, a French minister reported back to the Council of Ministers that "Mexico is a country which it is already [sic] necessary to take account of. Its population is equal to that of France. . . ."[32]

The attractiveness of an area may, of course, be fortified by the decreasing accessibility or attraction of other areas. The efforts of Great Britain in 1965–1968 to recover ground in South America were all the more necessary because of diminished opportunities in Africa, the Middle East, and Asia. Sir George Bolton's statement

[29] John D. Wirth, "A German View of Brazilian Trade and Development, 1935," *The Hispanic American Historical Review,* XLVII (2), May 1967, pp. 225–235. Today, on the other hand, the views of German leaders on the future of Latin America seem to be somewhat more reserved or sober than those of leaders in other industrial countries.

[30] Some of these population projections may be off by a sizable amount. The Brazil 1970 census showed that the annual population increase, thought to be well over 3 percent, was probably closer to 2.7 percent. *Visión Letter,* April 14, 1971, p. 1.

[31] *Foreign Investment in Latin America: Past Policies and Future Trends,* Report of a Regional Meeting of the American Society of International Law, published by the Virginia Journal of International Law, 1970, p. 79.

[32] *Le Monde,* December 11, 1970.

on the future of Latin America cited above has its counterpart in an earlier statement by him: "Our traditional eastward lines of communication are in jeopardy. It, therefore, becomes imperative that we should reconsider our whole attitude toward Latin America, the only area left in the world which combines richness of resources with undecided international foreign policies." [33]

The renewal of Japanese interest in Latin America after World War II was partly motivated by the return of Japanese emigrants from the Asian mainland and the unavailability of other migration outlets,[34] and by the loss of Asian mainland resources. A vigorous South African political, economic, and cultural campaign in 1966 and 1967 to promote closer relations with Latin America, especially with Argentina and Brazil, was clearly related to its fear of isolation and to the actual and threatened boycott of it by a number of the African countries. South Africa switched to Latin America for coffee and cocoa formerly imported from Kenya and Ghana and has shown an interest in Argentinian oil.[35] Mrs. Indira Ghandi's visit to South America and the Caribbean in September and October of 1968 was motivated in part by a desire to avoid too great a "dependence on the dominant economies." [36]

The impressive month-long Canadian ministerial mission to Latin America [37] in late 1968 marked, according to Mr. Mitchell Sharp, minister of external affairs, a turning point in Canada's relations with Latin America and was not to be viewed simply as a commercial mission.[38] In the Trudeau administration's review of Canadian foreign policy, Canada's projected increase in foreign aid to less-developed countries was viewed as a contribution to peace and international welfare and as a Canadian alternative to its current

[33] Cited by Daniel James, "Europe Over Latin America," *Interplay*, December 1967, I (5), p. 8.

[34] James Lawrence Tigner, "The Ryukyuans in Argentina," *The Hispanic American Historical Review*, XLVII (2), May 1967, pp. 218ff.

[35] *Le Monde*, December 29, 1967; and *The Economist*, September 17, 1966.

[36] *India News* (Embassy of India, Washington, D.C.), October 4, 11, and 18, 1968.

[37] Specifically to: Argentina, Brazil, Chile, Colombia, Peru, Venezuela, Mexico, Costa Rica, and Guatemala.

[38] *Visão*, December 6, 1968, p. 52; and *The Christian Science Monitor*, December 7, 1968.

60

level of commitment to NATO.[39] The Third World was to be the beneficiary of a reduced contribution to Europe. The question of Canadian membership in the OAS received renewed attention. The Liberal administration had long taken a favorable "in principle" attitude to this measure [40] but had concentrated more especially on Caribbean relations and, no doubt, would have found Canadian relations with Cuba and the United States complicated by OAS membership. Galo Plaza, secretary general of the OAS, made a special trip to Canada to urge the Canadian government to seek admission to the OAS [41] but the Canadian ministerial mission to Latin America reported to Ottawa that Latin Americans did not feel that Canadian membership in the OAS was of major importance for Latin–Canadian relations. Prime Minister Trudeau had himself specifically indicated that the aim of the Canadian mission was to strengthen *bilateral* relations with Latin American countries.[42] This position was reiterated a year later in unmistakable language: "Canada's Latin American policy will . . . be based on *direct* contact with the continent to the South. . . ." [43] [Emphasis added.] Canada's 1970 white paper on foreign policy contented itself with looking forward to a rapid improvement in Canadian knowledge of Latin America which would render Canadian participation in the OAS more useful should Canada at some future time opt for full

[39] Roy A. Mathews, "A New Atlantic Role for Canada," *Foreign Affairs,* 47 (2), January 1969, p. 346.

[40] "I have no doubt whatsoever that membership in the OAS is part of the ultimate destiny of Canada as a country of the Western Hemisphere." Former Secretary of State for External Affairs Paul Martin, *External Affairs* (Ottawa), XIX (7), July 1967, p. 265.

[41] *Economist para América Latina,* December 11, 1968, p. 21.

[42] *External Affairs* (Ottawa), XX (8), August 1968, p. 333. Canada's increasing interest in Latin America is reflected in Colin I. Bradford, Jr. and Carolyn Pestieau, *Canada and Latin America: The Potential for Partnership,* Canadian Association for Latin America, Toronto, 1971.

[43] *Ibid.,* XXI (6), June 1969, p. 258. This Canadian statement was written before Jamaica was admitted to the OAS after several months of negotiations rendered difficult because of Jamaica's consular and commercial relations with Cuba, which it had no intention of discontinuing. Insofar as Canadian membership in the OAS has been inhibited by complications anticipated from its relations with Cuba, the admission of Jamaica may suggest that these problems are not insuperable. Chile's recognition of Cuba, although taken without consultation with the OAS, could reinforce this conclusion.

61

membership. In the meantime, the Canadian government indicated, in 1971, its interest in fuller participation in Pan-American activities by informing the Inter-American Development Bank that it was prepared to become a full member of the bank, by announcing that it would join the Pan-American Health Organization, and by expressing its interest in having a permanent observer at the OAS.

3. *United States Preemption*

Canadian hesitation to join the OAS is linked to the position of the United States in Latin America and in the OAS. "Until now our prudent intuition or our cowardice has led us to believe that we already have enough of our own worries and enough divergences of opinion with the United States without joining the OAS." [44] This sensitivity to the United States interest in Latin America and to the capabilities that the United States can bring to bear in promoting its interests in the region was already well developed by the mid-nineteenth century in Great Britain.[45] It was still viewed in 1965 by the Parry Committee as a source of British passivity in its relations with Latin America: "It is often held that since Latin America is within the sphere of influence of the United States, there is not much point in the British interesting themselves in the area. This is a view which is not shared by other European countries, nor is it held in the United States itself." [46]

The visits of European statesmen to Latin America have sometimes been accompanied by statements that imply a danger that these visits will be viewed by the United States as an attempt to undermine its position in the area. An Italian semi-official foreign affairs publication pointed out in advance of President Saragat's 1965 visit to Latin America that "nothing would be more absurd than to wish to create in this sector an alternative to the role of the United States of America." [47] During his 1966 visit to Latin

[44] John W. Holmes (Director, The Canadian Institute of International Affairs), "Le Canada dans le monde," *Politique Etrangère,* 33 (4), 1968, p. 304.

[45] D. C. M. Platt, "British Diplomacy in Latin America Since the Emancipation," *Inter-American Economic Affairs,* 21 (3), Winter 1967, pp. 23–25.

[46] University Grants Committee, *Report of the Committee on Latin American Studies,* London, HMSO, 1965, p. 7.

[47] *Esteri* (Rome), August 30, 1965, p. 2. Nonetheless, the *LeMonde* correspondent in Rio de Janeiro alleged that Foreign Minister Fanfani, who accompanied President Saragat, did not hide his view that Brazilian policy was too strictly aligned on Washington. *Le Monde,* September 14, 1965.

62

America, Foreign Minister Michael Stewart, in response to a tendentious question from a French correspondent, replied that British and American interests in Latin America were not opposed and that "this was understood in Washington." [48] General Franco's sensational offer to Latin America in November 1965 of one billion dollars in credits was called the "H program," the two parallel lines of the H symbolizing the cooperating, and not competing, programs of Spain and the United States. [49] When General de Gaulle, prior to his 1964 Latin American trip, sought to enlist German cooperation in the trade drive that France planned in Latin America, Chancellor Erhard feared that the United States would object, and it appears that it was not until he had talks with President Johnson that he informed General de Gaulle that Washington welcomed this action. [50] More recently, despite a decline in the United States ability to make its preferences felt, Japan is said to have withheld purchases of ore concentrates from United States mines that had been nationalized in Latin America. [51]

Countries whose relations with the United States are less close or less friendly are not so inclined to worry about actual or imagined United States sensitivities. But even France is said to have given assurances to President Johnson that General de Gaulle's trip to South America would not be the occasion for the exercise of anti-Anglo-Saxon diplomacy. [52] In fact, of course, General de Gaulle was not entirely inhibited from speaking his mind and if he warned Latin nationalism against exhausting itself in "xenophobia against its great North American neighbor," he also warned the Latin nations not to "fall victim to one of the rival hegemonies both of which want to dominate under pretext of [an] ideological struggle . . . which serve[s] to cover up hegemonist pretensions." [53]

The concern for possible United States sensitivities seems more a desire to avoid gratuitous friction than a willingness to sacrifice

[48] *Le Monde,* January 7, 1966; and *The Economist,* January 15, 1966, p. 195.

[49] *The New York Times,* March 2, 1966.

[50] *The New York Times,* February 16, 1964.

[51] *Latin America* (London), July 2, 1971, p. 211. On the other hand, threats of United States retaliation are said no longer to worry Swedish businessmen or the Swedish government. *Ibid.,* p. 212.

[52] *The Evening Star* (Washington, D.C.), March 12, 1964.

[53] Leo Hamon, *Review of International Affairs* (Belgrade), XVIII (402), January 5, 1967, pp. 11–12.

major economic or political benefits to United States interests or policy preferences in Latin America. The substantial British, Canadian, Spanish, Japanese, and French commerce with Cuba, and European sales of military goods to South America are hardly consistent with the view that the United States has imposed its Latin American policy on the nonhemispheric countries.[54]

The existence of United States pressure is indisputable, but sometimes such pressures may be alleged in order to conceal, at least publicly, other motives. According to a French statement, a plan to install a Renault plant in Cuba fell through only because the French government feared reprisals against French auto sales in the United States.[55] Whether this was in fact the case or was an attempt by France to bring pressure to bear on Cuba for restitution of French-owned property (see section 6 below) may perhaps be viewed as uncertain.

Similarly, domestic political motives may lie behind actions attributed to a threat of American punitive measures. Thus in July 1968 the French transport ministry explained its abandonment of French tourist and youth flights to Cuba by reference to the fact that one-third of Air France traffic is with the United States and that 70 percent of the passengers on these flights are Americans. The French ministry did not claim that United States pressure had been exercised but that Americans "would" not appreciate such trips being organized on French soil and that the ill will of *"leurs grandes agences de voyage"* "could" have disagreeable consequences, thus attributing a degree of both power and patriotism to United States travel agencies that no doubt would have astonished them had they been aware of the attribution. In fact, the cancellation of French

[54] In 1971 the United States lifted its ban on the import of French products containing nickel because France agreed to stop importing Cuban nickel. *Latin America* (London), February 5, 1971, p. 43. This French compliance, after several years of importing Cuban nickel, resulted from France's interest in associating American, Canadian, and Belgian capital in developing its New Caledonian nickel mines. French substitution of its own New Caledonian sources for Cuban nickel is expected to cut Cuban exports to France by about 40 percent. Refusals by United States-owned enterprises in France to sell to Cuba are, on the other hand, clear cases where United States policy has adversely affected French interests. *Le Monde,* August 27, 1971.

[55] *Le Monde,* March 7–8, 1965.

64

student flights was demanded by a UDR deputy following the May 1968 students riots in France, on the grounds that French students were receiving guerrilla training in Cuba.[56]

Europe's willingness to challenge or ignore the United States in its relations with Latin America is facilitated by the increasing frequency with which Latin American governments signal their desire to establish closer relations with the nonhemispheric states and to decrease their dependence on the United States. Already in 1964 it was possible for President Valencia of Colombia, by no means the most active South American state in developing extra-hemispheric relations, to draw attention in his year-end review to trade treaties with Spain and Finland; technical cooperation negotiations with West Germany and Israel; economic agreements drafted with Denmark, the Netherlands, Great Britain, Ireland, Italy and France; the reception of special missions from West Germany, India, Australia, and Canada; negotiations to establish relations with Kuwait and Ivory Coast; and steps taken to develop relations with other newly independent states of Africa, Asia, and Oceania. President Frei of Chile broke a 20-year-old custom when he began his important 1965 presidential trip to Europe without first visiting Washington. Similarly, President-elect Lleras Restrepo of Colombia avoided Washington in setting out on his 1966 preinaugural trip to Spain, France, and Portugal, although he flew via Caracas and New York. Since then, many of the Latin American states have made unmistakably clear their interest in economic and diplomatic relations with Europe, Japan, and the Soviet bloc countries. Galo Plaza, secretary general of the OAS, while in Paris to make a plea for more European economic and technological help for Latin America, pointed out that "Latin America more and more looks toward Europe and other continents for mutually beneficial relations. . . ." And to make sure that his meaning was not lost, he added: "Latin America is not, nor will it ever be, the private domain

[56] The cancellation of Cuban flights in 1968 is discussed in *Le Monde,* May 25–26, 1969. United States punitive measures against French firms that engaged in clandestine reexportation of United States products to Cuba seems neither very swift nor overly severe. Two large French companies that reshipped United States chemical fertilizers to Cuba in 1968 were not penalized until 1971 when they were banned from trade with the United States for six months in one case and nine months in the other. *Los Angeles Times,* August 5, 1971.

or the backyard of any power." [57] Latin American ministers of foreign, economic, and defense affairs are no strangers to Europe. The visit of Foreign Minister Costa Méndez of Argentina in the spring of 1969 to West Germany, France, Rumania, Italy, and Spain underlined Argentinian preference for European capital and shows an itinerary typical of recent Latin American ministerial visits. Prior to and during General de Gaulle's Mexican and South American tours, the Latin American governments took care to reassure the United States on their forthcoming conversations with him. [58] In 1967 the Brazilian minister for foreign affairs did not attend the Algiers meeting of the Seventy-Seven (less-developed countries) in order not to associate his country with possible condemnations of United States policy. [59] It is doubtful that these types of Latin American concern would repeat themselves today on parallel occasions.

4. *"We Are Far Away"*

The nonhemispheric countries have sometimes exhibited an exaggerated sense of their distance from Latin America and of the closeness of the United States to it. This on occasion served to encourage their inaction in Latin America or at least to create a sense of an obstacle to be overcome in pursuit of national objectives. North Americans, on the other hand, sometimes underestimate their considerable distance from much of the Latin world—New York is closer to Istanbul and Moscow than it is to Montevideo.

In 1867, speaking of Central America, Lord Palmerston had said, "They [the United States] are on the spot, strong deeply interested in the matter. . . . We are far away, weak from Distance. . . ." [60] Whatever geopolitical justification this may have had, it hardly applied to some parts of South America. Forty years later, the

[57] *The New York Times,* November 17, 1970. The secretary general's statement was underlined by the appearance while he was in Europe of a European edition of *Visión* in four languages, English, German, French, and Italian.

[58] Jean Meyriat, "France and Latin America," in Claudio Véliz (ed.), *op. cit.,* p. 430. The Latin American governments may have been unduly concerned about United States apprehensions. Prior to General de Gaulle's Mexican trip, President Kennedy had urged the General to increase French economic participation in Latin America and had emphasized the special opportunities open to France because of Latin American affinities with French culture. *The Evening Star* (Washington, D.C.), February 17, 1964.

[59] *Le Monde,* October 7–8, 1967.

[60] Cited in D. C. M. Platt, *op. cit.,* p. 25.

author of a chapter on Latin American history in *The Cambridge Modern History* (1910) could still write: "The River Plate is, by sea, geographically as near to Bordeaux or Southhampton as to Washington or New York, and in effect much nearer; at the present time, United States diplomatists and officers find that the most convenient route from New York to Buenos Aires is through Southhampton." [61]

The decline of British investment and commerce in South America after World War I and World War II seems to have produced a sense of great physical distance from Latin America. The London *Economist,* speaking of Britain's need to restore its Latin American relations, could refer to Latin America's "remoteness from Britain" and its "closeness to the United States" and merge with the idea of Latin America being politically the United States "backyard" a sense of Britain's physical distance from the subcontinent. APSA, the Peruvian airline, advertising in Great Britain, headlines a full-page advertisement with "The South American market is far away but. . . ." [62] Similarly, a French observer notes that France, on the whole, is indifferent to "far off Latin America." [63] And a Soviet writer, referring to recent "suspicious" West German contacts with Argentina, especially the Siemens contract (see note 47, Chapter 3), asks: What is Bonn looking for "in this distant region?" [64] feeling, perhaps, that anyone who travels *that* far must have some rather special designs, possibly an insight arrived at from observations of increased Soviet contact with the Latin area. Peking, too, feels itself separated by great distances from Latin America. "Though China and Chile are separated by tens of thousands of miles [li], yet the friendly ties between the two peoples can by no means be cut off by the vast Pacific Ocean." [65]

[61] F. A. Kirkpatrick, "The Republics of Latin America: Historical Sketch to 1896," in *The Latest Age* (Cambridge Modern History, Vol. XII), New York, 1910, p. 684.

[62] *The Economist,* October 3, 1964, and April 26, 1969.

[63] Jean Meyriat, *op. cit.,* p. 440. President Pompidou was probably more concerned with defending the utility of the supersonic Concorde than he was with France's relations with Latin America when he praised the Concorde for the favorable effect it would have on France's relations with Latin America and Asia by bringing these continents closer. *Le Monde,* May 9–10, 1971.

[64] *Pravda,* April 14, 1969, p. 5.

[65] *People's Daily* (Peking), January 7, 1971. In fact, it was not "the vast Pacific Ocean" that Peking's delegation to the inauguration of President

First steps toward establishing relations with a region also seem to suggest that considerable distance are being traversed. President Archbishop Makarios of Cyprus, in visiting Bogotá in 1966, thought that trade possibilities existed "despite the distance" separating the two countries. And President Kenneth Kaunda of Zambia, second African head of state to visit Latin America, also saw a promising future for African–Latin American relations, despite the distance separating the two continents.[66] Probably the Archbishop does not feel himself in so distant a region when in New York, which is about the same distance from Cyprus as is Bogotá; nor President Kaunda so distant in London, which is just as far from Lusaka as substantial parts of Latin America.[67]

Foreign Minister Hilgard Muller of South Africa, on the contrary, anxious to consolidate relations with Argentina and Brazil, emphasized in his 1966 visit to Buenos Aires and Rio de Janeiro that South America was a "neighbor," albeit a neighbor across the seas, and felt that he had to provide for his auditors—and perhaps for himself—an unaccustomed perspective on the geography of the world by pointing out that the distance between South Africa and the east coast of South America was less than between South Africa and many of its trading partners. Indeed, the Cape is closer to Rio than to Cairo, and Johannesburg closer to Brazil than to London.

A "neighbor," it appears, can be any country between which and oneself there is no intervening land mass. Thus a French official contemplating Tahiti and the possible opening of direct air service from Chile was able to refer to France as Chile's "neighbor" in the Pacific; and Foreign Minister Vasco Leitão da Cunha of Brazil found the possibility of communism on the West Coast of Africa especially alarming since the African West Coast countries are "neighbors" of Brazil.

If the intervening spaces are not empty there is still the pos-

---

Allende had to cross. It flew from Peking via Asia, Europe, Africa, the Atlantic, the South American east coast, and across the Andes to Santiago.

[66] *Le Monde,* December 18–19, 1966. President Kaunda was preceded by President Senghor of Senegal, who visited Latin America in 1964.

[67] Distance as perceived may, of course, depend on cost, time, and travel facilities. In the mid-sixties, the number of international plane flights weekly between Latin American countries and Asia was 8, Africa 37, Europe 119, and the United States 299. Johan Galtung, Manuel Mora y Araujo, Simon Schwartzman, "El Sistema Latinoamericano de Naciones: un análisis estructural," *América Latina* (Rio de Janeiro), 9 (1), January–March 1966, p. 71.

sibility that neighborliness may be claimed by virtue of membership in the same hemisphere. Foreign Minister Costa Méndez of Argentina pointed out that by historical legacy Argentina's bond is with Europe but on the other hand with the United States Argentina has the bond of being hemispheric "neighbors." In a similar vein a Canadian ambassador presenting his credentials to a Central American president was able to affirm that "geographically we are neighbors." Foreign Minister Muller had supposed that South Africa and Argentina were neighbors because of a common membership in the Southern Hemisphere [68] but for President Nixon it is the United States and Latin America who "share a concept of hemispheric community." Following the disastrous Peruvian earthquake of 1970, President Nixon referred, in a special statement, to "Peru, a neighbor nation in this hemisphere." [69]

In the modern world, distance would seem to have a somewhat attenuated significance given the contemporary technology of transport and communication.[70] Japan, whose distance from Latin American east and west coast ports is far greater than that of any other important trading partner of Latin America (Yokohama to Buenos Aires, 14,000 steamship miles!), has in the postwar period become a principal buyer, seller, and investor in Latin America. Supplementing its huge oil tankers with specially designed freighters of 100,000 tons for the shipping of ores, Japan has adapted to the fact that some 70–80 percent of its imports are raw materials and that its average raw material hauling distance rose from 3,520 miles in 1925 to 5,800 miles in 1966.[71] Latin American ports are thus separated from Japan by more than twice the average of Japan's raw material transport distance. Symbolic of how little this has discouraged Japanese businessmen is the fact that signs in Managua's Gran Hotel are in three languages: Spanish, English, and— Japanese.[72]

[68] *El Cronista Comercial* (Buenos Aires), July 22, 1966.

[69] *The New York Times*, February 19, 1970, and July 14, 1970.

[70] For a discussion of this theme, especially in a national security setting, see Albert Wohlstetter, "Illusions of Distance," *Foreign Affairs*, January 1968, pp. 242–255.

[71] Japanese Ministry of Transport. Approximately one-third of Japanese trade transits the Panama Canal. *United States Congressional Record— Senate*, July 21, 1967, p. S-10025. Japanese transport technology does not mean that Japan has overlooked the advantages to her of nearby Alaskan oil, timber, and other resources.

[72] *Los Angeles Times*, October 11, 1965.

5. *"No Policy Is the Best Policy"*

The ascription of political and other objectives to governments and private groups sometimes suggests a clarity of purpose and a firmness of intent that scarcely correspond to the real frame of mind of political leaders or to the actual state of planning and activity in complex organizations. Foreign affairs minister Amintore Fanfani, in his report of January 1967 to the Italian parliamentary commission on foreign affairs, listed improved relations with Latin America as the second of three major goals of Italian foreign policy in the period 1965–1966. Italian commentators, however, despite high-ranking official Italian visits to Latin America, saw few examples of significant initiatives and viewed Italian foreign policy as being rather more consistent with a well-known slogan of Italian political circles: No foreign policy is the best foreign policy, a slogan justified by the rhetorical query: Who else can claim to have only friends in the world? [73]

Some observers of Great Britain's activity in Latin America have felt it was "not backed by any discernible British policy" and justified a Chilean remark that "France has the will but not the resources, Germany the resources but not the will, Britain neither." [74] A tendency to view the pursuit of trade, investment, and construction contracts ("economics") as equivalent to not having a policy accounts in part for an impression of passivity in Great Britain's policy toward Latin America. In fact British diplomacy in Latin America has had a fairly consistent aim over the last 100 years— the protection of British subjects and their trade and investments. Britain, until after World War II, largely left its businessmen and goods to find their own markets. This policy reinforced the impression of passivity. After World War II, however, "a tradition of diplomatic assistance to commerce and investment . . . developed which would have seemed inconceivable thirty years ago." [75] This brought additional means into play without altering government objectives in Latin America.

[73] Cavazza, *op. cit.,* pp. 35–37 and 83–84; and Arrigo Levi in *Interplay,* October 1967, I (3), pp. 41–42.

[74] *The Economist,* October 3, 1964, p. 20; and *The New York Times,* January 16, 1966.

[75] D. C. M. Platt, *op. cit.,* p. 28. For an extension of the discussion to British policy in other areas as well, see the same author's *Finance, Trade, and Politics in British Foreign Policy, 1815–1914,* New York, 1968.

Japan, too, is sometimes viewed as a country without a foreign policy because until recently its concern in the world has been largely confined to selling its goods and acquiring raw materials. A Japanese foreign office official has defended Japan against the charge of being a timid giant: "There are definite advantages to our policy of emphasizing economics. . . . You cannot really say we don't have a policy. We have a great deal of initiative in the economic sense. . . ." [76] The timid giant is at any rate not timid with respect to its investment policy in Latin America, where perhaps more than in other areas a major motive has been access to raw materials without too much regard for immediate profits. [77]

Specialists in Latin American affairs are generally little content with the Latin American policies of their own governments. They find them to be unclear, vacillating, and indifferent to Latin America and executed by officials insufficiently trained and informed on Latin American affairs. These criticisms, often true, nonetheless reflect sometimes a certain *parti pris* not readily shared by political leaders whose concerns extend beyond specific regional interests; and perhaps reflect, too, an unwillingness to recognize that passive diplomacy can also be a policy.

6. *Protection of Nationals*

The protection of nationals and their interests abroad is a routine responsibility of government, but the vigor with which it is pursued and the occasions on which it is exercised are sometimes matters of larger government policy and frequently are associated with other foreign objectives. The French blockade of 1838–1840 in the Río de la Plata was ostensibly to protect France's 5,000 nationals in Buenos Aires against obligatory military service, but was in fact motivated by commercial considerations. [78] The collection of defaulted debts owed to their nationals has provided other occasions for the military reaction of European governments, the last of which

[76] B. Krisher, "How Japan Sees the Future," *The New Leader*, February 27, 1967, p. 9. See also Kei Wakaisumi, "Japan Beyond 1970," *Foreign Affairs*, April 1969, p. 509.

[77] Yoshinori Ohara, *Japan and Latin America*, The Rand Corporation, RM-5388-RC, 1967, pp. 42–43. On the Japanese rush for investment at any price and governmental guidance on this policy, see also the Japan Survey, *The Economist*, May 27, 1967, pp. xix–xx.

[78] Nestor S. Colli, *La Política Francesa en el Río de la Plata: Rosas y el Bloqueo de 1838–1840*, Buenos Aires, 1963, pp. 40, 139.

71

was the British, German, and Italian blockade of Venezuela in 1902.

Occasions for restitution continue to exist, but diplomatic and economic instruments have now replaced military pressure. In 1965 the Chilean government returned to German ownership property confiscated during the war in 1943. In return for this the government of the Federal Republic of Germany agreed to renegotiate the Chilean foreign debt. In Brazil, Governor Carlos Lacerda of Guanabara returned in 1965 German property seized during World War II. And in the same year the Brazilian government returned to the Bank of Tokyo Japanese funds that had been confiscated during the war. The contemporary economic position in Latin America of the losers of World War II has thus permitted compensation for losses suffered two decades earlier.

The British-owned Antofagasta (Chili) and Bolivian Railway accepted in 1967 an unsatisfactory compensation for properties and investments taken over by Bolivia. It is indicative of the limited British economic activity in Latin America that in warning the Bolivian government in 1966 against delaying a settlement, the company had to refer largely to the negative effect this would have on credits negotiated by other governments.[79]

France in 1965 obtained compensation for its citizens holding stock in the Victoria–Minas and São Paulo–Rio Grande Railway Companies, and in 1966 the Brazilian government also asked Congress for funds to indemnify French shareholders in the Port of Pará, which had been nationalized in 1940.[80] On the other hand, an apparent French attempt to exert pressure on Castro for the indemnification of nationalized French property, valued at about $50–80 million, failed. The French agency COFACE [Compagnie française d'assurance et de crédit pour le commerce extérieur] held up for 15 months insurance on credits for a Krebs et Cie contract to build a fertilizer and insecticide plant for Cuba, in order to bring pressure to bear on Castro. Cuba, however, procured the fertilizer plant from Britain.[81]

---

[79] Annual statement of the chairman. *The Economist,* October 15, 1966, pp. 314–315, November 18, 1967, and October 12, 1968, p. 102.

[80] *Le Monde,* July 6, 1966, October 7, 1966, and October 5, 1966.

[81] *Le Monde,* November 18, 1965. The Cuban ambassador to France rejected *Le Monde's* imputation of a political motive for COFACE's behavior, but no French spokesman issued a similar denial. *Le Monde,* November 23,

In 1965 the new Dutch ambassador to Cuba announced that the Netherlands would seriously consider the extension of long-term commercial credits to Cuba. Interpretations of this as a prelude to an effort to secure compensation for nationalized Dutch properties were not entirely laid to rest by his accompanying statement that no plans for the negotiation of a compensation agreement existed.[82]

These efforts by the Dutch and the French to salvage something from Cuban confiscations may have been encouraged by Castro's references in the first half of 1964 to the possibility of compensation for United States properties. In a speech of January 2, 1964, Castro indicated that he might be willing to provide compensation for nationalized United States properties if trade was restored with Cuba. In April he repeated this theme to a correspondent of the American Broadcasting Company and in July to a *New York Times* correspondent.[83] That compensation for some Cuban confiscations may be paid is suggested by a statement of Foreign Affairs Minister Mitchell Sharp in January 1971 that Canada and Cuba would begin negotiations on a lump sum payment for property of Canadian citizens taken over by Cuba.

The United States has in recent years largely relied in Latin America on the importance of its private investment flows, its trade, and its aid programs to protect United States investors. However, the pressures inherent in these transactions did not, in fact, always prevent uncompensated expropriations. The diffidence of the United States government in its application of pressure, especially following Brazilian expropriations in 1962, led the Congress to pass the Hickenlooper Amendment to the Foreign Assistance Act of 1961. The Amendment made it mandatory for the President to cut off grant aid and sugar quota purchases from any government that expropriated United States property without full and timely compensation in convertible foreign exchange. By falling back on rather strained legalisms the Executive branch of the government has been able to avoid invoking the Hickenlooper Amendment in cases where the Amendment called for presidential action. Nonetheless, the

---

1965. A coolness arising in 1971 between the Spanish and Cuban governments has also been attributed, among other matters, to Spanish pressure for indemnification for property confiscated from Spanish nationals.

[82] *Latin American Times,* September 7, 1965.

[83] Andrés Suaréz, *Cuba: Castroism and Communism, 1959–66,* Cambridge, Mass., 1967, pp. 192, 210–211.

Brazilian cases of 1962–1963 and the Hickenlooper Amendment may have been responsible for the fact that in 1963 in Peru "the U.S. Government, without any announcement, started a stop-and-go policy on the Aid program, depending on the status of the oil negotiations. . . ." [84] However, when Peru finally took control of the International Petroleum Corporation in 1968 no action was taken by the president of the United States under the Hickenlooper Amendment, which, in fact, has been invoked only once in the eight years of its existence (Ceylon, 1963).

Governmental support and protection abroad of private interests lay governments open to the charge that their overall policies in the region are largely designed for the benefit of big business and are at the cost of the national welfare. Such charges are all the more plausible if both government and business are powerful and active in a foreign region. Thus the United States interventions in the Caribbean during the first two decades of the century lent themselves more especially to the charge of dollar diplomacy. Nevertheless, a recent study of the period concludes that United States interventions in the internal affairs of Caribbean countries were largely motivated by political and national security considerations and not primarily to support United States corporations operating in the area. [85] Still, it is apparent that in small countries not involved in major political issues with the United States, much of United States policy and action will turn out to be in connection with and in support of United States private citizens and corporations. When United States government relations with a country are relatively unimportant it is easier for a private corporation or a United States citizen to get intervention on its or his behalf since the political stakes that might be disturbed are quite limited.

Speaking of the present period, a former government official points out that there has been a diminished "responsiveness of the United States government to the cries for protection against na-

[84] Carlos Gibson, Minister Counselor Financial of Peru, in American Society of International Law, *op. cit.,* p. 48. See also p. 33. This regional meeting of the society brought together a number of Latin American and North American representatives of government, business, and law with a considerable range of views on the legal, political, and moral issues before the meeting.

[85] Dana G. Munro, *Intervention and Dollar Diplomacy in the Caribbean, 1900–1921,* Princeton, N.J., 1964. See especially Chapter 12 and pp. 530–535. See also Bryce Wood, *The United States and Latin American Wars 1932–1942,* New York, 1966, pp. 1–4.

tionalism of United States companies abroad. American business is realizing that Washington and its embassies are of questionable value in a Latin American scuffle." [86] The reluctance of recent Democratic and Republican administrations to take a hard line in reprisal for expropriations or for seizures of United States fishing vessels underlines that Executive policy in Latin America is not always responsive to United States business. In 1971, however, the "soft line" of the State Department was apparently overruled and United States Export-Import Bank credits for the purchase of three Boeing jet aircraft were refused to Chile, and the United States abstained on World Bank loans for Guyana and Bolivia and on an Inter-American Development Bank loan to the latter. All three of these countries had recently expropriated United States properties. In the case of Chile, United States action was clearly intended to force President Allende to announce his compensation plan for nationalized copper properties. That this involved the likely loss to the United States aircraft industry of a $21 million sale suggests that United States action was probably motivated by longer term calculations affecting United States investments in Latin America and not only those properties recently nationalized. These measures did not serve simply to protect private interests. The United States government has its own interest in avoiding tax and insurance losses and negative effects on the balance of payments resulting from expropriations. Nor does the fact that private groups in the United States solicit and often receive special advantages from the United States government—special trade policies, tax privileges, assistance in collecting bad debts, credit and investment insurance, and other facilities for the promotion of trade and investment—mean that they shape the main lines of its policy in the region. The principal directions of that policy were in the decade of the Alliance for Progress affected more by the cold war, by the advent of Castro and sporadic guerilla outbreaks, by the political importance of the military in Latin American affairs, by strategic considerations, and not least, by the almost inextinguishable faith that United States responsibilities and capabilities extend to the moral and practical guidance of the Latin American states. [87]

[86] George C. Lodge, *Engines of Change: United States Interests and Revolution in Latin America,* New York, 1970, p. 295. See also pp. 292–304.

[87] See Chapter 11.3 for a discussion of this last theme; and Chapter 12 for further discussion of the response of government and the international and multinational corporations to expropriation.

Part II

INSTRUMENTS

5. The Migrant Presence

SOMETIMES as a conscious instrument of national policy and sometimes simply as an unplanned consequence of their presence,
migrants to Latin America have often benefited—and occasionally
harmed—their homelands both economically (section 2 below)
and politically (section 3 below). We first examine the extent and
character of these migrations to Latin America.

1. *Numbers*

When Latin America achieved independence, only about 20 percent of its population was of European—mostly Spanish and
Portuguese—origin.[1] But the large-scale migrations from many
parts of the world to Latin America, especially toward the end of
the nineteenth century, in the years just before World War I, and
again after World War II [2] (see Tables 5.3 and 5.4) markedly

[1] Artur Hehl Neiva, "International Migration Affecting Latin America,"
in Clyde C. Kiser (ed.), *Components of Population Change in Latin
America,* The Milbank Memorial Fund Quarterly, XLIII (4), October 1965,
Part 2, p. 122. R. Kuczynski estimated Central and South American
population in the period 1825–1835 to be: European origin, 5 million;
African origin, 17 million; indigenous population, 8 million; *mestizos,*
6 million. *Population Movements,* Oxford, 1936, p. 90.

[2] Because of the construction program under the Pérez Jiménez regime,
migration in the fifties was directed in an unusual degree to Venezuela, which
received almost a half million immigrants in the years 1952–1956, as compared with less than 200,000 for Argentina and about 350,000 for Brazil.
Anthony T. Bouscaren, *International Migrations Since 1945,* New York,
1963, p. 151.

increased the physical presence and the political and economic involvement with Latin America of a number of other countries. Both the opportunities open to governments to send "surplus" populations to Latin America and migrations that took place on a purely private basis introduced the nonhemispheric states to a variety of new relations with the Latin republics.

With the important exceptions of Argentina and Venezuela the foreign born are not a large proportion of the population of the Latin American republics; [3] they are a smaller proportion than are the foreign born in Canada and the United States (see Table 5.1). Further, in most Latin American countries a substantial part of the foreign born are made up of migrants from other Latin American countries (see Table 5.2) whose language and culture are often not very different from those of the host country.

What gives the foreign born in Latin America special political significance is that the great majority have remained nationals of their country of origin and that their descendants often maintain a close connection with the land of their parents and grandparents. In the United States (1950) and in Canada (1951) close to 80 percent of the foreign born were United States and Canadian citizens. In Latin America the situation is the reverse. Typically, the Latin American censuses for the years around 1950 show the great majority of foreign born, about 85–90 percent, as citizens of their country of issue. Only in Mexico (1950) and Cuba (1953) do the foreign nationals among the foreign born drop as low as 58 percent and 65 percent respectively (see Table 5.1).

This striking difference between the citizenship status of migrants to North America and South America is not accounted for by differences in age structure or in recency of immigration. Nor do data on naturalization by age groups support the view that avoidance of military service explains the observed differences between North American and South American immigrant behavior. There are some differences in the propensities of various immigrant nationalities to acquire Latin American citizenship, but they are not very striking and the great majority of the foreign born of each nationality retain their original citizenship. In Brazil, 1940, the percentage

[3] In 1930 one out of every four Argentinians (26 percent) was an alien of European origin. Imre Ferenczi, *World Statistics of Aliens, A Comparative Study of Census Returns, 1910–1920–1930,* International Labour Office, Geneva, 1936, Table 8, p. 46.

TABLE 5.1
PERCENTAGE OF POPULATION FOREIGN BORN AND EUROPEAN BORN
AND PERCENTAGE OF FOREIGN NATIONALS AMONG FOREIGN BORN

| Country | Year | Percentage of Population | | Percentage of Foreign Nationals Among Foreign Born |
		Foreign Born	European Born	
Argentina	1947	15.33	12.04	—
	1960	12.82	—	—
Boliva	1950	1.31	0.14	80.1
Brazil	1950	2.34	1.86	89.3
Chile	1952	1.75	1.07	93.1
	1960	1.43	—	—
Colombia	1951	0.44	0.06	90.9
	1961	0.42	—	—
Costa Rica	1950	4.15	0.42	100.5 [a]
Cuba	1953	3.95	1.55 [b]	64.8
Dominican Republic	1950	1.62	0.09	94.4
Ecuador	1950	0.73	0.13	—
El Salvador	1950	1.04	0.02	97.1
Guatemala	1950	1.08	0.04	—
Honduras	1950	2.40	0.09 [b]	99.6
Mexico	1950	0.71	—	57.8
	1960	0.64	—	—
Nicaragua	1950	0.96	0.03	72.9
	1963	0.81	—	—
Panama	1950	6.22	0.60	92.7
	1960	4.16	—	—
Paraguay	1950	4.08	1.08	87.0
Uruguay	1963	6.41 [c]	—	—
Venezuela	1950	4.15	2.43	93.0
	1961	7.41	—	—
Canada	1951	14.70	—	21.4
	1961	15.60	—	37.1
United States	1950	6.87	—	19.9
	1960	5.41	—	30.3

[a] *Sic.*
[b] European nationals.
[c] Percent aliens.
SOURCES: Pan American Union, *La Composición étnica de los países latino-americanos,* 1963, p. 95; U.N. *Demographic Year Book,* 1963 and 1964, *Canada Year Book,* 1967; *Statistical Abstract of the United States,* 1967.

of foreign born who were naturalized varied from 3 percent for the Japanese [4] to 22 percent for Austrians, with most nationalities

[4] This figure was 7 percent in 1958. Census Commission of the Japanese Colony in São Paulo, *The Japanese Immigrants in Brazil,* Tokyo, 1964. The number naturalized is not given directly but has been inferred from data on voters. Table headings are in Japanese and English. The census date is

falling between 7 and 14 percent. The propensity of migrants to become naturalized varies a little among the Latin republics. In Mexico (1950), among almost all nationalities, the proportion of naturalized foreign born is larger than in Brazil, Chile, and Venezuela, but the naturalized are still a minority.[5]

The failure to become naturalized is in part related to the substantial proportion of immigrants to Latin America who plan to and do return to their country of origin.[6] During the years 1946–1954 the rate of return from Latin America was only about 15–20 percent for Spanish, Italian, and Portuguese migrants but approximately 50 percent for other European nationalities.[7] Migrants who never return to their native land continue to preserve this option and also hesitate to become citizens because of obstacles and disincentives to naturalization. Fees, bureaucratic delays in the processing of applications, and the fact that naturalized citizens do not always acquire the full privileges of native born citizens act as disincentives.[8] One of Argentina's most enthusiastic supporters of European immigration, Juan Bautista Alberdi ("to govern is to populate"), helped to write the Argentinian Constitution of 1853 of which Article 20 guaranteed aliens the same civil rights as

---

June 1958. This remarkable volume, one of the world's more ambitious private censuses, deserves to be better known.

[5] The foregoing paragraph is based on 1950 data on foreign born and foreign nationals in Brazil, Bolivia, Venezuela, and Mexico in Pan American Union, *La estructura demográfica de las naciones Americanas,* Washington, D.C. 1960, and on 1940 data on foreign born and foreign nationals in Brazil in Geraldo de Menezes Cortês, *Migração e colonização no Brasil,* Rio de Janeiro, 1958, p. 47.

[6] Early Italian migrants sometimes took advantage of the seasonal differences between Italy and Argentina to become intercontinental migratory agricultural laborers. These "golondrinas" may have constituted about 15 percent of Italian migration to Argentina in the last half of the nineteenth century.

[7] Christopher Tietze, "The Role of Immigration in Latin America's Population Pattern," in Margaret Bates (ed.), *The Migration of Peoples to Latin America,* Washington, D.C., 1957, pp. 40–41. Venezuela (1950–1955) had an overall reemigration rate of 62 percent, with an Italian rate of 39 percent. Italian return rates for Argentina, Brazil, and Uruguay were 27 percent, 26 percent, and 20 percent respectively. Spanish reemigration from Latin America (1955–1959) was 20 percent, Portuguese (1946–1960) 12 percent, and Japanese less than 10 percent. Artur Hehl Neiva, *op. cit.,* p. 128.

[8] Fernando Bastos de Ávila, S.J., *La inmigración en América Latina,* Pan American Union, Washington, D.C., 1964, pp. 293–294.

TABLE 5.2

Place of Birth of the Foreign Born in Latin America

(in thousands)

Place of Birth	Argentina 1947	Brazil 1950	Chile 1952	Colombia 1964	Mexico 1950	Mexico 1960	Peru 1940	Venezuela 1950	Venezuela 1961
Austria	33.2	17.4	1.5	0.6	[a]	[a]	0.3	1.3	[b]
France	33.5	8.6	3.4	1.7	2.9	4.2	0.8	4.7	[b]
Germany	51.6	65.8	13.0	3.9	4.6 [a]	6.7 [a]	2.2	4.3	[b]
Great Britain	11.4	5.4	2.2	0.6	2.3	2.4	1.1	3.5	[b]
Italy	786.2	242.3	11.6	2.9	2.1	3.5	3.8	43.9	122.5
Poland	111.3	48.8	1.7	0.9	3.5	4.3	0.5	3.9	[b]
Portugal	25.3	336.9	[c]	[c]	0.3	[c]	0.1	11.0	44.2
Spain	749.6	131.6	22.4	7.4	37.5	49.6	2.5	37.9	178.0
USSR	109.2	48.7	1.8	0.3	3.1	[b]	0.1	2.9	[b]
Europe, other	111.9	58.8	12.1	4.2	3.8	6.1	2.2	14.0	[b]
Japan	5.2	129.2	1.7 [d]	0.4	2.0	2.2	17.6	0.04	[b]
Lebanon, Syria [e]	65.7	44.7	3.4	2.1	6.8	5.1	0.7	3.1	[b]
Central and South America	323.3	58.1	20.0 [f]	39.1	16.1 [g]	[b]	17.1	65.0	106.4 [h]
U.S. and Canada	6.3	8.4 [i]	2.2 [j]	7.9	89.6	97.9 [j]	1.4	11.1	[b]
Others	12.2	9.3	6.9	2.0	8.1	40.5	12.4	1.7	105.8
Total	2435.9	1214.0	103.9	74.0	182.7	222.5	62.7	208.7	556.9

[a] Austria included in Germany.

[b] Included in "Others."

[c] Included in "Europe, others."

[d] Includes Asia other than China and Near East.

[e] And other Near East countries (Jordan, Iraq, Palestine, Turkey).

[f] South America only.

[g] Central America only.

[h] Includes Colombia only (106.4 thousand).

[i] Includes Puerto Rico.

[j] United States only.

Sources: Pan American Union, *La Estructura Demográfica de las Naciones Americanas*, I (3), Washington, 1962; U.N. *Demographic Yearbook* 1963; República del Perú, *Censo Nacional de Población y Ocupación 1940*, Vol. I; República de Colombia, *Censo Nacional de Población 1964, Resumen General*, 1967.

Argentine citizens. At the turn of the century, however, labor disturbances and a general strike in which immigrants played a large role led to the limiting of immigration and in 1902 to the Ley de Residencia which permitted the government to deport foreigners who disturbed the public order.[9] The contemporary fragility of the rights of naturalized citizens is illustrated in the enforcement of Argentina's law for the suppression of communism (Law of August 22, 1967). Naturalized Argentinians convicted under this law are considered foreigners and can be expelled at the end of their punishment.[10]

There seem to be substantial differences in the attitudes of migrants toward the Latin republics and toward the United States and Canada. These differences are probably related to economic and political differences in the host countries and help account for the greater disposition of migrants to North America to acquire citizenship. In the post-World War II period only 8 percent of Italian migrants to Canada and the United States returned to Italy as compared with 30 percent from Latin America.[11] These variations in attitude toward the host countries may be more important than legal and administrative obstacles to naturalization. Although Article 129, paragraph IV, of the Brazilian constitution of 1946 (Article 140 of the constitution of 1967) facilitates the acquisition of citizenship by Portuguese migrants, the rate of naturalization in Brazil of Portuguese migrants has been one of the lowest among the various immigrant groups.

Political circumstances sometimes give migrants greater incentive to establish themselves juridically in their new country. The Spaniards who went to Mexico after the Spanish Civil War largely became citizens of that country. In Peru, Spaniards in the period of the Civil War, Germans after 1933, and Italians during the war years 1941–1945 account for a large number of naturalizations.[12]

Second- and third-generation Latin Americans may also repre-

[9] Samuel L. Bailey, "The Italians and Organized Labor in the United States and Argentina: 1880–1910," *The International Migration Review,* I (3), Summer 1967, pp. 58–62.

[10] Jacques Arnault, *Journal de voyage en Amérique latine,* Vol. 1, Paris, 1969, p. 119 and p. 163.

[11] Giuseppe Lucrezio Monticelli, "Italian Emigration: Basic Characteristics and Trends with Special Reference to the Last Twenty Years," *The International Migration Review,* I (3), Summer 1967, p. 19.

[12] República Peruana, *Anuario estadístico del Perú,* Lima, 1953, p. 115.

sent a foreign presence, one that depends on the degree to which they maintain overseas links. In Brazil, 1940, almost half a million persons of German descent and 300,000 persons of Italian descent of the *third and higher* generations customarily spoke German and Italian in their homes.[13] In Argentina, where it is generally estimated that 30–40 percent of Argentinians are of Italian descent,[14] the Italian presence was strong enough for Perón to consider making Italian the second national language of Argentina. Brazil has only about 300,000 Italian nationals, but 5 million Brazilians are estimated to be of Italian descent, and in Uruguay, with 30,000 Italian nationals, over 350,000 are of Italian descent.[15]

Of the estimated 600,000 Japanese in Brazil, approximately 70 percent are second-, third-, and fourth-generation Japanese–Brazilians, the majority of whom marry among themselves.[16] The German foreign born in Latin America numbered in 1950 less than 150,000, but the Nazi *Auslandsorganisation* had estimated in 1936 that there were about one million persons of German descent in Latin America, the great majority in Brazil (800,000), with 150,000 in Argentina and 30,000 in Chile.[17] In Bolivia, Germans constituted in 1950 the largest single group of European foreign

---

[13] Geraldo de Menezes Cortès, *op. cit.*, p. 51. See also Octavio de Moreas, "Immigration into Brazil," in Margaret Bates (ed.), *op. cit.*, p. 63, on the high frequency of use of foreign languages in the home in Brazil, all the more striking since approximately one-third of all immigrants to Brazil in the four decades preceding 1940 were Portuguese, whose descendants are hardly likely to speak a foreign language. For Portuguese immigration to Brazil, see "Imigrantes entrados, 1884–1963," in *Anuario estatístico do Brasil,* 1964.

[14] See Basilio Cialdea, "Le relazioni politiche con l'America Latina," *Il Veltro,* V (1–2), January–February 1961, p. 106; and Monticelli, *op cit.,* p. 21. *Successo,* May 1967, p. 48, however, gives an estimate of 50 percent.

[15] Basilio Cialdea, *op. cit.*, p. 106; and Monticelli, *op. cit.*, p. 21.

[16] Of male and female married Japanese descendants in Brazil, 7.6 percent and 1.6 percent respectively are in interethnic marriages. (The corresponding figures for Japanese first-generation immigrants in Brazil are 2.6 percent and 0.4 percent.) Census Commission of the Japanese Colony in São Paulo, *op. cit.,* Table 1, p. 6, and Table 276, p. 356. A later estimate (1958–68) gives 18 percent of nisei men and 8 percent of nisei women in interethnic marriages. Thomas G. Sanders, *Japanese in Brazil,* American Universities Field Staff, Report XIV (3), p. 3. During the sixties, Japanese and Japanese descendants in Brazil were commonly estimated at 600,000. Today one increasingly finds the number 700,000 cited.

[17] Alton Frye, *Nazi Germany and the American Hemisphere, 1933–1941,* New Haven, 1967, p. 65.

85

born, and in Chile and Colombia they were surpassed only by the Spanish. Nor does a foreign presence necessarily become diluted in time due to a lower birthrate of the immigrant descendants as compared with the older sectors of the population. In Rio Grande do Sul, in the interwar period, areas with large populations of Italian and German descent had both lower death rates and much higher birth rates than *municipios* that were predominently Luso-Brazilian.[18]

The immigrant presence varies, naturally, according to its degree of concentration in geographical areas or occupational sectors. Of all Japanese nationals overseas (1960), 77 percent were in Latin America. Of all Japanese nationals in Latin America, 85 percent lived in Brazil,[19] and of all Japanese nationals and descendants in Brazil, 76 percent lived in the state of São Paulo, where they constituted about 3 percent of the state population and about 10 percent of the rural population.[20] In the Brazilian population at large they constitute one out of every 140 Brazilians. In 1900 and 1960, Italians were only 3 and 7 percent of the Brazilian population but they constituted 16 and 15 percent of the population of the state of São Paulo. Today, Italians commonly speak of the city of São Paulo as being half Italian. Early in the century, Buenos Aires was said to be the largest Italian city after Rome. Its population and that of Rosario were about one-fourth of Italian origin.[21] In rural areas as well, especially in Brazil, Argentina, and Chile, immigrants often founded settlements and colonies which, being inhabited by single national groups, tended to reproduce many aspects of life in the homelands.

The magnitude of Italian migration to South America has sometimes tended to obscure the renewal of the Hispanic element in the continent by continued Spanish emigration. The number of Italian nationals in Latin America is not much greater than the number of

[18] Emilio Willems, "The Positive Contribution by Immigrants," in *Brazil*, UNESCO, Paris, 1955, p. 142.

[19] *Japan Statistical Yearbook*, 1963, Table 23, p. 43.

[20] *Visão*, May 26, 1967, p. 26. A 1969 Japanese Foreign Ministry estimate gives the number of Japanese nationals and descendants in the city of São Paulo in 1967 (population, 5.4 million) as about 100,000, and the number in the state of São Paulo (population 6.6 million) as about 520,000 in 1968, that is, 8 percent of the state population.

[21] Geraldo de Menezes Cortês, *op. cit.*, p. 40; Basilio Cialdea, *op. cit.*, p. 106; Samuel L. Bailey, *op. cit.*, p. 59.

Spanish nationals. In 1967 Italian and Spanish nationals were concentrated in the following countries:

	Italian Nationals [22] (in thousands)	Spanish Nationals [23] (in thousands)
Argentina	1,285	800
Brazil	297	244
Chile	16	not given
Cuba	not given	102
Mexico	not given	70
Uruguay	30	131
Venezuela	185	166
Others	20	not given

The contributions of France and Great Britain to the Latin American migrant presence were far less than those of Germany and of the more agricultural and less developed European lands. French and British migrations have been closely linked to the trade and investment activities of the two countries in South America and have, therefore, come from wealthier strata than the migration from the other European countries. Argentina, it has been estimated, has more than 80,000 persons of French descent, and Chile perhaps 10,000.[24] Descendants of British immigrants are scattered in substantial numbers throughout most of Latin America, as the not infrequent British names in Latin countries attest, but it is in Argentina, too, that the British migrant presence is strongest. Argentina is believed to have the largest population of British origin of any country never under British rule, and the older British presence has been fortified by an estimated 30,000 "comfortably off" British passport holders living in Argentina in 1968.[25] Current British emigration in 1964–1967, a little less than 200,000 annually, sent about half of its migrants to Commonwealth countries. Of the remaining half, only about 3 percent, that is, about 3,000 persons annually, went to Latin America as compared with 15,000 persons to South Africa.

[22] *Economist para América Latina,* Supplement on Italy, April 16, 1969, p. 39.

[23] Director, Instituto Español de Emigración, cited in *Le Monde,* November 12–13, 1967.

[24] Jean Meyriat, "France and Latin America," in Claudio Véliz (ed.), *Latin America and the Caribbean,* New York, 1968, p. 436.

[25] *The Economist,* September 25, 1965, Supplement, p. xxxiv; August 31, 1968, p. 44; and January 11, 1969, p. 4.

TABLE 5.3

NUMBER OF MIGRANTS TO LATIN AMERICA
(TO 1946)

To	Years	Number of Migrants (in thousands)
Argentina	1856–1946	6,651
Brazil	1821–1945	4,760
Chile	1850–1910	61
Cuba	1901–1937	872
Mexico	1911–1946	255
Paraguay	1881–1931	26
Uruguay	1836–1932	713
Canada	1851–1946	6,701
United States	1820–1946	38,570

SOURCES: Victor Audera, *La Población y la inmigración en Hispano-América,* Madrid, 1955, p. 48. Lines 6 and 7 from A. M. Carr-Saunders, *World Population,* Oxford, 1937, p. 49.

TABLE 5.4

NUMBER OF MIGRANTS TO LATIN AMERICA
(1946–1960)

To	Number of Migrants (in thousands)
Argentina	801
Brazil	704
Colombia	238
Uruguay	70
Venezuela	623

SOURCE: Artur Hehl Neiva, "International Migrations Affecting Latin America," *Milbank Memorial Fund Quarterly,* XLIII (4), October 1965, Part 2, p. 128.

The major wave of migration to Latin America that followed World War II has subsided. Although 58,000 Japanese migrated to South America (essentially to Brazil) between 1953 and 1966, in the last years of the period migration dropped to less than 1,000 annually.[26] Recent German migration to Central and South America has been small, a little over 3,000 in 1966, with over 4,000 returning to Germany from the Latin republics for a net loss of about 1,200; and a little less than 3,600 in 1968 with over 3,600 return-

[26] Japanese Foreign Ministry. See also *Japan Times* (Tokyo), November 1, 1966.

ing for a net loss of about 100.[27] Italian migration to Latin America also showed more exits than entries during the period 1961–1966.[28]

The great bulk of migrant labor from South and Southeastern Europe was captured by the expanding economies of Western Europe, more especially by Germany, France, and Switzerland. In 1964, 87 percent of Spain's emigration was intra-European as compared with only 41 percent in 1959. The corresponding figures for Portugal are 67 percent and 11 percent.[29] Between 1961 and 1965, Portuguese emigration to Brazil declined steadily from 15,000 to 2,000, while Portuguese migration within Europe (mostly to France) rose from 6,000 to 62,000 (legal) migrations. Migration to Brazil has also suffered, but less demonstrably, from the Portuguese government's attempt to check migration to Latin America and to steer it toward Mozambique and Angola, a policy that it had already initiated without great success prior to World War II.[30]

Although Italy and Japan are still interested in migration to Latin America they have both looked toward a new outlet, Australia. Prime Minister Sato's visit to Australia in 1967 was in part prompted by a desire to obtain liberalization of Australian immigration rules; and the flow of Italians to Australia was one factor in Argentina's convocation in 1969 of diplomats from Italy, Spain, Holland, West Germany, France, and Japan to present a new immigration program to them.[31] Argentina is torn between its desire to maintain a selective immigration policy and the desire to increase its low 1.5 percent population growth rate. Other Latin American countries have faced similar problems created by a more restrictive policy than existed prior to 1914 and by a failure to attract enough

[27] *Statistiches Jahrbuch für die Bundesrepublic Deutschland,* 1968, p. 57, and *ibid.,* 1970, p. 56. German emigrants to Latin America in 1966 and 1968 were 4 and 5 percent of all German emigrants. This proportion is fairly close to the 5–6 percent in sample surveys of Germans interested in migration who say they would choose Latin America.

[28] Giuseppe Lucrezio Monticelli, *op. cit.,* p. 19.

[29] Pierre Grandjeat, *Les Migrations de Travailleurs en Europe,* Paris, 1966, p. 92.

[30] Artur Hehl Neiva, *op. cit.,* p. 126; *Le Monde,* January 29, 1966, and August 28–29, 1966; and *Economist para América Latina,* August 25, 1967, p. 38.

[31] Norman A. Ingrey in *The Christian Science Monitor,* February 25, 1969.

of the skilled and urban workers that they desired. When Senator Edward Kennedy stated in 1966 that the Intergovernmental Commission for European Migration (ICEM) had largely completed its task, Brazil, Chile, Ecuador, and Costa Rica sharply dissented and pressed Latin American needs for more skilled manpower.[32]

Japanese and Italian migrations to Latin America have in fact in recent years more fully met Latin American requirements for skilled labor and technical capabilities than had their earlier migrations. But the availability of skilled workers for overseas migration is limited by the fact that many of the intra-European migrants belong to this category and find a greater and closer reward in Europe than overseas. In Portugal, the literacy of migrants is well above that of the general population, and more than 50 percent of Greek emigrants in 1963 were classed as industrial workers with some secondary education.[33] Nonetheless Latin America does continue to receive trained immigrants. ICEM relocated more than 1,500 skilled European technicians in Latin America in 1968, partly as a result of vocational adaptation courses provided by the Spanish government.[34] Despite Brazilian requirements that migrants be experienced farmers or skilled workers, Brazil still receives about 31,000 migrants annually, mostly from Portugal, Japan, Italy, and Spain.[35]

2. *Economic Benefits*

The departure of migrants from their homelands frequently alleviated economic stresses and the political strains attendant upon them. Italian, Spanish, Portuguese, and Japanese migration to Latin America (and elsewhere) reduced, if it by no means resolved, unemployment and pressure on the land.[36] However, these benefits

[32] *The New York Times,* November 16, 1966.

[33] Pierre Grandjeat, *op. cit.,* p. 54. However, the urban status of many of these workers is relatively recent.

[34] ICEM was established in 1951 and between 1952 and 1968 was responsible for sending 5,440 migrants to Colombia, 116,624 to Argentina, 109,702 to Brazil, 8,703 to Chile, 13,825 to Uruguay, and 70,968 to Venezuela. The effort made in 1968 to provide 1,500 skilled workers to Latin America cost $1.3 million, that is, an average of $867 per migrant. Et. de la Vallée Poussin, "Les nouvelles tâches du CIME: l'Emigration sélective," *International Migration,* VI (4), 1968, p. 205; and Alberto Galindo, "Hay que Importar Tecnología," *ibid.,* p. 239.

[35] *United States Congressional Record—House,* June 21, 1967, p. H-7718.

[36] Emigration, however, is sometimes not without cost to the mother-

from the emigration of "surplus" populations are sometimes secondary to later economic benefits that accrue to the homeland from the presence of its nationals and their descendants abroad.

Overseas migrants facilitate trade relations of the homeland with the countries in which the migrants are located. This may begin with the exporting of consumer goods that the migrants have been accustomed to at home, especially foodstuffs and household items.[37] Nonimigrants also may acquire a taste for these exotic products. This minor trade provides a basis for commercial relations and for the development of trading companies that introduce more important forms of commerce.[38] Naturally this process played an especially important role in those countries where the immigrant population was heavily represented among the industrial entrepreneurs. In 1895 in Buenos Aires more than 90 percent of industrial entrepreneurs were of immigrant origin, a figure that was still over 60 percent in 1935. Immigrants were also heavily represented among merchants.[39] In São Paulo, on the other hand, in the same period (1893) foreigners were only 19 percent of capitalists and only 31 percent of proprietors.[40] A contemporary Indian

land, especially if the migrants are skilled workers or if the government has other plans for them. A recent study made for the Italian Ministry of Labor estimated that the average Italian emigrant represents a capital investment of about $8,000 by the time he leaves. *The Times* (London), May 5, 1971.

[37] Portugal's trade with Brazil never got much beyond this stage and the later failures of her trade with Brazil have apparently been related to the decline in the former demand for traditional Portuguese products, some of which are now produced in Brazil. *Economist para América Latina*, July 9, 1969, p. 34.

[38] Carlos Martí Bufill, *Nuevas soluciones al problema migratorio*, Madrid, 1955, pp. 318–320 and p. 385. The statistical evidence on the effect of emigration to Latin America on Spanish trade provided in the foregoing work is not persuasive, but the existence of the process seems clear enough.

[39] Oscar Cornblit, "Inmigrantes y Empresarios en la Política Argentina," *Desarrollo Económico*, 6 (24), January–March 1967, p. 657 and p. 665.

[40] Florestan Fernandes, "Rapports de Races au Brésil: Mythes et Realité," *Les Temps Modernes*, 23 (257), October 1967, p. 692. Data for more recent years on the immigrant role in Latin American industry and commerce are reviewed in S. M. Lipset, "Values, Education, and Entrepreneurship," in S. M. Lipset and Aldo Solari (eds.), *Elites in Latin America*, New York, 1967, pp. 24–25. A still more recent study, James Petras, *Politics and Social Forces in Chilean Development*, Berkeley and Los Angeles, 1969, contains an interesting table (p. 96) showing that 78 percent of Chilean entrepreneurs are first- or second-generation immigrants. In the case of the large enter-

appeal to merchants and traders of Indian birth or descent to increase their imports and distribution of Indian goods in the countries where they live and do business is the application of a quite old pattern for the stimulation of foreign commerce.[41]

The full extent to which national colonies facilitate trade relations for the homeland is difficult to establish. When a competitive situation exists, it is understandable that migrants and their descendants may favor imports from their various homelands. This may be due not only to a residual loyalty but also to the fact that knowledge of or confidence in goods from one's own homeland may be greater. Certainly governmental and business observers affirm such a relationship in the Latin American case. In a 1964 roundup on the status of French imports to Latin America, the French attachés in Bolivia, Paraguay, and Peru attributed the competitive difficulties of France to the handicap of the small French colonies in these countries. Thus in Bolivia, the French are outnumbered 50 to 1 by the Germans.[42] An official of the Chambre de Commerce France-Amérique Latine explains Germany's greater success than France in Latin America by, among other things, its immigrants and the fact that they "never lose memory of their origin." [43]

Similarly, it is generally assumed, probably with good reason, that it is the large Italian community in Argentina that has enabled Italy to stand so well in the Argentinian import market. In the years 1962–1966 Italy ranked second two times and third three times in exports to Argentina, the United States and Germany being its chief rivals. This is a better showing than Italy made in Latin American countries with smaller Italian communities.[44]

---

prises, this figure drops to 59 percent. West European, Spanish, Jewish, and Arab entrepreneurs account (in that order) for most of the migrant entrepreneurs. Data in this field, including those cited in the text above, are generally deficient since they do not provide comparable rates for immigrants and nonimmigrants.

[41] *The Indian Export Trade Journal,* XIX, September–October–November 1965, p. 1.

[42] *Moniteur officiel du commerce international,* September 16, 1964, pp. 3598, 3616, and 3620.

[43] André Fines, "La France et l'Amérique Latine, relations commerciales, concours technique," *Revue Juridique et Politique,* 18 (3), July–September 1964, p. 446.

[44] IMF, *Direction of Trade Annual 1962–66.* When Italy was still a colonial power she was said to have derived more economic benefits from

The British, in attempting to revive their former trade position in Latin America, have also been aware of the utility to them of strong British strains dating from the nineteenth and early twentieth centuries in the business circles of various Latin American commercial centers,[45] although some have deplored attempts to rely on sentimental relations in a period when other devices are thought to be more important for commercial success.

Japan's trade position in Brazil similarly seems to be associated with a strong immigrant presence in that country. Thus Brazil is the only major Latin American country in which Japan generally outranks the United Kingdom in export levels.[46] The Japanese government has not relied on a private, spontaneous process to achieve economic benefits from the overseas Japanese in Brazil. In addition to continuing to promote migration to Brazil it has opened offices in São Paulo to help place Japanese engineers and technicians in Brazilian firms. The willingness of Japan to encourage the emigration of high-skill personnel needed at home is almost certainly related to the expectation that specialists accustomed to work with Japanese techniques and equipment will provide a link that will promote Brazilian dependence on Japanese goods. Future economic benefits are apparently expected to more than compensate for the losses such migration imposes on the domestic labor supply and present production.[47]

Foreign direct investment activity in Latin America is also linked to the immigrant communities. In developing and operating enterprises abroad, foreign capitalists find that their own migrant

---

her "colony" in Argentina than from her African colonies, and without the costs and vexations imposed by dominion over a territory. Emile Boix, cited in J. F. Normano, *The Struggle for South America,* London, 1931, p. 77.

[45] See, for example, *The Times* (London), December 1, 1966.

[46] IMF, *op. cit.*

[47] For the Japanese program for placing technical workers in Brazilian industry, see *The Christian Science Monitor,* December 12, 1968. On problems of Japanese labor supply, see *The Economist's* special survey on Japan, Part II, June 3, 1967. Japan still employs a considerable part of its labor force in small firms. Economies in the use of labor may still be available in the future as the size of enterprises increases, and this may explain Japanese willingness to encourage migration of relatively scarce segments of the labor force.

nationals (or descendants) are, because of familiarity with the local language, culture, and politics, an important resource, especially for middle management jobs.[48] The chief of Japan's 1965 economic mission to Brazil expressed a hope that the Japanese colony would facilitate Japanese investment in that country.[49] By 1968, in addition to the use of local Japanese in Japanese enterprises in Brazil, new Japanese investments were being promoted by combining private investments funds in Japan with the private investment interests of Japanese–Brazilians, now long enough in Brazil to have acquired significant amounts of capital.[50]

It is not accidental that the three nations with the most pronounced investment interests in Latin America (relative to their overall foreign placements)—Germany, Japan, and Italy—also have substantial immigrant presences in Latin America. In the case of Japan the connection is clear since Japanese investment has been proportioned to the liberality of a country's policies toward Japanese immigration.[51] And in the case of German and Italian funds it appears that much of the money that entered Latin America after 1955 "flowed into these countries in the wake of postwar immigration—largely German and Italian—frequently by way of Switzerland." [52] Still, it is evident from the cases of Spain and Portugal that large-scale emigration to Latin America is by no means sufficient to ensure a strong position in Latin American trade and investment. Some Spanish circles attribute to the lower educational and technical levels of Spanish migrants Spain's failure to benefit economically as much as Italy from its overseas nationals and descendants.[53] It is doubtful that this explanation is adequate. The lower educational and technical levels of the Spanish migrants probably reflected a lower capability of the Spanish economy to exploit overseas oppor-

---

[48] Robert J. Alexander, *Labor Relations in Argentina, Brazil, and Chile,* New York, 1962, p. 54.

[49] *Latin American Times,* September 22, 1965.

[50] *Visión,* August 30, 1968, pp. 34–35.

[51] *Bank of London and South America Review,* 3 (36), December 1969, p. 731. In recent years, however, financing the development of natural resources seems to have been more important in shaping Japanese investment policy.

[52] Penelope Roper, *Investment in Latin America,* The Economist Intelligence Unit, London, 1970, p. 7.

[53] *Latin American Times,* September 20, 1965.

tunities.[54] Besides, Spanish emigration to Latin America has also included substantial numbers of professional and middle class persons whose emigration was politically motivated (see section 3 below).

One economic benefit received by nations from their emigrant populations is more direct and tangible. This is the remittances sent back by the emigrants to their families and relatives. These transfers play a large role in the story of the first great European waves of migration to the Americas and were one of the first benefits that in the nineteenth century increased governmental interest in migration to Latin America and the United States. The remittances were sufficiently large to be accounted, in the case of Argentina, a significant factor draining potential capital and helping to explain the failure of Buenos Aires to "take off" economically in the pre World War I period.[55]

After World War II and especially during the late sixties remittances once again became an important factor in international economic transactions.[56] In Greece, private transfers in 1967 had a positive balance of $236 million as compared with only $86 million for tourism.[57] In the same year private transfers to Italy were 40 percent of the large amount ($1.1 billion) that Italy earned from tourism, a principal item in its balance of payment. In Spain private transfers ($446 million) had about the same ratio to travel earnings as in Italy. Portugal, with a population only one-fifth the size of Italy

[54] This is not to deny that migrant educational and economic levels influence the economic and political role they play in their new country.

Worth noting here is an unusual phenomenon: First-generation Japanese migrants in Brazil had an extraordinarily low rate of illiteracy (1.5 percent, 1958). This rate increases with successive generations. Second- and third-generation Japanese illiteracy in 1958 was 2.6 percent and 6.9 percent, respectively. With progressive "Brazilianization" the Japanese community has become less literate. See Census Commission of the Japanese Colony in São Paulo, *op. cit.,* Table 8, p. 50.

[55] James R. Scobie, "Buenos Aires of 1910: The Paris of South America That Did Not Take Off," *Inter-American Economic Affairs,* XXII (2), Autumn 1968, p. 12.

[56] Cf. G. Parenti, *The Role of Emigrant Remittances in the Economic Development of European Countries,* U.N. 1965.

[57] International Monetary Fund, *International Financial Statistics,* XXI (11), November 1968.

and one-third the size of Spain, had private transfers ($207 million) approximately one-half of Italy's and Spain's.[58]

The great increase in the positive balance of private transfers in the middle sixties in Spain, Portugal, Italy, Greece, and Turkey has been due to the wave of migration to, and remittances from, Western Europe, especially Germany, Switzerland, and France. But in earlier years transfers from Latin America and North America played a greater role. In 1914, emigrant remittances to Spain were equal to half the value of its foreign trade, and in 1952, when remittances were reduced to a much lower level, they were still $75 million, more than double the earnings from tourism and about 20 percent of foreign trade.[59] In 1963 Italy received approximately $30 million in remittances from Latin America, an amount equal to about 10 percent of the value of Italy's exports to Latin America in that year.[60] In 1957, Portugal received about $10 million in transfers from Brazil, roughly three times the value of its negligible exports to that country.[61]

Public benefactions by returned emigrants and by various private emigrant groups are an additional source of economic return to the mother country from her emigrants, a source difficult to measure but apparently not trivial. In Ramosierra (Castile) the philanthropy of emigrants and *Indianos* (emigrants returned from Latin America) was held up as an example to others. Emigrant donations enabled Ramosierra to build an adequate drainage system in 1919 when its provincial capital still did not have one.[62] In 1966, following the devastating floods in North Italy, the relatively small Italian colony in Mexico donated $320,000 to Florence and Venice.[63]

[58] International Monetary Fund, *ibid.;* see also Guy Caire, "Industrialisation et échanges extérieures," *Revue Tiers-Mondes,* VIII (31), July–September 1967, p. 544.

[59] Carlos Martí Bufill, *op. cit.,* pp. 321–322.

[60] IMF, *Direction of Trade 1962–66,* p. 218; and *Visión,* May 24, 1966, p. 4.

[61] José Honório Rodrigues, *Brazil and Africa,* Berkeley and Los Angeles, 1965, p. 303; and IMF, *Direction of International Trade 1938, 1948, 1955–58.*

[62] Michael Kenny, *A Spanish Tapestry: Town and Country in Castile,* New York, 1961, pp. 43–44; Carlos Martí Bufill, *op. cit.,* p. 385, also lists *obras sociales* by migrants (together with their remittances to and investments in Spain) as a significant economic return.

[63] *Los Angeles Times,* December 8, 1966. Private philanthropy is apparently more generous than public philanthropy. In the preceding year

3. *Political Significance*

Large immigrant colonies in Latin America have sometimes provided inspiration or support for European—mostly German, Italian, and Spanish—aspirations toward political influence over the southern continent. Whereas Italian and Spanish hopes were largely based on emigration that had developed independently of governmental political ambitions, German emigration to Latin America in both the Imperial and the Nazi periods was in part fostered to facilitate German ambitions in the subcontinent.[64] None of these attempts was particularly successful, and where they had a temporary apparent success, this was due more to the independent interests of Latin American political leaders than to European manipulation of them or of the migrants and their descendants.

The retention by migrants of their original nationalities suggests that they maintain a loyalty toward the mother country that renders them especially useful to her. This is not necessarily the case. Failure to become citizens was associated with lessened political participation in Latin America and with political apathy and this made some immigrant groups politically less influential and therefore less useful to the homeland than they otherwise might have been. Thus Italian migrants were not effective in spreading Fascist doctrine in South America.[65] In Brazil, German and Japanese "racial cysts" were

---

the Italian government had donated about $20,000 to the flood-racked province of Rio Grande do Sul (Brazil). *Latin American Times,* September 7, 1965.

[64] On German interests in Latin America and the use of German settlers, see for the Nazi period, Alton Frye, *op. cit.,* especially Chapters 5, 7, and 8; and for both the Imperial and Nazi periods, *Der Deutsche Faschismus in Lateinamerika, 1933–1943* [East] Berlin, 1966. See also Albrecht von Gleich, *Germany and Latin America,* The Rand Corporation, Santa Monica, RM-5523-RC, June 1968, pp. 5–10, 14–20; and on Italy, Fabio Luca Cavazza, *Italy and Latin America,* The Rand Corporation, Santa Monica, RM-5400-RC, November 1967, pp. 6–25.

[65] See Cavazza, *op. cit.,* p. 21. In 1925 less than 10 percent of male adults voted in national Argentinian elections; in 1935 about 35 percent; in 1945 about 50 percent. Although other factors are influential, these figures reflect increased political participation as nonnaturalized first-generation immigrants gave way to their descendants. Eldon Kenworthy, "Argentina: The Politics of Late Industrialization," *Foreign Affairs,* 45 (3), April 1967, p. 470. Immigrants, especially Italians, were, however, very active earlier in labor organizations and labor activities. Cf. Samuel L. Bailey, *op. cit.,* pp. 64–66.

viewed by Brazilians as stimulating a political interest in their destinies by the mother countries that might lead to German and Japanese satellite states or colonies on Brazilian soil. But self-isolation, while rousing apprehensions, at the same time reduced political effectiveness. Immigrant contributions to Brazil consequently have been largely in economic development and cultural life, and the political development of Brazil has been little affected by them.[66] In Argentina socialist leaders were well aware of the importance immigrant naturalization would have for the success of their parties but were politically too weak to be able to get the naturalization process simplified or to overcome migrant unwillingness to face the necessary administrative complications.[67]

In any case, the political value of emigrants to their homeland is limited since they are not always sympathetic to it. Politically motivated emigrations have sometimes brought to Latin America, as elsewhere, emigrants and refugees antagonistic to the political or social structure that they left behind. In 1966, the United Nations commissioner for refugees estimated the number of refugees in Latin America at about 135,000.[68]

The emigration from Spain following the Civil War of 1936–1939 took to Mexico 30,000 and to South America 40,000 Spanish emigrés. Given the low rate of naturalization in Latin America, it is striking that of the post-Civil War Spaniards who migrated to Mexico only about 200 were, in 1967, estimated to have retained their Spanish citizenship.[69] This juridical breach with their homeland and legal assimilation into the Mexican nation was, of course, easier given Mexico's refusal to recognize the Franco regime and its continuous recognition after the Civil War of a Republican government-in-exile. The attitudes of the Spanish emigrés in Mexico City toward Spain have been all the more important because professional and white collar Spanish emigrés tended to settle in Mexico

[66] Emilio Willems, *op. cit.,* pp. 144–145; see also J. F. Normano, *op. cit.,* p. 96 and p. 120.

[67] Oscar Cornblit, *op. cit.,* pp. 678–679.

[68] *Marcha* (Montevideo), September 25, 1966, p. 11. A refugee is defined as a person who leaves his place of origin for reasons of racial, religious, or political persecution. Between 1965 and 1970 the worldwide number of refugees increased by about 70 percent, particularly because of events in Africa.

[69] Stephen Clissold, "Spain and Latin America," in Claudio Véliz (ed.), *op. cit.,* p. 433.

City (and Spanish workers in France) and were articulate representatives of their political and cultural views. Such exiles can be damaging critics of the regimes they flee, especially when they have an international reputation.[70] On the other hand, the Republican emigration to Mexico has contributed substantially to developments in Mexico in the theater, art, and literature.[71] Thus the unfavorable views of Spain expressed by embittered exiles are, perhaps, balanced by the cultural impact in Latin America of the Spanish Republican exile presence and its many distinguished representatives, and this indirectly benefits the homeland and its political regime. "The [Republican] emigration has destroyed the myth of Spanish decadence." [72] Similarly, it is hoped, perhaps with less justification, that the Portuguese colony in Brazil will prove to be Portugal's best instrument in spreading a favorable, up-to-date image of Portugal.[73]

A more recent political emigration also illustrates the simultaneous positive and negative impact of an immigrant presence on the image of the homeland or its political regime. After North Africa gained independence, the French of Algeria, Morocco, and Tunisia (les colons, les pieds-noirs) returned in great numbers to France—about 1.4 million by 1966. About 75,000 others have settled abroad. In Argentina a combination of Argentinian ineptness and immigrant inexperience led to initial disappointments and only 1,500 pieds-noirs have settled (1968) there, with a still smaller number in Chile. Canada, on the other hand, received 12,000 and Spain about 50,000. Although for the most part bitterly anti-Gaullist, and to that extent an embarrassment to the French

[70] See, for example, "España: cultura muerta," *Marcha*, February 11, 1966, p. 30, and the novel *Señas de Identidad*, both by the Spanish novelist Juan Goytisolo.

[71] Vicente Llorens, "Entre España y América: La emigración Republicana de 1939," *Mundo Nuevo*, No. 12, June 1967, pp. 61–65. See also Juan Bautista Climent, "España en el exilio," *Cuadernos Americanos* (Mexico), XXII (1), January–February 1963, pp. 91–108; and Jacinto Luis Guereña, "Acerca de la emigración intelectual española," *Política* (Caracas), IV (48), April 1966, pp. 65–72. Bautista Climent does not agree with Llorens concerning the difficulty of Spanish integration in Mexican life. "We are so dispersed through the social environment and in Mexican life that we lack adequate knowledge of the activities of Republican exiles" (p. 107).

[72] Juan Bautista Climent, *op. cit.*, p. 106.

[73] Adriano Moreira, "Aspectos negativos da imagem recíproca de Portugal-Brasil," *América Latina* (Rio de Janeiro), 10 (1), January–March 1967, p. 54.

99

government, the French North Africans nonetheless constitute an advertisement for French capabilities and culture.[74]

A different form of dualism is represented by the German case. Here two streams of politically motivated migrations, that of 1933–1939 and the postwar German migration, carried to Latin America bitter ideological, political, and racial enmities.[75] These enmities have given Germany diplomacy in Latin America many difficult moments and have more especially made difficult the important objective of building a new German image.[76] The belief that Martin Bormann and other important Nazis are in hiding in Latin American countries, the existence of German settlements in Paraná inhabited by nationalist elements, the assassination of a German industrialist in Rio de Janeiro in 1967, the finding in 1965 of the body of an apostate Nazi in Montevideo, the international scandal provoked in 1966 by deaths and alleged tortures in the German Colonia Dignidad, south of Santiago de Chile, and similar events indicate the problems of the Federal Republic arising from some of its nationals and ex-nationals resident in Latin America.[77]

Politically motivated migrants and refugees are not the only ones who carry with them unfavorable views of their homeland or who

[74] "The [Algerian] immigrant [in Argentina] does not abandon France. He brings it with him. . . ." Léo Palacio, *Les pieds-noirs dans le monde,* Paris, 1968, p. 73. See also Chapter 5, pp. 67–74. One of the few results in Argentina of de Gaulle's *la mano en la mano* was a migration agreement between France and Argentina for the reception of additional families of French Algerian refugees. Under the accord they and the land they receive are exempt from Argentine taxes for five years. *France–Argentine* (Buenos Aires), No. 133, August–September 1965.

The failure of Argentina and other Latin American countries seeking skilled rural and urban immigrants to capture more of the French North African emigration was a minor disaster for their immigration policies. It also represented the loss to France of an outstanding opportunity to strengthen her weak physical presence in Latin America.

[75] Naturally, this does not imply that all German migrants of the 1933–1939 period were anti-Nazis and all those of the post-1945 period were Nazis fleeing defeat. The latter constituted a small but politically well publicized group.

[76] See von Gleich, *op. cit.,* pp. 36–40.

[77] For a running account of the Colonia Dignidad affair, see the issues of *Le Monde* for March 14 to March 25, 1966. The Colonia Dignidad reappeared in the news in a similar context two years later. A recent account of Nazi groups active in Chile and Argentina is provided by Alain Pujol in *Le Figaro,* September 1, 1970.

are capable of causing embarrassment to its government. Voluntary and nonpolitical migrants too have in many cases left their native land because of dissatisfaction with their lot and the expectation that they can better themselves abroad. They often harbor critical feelings toward their native land, but more especially toward its government and official class.

Needless to say, foreigners living in Latin America who are not alienated from their own government and country may still fail to win friends for them. Partly this will depend on personal qualities and various national capabilities for understanding and adapting to Latin American life; partly it will depend on the special loci some national groups occupy in Latin American countries. The United States physical presence in Latin America is much smaller than that of many of the nonhemispheric countries, although in Colombia it is tied for first and second place with the Spanish foreign population and in Mexico it is by far the largest (see Table 5.2). The United States presence, however, is more mixed than that of many of the nonhemispheric countries—businessmen, the military, managers, professionals and technicians, both governmental [78] and private, Peace Corps members, retired persons (especially in Mexico), and, of course, tourists. The United States is also heavily represented both in the Latin American Catholic priesthood, which is made up in substantial measure—about 1 in 3—of foreign priests, especially Spanish, German, and Dutch, as well as North American,[79] and in the Protestant church and missionary groups. In 1960 there were in Latin America from the United States about 2,300 Roman Catholic

[78] In July 1969 President Nixon ordered a 10 percent reduction in the number of American direct-hire civilian personnel abroad. The United States military mission personnel in Latin America was reduced from 800 in 1969 to about 500 by July 1970. United States Department of State, *Bulletin,* August 4, 1969, p. 92 and p. 100.

[79] For the number of foreign Catholic priests in Latin America and their national origins, see Isidoro Alanso *et al., La Iglesia en Perú y Bolivia,* Freiburg (Switzerland) and Bogotá, 1961, p. 59 and pp. 196–197; Gustavo Pérez Ramírez and Yván Labelle, *El problema sacerdotal en América latina,* Freiburg (Switzerland) and Bogotá, 1964, pp. 22–23; Emile Pin and François Houtart, *The Church and the Latin American Revolution,* New York, 1965, pp. 156–157; and Luigi Einaudi, Richard Maullin, Alfred Stepan, and Michael Fleet, *Latin American Institutional Development: The Changing Catholic Church,* RM-6136-DOS, The Rand Corporation, Santa Monica, October 1969, p. 17.

101

missionary personnel and in Brazil alone about 1,500 Protestant missionaries.[80] This is not a very high degree of concentration compared with the 400 Canadian-trained priests who worked at one time in the Dominican Republic.[81] The overall effect on national reputation of these varied types of persons with their different relations to the Latin societies can hardly be determined from available studies. Indeed, it is not at all clear to what extent contacts with foreigners determine Latin American attitudes toward the countries they represent, and how influential these contacts are as compared with stereotypes derived in the home, from literature, from the mass media, and from ideological and political considerations.

The retention by immigrants of their original nationality sometimes burdens the government of their homeland with unwelcome responsibilities. When President Saragat visited Venezuela in 1965 he agreed to a special aid program for Italian immigrants and was pressed to study a proposal by which the Italian government would extend its welfare benefits to its nationals in Venezuela.

Migrants, however, are not always a negative or simply a neutral feature in their country's political relations with the Latin republics. Migrations to Latin America have opened the road to diplomatic relations, especially for countries such as Japan and China,[82] whose official relations with the subcontinent would otherwise have been delayed. Emigrant colonies also provide politicians and officials in the homeland with a convenient reason for overseas visits that can be utilized for diplomatic activity that might otherwise be difficult to initiate.

The security of a country's migrant nationals has been used not only to justify hostile interventions [83] but also to justify what some

[80] W. Phillips Davison, *International Political Communication,* New York, 1965, p. 244.

[81] John D. Harbron, "Canada in Caribbean America: Technique for Involvement," *Journal of Inter-American Studies and World Affairs,* 12 (4), October 1970, p. 479.

[82] Between 1850 and 1875 about 100,000 Chinese men were brought to Peru for agricultural work and railroad construction. Chinese migration was cut off by Peru in 1922. Early Chinese migration contrasts sharply with early Japanese migration of immigrants with families, education, and some capital. David Chaplin, *The Peruvian Industrial Labor Force,* Princeton, N.J., 1967, pp. 61–63.

[83] See, for example, Chapter 4.6.

might view as excessive cordiality. General Franco has explained his economic and diplomatic relations with Cuba by the need to maintain "correct" relations with Cuba in order to protect Spain's thousands of nationals living there.[84] Similarly, Jamaican interest in maintaining official relations with Cuba both while applying for and after admission to the OAS was explained by the fact that several thousand Jamaicans live in Cuba.[85]

It is apparent that the political benefits derived by the home-land from their emigrants in Latin America have been quite modest, especially when compared with the economic benefits that they have conferred. The limited, although by no means negligible, eco-nomic and political roles played by Italy and Spain in contemporary Hispanic America and by Italy, Portugal, and Japan in Brazil under-line the fact that a large migrant presence, even when, as in the case of Portugal and Spain, it is supported by ethnic, linguistic, and cultural bonds, does not by itself assure a major impact of the homeland on the host country similar to that of the Western in-dustrial powers, the United States, Great Britain, Germany, and France.

[84] *The New York Times*, July 15, 1967. These correct relations did not prevent Cuba from jailing four Spanish officials. *Le Monde*, January 15–16, 1967. Spanish exports to Cuba rose from $12 million in 1958 to an average of $57 million in the two years 1965–1966, possibly another reason for maintaining correct relations. IMF, *Direction of Trade 1958–1962* and *Direction of Trade 1962–1966*.

[85] *Visión*, December 8, 1967. Jamaica became the 24th member state of the OAS in 1969, bringing to four the number of English-speaking members: United States, Trinidad–Tobago, Barbados, Jamaica.

6. Affinities

THE meetings of statesmen and other representatives of nations are fertile occasions for the affirmation or, if necessary, the discovery and revelation of national affinities often little suspected by the rest of the world. Useful as courtesies that flatter host or guest, these references also serve, perhaps more especially in the Latin American case, to overcome feelings of estrangement and a sense of the social and physical distance that separates peoples.[1]

The discovery of affinities is particularly useful and demands a certain ingenuity precisely in those instances where their existence is least evident. Peru's former president, Fernando Belaúnde, whose country harbors fewer Italian immigrants than Argentina, Brazil, and Venezuela and who was, therefore, unable to refer to a large Italian immigrant presence as a tie between his country and that of a distinguished visitor, President Saragat of Italy, was able to evoke, nonetheless, if not an historical connection, at least an historical parallel. "It has been said," recalled Belaúnde, "that the Incas were the Romans of America, and actually there are amazing similarities between the two civilizations. . . . The visit of President Saragat is a reminder of the old empires which now unite, joining old Imperial Rome to millenary Cuzco."[2]

Millenary Cuzco has been evoked, too, on behalf of the Japanese presence in Latin America. More than historical similarities, a common origin, a racial bond between the Incas and the Japanese

[1] See in this connection Chapter 4.4, "We Are Far Away."
[2] *Latin American Times,* September 10, 1965.

has sometimes been alleged in Japan and this is introduced as a powerful link between the two shores of the Pacific by Susumu Hani [3] in *Bride of the Andes,* one of his two films dealing with the Japanese presence in less-developed countries. Exploiting in dramatic fashion the existence of the Mongolian spot [4] in both Japanese and Peruvian highland babies, the film also underlines the sympathy between Japanese and Indians evoked by a similar skin color,[5] and in an unusual Japanese intrusion into the domestic political sphere in Latin America this sympathy is contrasted with the contempt of some white or light-skinned Peruvians for the dark-skinned Indians.

The tracing of relations is often a competition to establish contacts at as early a date as possible. Japanese seeking an early political link with Latin America refer to the rescue by a Spanish galleon sailing from the Orient to Mexico of two Japanese who are thought to have landed in New Spain in 1578. Following the shipwreck of another galleon on the Japanese coast, Japan's ruler sent in 1609 a trade mission and an ambassador to the viceroy of New Spain.[6] Japanese also refer to a Japanese mission to Rome some 350 years ago which visited Mexico both on its outward and on its return trip.[7] Similarly a newly arrived ambassador of Nationalist

[3] Susumu Hani is the director of *Bad Boys* (Cannes, 1962), *She and He* (Berlin, 1964), and more recently, *The Bees.* His *Bride of the Andes* followed upon his African film, *Song of Bwana Toshi* (1964).

[4] The Mongolian or blue spot of irregular and diffuse outline is found in the lumbar and sacral regions and buttocks of most infants of the yellow and some other races. It disappears after several years.

[5] The Japanese sense of at-homeness in Latin America stimulated by similarity of skin color is noted by a Japanese woman visitor to Mexico in the following terms: "White skin suggests a certain remoteness. When I went to Mexico, where most women are not white skinned like the Americans, I felt more at home seeing them. I felt more comfortable." Cited by Hiroshi Wagatsuma in "The Social Perceptions of Skin Color in Japan," *Daedalus,* Spring 1967, p. 424.

[6] Nobuo Ito, "Japan's Trade Relations with Latin America," *The Inter-American Scene,* 2 (4), Fall 1970, pp. 7–8, and *National Geographic,* 140 (1), July 1971, pp. 134–135.

[7] *Keidanren Review* (Tokyo), No. 5, 1966, p. 66. Future Japanese statesmen visiting Latin America may be able to evoke a Japanese–Latin American contact occurring some four to five thousand years before Columbus. It appears that prehistoric Ecuadorian pottery may have been influenced by Middle Jomar visitors from Kyushu, Japan. See Betty J. Meggers and Evans Clifford, "A Transpacific Contact in 3,000 B.C.," *Scientific American,* January 1966, pp. 28–35. Another contender for honors in early contacts

China to Mexico is able to establish a closer rapport with his host country by referring to the use in China "hundreds" of years ago of Mexican silver coins.⁸ The ambassador from Taiwan was presumably referring to the Acapulco trade with China in the sixteenth century and the existence in Acapulco during this period of a small Chinese colony, the forerunners there of the international jet set.

That relatively early historical links between Latin America and Asian countries are not as difficult to establish as one might suppose was further illustrated on the occasion of Mrs. Indira Ghandi's state visit to Brazil in 1968. Mrs. Ghandi was able to surround the development of an essentially new relation between India and Brazil with an aura of past history: "The links between Brazil and India . . . were forged 468 years ago by Pedro Cabral, who set out to look for us but found you. He sailed from Portugal and touched your shores before landing . . . in India. . . . His voyage on two oceans etched great arcs which bind us. A common name unites us to the original inhabitants of this continent." ⁹

The important African presence in Central America, the Caribbean, and South America has been exploited only modestly on both sides of the South Atlantic. This is, of course, more a reflection of the limited importance that Latin America and Africa still have for each other than it is of any difficulty in finding historical links between these two world regions—links too evident to be forgotten but less suited for memorialization than most.

More agreeable to recall than the enforced migration of Africans to the Americas is the return movement in the eighteenth and nine-

---

with Latin America is the Middle East. A contact with the Brazilian coast has been claimed on behalf of the Phoenicians. *The New York Times,* May 16, 1968. Polish scientists have entered a tentative claim for an early North African contact with Latin America. *The New York Times,* December 3, 1969. Two Soviet scientists believe ancient Tibetan maps and Asian use of tobacco suggest that "discovery of the Americas possibly belongs to ancient Asian adventurers." *The New York Times,* July 12, 1970. And an American scholar, on the basis of an inscription in the Smithsonian Institution, has entered the Jews in the discovery-of-America sweepstakes. *Los Angeles Times,* October 19, 1970. Another professor, from Mexico City, affirms a possible contact between the Maya and the Mediterranean about A.D. 700 on the basis of what appears to be a Star of David on the earring of a statue of a man. *The New York Times,* March 23, 1971.

⁸ *Latin American Times,* August 17, 1965.

⁹ *India News* (Embassy of India, Washington, D.C.), October 4, 1968.

106

teenth centuries of Brazilians to the west coast of Africa, particularly to Lagos—which still has its Brazilian Quarter—but also to other parts of Nigeria, to Dahomey, Sierra Leona, Senegal, and the Ivory Coast where they sometimes became a political irritant to the English and French. About 15,000 descendants of these Brazilians live today in Lagos and perhaps another 10,000 in the rest of Nigeria, some of whom maintain a sufficient Brazilian identity to be organized in the *União Descendentes Brazileiros*.[10] But this connection has played only a small role, symbolically and otherwise, in strengthening Brazilian–African relations. In 1960 and 1961 President Jânio Quadros and his foreign minister, Afonso Arinos, sent diplomatic, economic, and cultural missions to a number of the African states. These attempts to move Brazil into a new diplomatic and cultural orbit and to exploit historical, racial, and cultural affinities between Brazil and Africa foundered on presidential vacillation and on congressional support for Portugal's position in its African territories. The Africans were, in any case, largely ignorant of and indifferent to Brazil.[11]

Like Quadros, Mr. Hugh Shearer, prime minister of Jamaica, also had a special interest in African relations, but just as Europe, Japan, the United States, and Portugal continued to dominate Brazilian foreign interest, so Canada, Great Britain, and the United States have continued to play the same role in the Jamaican case. The principal Jamaican relation with Africa is, in fact, not of governmental but of popular origin. The Rastafarians, a religious-political sect that claims an Abyssinian birth, numbering only a few hundred in 1950 and now counted in the thousands, worship the Negus, Ras Tafari, the Emperor Haile Selassie.[12] The worship of Emperor Selassie by the politically not insignificant Rastafarians

[10] Antonio Olinto, *Brasileiros na África*, Rio de Janeiro, 1964. Cf. especially, pp. 161–170, 180–183, and 211–216. The part of Lagos that Olinto refers to as the Brazilian Quarter is also called, due to its mixed composition, the Syrian Quarter.

[11] José Honório Rodrigues, *Brazil and Africa*, Berkeley and Los Angeles, 1965, pp. 308–337.

[12] The Rastafarians have for a number of years looked forward, not too actively, to "repatriation" to Ethiopia. In 1955, the emperor set aside 500 acres in Ethiopia for the settlement of his worshippers. Sheilah Kitzinger, "The Rastafarian Brethren of Jamaica," *Comparative Studies in Society and History*, IX (1), October 1966, pp. 32–39. See also James A. Mau, "Images of Jamaica's Future," in Wendell Bell (ed.), *The Democratic Revolution in the West Indies*, Cambridge, Mass., 1967, pp. 206–207.

in Jamaica gave the Jamaican part of the emperor's Caribbean visit in 1966 a special interest.

Latin American countries that are predominantly of Spanish and other European origins do not usually emphasize the African component of their populations. Castro, however, in putting out signals in 1966 for the acceptance of Cuba as a member nation of the Organization of African Unity provided as a secondary justification the fact that "African blood runs in the veins of half of the Cuban people." [13] Castro, however, apparently has no intention of permitting the African racial component in Cuba to divide national loyalties. Stokely Carmichael was given an impressive welcome in Havana in 1967 but subsequently Eldridge Cleaver was treated coolly and was not officially received by Castro. Black Panthers in Cuba have been prevented from propagandizing their positions on black culture and black power. [14]

The Latin American and African countries have connections based largely on their competitive and cooperative relations as Third World countries and, in a number of cases, as producers of tropical products and of minerals. These factors dominate their association, which is little affected by sentiments based on cultural or racial ties. Where steps have been taken to exploit the latter, they have generally in the past been initiated from the Latin American and not the African side. In political, economic, and cultural relations, Latin America generally played vis-à-vis Africa the role of an advanced region and Africa that of the less developed area. For some of the new Caribbean states with large black populations a more equal reciprocal relationship appears to be developing with black Africa. Zambia has recruited personnel for her local government in Guyana and in other Caribbean states. [15] Guyana in turn has shown an interest in developing cultural relations with Africa [16]

[13] *Le Monde,* January 30, 1966. Castro's bid for Cuba to join the Organization of African Unity followed invitations to Cuba and five other Latin American countries—Chile, Guatemala, Mexico, Uruguay, and Venezuela—to attend, as observers, the Afro-Asian Conference in Bagdad the preceding year.

[14] Harry Hamm, "Kuba und die radikale Linke des Westens," *Frankfurter Allgemeine Zeitung,* March 25, 1970, p. 2.

[15] *The New York Times,* January 31, 1971

[16] When an African ballet company arrived at the airport in Guyana, they were met by Guyanese officials almost all of whom had dressed in flowing African garments. The ballet company, however, emerged from the plane in business suits. *Los Angeles Times,* January 21, 1971.

as it attempts to develop a new national consciousness. This has not meant that black Guyanese are insensitive to their own national duality. When Stokely Carmichael, invited to speak before a group of radical Guyanese blacks, affirmed that the black radical movement ought to be separate from the Asian (Indian) one, criticism was vehement and his audience left.[17]

For the countries that primarily colonized Central and South America, Spain and Portugal, the ties of blood, language, culture, and history hardly need to be ingeniously rediscovered. The recollection of the ties, however, has not always been favorable to the mother country.

In some Latin American countries with substantial Indian and *mestizo* populations, the contemporary Spanish are the descendants of conquerors and destroyers. This seems to have been least easily forgotten and forgiven in Mexico, where negative attitudes toward official Spain led to and were reinforced by Mexico's reception of the single largest body of Republican exiles and by her refusal to recognize the Franco regime.[18] It has not been uncommon for well-to-do Mexicans to give Indian names to their children, and in the presidential palace of Mexico there are portraits of Indian leaders but not of their Spanish conquerors. The body of Peru's conqueror, Pizarro, is proudly displayed in Lima's Cathedral, but in Mexico, Cortés' body is inconspicuously entombed in a convent. Carlos Fuentes has remarked that Cortés is a more controversial figure in Mexico than a presidential candidate is in the United States.[19] Tensions between Mexican and Spanish historians burst once more into the open at a recent (1969) meeting when a

[17] *Marcha,* January 29, 1971, p. 20.

[18] Mexico's intransigent position on the recognition of the Spanish government is echoed by its position with regard to the Vatican. It and Guyana are the only Latin American countries that do not have relations with the Vatican. The visit of Eugene Cardinal Tisserant to Mexico in 1964 and a later visit by Cardinal Confalonieri were said to involve attempts to reestablish not only Vatican relations with Mexico but also relations between Spain and Mexico.

[19] Selden Rodman, *Mexican Journal,* New York, 1958, p. 193. Mexico's sensitivity to Spain's colonial role and to her conqueror Cortés has been matched more recently in some Peruvian leftist and nationalist circles. Jorge Luis Borges comments, after visiting Lima, "In Peru they asked me seriously: 'Are you on the side of Pizarro or Atahualpa?' " Selden Rodman, *South America of the Poets,* New York, 1970, p. 20.

Mexican historian denounced Cortés as a "syphilitic dwarf" who had concealed his inferiority under a cloak of arrogance and aggression.[20]

There seems little doubt that the extraordinarily small number of Mexican students who study in Spain (see note 50, Chapter 9) as compared with students from other Latin American countries, is in part related to these tensions between the two countries.

When Prince Juan Carlos of Spain visited the OAS headquarters in Washington, the Mexican foreign minister refused to meet him,[21] but Mexico's official coolness to Franco's Spain does not seem to have harmed, and may have improved, her relations with the Spanish people. In any case it appears that Spaniards most appreciate, among foreign people, the Mexicans and the French. Among South Americans they prefer the non-Spanish speaking Brazilians to Argentinians and other South Americans.[22]

After the defeat of Germany and Italy in World War II, Spain substituted cultural and linguistic themes for the more militant nationalistic emphases of the Falange. But this has not entirely erased the reserve that some Latin Americans feel toward contemporary Spain. General Franco's statement that Spain has never been colonizer or colonialist but a civilizer "which is quite a different matter"[23] is likely to be no more convincing to many Latin Americans than to the people of Equatorial Guinea whose newly gained independence provided the occasion for the statement.

Various forms of nativism in the Indian lands of Latin America and the presence in them and in the other Latin American countries of a variety of African and European stocks have also led Spain to

[20] The *Los Angeles Times,* February 27, 1969. See also in this connection Arthur Whitaker, *Spain and Defense of the West: Ally and Liability,* New York, 1961, p. 344. For a brief account of a modern "confrontation" between Cortés and his royal victim Cuauhtémoc, whose bones were alleged to have been found in 1949 but, in the midst of bitter controversy, were rejected as unauthentic by two government scientific commissions, see Lewis Hanke, "The Bones of Cuauhtémoc," in *Encounter,* XXV (3), September 1965, p. 79.

[21] *Latin America* (London), February 5, 1971, p. 48.

[22] Based on tables from Salustiano del Campo, "On the Assimilation of Immigrants in Cataluña." These tables are reproduced, from a typescript copy of del Campo's paper, by James A. Michener, *Iberia,* New York, 1968, pp. 562–563.

[23] *Le Monde,* July 23, 1968.

recognize that blood ties provide a less convincing or compelling bond than linguistic and cultural affinities. In Spain, *El día de la raza* has given place to *El día de la Hispanidad*. Characteristically, the Mexicans have retained the old name since they take *la raza* to refer to the Aztecs and not to the Spanish.[24]

Spain has attempted to give her links with Latin America a juridical framework through treaties of double nationality. Under both the monarchy and the Second Republic the Spanish civil code [25] had defined as Spanish nationals persons born outside of Spain whose fathers or mothers were Spanish nationals. The treaties of double nationality go further and provide for special access to the rights of Spanish citizenship for citizens of Latin American countries that have signed the double nationality treaty (with reciprocal rights for Spaniards overseas). The language of these treaties appeals to a sentiment of hispanic unity whose existence is not for one moment doubted:

> Whereas . . . the Spanish in Peru and the Peruvians in Spain do not feel themselves to be foreigners. . . . Whereas . . . the Spanish in Nicaragua and the Nicaraguans in Spain feel themselves to be in their own Fatherland. . . .[26]

These treaties of double nationality were for some Spaniards only a step toward *"la supranacionalidad Hispánica"* which would unite countries "that constitute a community with deep roots in history, with a communion of blood, culture, language, religious beliefs, political institutions, a common past, the same conception of life and of man, and above that . . . the same destiny in the world. These conditions for supranationality can only be successfully found in these privileged regions of the planet." [27] Similar senti-

[24] Julian P. H. Rivers, "Race, Color, and Class in Central America and the Andes," *Daedalus,* Spring 1967, p. 542.

[25] Article 17, Paragraph 2, as amended December 9, 1931.

[26] Treaty on Double Nationality Between Spain and Peru, May 16, 1959, and Treaty on Double Nationality Between Spain and Nicaragua, July 25, 1961. Portugal and Brazil went even further in a treaty of considerable political importance, signed in September 1971, that gave citizens of one country equal rights in the other, including the right to vote and hold office. *Latin America* (London), September 17, 1971, p. 300.

[27] J. M. Yepes, "Doble Nacionalidad o Supranacionalidad," *Mundo Hispánico* (Madrid), No. 142, January 1960.

ments in favor of a Hispanic Commonwealth have been expressed, although less frequently, in Latin America.[28]

These insistent appeals to ties forged many years ago to justify claims on the loyalty of Hispanic Americans betray how little Spanish aspirations in Latin America have been fulfilled. Still, 300 years of physical presence of one of the most distinctive societies and cultures of Europe are by no means easily erased; links between Spain and many of the populations of Latin America are much too strong not to have had substantial effects on Spanish relations with Latin America.[29] That Spain's importance to Latin Americans seems nonetheless relatively modest compared with that of the United States, the other Western European powers, and Japan is a measure of how much commerce, investment, economic and political power have counted in comparison with the linguistic, religious, and cultural–historical ties that relate Hispanic America to Spain, past and present.

Like Spain, Portugal has sought in a closer relation with its former colony, Brazil, to resolve its political and economic isolation and limitations. Portuguese Premier Marcello Caetano's five-day state visit to Brazil in 1969 prompted Lisbon newspapers to urge Brazil and Portugal to give a juridical–political structure to the Portuguese-speaking world and to form a commonwealth including Brazil as well as Portugal's African territories, and to end a condition in which "we are brothers and hardly know each other." [30]

But Portuguese interest in establishing closer ties with Brazil has been hampered by official and unofficial preoccupation with the glories of the sixteenth century and by the largely sentimental invocation of Brazilian ties with Portugal. This has produced Brazilian conceptions of the Portuguese that to the latter are "extremely wounding and painful," attitudes reciprocated by some Portuguese who view the Brazilians as improvident, careless, lazy, and irresponsible singers of popular songs.[31]

[28] See, for example, the work of the Argentinian Mario Amadeo, *Por una convivencia Internacional: Bases para una communidad Hispánica de Naciones,* Madrid, 1956, especially pp. 221–224.

[29] For example, Latin American assistance to Spain in achieving United Nations membership and its support of Spain in its conflict with Britain over Gibraltar; relevant also is the fact that more Latin American students study in Spain than in all other countries of Europe put together, including the Communist countries (see Chapter 9.5).

[30] *The New York Times,* July 9, 1969. See also Chapter 2.2.

[31] Adriano Moreira, "Aspectos Negativos da imagem recíproca de Por-

Such reciprocally uncomplimentary views do not imply that political and economic elites on both sides of the Atlantic are un-affected by the past historical connections between their countries, but the past seems to have a more compelling influence when it is fortified by common economic and political interests, or when Spain and Portugal become, like France, a European *pied-à-terre* for Latin Americans who seek temporary absorption into a European society.

France stresses the unity of all lands that participate in a common "cultural latinity" (*latinité*) thus opposing itself to Spain's emphasis on Latin American *Hispanidad* and largely ignoring the highly mixed ethnic and cultural character of the Central and South American populations. In this France has been supported by some Latin Americans. In 1959 President Prado of Peru sought to promote *latinidad* as a community of peoples of Latin language, much to the satisfaction of the then French minister for foreign affairs.[32] The joint communiqué of the Chilean–French Mixed Commission issued at the end of its 1967 meeting did not hesitate to speak of "Latin America and Europe which . . . participate in a common origin." [33] In a similar spirit, M. André Malraux, then minister of state for cultural affairs, while in Mexico in February 1966, emphasized in his press conference that were France to disappear, the link that held together the *latinidad* of the Latin Americans would also disappear. As *Política* pointed out, the minister for cultural affairs did not explain "the common denominator . . . between a Quechua peasant, a Tarahumara Indian, and Marcel Proust. . . ." [34] Even in countries with a largely European composition affirmations of a stronger link to France than to other European countries is viewed as suspect by a French observer. Faced with the remark of an Argentinian theater director that "We are . . .

tugal-Brasil," *América Latina* (Rio de Janeiro), 10 (1), January–March 1967, p. 54.

[32] See Fabio Luca Cavazza, *Italy and Latin America,* The Rand Corporation, RM-5400-RC, November 1967, p. 87.

[33] *Le Monde,* November 11, 1967.

[34] *Política* (Mexico), March 1, 1966, pp. 49–50. There is irony in the fact that Malraux's statement was made on a visit to Mexico and Guatemala to arrange for an important Mayan exhibit in Paris. Malraux apparently had not taken the hint given by President Belaúnde to General de Gaulle that the *latinité* of Peru was not quite evident to him. Marc Blancpain, *Aujourd'hui, L'Amérique Latine,* Paris, 1966, p. 13.

children of France more than of Italy and Spain," this observer remarks: "This denial of Italy and Spain and this choice of a French filiation seemed to me to express the desire to attach oneself in the cultural sphere . . . to what one believes is most prestigious." [35]

French references to *latinité* or *latinidad* and her use of *Amérique latine* and *América Latina,* a denomination consecrated by use in South America itself, provoked, especially in the past, sharp Spanish reactions. The question of nomenclature was raised at the First (1914) and Second (1921) Hispanic Congresses of History and Geography in Seville. "Who is the author of these new expressions which have been unfairly circulated. . . . It is not our intention to examine this. But we will call attention to the fact that the French adopt them with rare unanimity and fervor." [36] This intransigent Spanish speaker also rejected the use of "Ibero-American" to embrace the Spanish and Portuguese in America and contended that "Hispanic" was entirely adequate to cover both. It appears that the expression *América Latina* was devised about 1855 by a group of South American intellectuals who were replying to Gobineau's disparagement, in his *Essay on the Inequality of the Human Race,* of French and Iberian mixing in America with "inferior indigenous races.[37]

Frenchmen more concerned with France's economic interests in Latin America and less impressed by the spiritual affinities so evident to Malraux, have found other bonds that in their opinion enable France and the Latin republics to understand each other: France, like Latin America, has a large agricultural population, public and private enterprise exist happily together, and France does not have, like the United States, the mystique of private enterprise.[38]

[35] Jacques Arnault, *Journal de voyage en Amérique latine,* Vol. 1, Paris, 1969, p. 144.

[36] Cited in J. F. Normano, *The Struggle for South America,* London, 1931, pp. 81–83. This lively work should be consulted for additional discussion of the "ideological," that is, national affinities struggle in Latin America during the first decades of the century.

[37] Arturo Ardao, "El Canadá y América," *Marcha* (Montevideo), October 1967. According to another theory, the expression *L'Amérique latine* was invented in France about 1870 by followers of Michel Chevalier, according to whom France had the historical duty to assume leadership of the Latin peoples. *Visión,* September 11, 1971, p. 4.

[38] *The Jeanneney Report,* Overseas Development Institute, London, 1964.

114

The Italians, who have at least an equal claim to represent latinity, have not stressed affinities of this ambiguous nature and have been more inclined to emphasize the bonds created by particular historical events. Although President Castelo Branco in his reception for President Saragat spoke of "the affinities that unite the Italian and the Latin American minds," [39] President Saragat in his reply recalled the role of the Brazilian expeditionary force in ousting the Germans from Italian soil during World War II, apparently willing to overlook that on August 22, 1942, Brazil had declared war on Italy as well as on Germany.[40]

Brazilian participation in World War II also provided a means for the Brazilian and Polish ministers of foreign affairs at their meeting in 1962 to evoke an image, otherwise difficult to conjure up, of Polish–Brazilian solidarity.[41] An earlier war provides the basis for an equally unexpected relationship—between Mexico and the Irish. An annual ceremony marks Mexican remembrance of the St. Patrick's Battalion of about 100 Irish in General Winfield Scott's invading army, who went over to the Mexicans in the United States–Mexican War of 1847.[42]

United States officials, conscious of the Protestant and North European origins of the United States, generally avoid attempts to claim affinities of a cultural, ethnic, or religious character although the election of a Catholic president by the United States in 1960 did create a distinct stir in Latin America.[43] The progressive diversification of the populations of the two Americas and the com-

[39] *Latin American Times,* September 28, 1965.

[40] In Uruguay President Saragat had at his disposal a reference to Garibaldi's arrival, more than 100 years before him, on the shores of the Plata with 600 men to aid Montevideo's struggle against Rosas. Unfortunately, such a reference had less welcome connotations on the Argentinian side of the Plata. *La Stampa,* however, reported the president's arrival in Montevideo under the heading: "In this land the name of Italy is bound to Garibaldi who evokes once more . . . glorious struggle for democracy." *La Stampa* (Turin), September 15, 1965.

[41] Viagem do Ministro das Relacões Exteriores, *Revista Brasileira de Política Internacional,* V (18), June 1962, p. 341.

[42] *Latin American Times,* September 14, 1965.

[43] R. Richard Rubottom, Jr., "An Assessment of Current American Influence in Latin America," *The Annals of the American Academy of Political and Social Science, Vol.* 366, July 1966, p. 118.

mon possession of immigrant groups from the same foreign lands have not provided as much of a sense of kinship as one might have supposed.[44] Nor does the sizable population of Latin American origin in the United States seem to have created a sense of kinship. Of the 24.5 million immigrants who entered the United States in this century, 11 percent were from Latin America, and during the sixties this figure rose to 38 percent.[45] A recent United States Census report shows that 9.2 million Americans, that is, 5 percent of the population, identify themselves as having an origin in a Spanish-speaking country, although 80 percent were born in the continental United States or Puerto Rico.[46]

United States and Latin American spokesmen seek a common bond in their membership in the New World and its differences from the Old World. Spokesmen for the two Americas both refer to their common reception of Europeans and other migrants who sought in both parts of the New World opportunities for personal freedom and economic advancement and release from the restrictive social and political life of the Old World. And both sets of spokesmen can equally refer to wars that provided political liberation from the sovereignty of European powers. "We are all, I think," pointed out former Secretary of State Dean Rusk, "keenly aware of the close and special relationship we have with our neighbors in this Hemisphere. It is a relationship shaped from a common heritage in revolution, from a shared belief in social

[44] The presence common to the United States and a number of the Latin republics of a sizable population of African origin seems to have been equally ineffective. The isolation of the American Indians from United States life and their small number have of course prevented the Indian in the United States from representing a point of commonality with Latin America. On the contrary, the substantial presence of Indians and *mestizos* in the Central American and Andean republics marks for these countries a separation from, and not an affinity with, the United States.

[45] Gustavo R. Gonzalez, "The Migration of Latin American High-level Manpower," *International Labour Review,* 98 (6), December 1968, p. 552.

[46] For 70 percent of this group, Spanish is the mother tongue and 50 percent speak Spanish at home. A little more than 5 million are Mexican–Americans and about 1.5 million Puerto Ricans. Cuba accounts for almost 600,000 as do also Central and South America. Approximately one and a half million "other Spanish" are not further identified but presumably include many persons whose forebears came from Spain. United States Department of Commerce, *Persons of Spanish Origin in the United States,* P-20, No. 213.

116

justice, and from a deep respect for personal dignity. These traditions and beliefs are common to the Hemisphere." [47] Evoking similar themes, Governor Rockefeller, during the course of a tension-laden trip to Latin America, affirmed repeatedly, if somewhat vaguely, that "we in the Western Hemisphere have common backgrounds, heritages and beliefs and, I believe, a common destiny," [48] President Nixon in a report to Congress on foreign affairs recalled that our "unique relationship [with Latin America] is rooted in geography, in a common Western heritage and in a shared historical experience of independence born through revolution." [49] And President Lleras Restrepo of Colombia, in an exchange of toasts, recalled that "the Americas were once called 'land of hope,' and I am sure this title can and should be preserved as the symbol and guide of our common conduct." [50]

These themes now have a less compelling air than they once possessed. The Old World is no longer the seat of imperial dynasties and ancient privilege. For many, a "land of hope" is a welfare state with an old-age pension rather than a land of more exuberant possibilities. Besides, Peru is no longer a word synonymous with untold wealth, and the gold with which New York streets were once paved has long ago worn thin. Still, for some Latins and North Americans the development of new regions in Latin America, the feeling for large spaces and unlimited possibilities,[51] the flair for the gigantic, still shape a sense of kinship, although probably a declining one. For Europeans (and some North Americans) it is still a shock to find that the "little" countries of South America are very large: "little" Paraguay is larger than Italy, Belgium, and Holland combined, and Bolivia is as large as France, West Germany, Italy, Belgium, and Holland together.[52] Nonetheless the progressive widen-

[47] *Hearings,* Committee on Foreign Relations, Senate, 90th Congress, First Session on Senate Joint Resolution 53, March 17 and 21, 1967, p. 9.

[48] *Los Angeles Times,* June 20, 1969.

[49] *The New York Times,* February 19, 1970.

[50] United States State Department, *Bulletin,* July 7, 1969, p. 12.

[51] The contribution of continental riches to *"la conciencia continental americana frente a Europa"* has been noted by Julio Ycaza Tigerino, *Sociología de la Política Hispanoamericana,* Madrid, 1962, pp. 316–318.

[52] Nonetheless some Latin Americans, impressed by the size of the United States, find that "the European nations are small, *like our own"* [emphasis added]. Mariano Grondona, "América latina como región," *Visión,* September 25, 1970, p. 63.

117

ing of the income differences between the United States, Europe, and Japan on the one hand, and Latin America on the other, serves to underline that some affinities do not so much run north and south within the New World, as east and west across the Atlantic and the Pacific, uniting in a common industrial civilization the northern countries of the New and Old Worlds.

7. Advocacy

A SENSE of dependency has rendered the Latin American countries appreciative of any country that could claim to promote their interests. The foreign powers, seeking to improve their position in the Latin American world, compete for the title of special advocate of Latin American economic interests. So widespread is this competition that it raises the question before whom do these spokesmen for Latin America plead—all the relevant parties have enlisted themselves in the ranks of the advocates.

Italy, more than most, has had a continuing reputation for being Latin America's defendant and spokesman, especially before the EEC.[1] Italy has gained this reputation in part because, not having a set of preferentially treated client states stemming from former colonial possessions, she has been in a better position than France and Great Britain to advocate Latin American claims. The visit of President Giuseppe Saragat and Foreign Minister Amintore Fanfani to South America in 1965 was especially an occasion for affirmations by the Italian press that Italy was the true spokesman in EEC for South American interests. "Italy defends the interests of South America in the EEC" against the competition of "numerous African countries . . . introduced into the Common Market by the will of General de Gaulle. . . . Italy has always followed a . . . policy that takes account of South American interests and their need to overcome African competition . . . in coffee, tea,

[1] The reader is reminded that the discussion of Caribbean relations with the EEC (Chapter 1.1) is relevant to the present chapter.

tropical fruits and minerals." [2] In Brazil General Castello Branco used the occasion of President Saragat's visit to affirm that the affinities uniting the Italian and the Latin American minds were a special qualification for Italy to become the interpreter in Europe of Latin American economic aspirations. [3]

Nonetheless, the Latin American governments do not exactly view Italian representation as having produced significant gains for them in the EEC. A hint of threat sometimes accompanies Latin American demands for a more vigorous advocacy of its interests. Thus Adelbert Krieger Vasena, former Argentine minister of economics and labor, adds, after noting certain economic measures taken to consolidate Argentinian relations with Italy: "We hope that Italy on its part will *prudently* [emphasis added] interpret the problem created by the excessive agricultural protectionism of the European Common Market." [4]

France has also attempted to establish itself as a spokesman for Latin American interests. In his Mexican and South American visits de Gaulle expressed his intention to lower EEC barriers to foodstuffs and raw materials. France's need to establish itself as a spokesman for Latin America was all the greater because the policies that it in fact defended in the EEC and especially its promotion of special economic privileges for the associated African, mostly francophone, states, [5] and for its Antilles departments, brought it into sharper conflict with Latin American interests than did the policies of other EEC countries. In some cases France did not succeed in excluding Latin American tropical products from the EEC but only from France itself. Although the French Caribbean departments are formally part of the EEC by virtue of Article 227 of the Treaty of Rome, special regulations make this in fact an association rather than a full membership. Consequently, Germany and Italy were able to secure their bananas from Latin America much more cheaply than was France from its own Caribbean territories. [6] France, how-

[2] *La Stampa* (Turin), September 17, 1965.

[3] *Latin American Times,* September 28, 1965.

[4] *Successo,* May 1967, p. 45.

[5] About one-half of all exports to the EEC from the African associated states are received by France.

[6] Ecuador is the world's leading exporter of bananas, accounting in 1968 for about 22 percent of the world's $500 million export market. Central American countries account for another 36 percent. *Ceres,* II (2), March–April 1969, p. 17. In 1967 the c.i.f. cost of Latin American bananas at West

120

ever, was able to keep these bananas from being trans-shipped within the Common Market.[7]

Reviewing France's trade relations with Latin America, a French observer remarked that at UNCTAD I, Geneva, 1964, France defended Latin American economic interests and particularly stressed guaranteed commodity prices. A British observer, however, found that at Geneva in 1964 British intervention resolved the differences between industrialized and developing countries, especially Latin America, and that the United Kingdom had had a positive approach toward commodity stabilization schemes.[8] Unfortunately for Latin America the combined representation and advocacy of her interests by Italy, France, and the United Kingdom did not enable her to penetrate more fully the EEC and Commonwealth markets.

Four years later at UNCTAD II, New Delhi, 1968, France, through its finance minister, Michel Debré, made clear that although it might be willing to consider some generalized system of preferences, special preferential arrangements for the associated EEC countries must continue; nor was France willing to abandon the system of reverse preferences by which these latter states gave preferences to the exports of the EEC countries. The discovery of a substitute system will be "a long and arduous task, filled with great difficulties." [9]

Similarly, the United Kingdom, while accepting in principle a generalized system of preferences for the less-developed countries, took the position that it was up to the Commonwealth countries to weigh the relative advantages of any new schedule of preferences against those presently enjoyed, and that in fact the Commonwealth countries had decided that they did not wish to abandon their system of Commonwealth exchanges.[10] Thus the special interests of differ-

---

German ports was about $138 a metric ton, and the corresponding figure for French Caribbean bananas at French ports was $209.

[7] In trying to secure the free movement of Antilles' products into the EEC, the French government used the departmental status of Guadaloupe and Martinique to promote a geographical conception of some originality: The French Antilles are *"l'Europe tropicale." Le Monde,* August 9, 1966.

[8] Jean Meyriat, "France and Latin America" in Claudio Véliz (ed.), *Latin America and the Caribbean,* New York, 1968, p. 437; and James C. Hunt, "Britain and Latin America," in *ibid.,* p. 446.

[9] *The New York Times,* February 6, 1968.

[10] *The New York Times,* February 7, 1968; and *Le Monde,* February 8, 1968.

ent groups of underdeveloped countries, and not only the policies of the industrialized countries, are involved in the satisfaction (or nonsatisfaction) of Latin American demands. This was already evident in Third World discussions preceding the formulation of the Charter of Algiers [11] drawn up by the Seventy-seven (less-developed countries) in preparation for UNCTAD II.

Germany has not made a special point of affirming its support for Latin American interests in the Common Market, but has, on occasion, found such statements a useful means of expressing its pleasure for some Latin American act of political utility. When the Argentinian foreign minister Costa Méndez preceded his visit to Bonn by a visit to West Berlin, the Federal Republic expressed its sympathetic support for Argentina's concern about Common Market decisions.[12]

The United States found it easy at New Delhi to support a general system of preferences for the Third World and to come out strongly against the system of inverse preferences applied to the associated EEC states. The United States was thus generally in opposition to France and Great Britain on those matters, although its status in Latin American eyes was tarnished by its unwillingness to give Latin America privileges in the United States market similar to those enjoyed by the African countries in the EEC and the former British colonies in the Commonwealth markets. France attempted to mitigate the blows to its position as an advocate of Latin American interests by again stressing the need for price stabilization of products important to the Third World, and the United Kingdom acquired credit for its support for the progressive untying of aid (see Chapter 10.7). It was the Netherlands, however, which, at New Delhi, broke the solidarity of the Common Market Six and declared itself in favor of the abolition of inverse preferences as applied to the African countries associated with the EEC, and which, a year later, came out for generalized preferences.[13] Sweden at New Delhi argued that "joint action from all industrialized countries with the aim to abolish customs tariffs on tropical products must

---

[11] The Charter of Algiers, adopted in October 1967, is reproduced in ECLA, *Economic Bulletin for Latin America,* XIII (1), June 1968, pp. 115–128.

[12] *Primera Plana* (Buenos Aires), April 1–7, 1969, p. 10.

[13] *Le Monde,* March 1, 1968, and May 31, 1969.

be given high priority as well as the abolition of tariffs on industrial raw materials. . . . In our view a preferential system should be extended to all developing countries by all the major industrial countries." [14] And in 1969 Japan voted with the Third World against the United States, France, the United Kingdom, and the Federal Republic of Germany (with other industrial nations abstaining) on a procedural matter of interest to the Third World bearing on an UNCTAD report.[15] In UNCTAD, then, it was primarily countries that had not made a special profession of advocating Latin American trade interests that were, in fact, the most vigorous on behalf of international trade reforms sought by Latin America. For the most part the rivalry of the Western European industrial countries to establish themselves as advocates of Latin American economic interests did not win them particular credit in Latin America with, perhaps, the exception of Italy.

Latin American reserve was little altered when, in 1969, the United States resumed its advocacy of generalized tariff preferences for the Third World through its delegate to the OECD and by a well publicized statement by President Nixon.[16] This time the United States went beyond its New Delhi position in indicating that if the OECD countries did not agree to support global preferences, the United States "will be prepared to consider other alternative actions" that would give Latin America alone preferential treatment by the United States.

The resistance of several of the industrial countries to general concessions for the Third World weakened in 1970. The United States had, however, to abandon its insistence that the industrial

---

[14] Royal Ministry for Foreign Affairs, *Documents on Swedish Foreign Policy 1968,* New Series I:C:17, Stockholm, 1969, pp. 248–249. On the other hand, Sweden was not so forthcoming on questions of shipping, important to Brazil and some other Latin republics. "We cannot accept practices of flag discrimination." *Ibid.,* p. 253. About 65 percent of international shipping is accounted for by the developing countries; but these countries have only a 7 percent share in the world shipping fleet. See L.M.S. Raywar *et al., Shipping and Developing Countries,* Carnegie Endowment for International Peace, New York, 1971. However, Brazil's vigorous program for attaining shipping independence is saving her about $100 million annually in foreign currency expenditures.

[15] *Le Monde,* February 12, 1969.

[16] *The New York Times,* November 11, 1969.

countries draw up a common set of preferences, and agree to each nation making its own individual concessions. This process led to inequities, and the United Kingdom withdrew duty-free exemptions on man-made fibers and wool textiles after finding that other industrial countries, including the United States, did not follow suit. The United States has not included textiles, shoes, and petroleum products among its concessions but it did, on the other hand, reluctantly agree to make tariff concessions to those less-developed countries that grant reverse preferences to the EEC (or in the case of the Commonwealth countries to the United Kingdom) while expressing the hope that reverse preferences would be abolished "over a reasonable period." This United States concession was, of course, advantageous to Africa but not to Central and South America.

The insistence of the European nations that each industrial country draw up its own list of concessions has led to joint Latin American pressure on the United States, and to the Latin American organization of additional conferences to enable the republics to place their demands jointly before the EEC and other industrial countries.

Japan may have derived some political benefit from being the first to announce general preferences, but implementation, it turned out, was only to occur "no later than October 1" [1971]. In the meantime, Holland more or less forced the EEC to institute its schedule of tariff preferences for the less-developed countries on July 1, 1971, although the other members of the EEC were evidently not eager to take action any sooner than necessary.[17]

Although the United States was, together with Scandinavia and Switzerland, in the forefront of the battle for the abolition of regional preferences, it has been laggard in following the example of Japan and the EEC. The nonmonolithic character of the United States government is not always appreciated in Latin America, and the discrepancy between Executive promises and Congressional action has been very unfavorably interpreted. These unfavorable in-

---

[17] The duty-free entry to the EEC of manufactured and semimanufactured products of the less-developed countries will still leave preferential advantages for the agricultural exports of EEC associate member states. The EEC has set a dollar limit to manufactured Third World imports. The United States will presumably operate on a system of specified items. The Japanese system is a mixture of both methods. *Visión Letter,* April 28, 1971, p. 3.

terpretations were rendered all the more plausible by the apparent disinclination of the Nixon administration to continue in 1971 its earlier pressure on Congress and, finally, by its inclusion of Latin America in the 10 percent import surcharge imposed in its August 1971 measures against a rapidly increasing negative balance of payments.

8. Models

SOME of the nonhemispheric countries competing for a favored position in Latin America are able to urge or imply that relations with them have a particular value for Latin America because of special national experiences or talents that have a Latin American application.

No country has more persistently traded on this than Italy. Several elements enter into the claim: Italian experience in economic planning, the Italian "opening to the Left" without sacrificing political stability and economic development, and above all, Italy's experience in developing the Mezzogiorno, its underdeveloped southern regions,[1] the problems of which are equated with those of Latin American countries seeking to escape cultural and industrial backwardness. Unfortunately, the two decades that have elapsed since the creation in 1950 of the Cassa per il Mezzogiorno have not resolved the problems of the Italian south, where per capita income is still approximately one-half of the northern figure. Indeed, Italy's experience in rehabilitating the south has been used on the one hand to demonstrate to Latin Americans Italian leadership in economic development, while at the same time Italian failures and difficulties in the south have been advanced to explain the limited Italian ability to provide economic aid. Speaking at UNCTAD II at New Delhi in 1968, the Italian undersecretary for foreign affairs urged realism in setting aid objectives and observed that Italy "has not yet entirely

[1] See Fabio Luca Cavazza, *Italy and Latin America,* The Rand Corporation, Santa Monica, RM-5400-RC, November 1967, p. 88.

126

resolved the South Italian problem which was recently aggravated by the earthquake in Sicily." [2]

Italian experience in economic planning has hardly been more successful. [3] The 1955 Vanoni Plan was largely a failure since it provided no means for imposing conformity with it, nor has this changed in the last quinquennial plan. It is doubtful that the Italian administrative process and Italian planning experience have provided models for Latin American planners. On the other hand, Italy's mixed economy and use of semiautonomous state agencies provide it with an economic experience relevant to Latin American patterns.

France has relied largely on claims to spiritual and cultural leadership rather than on special experience adaptable to Latin American advantage. French officials have, however, reminded South America that France's experience during her years of colonial administration and more recently her experience in technical, cultural, scientific, and educational aid to her former colonies are at the disposal of the Latin American countries. France has also pointed out that her experience in planning may appeal to developing countries that are dissatisfied with market mechanisms but dislike the rigidities of Soviet planning. "But this does not imply that France should impose herself as a model; merely that there are ways in which she may play a useful role." [4]

The Chilean minister of foreign affairs, Gabriel Valdés, in a speech in Paris noted a rather different inspiration from French experience. "France [i.e., de Gaulle] is doing in the world what we would like to do and what other Latin American nations would like to do . . . even if they do not always recognize it." [5]

Gabriel Valdés' chief, President Frei, speaking in Bonn in 1965, found that German experience and German qualities were equally inspirational. "Chile has always admired Germany's working ability, its industrial power, its scientific spirit, and its technical abilities. . . .

[2] *Le Monde,* February 8, 1968.

[3] See J. LaPalombara, *Italy: The Politics of Planning,* Syracuse (New York), 1966.

[4] *The Jeanneney Report,* Overseas Development Institute, London, 1964, p. 23. For an analysis of the French experience in planning, see Stephen S. Cohen, *Modern Capitalist Planning: The French Model,* Cambridge, Mass., 1969.

[5] *Le Monde,* October 7, 1967.

What happened after the war has . . . turned this admiration into astonishment. All Chileans have observed . . . the German miracle. . . . It is even more important to see that Germany is solving its problems in the framework of human rights and a democratic regime. . . ." Heinrich Gewandt, the Hamburg CDU deputy who played a role in Frei's election, relates that five years earlier, in 1960, he had given Frei a detailed account of how the Federal Republic of Germany had solved its problems and of the social and political ideas of German Christian Democracy, and that this account of German experience had greatly impressed Frei. It was also Heinrich Gewandt who later, in 1963, a year before Frei's election, conducted Frei through Germany on a private information tour.[6] Former President Onganía, equally impressed by German experience, is said to have given his minister, Alsogaray, the mission of reproducing in Argentina the "German miracle."[7] A leading São Paulo businessman explains the presence in his office of a photograph of West German Chancellor Erhard: "It's not the chancellor we admire, but the author of what is called the German miracle. Why shouldn't we be able to do what he has done?"[8]

In some cases the experiences of the industrial countries that are relevant to Latin America are of a quite specialized character. Thus France's experience in subway construction has been applied in several Latin American countries and Japan's success in building and operating high-speed interurban trains in Japan has interested Brazil, which seeks a high-speed train between Rio de Janiero and São Paulo.

The Russians have not emphasized Soviet planning techniques as a model for Latin American emulation. Rather, the Soviets have pointed to the Russian Revolution and to the later economic and political development of their country as an example for the underdeveloped world and as a model for the accumulation of capital

[6] Heinrich Gewandt, "Mein Freund Frei," *Die Welt,* July 17, 1965, p. 3.
[7] *Le Monde,* July 13, 1966. The "Japanese miracle," perhaps even more impressive than the "German miracle," has not led, apparently, to Japanese claims to be a model for Latin America. ECLA, however, has published a study of "Export Promotion in Japan and its Application to Latin America," *Economic Bulletin for Latin America,* XV (1), 1970. See especially Chapter VI, "Applicability of Japan's Experience to Latin America," pp. 98–102.
[8] Marc Blancpain, *Aujourd'hui, L'Amérique Latine,* Paris, 1966, p. 304.

required for industrial development. However, the availability of Western capital and economic aid for industrial development made the Soviet model increasingly irrelevant. The Soviets consequently included aid from Western countries as an integral part of their theory of Third World progression to socialism.[9]

Until the early sixties the Russians urged the Third World toward expansion of the public sector and recommended nationalization of foreign and domestic private property without compensation as a means to increase savings. Increased experience in the Third World led to doubts about the wisdom of "ultra-revolutionary haste" in resolving complex economic problems. Flexibility is now preferred to rigid, centralized controls, and Moscow commended the UAR for promoting private investment in industry and for partially freeing the private sector from rigid controls. The Russians point out that hasty nationalization incurs losses in production and services. The Russians note, too, that large public sectors and state-managed economies breed a "bureaucratic bourgeoisie" that "regards the public sector not as a means for political and economic transformation of the country but as a field for personal advancement and profit which results in widespread corruption and other costly abuses. . . . But [Moscow] is not ready to tolerate any inroads on the public sector or relaxation of restrictions on domestic and foreign business if they are associated with reorienting a country politically and economically away from the USSR." [10] Soviet desire to check a too hasty expansion of the public sector is matched by doubts concerning the applicability of Soviet planning experience. "In many of them [Third World countries], among those also that have chosen the non-capitalist path of development, the prerequisites are still lacking which are essential for all-national central planning. Therefore, the application of modern Soviet methods of planning is extremely difficult in these countries, at times even absolutely impossible." [11]

[9] Herbert S. Dinerstein, *Soviet Policy in Latin America,* The Rand Corporation, Santa Monica, RM-4967-PR, May 1966, pp. vi–vii.

[10] Elizabeth K. Valkenier, "New Soviet Views on Economic Aid," *Survey,* No. 76, Summer 1970, pp. 27–29. This paper and the citations therein are a valuable guide to the evolution of Soviet aid doctrine.

[11] V. Popov [Utilization of Soviet Experiences in Planning in the Developing Countries] in *Planovoye Chosyaistvo* (Moscow), No. 5, 1970, p. 22, cited in Harry Zinger, "Planning in Developing Countries," *German Foreign Policy,* (East Berlin), 10 (1), 1971, p. 64.

It is not the major industrial countries alone that are able to claim relevance for their historical experiences and special accomplishments. In signing, in 1970, a new two-year extension of an agreement between Israel and the OAS, Israeli Ambassador Rabin pointed out that the agreement afforded Israel "a good opportunity . . . to share the knowledge we have gained through our own economic and social development." [12] Israel's economic assistance activities has enabled her to apply her experience in agricultural problems, including the use of water resources and irrigation, in problems of communal development and regional planning, in the development of cooperatives and labor unions, and in education and youth work along *gadna-nachal* patterns.[13] Israeli technicians have also transferred the experience of the *moshav* or cooperative village to Latin America. Israel is one of the original partners of the Alliance for Progress and 40 percent of Latin Americans (over 1,200 in 1963–1966) receiving development training outside the Western hemisphere received it in Israel under various Alliance and bilateral programs.[14]

These various nonhemispheric claims to special national experiences with significant contemporary Latin American applications have no real counterpart in the United States. Although North Americans point to parallels in South and North American development (Chapter 6) and publicize the relevance of their industrial–scientific–organizational capabilities, they seem less inclined (or able) to lay claim to a unique national experience that has special relevance for current Latin American economic development.

[12] *The New York Times,* July 15, 1970.

[13] *Gadna* is the Israeli paramilitary organization for upper grade school children; *nachal* is a two-year military service system in which soldiers devote one year to agricultural work in outlying regions. For the training of Latin Americans in Israel in *gadna* and *nachal* courses and for technical assistance by Israeli officers to Bolivia and Ecuador, see Edward B. Glick, "The Non-Military Use of the Latin American Military," in Norman A. Bailey (ed.), *Latin America: Politics, Economics, and Hemispheric Security,* New York, 1965, pp. 181–182.

[14] José A. Mora, former secretary-general of OAS, cited in *The New York Times,* June 26, 1967. See also *Le Monde,* June 18, 1966; and Alliance for Progress, *Weekly Newsletter,* August 8, 1966, p. 3.

9. Cultural Programs

THE cultivation of a national presence abroad through cultural programs is usually presented as a means to promote international communication and the advancement of the arts and sciences. Nonetheless it is generally understood to serve political ends. It is this, of course, that explains the otherwise curious insistence on the part of nations to reciprocate with cultural missions of their own those that have been received from other countries. This is less a repayment of cultural debts than it is a demand for an equal opportunity to impose one's own presence.

1. *France*

In no Western country have convictions of one's own cultural excellence and the political value of cultural programs combined so well to make cultural diplomacy a major instrument of policy as in France. The relation of France's cultural programs to international objectives was expressed with little regard for customary polite formulas by the director of cultural affairs for the French Foreign Ministry (1964): "The expansion of France's language, the spread of her culture and ideas, the attraction of her literature, her science, her technology and her art, the value of her methods of training men, constitute . . . essential means of action for her foreign policy. Cultural action is closely linked with the political and economic action which it precedes, supports and completes.

131

It contributes directly to the power of our country in the international sphere." [1]

Although cultural diplomacy is often thought to serve primarily political ends, the attention given in the above statement to the economic value of France's cultural diplomacy is repeated in an even more emphatic manner in a more recent (1970) French statement:

> Why is France willing to make such a considerable effort in the field of cultural activity?
>
> Political reasons? . . . French action in this area does not tend . . . toward a political objective: she supports and favors a grouping of states which have a common interest in making the French language respected. . . .
>
> Preoccupations of an economic and commercial character? Why deny it? . . .
>
> Foreign students trained in our culture and techniques thanks to scholarships of the Ministry of Foreign Affairs are . . . the best ambassadors of French products, as well as of our methods and technical procedures. Doctors prescribe French medicines, engineers suggest the purchase of French machines. . . .
>
> But it is not purely for the sake of commercial ends that France pursues its cultural activities. . . . Its experience is the fruit of its consciousness of its civilizing mission. . . . [2]

Support of French cultural programs at all governmental levels— budgetary, administrative, and political—reflects the seriousness with which this instrument is regarded. Between 1958 and 1968 the French budget for cultural relations rose from 180 million to 575 million francs. [3] The Latin American share was modest but increased from 24 million francs in 1964 to 42 million in 1967.

[1] Cited in Maurice Adelman, "Talking Culture with the French," *The Times Literary Supplement* (London), March 21, 1968, p. 287.

[2] Suzanne Balous, *L'action culturelle de la France dans le monde*, Paris, 1970, pp. 175–176. In the cited statement the author appears to be referring not only to France's cultural programs proper but to her technical cooperation programs as well. This book provides the most up-to-date review of French activity in the field of cultural relations. An earlier work is still useful: Louis Dollot, *Les relations culturelles internationales*, Paris, 1964, especially Chapter 2.

[3] Different figures are sometimes cited due to the inclusion of credits for technical cooperation (aid) with expenditures for cultural relations. With

The leading place given to the French language as a tool of French cultural expansion is reflected in French budgetary actions and in official and private discussions. "French culture doubtless would not have been so widely acknowledged . . . had it not . . . a universal inclination. This universality is . . . linked to its means of expression, the French language." [4] "Every decline in the language not only bears witness to a decline in national vitality but also increases it. . . . France . . . sees in the defense of the French language an action necessary to safeguard the very existence of the nation. It sees in it, too, the indispensable condition for the maintenance and, if possible, the expansion of exchanges of all types, economic as well as cultural. . . . The struggle for the defence of the French language no longer appears as a rearguard action retarding, at the most, the advance of an adversary assured of victory." [5] In Senate budget debates particular attention is paid by the senators to the effectiveness of French language diffusion, and members of the Senate have asked France's cultural attachés to report on this every two or three years. [6] There are probably few countries whose first minister (later, president) would take the time, as did M. Georges Pompidou, to preside over an inter-ministerial committee devoted to the study of the expansion and diffusion of French books and public libraries. [7]

The creation in 1967 of the Association internationale des parlementaires de la langue française uniting parliamentarians of some 20 countries with substantial French-speaking populations, gives political value to a common use of the French language. The French government has, however, proceeded cautiously to avoid any appearance of reestablishing a colonial relationship between France and its former possessions. Nonetheless it seems to believe that learning French develops a sentimental attachment both to the

---

both included the expenditures in 1968 were two billion francs. See Suzanne Balous, *op. cit.,* p. 12 and pp. 174–175.

Budget data, here and later in the chapter, are not in constant francs, marks, etc. All francs are, however, New Francs.

[4] French Information Office, *Cultural and Technical Cooperation,* 1965, p. 7.

[5] Jacques Vernant, "La langue Française et le destin national," *Revue de Défense Nationale,* 26, May 1970, pp. 805–806.

[6] *Le Monde,* November 24, 1966.

[7] *Le Monde,* January 26, 1968. Of course, President Pompidou is a graduate of the École Normale Supérieure, a former schoolmaster at the lycée Henri IV, and editor of an anthology of French poetry.

language and to the culture and that an ability to use French was associated in the African colonies with less rebellious attitudes toward France. Indeed the former French colonies do appear to have a greater cultural identification with France than do the British colonies with Britain.[8]

Naturally in Latin America the French language is not expected to play as great a role as in Africa or in Southeast Asia, and in 1968 approximately two-thirds of 33,000 French teachers abroad supported by the French government were in Africa and only 639 in South America. This distribution results from the very heavy teaching commitments France made to her former colonies. A shift, however, in favor of Latin America has taken place. The number of French teachers in Latin America rose from 649 in 1969 to 809 in 1970, the latter figure being approximately double the 1964 level.[9]

The Alliance Française in Latin America has a vigorous program that seeks to maintain and extend the receptivity of Latin Americans to France, its language, and its culture.[10] In 1969 it had more than 300 centers with 120,000 students. In 1968 Brazil, with 40 centers and 35,000 students, and Argentina, with 149 centers and 21,000 students, were principal beneficiaries of Alliance Française activity. In addition to the centers with their language teaching and cultural activities, 15 lycées and colleges with 15,000 students in the major cities of South America provide a full secondary education for Latin American youth and the children of French living in Latin America.[11]

[8] Ali and Molly Mazrui, "The Impact of the English Language on African International Relations," *The Political Quarterly,* 38 (2), April–June 1967, pp. 140–155. In 1969 representatives of some 30 countries with French-speaking populations met to create another agency for cultural cooperation. This came into being in 1970 as L'agence de coopération culturelle et technique des pays francophones, which has been joined by 22 states "conscious of the solidarity that unites them through usage of the French language." *Le Monde,* February 2, 1969, and March 23, 1970. France contributes 45 percent of the budget, Canada 33 percent. *Le Monde,* July 4–5, 1971.

[9] *Le Monde,* May 9–10, 1971.

[10] The 1,200 centers of the Alliance Française throughout the world had a total budget of 180 million francs (about $56 million) in 1968. One-tenth of total revenue comes from the French government.

[11] Mention should at least be made of a variety of special organizations such as L'institut français d'Amérique latine (IFAL) in Mexico which

Seeking financial support in France for the teaching of French abroad the Alliance Française, in an appeal to French businessmen, asks how they expect to sell their products in Chile when Chilean businessmen do not even know the difference between the future and conditional tenses of the French language.[12] The premise of this appeal seems to be that Latin American businessmen should be taught French and not that French businessmen should learn Spanish. To be sure, in 1967 the French government took increased cognizance of foreign national pride by modifying the educational program in its foreign lycées. Although most of the instruction continues to be in French, courses on the literature and civilization of the host country are given in the language of that country. The new lycée in Buenos Aires was one of the first nominated for the new system.

The French Foreign Ministry does not rely simply on French programs and agencies to increase the use of the French language in Latin America. In its cultural accords with Latin American countries, France places special emphasis on obtaining a privileged position for the instruction of French in the official programs of primary, and more especially, secondary education.[13] In Uruguay, since 1963, French is taught for at least four years as the first obligatory language; in Colombia, since 1962, French is obligatory in the last two years of secondary school; in Venezuela, French is obligatory in the last two years of secondary education in the humanities division. It appears, however, that where school principals or students are free to choose a language, the great majority choose, not French, but English. This is the case in Brazil, and also in Venezuela in the science division where an English option exists and where French is rarely chosen. Similarly in Peru where only one foreign language is required the great majority of students choose English.[14]

The cultural presence of foreign nations in Latin America is represented not only by activities in Latin America, but also by the

---

recently celebrated its 25th anniversary. After starting as a center for research and scholarship, it has largely become a teaching institute.

[12] *Le Monde,* February 4, 1969.

[13] This is not only true of French cultural accords with Third World countries. France has also brought pressure to bear on West Germany to make French a first language in secondary schools.

[14] Suzanne Balous, *op. cit.,* pp. 158–159.

temporary transfer of Latin Americans to foreign countries for educational or other purposes. French university scholarships for Latin America increased from 156 in 1959 to 476 in 1964, to 809 in 1967, and to approximately 1,700 in 1970.[15]

France also receives a substantial number of Latin American intellectuals for whom Paris is, much more than other European capitals, a major attraction.[16] French intellectuals, especially those of left political orientation, reciprocate this with an interest in Latin American cultural and political events. A common antagonism to the United States often adds to the sense of political solidarity thus developed. The 1968 Havana Cultural Congress had a French delegation sixty strong, larger than Cuba's and six times larger than the Soviet delegation.[17] Probably more than those of other countries, French writers, professors, scientists, and students are active, if only to sign petitions, in the support of Latin American activities of a nationalist-left persuasion. When President Costa e Silva of Brazil forced the retirement of a number of Brazilian university teachers and scientists, some 240 French physicists alone sent a joint letter of protest to the president.[18] That Brazilian intellectuals feel they will be accorded an especially sympathetic hearing in France was indicated by the arrest of a group of Brazilians for sending articles, charging Army torture, to several American, British, and French newspapers and journals. Of the seven publications to which the articles had been sent, four were French, two British, and one American.[19]

In 1971 a large group of outstanding French left intellectuals, together with a number of Latin American writers, wrote to Castro to express their "shame and anger" at the persecution of the Cuban

[15] *Ibid.*, p. 105 and pp. 162–163; and *Le Monde,* May 9–10, 1971. To these should be added over 1,500 bursaries for technical training under the technical cooperation portion of France's aid programs to the less-developed countries. See OECD sources cited in note 66 below.

[16] For one interesting portrait of Latin American student and expatriate life in Paris, see the novel of the Colombian writer Eduardo Caballero Calderón, *El buen salvaje,* Barcelona, 1966 (Premio Eugenio Nadal, 1965).

[17] Adolfo Sánchez Vásquez, "Impressiones Sobre el Congreso Cultural de la Habana," *Cuadernos Americanos* (Mexico), CLVIII (3), May–June 1968, p. 55; and *Le Monde,* January 26, 1968.

[18] *Le Monde,* July 27–28, 1969.

[19] *The New York Times,* March 6, 1970. The four French publications were *Le Monde, L'Express, Les Temps Modernes,* and *Esprit.*

poet Heberto Padilla. This had repercussions throughout Latin America where among some it reinforced appreciation for French concern with Latin America, and among others it undermined regard for both the French intellectual left and those Latin American writers who prefer to live abroad and whose names were prominent among the signers of the letter. The most extraordinary sequel to this affair was not so much Castro's angry reply to "you agents of the CIA" but a letter to Castro from a number of Spanish intellectuals expressing their solidarity with him on the issue. That politics makes strange bedfellows can hardly be more aptly illustrated.

2. *Germany*

When in 1958, the president of the German Bundestag set forth the principal lines of West Germany's cultural programs abroad, he distinguished two chief tasks: one, to maintain contact with Germans abroad, especially in Latin America, and two, to give foreigners a better understanding of Germans and Germany. The first task reflected, as contrasted with France, the large number of persons of German descent in Latin America, especially in Brazil. The second task was related to the need to reconstruct Germany's image and to support West Germany's drive to prevent the recognition of East Germany.

Although the Federal Republic is charged by the constitution with responsibility for cultural activities abroad, education and cultural activity at home are the responsibility not of the *Bund* but of the individual *Länder* (states). This has hampered the Federal Republic in its foreign programs and has complicated the task of signing cultural accords with foreign nations, the terms of which normally involve relations with German educational and cultural institutions that are under the control of the *Länder*.

Federal budgetary support for cultural work abroad rose from 3 million marks in 1952 to 32 million DM in 1958, to 128 million DM in 1961, and to 229 million DM in 1968, the last figure being almost exactly one-third of the total budget of the Foreign Ministry.[20]

[20] Budget figures for 1958 are from Dollot, *op. cit.*, p. 82, and for other years from *Bulletin des Presse- und Informationsamtes der Bundesregierung*, Bonn, No. 124, November 3, 1967, p. 1053, and No. 64, May 20, 1969, pp. 549–550.

Like France's Alliance Française and the United Kingdom's British Council, Germany has its private organization, the Goethe Institute, which serves governmental cultural purposes. After a long period of informal cooperation the Goethe Institute undertook in 1969 to do its work in contractual agreement with the Foreign Ministry which, however, retains its freedom to engage in independent cultural activity.[21]

Of 114 German cultural institutes throughout the world (1968), 18 are located in 9 Latin American countries, Brazil leading with 5 centers and Argentina with 3.[22] Like its British and French counterparts, the Goethe Institutes in Latin America have given a high priority to the teaching of the German language, but have found this objective heavy going. The dropout rate in German language courses is high and the concern of the Foreign Ministry with the unpopularity of German language study led to a government interest in developing a "basic German" that would be more suitable for instruction in foreign areas.[23] In 1967–1968 about 77,000 foreigners were studying German at the Goethe Institutes throughout the world.[24] If we make the risky assumption that the average number of students in Goethe Institutes is the same in Latin America as in other foreign countries, then there were in 1968 approximately 13,000 Latin Americans studying German in Goethe Institutes.

Prior to World War I Germany supported some 2,000 schools throughout the world and in 1968 only 260. Although mostly private, they receive government subsidies, and approximately one-third of all German cultural expenditures are devoted to them. In Latin America, school expenditures of 28 million DM (1967) supported 79 schools (almost one-third of the German world total) and 520 of the 1,350 German teachers provided by the Foreign Office.[25]

[21] *Ibid.*, No. 100, July 31, 1969, p. 864.

[22] Goethe Institute [Report ending December 1968], Munich, pp. 26–31.

[23] *The Economist,* March 16, 1968, p. 25. It is not only the Germans who run into difficulties. Complaints have been made that in language instruction abroad, French teachers overemphasize the subtleties of grammar rather than a practical knowledge of French. *Le Monde,* July 9, 1966.

[24] *Bulletin des Presse- und Informationsamtes der Bundesregierung,* Bonn, No. 64, May 20, 1969, pp. 549–550.

[25] *Auslandsschulverzeichnis, Stand 1969,* Munich, 1969; *Bulletin des Presse- und Informationsamtes der Bundesregierung,* Bonn, No. 11, October 13, 1967, p. 956; *ibid.,* No. 64, May 20, 1969, pp. 549–550; Albrecht von

Unlike the French lycées, the German schools in Latin America teach in the language of the host country, that is, in Spanish or Portuguese, although German is, of course, taught as a school subject. The German schools enjoy an excellent reputation in Latin America and most of the students are of non-German descent. Indeed the German Foreign Office claims that in Latin America parents register their newborn infants in the German school before doing so in the government birth registry office.

Germany encourages the completion of a German education through study in Germany itself. A second pillar of German cultural work, paralleling in the field of university study and university exchanges the work of the Goethe Institute, is the Deutscher Akademischer Austauschdienst (aided by the Humboldt Stiftung). In 1967–1968 they were largely responsible for the 23,648 foreign students studying in Germany, of whom about 2,500 received financial assistance from German sources.[26] In 1966 some 1,250 students from Latin America studied in German universities and professional schools.[27] Although Latin Americans were only 8 percent of Third World students studying in Germany they received almost 20 percent of the stipends provided by the Deutscher Akademischer Austauschdienst and constituted the largest body of Latin American students in Western Europe outside of Spain.

Germany maintains an active exchange program for scientists and teachers. In 1966 almost 300 German professors, teachers, and scientists taught and traveled in Latin America (exclusive of German teachers teaching in Latin American German schools) and close to a hundred Latin American scientists traveled in Germany.[28] The year 1969, the 200th anniversary of the birth of Alexander von Humboldt, was a particularly favorable year for such exchanges and for ceremonial German–Latin American meetings.[29]

Gleich, *Germany and Latin America,* The Rand Corporation, RM-5523-RC, June 1968, pp. 96–100.

[26] *Bulletin des Presse- und Informationsamtes der Bundesregierung,* Bonn, No. 64, May 20, 1969, pp. 549–550.

[27] *Ibid.,* No. 111, October 13, 1967, p. 956.

[28] *Ibid.*

[29] Alexander von Humboldt (1769–1859), the German scientist for whom the Humboldt Current is named, traveled in Latin America in 1799–1804 and is esteemed there partly because of his contributions to scientific observations in the Southern Hemisphere but also because of his influence on Simón Bolívar and his sympathy for Latin American independence.

Like France, Germany is very active in promoting theatrical performances, concerts, and art exhibits as part of its cultural programs abroad. In addition it distributes a large number of German films, books, and newspaper subscriptions. Its foreign broadcast service ranks sixth in number of hours per week of air time after Radio Moscow, Radio Peking, VOA, the UAR broadcast service, and the BBC.[30]

Unlike the Federal Republic of Germany, for which cultural programs are just one arm of diplomacy, East German attempts to secure the recognition of the GDR (German Democratic Republic) and the establishment of diplomatic relations have had to be pursued, for lack of any other basis, largely through its cultural activities. These have had, apart from Cuba, their best reception in Chile, although East Germany has also been able to keep a more or less continuous set of activities going in Colombia, Uruguay, and Mexico as well. The objective of the GDR's cultural diplomacy—recognition—has necessarily brought it into contact with governments that are opposed by the Communist parties of Latin America. As a result the GDR found itself bitterly criticized at the 1967 Havana Solidarity Conference.[31] In one respect the cultural programs of West and East Germany coincide. East Germany also contributes to the teaching of German and to the spread of the German language in some countries of Latin America.

3. *United Kingdom*

Like the Alliance Française and the Goethe Institute, the British Council, formed in 1934 to promote a wider knowledge of English, is a private organization receiving government subsidies. Its 1969–1970 budget of £13.7 million includes a very substantial government grant of £12.6 million and earnings and donations of £1.0 million. In addition it received during the budget year 1969–1970

[30] USIA, *31st Review of Operations, July–December 1968,* p. 8. For the weekly hours of air time, see note 55 below.

[31] For a compact and valuable review on a country-by-country basis of East German cultural diplomacy in Latin America, see Johannes Schlootz, "Die Kulturbeziehungen zwischen Lateinamerika und der DDR," *Viertel Jahres Berichte* (Forschungsinstitut der Friedrich-Ebert Stiftung), No. 30, December 1967, pp. 393–416. On East German difficulties at the 1967 Havana Solidarity Conference, see p. 416. On East German cultural activities see also von Gleich, *op. cit.,* pp. 109–115.

an additional £6 million for special work undertaken for the Ministry of Overseas Development and the Board of Trade, much of this, presumably, for acting as the overseas arm for three of the four British societies engaged in the British volunteer service program. Of £5.4 million spent on regional programs, Latin America received only £504,000, that is, about 9 percent, with Argentina and Brazil accounting for almost half of the Latin American expenditures, and Chile, Mexico, and Peru for a little over a quarter.[32]

Like the language instruction services of other countries the British Council believes that language cannot "be completely neutral. Something of the culture, attitudes, habits of thought it describes will influence those who speak it. . . . When we consider, sometimes enviously, the schools France and Germany have established around the world, we may overlook our immense advantage in being able . . . to teach a subject in universal demand. . . . We gain political, commercial, and cultural advantages from the worldwide use of English. . . ."[33] Because of their interest in teaching approximately the same language, the British Council and the United States Information Agency have cooperated since 1955 and some English language centers are financed by both agencies.

The Council maintains offices and schools in 16 Latin American, mostly capital, cities. It supports 13 adult education centers and assists some 85 additional schools in Latin America and a number of libraries operated by what it terms "anglophil societies." Its English instruction activities reached (1967–1968) 55,000 persons in Latin America, of whom 36,000 were in Argentina and Brazil.[34] British Council centers appear to be more successful than USIA centers in attracting elite students.[35]

In the fifties and early sixties relatively few Latin American

---

[32] The British Council, *Annual Report 1968/69, London,* p. 25, p. 27, and pp. 101–104. In 1971 the British Council was operating in 75 countries with a staff of 4,250. Its budget had risen to £16 million. In addition, it administered £8.5 million provided by the Overseas Development Administration of the Foreign and Commonwealth Office for aid to education. *The Economist,* October 23, 1971, p. 7.

[33] The British Council, *op. cit.,* pp. 11–12.

[34] *Ibid.,* pp. 53–61, pp. 66–67, p. 71, and pp. 81–85.

[35] Robert E. Elder, *The Information Machine: The United States Information Agency and American Foreign Policy,* Syracuse, 1968, p. 3.

students went to Britain to study.[36] In the academic year 1954–1955 British universities received only 95 full-time South and Central American students. By 1963–1964 this had risen to 192, to which should be added several hundred from British Caribbean territories. In 1967–1968 South and Central American students increased to 326 and students from British Caribbean countries to 535.[37] In addition the British Council assisted (1968–1969) some 12,500 overseas persons to visit Britain of whom 1,200 or a little less than 10 percent were from Latin America.[38]

Although British cultural diplomacy has not been as active in Latin America as that of France and the United States, both British governmental and private activity in Latin America have increased considerably since the initiative represented by the Committee on Latin American Studies and its report.[39] The five centers for Latin American studies recommended by the report have been created, including an Institute of Latin American Studies at the University of London.[40] These developments coincided with or were followed by other British initiatives in the Latin American field: the expansion in 1964 of Reuters Latin American press service; the intro-

[36] In the nineteenth century both England and France received a larger share of Latin American students studying abroad than they do today. Let us note, too, that in the mid-nineteenth century some Latin American countries sent a larger proportion of their students abroad than they do at present. In 1863 President Francisco Solano López of Paraguay sent 39 students to England and France. This was not, as one might suppose, primarily a military training operation. Only six of these students went to a military school (St. Cyr). Peter A. Schmitt, *Paraguay und Europa,* Berlin, 1963, pp. 86–88.

[37] *The Commonwealth Universities Yearbook 1965,* London, 1965, and *The Commonwealth Universities Yearbook 1969,* London, 1969, pp. 2650–2653. Students from Guyana (133) and British Honduras (17) have been included in the 535 students from British territories. A change in definitions used by the *Yearbook* does not materially alter the trend established by the figures cited in the text.

[38] The British Council, *op. cit.,* pp. 72–73.

[39] University Grants Committee, *Report of the Committee on Latin American Studies,* London, HMSO, 1965. This report is frequently referred to as the "Parry Report."

[40] This institute publishes very useful annual lists of theses, completed and in progress, on Latin American subjects; of staff research; and of teachers and syllabuses in the Latin American field, which taken together provide an excellent overview of current British academic interests in Latin America.

142

duction in 1967 of a Spanish language version of the London *Economist, Economist para América Latina,* which, until it ceased publication in 1970, claimed a wide readership in leading economic and political circles of the Latin republics; and the appearance in 1969 of the *Journal of Latin American Studies.* These developments, together with political and economic measures of the same period, reflect Britain's interest in reestablishing in some measure its former position in Latin America.

4. *Italy*

Despite, or perhaps because of, the large Italian immigrant presence in Latin America, the Italian government has only a modest cultural and information program in the subcontinent—a small number of cultural institutes (which succeed, nonetheless, in attracting elite members of the societies in which they are located), a fellowship program for study in Italy,[41] a substantial school program, and a book export program. An Italian public official and analyst of Italy's cultural diplomacy concludes that Italy does not have an operative cultural policy in the sense in which such policies exist in France, the United States, Great Britain, and Germany.[42]

Perhaps the most interesting and ambitious of Italian initiatives is the international Instituto Italo-Latinoamericano (IILA) with headquarters in Rome, whose members are Italy and 20 Latin American countries. Although intended to promote cultural, scientific, technical, economic, and social collaboration among the member countries, the Instituto is not without political significance. "It constitutes a dynamic conception of international relations and an effort toward a new type of increased contact between Europe and Latin America."[43] Developed and promoted by President Saragat and especially Foreign Minister Fanfani in 1965–1966 during the period of the "triangular policy" (see Chapter 2.1), the Instituto may yet find a political vocation as a partial implementa-

[41] In 1965, 205 scholarships were granted to Latin American students for study, mostly medicine and engineering, in Italian universities. Each was worth about $900 and they represented 12 percent of Italian government foreign scholarships. Fabio Luca Cavazza, *Italy and Latin America,* The Rand Corporation, Santa Monica, RM-5400-RC, November 1967, p. 55.

[42] Giuseppe Padellaro, *Informazione e cultura,* Milan, 1967, p. 36.

[43] Instituto Italo-Latinoamericano (brochure), Rome, n.d., p. 1. The Instituto is financially supported by all its members. An initial agreement was subscribed to in 1966 and ratified in 1967.

tion of the Latin American–European leg of the triangular relation, a vocation that in time may find the means and the opportunity to become an Italian or perhaps a European organizational counterpart to the United States–Latin American relation represented by OAS. A mission sent by the IILA to the ECC in February 1969 may represent the first step in this direction.[44]

5. *Spain*

Spain, like Germany, has been badly divided by political passions and consequently has had special problems of cultural diplomacy in Latin America. Principally, these problems stem from the political origins and tendencies of the Franco regime as well as from the image of Spain as a stubborn adherent of religious, political, economic, and cultural conservatism. Spain is now attempting a reconciliation with both the non-Hispanic world and her own Civil War generation abroad.[45] Aided by donations from Picasso himself, she has announced her intention to enshrine Picasso and his work—including the Guernica canvas—in Barcelona. A museum in Barcelona has also been dedicated to the work of Miró, who has donated 40 of his canvasses.[46] Spain also has awarded a major literary prize to the Spanish novelist-in-exile, Ramón J. Sender. In *Operación España* Spain has undertaken to bring back from Latin America Spaniards who have not seen their homeland for more than 25 years.[47]

Naturally, Spain does not have to teach Spanish in Spanish-speaking Latin America although she pays considerable attention to

[44] *Economist para América Latina,* April 16, 1968, p. 52 (Special Supplement on Italy).

[45] One is reminded of an earlier gesture of Spanish reconciliation—her dedication of a statue to the liberator of her American colonies, Simón Bolívar.

[46] Miró, however, refrained from attending the gallery's inauguration. *Le Monde,* October 24, 1969.

[47] Operación España has been effected by ship. Perhaps only in Spain could one find a big-city (Madrid) newspaper touchingly describe this "most singular, tender and moving ocean passage" as "the most beautiful voyage that has been undertaken in recent years, with the exception of Apollo XI." *ABC* (Madrid), September 23, 1969. *ABC* added: "One thing is certain and that is that all the immigrants succeeded in America, for if they did not all get rich, they have all collaborated to maintain the alliance of culture, language and love that exists between our country and the Hispanic nations."

language purity.[48] In 1969 Spain had 31 Institutos de Cultura Hispánica in Latin America competing with the cultural institutes of the other Western European countries.[49]

The absence of a language barrier between Spain and Hispanic America has had important repercussions for Spain: The identity of language makes Spain an important attraction to Latin American students who wish to study in Europe. The approximately 12,000 Latin American students[50] who study in Spanish universities (1968–1969), a larger number than in all other European countries combined, are in part the consequence of scholarship programs and a cultural identification with Spain, but it appears that the opportunity to study in one's native language plays a major role.[51] In

[48] The importance that the Spanish, like the French, attach to their language made Spain all the more grateful to the South American republics whose representatives in the League of Nations succeeded in having Spanish accepted as one of the international languages, a success Spain could not have achieved by herself. Hendrik Riemens, *L'Europe devant l'Amérique Latine,* The Hague, 1962, pp. 172–173.

[49] Of these 31 Institutos, 6 are located in Argentina, 6 in Brazil, and 3 each in Chile and Mexico. Other Latin American countries have only one. Instituto de Cultura Hispánica, Madrid, personal communication to the author.

[50] Of these 12,000 students approximately 8,000 were resident in Madrid. The country of origin of some 2,900 Latin American students, possibly a biased sample, who passed through the Instituto de Cultura Hispánica in Madrid in 1968–1969 was, in percentages: Cuba, 13; Venezuela 10; Colombia, 9; Argentina, 8; Puerto Rico, 8; Peru, 7; Ecuador, 5; Haiti, 5; Chile, 4; Costa Rica, 4; Dominican Republic, 4; Nicaragua, 4; all others, 19. The small number of students from Mexico (2.5 percent) is notable and is probably related, among other factors, to Mexican–Spanish tensions. That Spain has been anxious to correct imbalances in the distribution of Latin American students seems indicated by the fact that 10 percent of the scholarships given to Latin American students in the last 15 years have gone to Mexico. Similarly less than 2 percent of the Latin American students studying in Spain in 1968–1969 were Brazilians, but Brazil has received 15 percent of Spanish scholarships. Instituto de Cultura Hispánica, Madrid, personal communication.

[51] It is not possible to determine from available data the relative influence of the various components of attraction—cultural and historical affinities, language identity, distance, cost of travel and of living, national prestige, subsidization through scholarships. Information on hypothetical travel choices made by Latin Americans suggest that language identity plays a substantial role. The number of Central and South American students who go to Mexico to study also suggests the importance of language in their choice.

145

addition to scholarships, the Instituto de Cultura Hispánica provides Latin American students in Spain with special student residences. Although the Spanish government has been active in providing incentives for Latin American students to study in Spain, it is sometimes alleged by Latin American students in Spain that they are treated as provincials, a reaction not unlike that of some Commonwealth students studying in British centers.

6. The Soviet Union

Soviet cultural exchange programs with Latin America increased after the death of Stalin and the reversal by Khrushchev and Bulganin of the "hard" line of noncollaboration with noncommunist left groups. Cultural exchanges were, nonetheless, still less than 10 percent of all Soviet reported exchanges with noncommunist countries between 1953 and 1957. The number of exchanges dropped sharply in the first half of 1957 after the Soviet suppression of the Hungarian Revolution (1956), but in late 1957 the Soviets made a determined effort to overcome the effects in the West of this action by sending a number of its most distinguished musicians, composers, writers, chess players, and sportsmen to Latin America. At the same time Latin American writers and artists were accorded warm and flattering receptions in the Soviet Union that added to the effect of the Stalin Peace Prizes awarded to Pablo Neruda, former President Cárdenas of Mexico, and the Colombian writer, Sanin Cano.[52]

The Soviet Union ranks second (to Spain) among the nonhemispheric countries in the number of Latin American students it receives. It appears that about 2,500 Latin American students, of whom perhaps half are Cuban, study in the Soviet Union.[53] By giving a large number of their scholarships to Central and South American students from countries with small populations (for example, Guyana, Bolivia, Costa Rica) the Soviets achieve in these countries particularly impressive scholarship programs. The same technique

[52] Frederick C. Barghoorn, *The Soviet Cultural Offensive: The Role of Cultural Diplomacy in Soviet Foreign Policy*, Princeton, 1960, pp. 219–223.

[53] The Instituto de Cultura Hispánica, Madrid, citing a German source, estimates that about 6,000 Latin American students were studying in 1966 in the Communist bloc countries of Europe. According to *Newsweek* (October 19, 1970, p. 26) about 1,500 young Latin Americans annually receive scholarships to study in the Soviet Union.

146

of increasing impact has been used by Communist China in its cultural programs in Latin America. Thus in 1960–1961 as many Costa Ricans (224) as Mexicans were invited to visit China.[54]

Radio Moscow, which broadcasts to Latin America in Spanish, Portuguese, and Quechua, leads all international broadcasters with 1,899 hours of airtime per week, followed by Radio Peking in second place with 1,324 hours per week.[55] Between 1960 and 1962 Soviet broadcasts to Latin America increased sharply reaching in 1962 a total of 45.5 hours weekly in Spanish and 17.5 hours in Portuguese. By 1965 this had increased to nearly 100 hours of broadcast time in Spanish, Portuguese, and Quechua. In addition, East Germany also began broadcasting to the area in 1961.[56]

7. The Smaller Countries

Cultural exchanges are not the prerogative of the major industrial countries alone. The political and economic exigencies that increasingly bring a number of the smaller countries together also lead them to adopt the friendship and cooperation symbols of the larger powers. The visit of the Shah of Iran to Brazil in 1965 was the occasion of a joint communiqué announcing the creation of a Chair of Iranian Studies in Brazil and of Brazilian studies in Iran. In the same year the University of Costa Rica signed an agreement with Korea's Han Guk University by which courses on the Korean language and on Korean culture were to be taught at the University of Costa Rica and a Department of Central American studies was to be established at Han Guk University. In 1966 the UAR offered several three-month post-graduate scholarships to Panamanian stu-

[54] William E. Ratliff, "Chinese Communist Cultural Diplomacy Toward Latin America 1949–1960," The Hispanic American Historical Review, XLIX (1), February 1969, p. 59. Between 1963 and 1967 Communist China invited 183 delegations from Latin America and sent 21 in return. Cecil Johnson, Communist China and Latin America 1959–1967, New York, 1970, pp. 22–23.

[55] Third is Voice of America with 932 hours per week; fourth, the UAR with 779 hours per week; fifth, the BBC with 695 hours per week, and sixth, West Germany with 611 hours per week. USIA, 31st Review of Operations, July–December 1968, p. 8.

[56] Communist China began its broadcasts in Spanish to Latin America in 1957 with 7 hours of broadcast time per week and raised this to 28 hours per week in 1961. Chinese broadcasts in Portuguese to Brazil were raised from 10½ hours weekly to 28 hours weekly in 1966. Cecil Johnson, op. cit., pp. 9–10.

dents, but was not able to make provisions for travel expenses. An earlier UAR accord (1964) with Bolivia stipulated the establishment of a Spanish–Arabic center in Bolivia. To speakers of the major international languages some of these cultural arrangements may seem misplaced, and no doubt the limited points of political and economic contact sometimes induce the countries involved to increase them through cultural accords of more symbolic than practical value. Nonetheless the introduction of Japanese in a few French and Australian secondary schools might equally have seemed "symbolic" not so very long ago, although its practical value is now evident enough.

8. *The United States*

Unlike the Alliance Française, the Goethe Institute, and the British Council, the organization principally responsible for United States informational activities and cultural diplomacy abroad is not a private organization but a public agency, the USIA (United States Information Agency).[57] The USIA budget (estimated) for fiscal 1971 was $195 million. USIA expenditures are about one-sixth of Soviet expenditures in the same field.[58] Its objectives are "to help achieve United States foreign political objectives by (a) influencing public attitudes in other nations, and (b) advising the President, his representatives abroad . . . of foreign opinion. . . ."[59]

In 1969 USIA had missions in 190 localities, mostly large cities, throughout the world. Thirty-eight of these missions were in Central and South American cities. According to a 1961 survey the 11 libraries operated by these missions in Latin America contained about 175,000 volumes, had an annual attendance of 1.25 million persons, and a circulation of half a million volumes per year. In addition, 112 binational centers in Latin America also maintain libraries and provide cultural programs. These centers are sponsored by American residents together with nationals of the host

[57] Abroad the USIA is the USIS (United States Information Service).

[58] *The Rockefeller Report on the Americas,* 1969, Chapter 4, Section K. Budgetary comparisons should be treated with reserve due to the difficulty of arriving at comparisons covering common and precisely defined areas of cultural activity.

[59] Memorandum of President Kennedy, February 25, 1963, cited by Robert E. Elder, *The Information Machine: The United States Information Agency and American Foreign Policy,* Syracuse, 1968, p. 3.

148

country. They generate much of their funds from their own activities and from local contributions, with the rest of their financial support coming from the United States government.[60]

Like their French, German, and British counterparts, the USIA centers in Latin America are active in the field of language instruction both for the ordinary citizen and for various influential groups such as parliamentarians. In fiscal year 1969 USIA centers in Latin America taught English to 222,600 persons, a substantial increase over the fiscal 1960 figure of 130,900.[61]

Rivalry between French and English language instruction has occasioned mild political flurries from time to time. In 1966 William Benton, United States delegate to UNESCO, called on the United States to intensify the teaching of English as a major goal in the conduct of its foreign policy and attributed United States and British lack of emphasis on the teaching of English to the greater weight that they attach to cultural diversity. Benton's speech was viewed by part of the French press as an attempt to initiate a campaign against the expansion of the French language.[62] The following year France proposed a salary bonus for United Nations workers able to use both French and English. This move was opposed by the United States. Its principal effect seems to have been to increase interest on the part of the Latin American republics in having greater use made of Spanish in Assembly meetings.[63]

Latin America has been a major recipient of VOA (Voice of America) broadcasts and broadcast materials. In 1966 some 260 Latin American radio stations in 15 countries regularly reproduced VOA broadcasts and broadcast materials. Approximately 700 Latin American radio stations broadcast 11,000 hours weekly of taped VOA materials. In addition, VOA broadcasts directly from Washington.[64]

USIA publishes some 66 magazines and newspapers and dis-

[60] *Ibid.*, p. 10, and W. Phillips Davison, *International Political Communication,* New York, 1965, p. 255.

[61] United States Information Agency, personal communication.

[62] *The New York Times,* August 19, 1966.

[63] *Ibid.,* December 3, 1967.

[64] Robert E. Elder, *op. cit.,* p. 6. Despite this impressive degree of activity the *Rockefeller Report* notes that Radio Havana dominates the airwaves in Central America and the Caribbean. VOA ranks third after Radio Moscow and Radio Peking in number of hours of air time per week. See note 55 above.

149

tributes about 30 million copies of them annually in 28 languages. In the early sixties a substantial part of the printed materials sent to Latin America dealt with anti-Communist themes.[65]

Only the United States rivals Spain as a recipient of Latin American students. In 1965 there were about 13,600 Latin Americans at United States educational institutions, about one-quarter of whom were in graduate and professional studies. Fourteen percent received United States scholarships and 4 percent received funds from their own governments.[66] In 1968, there were approximately 2,900 Latin American students studying social sciences in the United States, an increase of over 1,000 since 1964.[67] In addition to students, over 700 professors and scholars from Latin America were at United States educational institutions and over 400 United States professors were attached to Latin American institutions.[68]

A Department of State program, the International Visitors (Leaders) Program, brings annually to the United States foreign

[65] Robert E. Elder, *op. cit.*, p. 8. In addition USIA supports the publication of commercial books. See section 9 below.

[66] See *Visão,* October 26, 1967, and *Política* (Caracas), V (49), May 1966. For students supported by technical assistance disbursements, see OECD, *Technical Assistance and the Needs of Developing Countries,* Paris, 1968, p. 48, and OECD, *Development Assistance 1968 Review,* Appendix III, Tables 16 and 18.

[67] Of the 2,900 Latin American students studying social sciences in 1968, 1,100 were in economics, 900 in education, 500 in political science and public administration, and 400 in sociology. *América Latina* (Rio de Janeiro), 13 (1), January–March 1970, p. 103.

[68] R. Richard Rubottom, Jr., "An Assessment of Current American Influence in Latin America," in *The Annals of the American Academy of Political and Social Science,* Vol. 366, July 1966, p. 119. For detailed tabulations of foreign students by country of origin and by country of study, see UNESCO, *Statistical Yearbook 1964.* Cuba, Mexico, Colombia, and Venezuela have contributed the largest contingents of Latin American students to United States universities, a distribution that suggests a substantial inverse dependence of number of student visitors on distance from the United States.

Foreign students in the United States probably have a different position in and relation to their host universities than do foreign students studying in European universities. Despite the large number of foreign students in the United States, they comprise less than 2 percent of the college population, whereas in France and Germany, foreign students are a sizable minority group, approximately 7 percent of the university student population. UNESCO, *Statistical Yearbook 1969,* p. 159.

nationals who are given an opportunity to travel in the United States. In fiscal 1969, 1,106 visitors from many parts of the world were brought to the United States, of whom 295, that is approximately one-quarter, were from Central and South America and the Caribbean.[69]

9. *Books, Movies, and the Press*

The identity of language between Hispanic America and Spain has been important for Spanish book exports and more recently in the export of radio and TV programs.[70] Spain's book industry accounts for about 15 percent of her exports to Latin America. A large part (79 percent in 1969) of her book exports goes to Latin America, Argentina alone accounting for (in 1964) more than one-fifth of Spain's sales in Spanish language countries.[71] These figures do not, however, necessarily signify a corresponding cultural influence since Spanish book production, like French, includes a substantial proportion (over 30 percent) of translated works, mostly from English and French. Spain's book exports to Latin America suffered earlier from her Falange-influenced censorship policy [72] and more recently from increased competition by government subsidized Mexican and Argentine publishers. More irritating to Spain is the Russian and Japanese practice of reprinting Spanish classics such as *Santa Teresa* and *Don Quixote* in Spanish and exporting them to Latin America. In addition, in almost all countries United States publishers provide the largest part of Latin American book imports and only in Brazil, Chile, and Venezuela (among the larger countries) does Spain even outrank the European countries (see Table 9.1).

Despite the reputation of Latin Americans, and particularly

[69] United States Information Agency, personal communication. For the development of this program, see Robert E. Elder, *The Foreign Leader Program: Operations in the United States,* The Brookings Institution, Washington, D.C., 1961.

[70] See, for example, *Latin American Times,* August 9, 1965; and *Visión,* November 24, 1967, p. 65.

[71] *El Libro Español* (Madrid), No. 146, February 1970, p. 90; and *Fichero Bibliográfico Hispanoamericano,* 7 (6), March 1968, p. 30. For Portuguese book exports to Brazil, see José Honório Rodrigues, *Brazil and Africa,* Berkeley and Los Angeles, 1965, p. 303.

[72] Eléna de la Sauchère, *An Explanation of Spain,* New York, 1964, pp. 301–302.

TABLE 9.1

VALUE OF IMPORTED BOOKS, PERIODICALS, AND NEWSPAPERS, PERCENT BY COUNTRY OF ORIGIN, FOR SIX LATIN AMERICAN REPUBLICS

To:	Argentina (1964)	Brazil (1964)	Chile (1963)	Colombia [a] (1963)	Peru [a] (1962)	Venezuela (1963)
From:						
United States	56.3	51.6	23.5	74.9	51.1	39.8
France	9.4	7.0	1.8	1.3	.7	5.7
Germany	2.4	7.8	3.8	1.5	1.9	4.0
Italy	11.3	2.1	1.1	4.9	.8	9.8
Spain	8.6	8.1	19.8	4.7	1.3	22.4
United Kingdom	6.1	4.2	1.0	5.1	1.7	1.7
Japan	.2	4.6	—	—	1.1	.1
Portugal	—	5.7	.1	—	—	.5
Argentina	[b]	3.2	32.1	1.4	31.1	8.2
Mexico	1.3	2.5	15.0	2.2	3.0	4.6
Others	4.4	3.1	1.8	4.0	7.3	3.1
Total percent	100.0	99.9	100.0	100.0	100.0	99.9
Total in millions	U.S. dollars 2.430	U.S. dollars 8.056	U.S. dollars 7.494	Pesos 6.548	Soles 31.769	Bolivares 16.140

[a] Books and periodicals only.
[b] Not applicable.
SOURCES: *Comercio Exterior Argentina 1964,* Buenos Aires; *Comercio Exterior 1964,* Rio de Janeiro; *Anuario de Comercio Exterior 1963,* Bogotá; *Comercio Exterior Año 1963,* Santiago de Chile; *Estadística de Comercio Exterior 1962,* Lima; *Boletin de Comercio Exterior No. 35,* Diciembre de 1963, Caracas.

Argentinians, as admirers of French culture, Argentina is only the 17th ranking country in the importation of French books and periodicals, and no other Latin American country ranks among the first 20. In effect all countries of French background, including the African republics, outrank Argentina, as do a number of non-French-speaking lands.[73] In 1968 only 6 percent of French exports of books and periodicals went to Latin America, as compared with 22 percent to North America. In no Latin American republic does the importation of French books, newspapers, and periodicals rank even second after the United States (see Table 9.1). To be sure, France is handicapped by the small size of the populations of French origin in the Latin American states, and where France com-

[73] *L'Année politique 1965,* Paris, p. 420.

petes on more equal terms (as with Great Britain) her showing is more in accord with her reputation. In South America Britain surpasses France only in Colombia and Peru although generally Britain outranks France in the Central American countries. The showing of Japan in Brazil (and even in Peru, where Japan's first major emigration to Latin America took place and where there is a Japanese population of 60,000) is not unexpected. Germany does well but its book exports seem to go largely to persons of German origin. The showing of Italy is also bound to its immigrant communities and it is only in Argentina, Venezuela, and Colombia that Italy ranks high among the European exporters of books.

Because the importation of books from abroad is influenced by the size of immigrant populations in the importing countries, the significance of importation data for judging the cultural preferences of the native population is limited, although the meaning of "native" in any New World context is ambiguous and requires definition in each case. The number of translations from foreign languages into Spanish and Portuguese avoids some of these difficulties of interpretation. Thus in Argentina Italy ranks second as a provider of books and periodicals, but Italian is only the fourth language with respect to translations into Spanish (see Table 9.2). In Argentina, Brazil, and Mexico translations from English account for about 50 percent of all translations, with translations from the French second, German third, and Italian fourth (Table 9.2). In Chile translations

TABLE 9.2

PERCENT OF ALL TRANSLATIONS PUBLISHED FROM SPECIFIED LANGUAGES IN FOUR LATIN AMERICAN COUNTRIES, 1960–1963

	Argentina	Brazil	Chile	Mexico
English	47.5	48.1	34.3	59.5
Russian	2.1	3.9	2.9	1.4
French	24.4	25.2	34.3	10.0
German	11.3	8.0	8.6	15.8
Italian	5.1	5.8	11.4	5.4
Other	9.6	9.1 [a]	8.6	7.9
Total percent	100.0	100.1	100.1	100.0
Total translations	1162	1656	105	1484

[a] Spanish, 2.5%.
SOURCE: UNESCO, *Statistical Yearbook 1964,* Paris, 1966, pp. 424–428.

153

from both French and Italian do better than in the more populous Latin American countries.

Notable changes have clearly taken place in Latin American patterns of book consumption: Forty years ago the library of the Faculty of Medicine in Buenos Aires was 50 percent French, 43 percent Spanish, about 5 percent Italian, and less than 1 percent German. Of the library's 28,000 volumes only 50 were in English! Similarly in Montevideo the medical library was 55 percent French, 27 percent Spanish, and 12 percent Italian. English and German were each only about 1 to 2 percent. Clearly these data support the reputation of French as the dominant foreign language of the educated circles of South America during that period.[74]

Foreign book imports in Latin America, together with increased Third World demands for economic concessions, led at the 1967 Stockholm meeting of the Berne (copyright) Union, to Third World demands that those countries that consider themselves economically unable to offer full copyright protection to foreign literary works should have the right to withdraw or restrict such protection provided such action was "for exclusively educational, scientific or scholastic purposes." This broad definition was, according to the (London) *Times Literary Supplement,* "an invitation to legalized theft." The British government opposed the protocol on developing countries but its Commonwealth associations made its opposition to Third World preferences hesitant and awkward.[75]

Book exports are not of interest to the exporting country simply for their cultural influence. In addition to their export and political value, there is a belief, apparently not well documented, that "trade follows the book." Technical books tend to create an interest in the technical products of the country in which the book is written.[76] This adds to the economic incentive for governments to facilitate

[74] J. F. Normano, *The Struggle for South America,* London, 1931, p. 258.

[75] See *Times Literary Supplement* (London), June 29, 1967, and July 6, 1967, p. 606. The secretary of the Publishers Association, London, addressed the following to the TLS: "British publishing houses are not charitable institutions and . . . are under no obligation to finance the development of another country's native skills in publishing and writing. . . . Economic aid should be given at the expense of taxpayers generally, not by stealing the property of a small section of the community." *Times Literary Supplement,* August 10, 1967, p. 732.

[76] R. E. Barker, *Books for All,* UNESCO, Paris, 1956, p. 38.

154

the exports of their publishers. For the United States government political incentives for the support of book exports seem to have been uppermost, although naturally United States publishers have a somewhat different view of export incentives. From 1950 to 1966 USIA provided financial support for the publication of almost 14,000 books (in 124 million copies), mostly by agreements to buy 5–20 percent of the editions for use in USIS centers. Most of this support, even in the case of those books published in English rather than in translation, went to books published abroad. Less than 4 percent of books supported were published in the United States.[77]

Under its Informational Media Guaranty Program USIA also instituted a program after the end of World War II by which United States publishers were able to sell books abroad (if they reflected favorably on life in the United States) for local currency and have the foreign currency exchanged for dollars by USIA. This program was abandoned in 1967 when the Senate voted down a revolving fund to be used for this purpose.[78]

The Soviet Union, an even more vigorous subsidizer and promoter of book exports, is estimated to produce about 100 million books annually in English, French, German, and Spanish.[79]

The price of some North American and European newspapers and magazines in Latin America suggests that their exportation has been subsidized, if only through special airmail rates. *Time, Paris Match, Der Spiegel, Corriere della Sera,* and numerous other continental and North American magazines and papers were available on Buenos Aires, São Paulo, and Rio de Janeiro bookstalls and kiosks, at a time when not a single British journal or periodical, which did not benefit from special airmail rates, was being carried.[80]

[77] Robert E. Elder, *The Information Machine: The United States Information Agency and American Foreign Policy,* Syracuse, 1968, p. 265.

[78] *Ibid.,* p. 268.

[79] William Benton, "Education as an Instrument of American Foreign Policy," *The Annals of the American Academy of Political and Social Science,* Vol. 366, July 1966, p. 37.

[80] *The Times* (London), April 1, 1966, p. 23. In 1971, the Banco Central of Chile issued a decree requiring that foreign magazines be imported by air and be dispatched not later than 15 days after publication. *Latin America* (London), March 19, 1971, p. 91.

155

Latin America's press, radio, and TV depend largely on foreign news services, primarily the United States AP and UPI, France's Agence France Presse and Britain's Reuters.[81] This dependence may be reduced by the impending organization of LATIN, a news agency sponsored by 13 newspapers in seven Latin American countries.[82]

Although in 1970 the United States had ten foreign correspondents in Latin America (as compared with only two a decade ago),[83] neither Latin Americans nor Governor Rockefeller in his 1969 report are content with the manner in which Latin American developments are represented in the United States press. Germany, whose relations with Latin America are far from being as close as those of the United States, had in 1968 eight newspaper and two radio and television correspondents in Latin America;[84] and the Soviet Union's TASS had, in 1964, permanent correspondents in eight countries of Central and South America.[85]

Latin editors have complained that Latin America gets a bad press in the United States. In the view of President Rafael Caldera of Venezuela: "The man in the street . . . generally receives the most unfavorable impression of [Latin America]. . . . Only deplorable incidents . . . gain prominent coverage. . . . Little is said about literary and scientific accomplishments. . . . Sometimes incidents which disrupt the normal activity of a country are not only reported; they are forecast, commented upon and, perhaps without wanting to, they are incited." [86] More relevant, perhaps, is that reporting often tends toward a wordy repetition of "background news" with limited attention to the new events that constitute the news proper. The executive producer of a United States TV news

[81] For information on the 155 news agencies of 80 countries as of 1964, see UNESCO, *World Press Newspaper and News Agencies,* Paris, 1964.

[82] *The New York Times,* January 15, 1970. The announced intent of LATIN is not to displace the international news agencies but to provide a complementary service on issues of primary interest to Latin Americans.

[83] Alliance for Progress, *Weekly Newsletter,* November 3, 1969, p. 2.

[84] von Gleich, *op. cit.,* p. 89.

[85] UNESCO, *op. cit.,* pp. 148–149.

[86] Alliance for Progress, *Weekly Newsletter,* June 15, 1970, pp. 2–3. The following year, President Balaguer of the Dominican Republic expressed identical sentiments before the Inter-American Press Association. Perhaps equally annoying to Latins are the typographical vagaries of United States papers. A *New York Times* story (December 11, 1970) from Chile refers to the country's third largest city (Concepción) four times as: conceptión, conception, Concepsion, Concepcion.

156

program unwittingly comments on this state of affairs: "Trend stories like Latin America are difficult to communicate." [87]

The movies provide another medium of foreign cultural influence in Latin America. Although Mexico and Argentina are active movie producers, only one major South American country, Colombia (1963) imported as much film (by value) from Mexico and Argentina as from the non-Latin American countries. In the other countries, United States films generally constituted more than 50 percent of film imports. Leaving the United States aside, Italy led in Argentina; Japan in Brazil; Mexico and then Spain together with Italy in Colombia; Mexico, Argentina, and then France and Britain in Peru; and Mexico, Britain, and Spain in Venezuela. [88] It is evident that apart from the United States no other single country plays a major role, a result similar to that in the Latin American import book market.

10. *Summary*

The cultural activities of the foreign powers in Latin America do not lend themselves to a simple summary statement, partly because the information available is not entirely comparable from country to country. The following may, nonetheless, place the foregoing material in better perspective.

(1) For the United States, the Soviet Union, Germany, and possibly Spain, political motives for their cultural programs seem uppermost. For France and Great Britain economic motives, as well as cultural and political interests, play a substantial part.

(2) The Soviet Union, the United States, and France provide the largest budgets for foreign cultural activity. France's commitments in Africa, however, drain much of its funds and the proportion allocated to Latin America is relatively modest.

(3) In Latin America, France, through its Alliance Française societies, has the largest number of groups or centers representing a foreign language and culture. However, the number of persons

---

[87] Malcolm Warner, "Decision Making in American TV Political News," in Paul Halmos (ed.), *The Sociology of Mass Media Communicators,* Sociological Review Monographs No. 13, University of Keele (England), 1969, p. 176.

[88] Based on the sources cited in Table 9.1. Comparisons are mostly for 1963 and 1964.

taking English language instruction at United States centers (222,-600) and British centers (55,000) far exceeds the 120,000 reported for the Alliance Française societies. France does well in Latin America's secondary school systems, but when a language choice is available to students they seem to prefer English.

(4) Spain and the United States attract by far the largest number of Latin American students. The Soviet Union is third, well behind them, with probably Germany in fourth place.

(5) The United States provides by far the greatest portion of foreign books and movies to Latin America and plays a large role in the provision of press services. Spain is second, well behind the United States, in the book export field. In the provision of political and economic literature to the politically minded intellectuals of Latin America, Western European countries probably have a lead over the United States and Spain.

(6) A generation or more ago the predominant influence of French culture in Latin America was rarely challenged as a fact. Today such statements, still frequently made, can no longer be supported by the available data. The prestige of French culture is still great, but France is no longer as influential as it once was in language instruction, literature, and various areas of art and science.

10. Aid

1. *The Aid Relationship*

THE transfer of assets, permanent or temporary, from donor to recipient countries is generally viewed as the core of development aid, and understandably so. Nonetheless, in addition to these financial or skill transfers, development aid creates a set of political ties that may affect interstate relations more fundamentally than do the economic transactions themselves. The process of soliciting or rejecting aid, of offering or refusing it, of justifying decisions and complaints before domestic and international public opinion, the formation of alliances and the development of conflicts and rivalries among the donors and recipients, the growth of national and international bureaucracies specializing in assistance activities and seconded by a small army of academicians who have made development economics into a new discipline, the multiplying of international conferences, the imposition of varying degrees of administrative control over foreign personnel, the proffering of advice with more or less insistence that it be followed, the utilization of aid by both donors and receivers to promote political and economic objectives extraneous to officially acknowledged aid objectives, the arousal among recipients and donors of aspirations and expectations that issue often in disappointment, aggravation and humiliation, the occasional triumphs of rewarded effort, of mutual satisfaction and esteem, are aspects of the assistance picture that often loom larger than the economic impact of the financial transfers.

Many of these transfers have been in any case simply a con-

159

tinuation, with some modification, of economic relations that have existed for many years. This is especially the case with those private transfers, such as direct investment, reinvestment of earnings, and trade credits, which are often included in aid statistics. Investments and trade credits may be guaranteed by the governments of industrial countries and thus facilitate private flows to the Third World, but the flows themselves are generally ordinary commercial transactions. The distinction between aid and trade is sometimes still further obscured. The Soviet offer to Brazil in 1966 of $100 million in credits for industrial equipment at 4 percent was the result not of Brazil's interest in Soviet trade credits, but of her attempt to salvage a favorable but nonliquid trade balance with Russia built up during the years following her 1959 trade agreement with the Soviets.[1] By contrast, outright grants, technical assistance, and governmental and multilateral loans with "soft" terms do establish relations outside the customary framework of private and governmental relations.[2]

The care with which language is chosen to describe aid relationships is one indicator of some of the political tensions that underlie financial transfers. "Underdeveloped" countries have become "less developed," "developing," and "Third World" countries. "Economic aid" has become "economic cooperation," and this implication of mutuality or symmetry in the relationship is sometimes made more explicit. Following a reduction of funds for the Alliance for Progress by the United States House of Representatives, three Latin American spokesmen, Galo Plaza, Carlos Sanz de Santamaría, and Patricio Rojas, in a joint statement reminded the United States that the Alliance involves the self-interest of all the peoples of America. "There are no givers on the one hand and receivers on the other. . . ."[3] In the same vein, an aid agreement between the Federal Republic of Germany and Ecuador provided for the movement of private investment funds and government loans from Ecuador to

[1] Marshall I. Goldman, *Soviet Foreign Aid,* New York, 1967, p. 160.

[2] They are, however, not necessarily novel. The loans of the European countries to the newly independent Latin republics might be viewed as development aid, and even technical assistance and Peace Corps types of enterprise have their early counterparts in the work of religious bodies and various social service groups. The almost two centuries of Jesuit work in Paraguay included technical assistance of a high order.

[3] Alliance for Progress, *Weekly Newsletter,* September 30, 1968, p. 2.

West Germany as well as from West Germany to Ecuador. The actual movement of funds, 16 million marks, was, however, in the latter direction.[4] The interest in mutuality or symmetry in the aid relationship is also reflected in the "Peace Corps in reverse," an arrangement by which volunteers from Third World countries, mostly Latin America, serve in the United States. All expenses of this operation, except travel between the Third World country and the United States, are borne by United States private and government agencies.[5]

The less-developed countries are, indeed, sometimes aid donors as well as aid recipients. Venezuela, a recipient of United States technical assistance in public administration, education, housing, and public safety, is in its turn a donor to other Latin American countries of technical assistance programs in vocational training, community development, agricultural credit, and rural education.[6] Brazil, a consumer of economic aid from the United States and from the nonhemispheric countries, donated 500 tons of rice to India in 1966.[7] She has provided several black African countries with football (soccer) coaches and has given a small number of scholarships to African students for study at Brazilian universities.[8] Brazil is a recipient of large amounts of development capital, but she sent a delegation to Mozambique and Angola with a view to the transfer of Brazilian capital and technical aid to these Portuguese territories.[9] Indeed, Brazil may be the only former European colony that now gives economic aid to its mother country. Brazil, Mexico, and Argentina, like Venezuela, have provided bilateral and multilateral aid to several of the other Latin republics. Brazil especially has been interested in improving its relations with and its status among the Latin American republics by increasing its aid activities in the region. India reciprocated Brazil's gift of rice in 1966 with the offer in 1967 of several scholarships for Brazilian engineers and technicians for study in India. Taiwan, at one time one of the major

[4] *Le Monde,* January 27, 1966.

[5] United States Department of State, *Bulletin,* August 21, 1967, p. 235.

[6] Agency for International Development, *United States Foreign Aid and the Alliance for Progress,* Washington, D.C., 1967, p. 37.

[7] *The New York Times,* April 21, 1966.

[8] Aaron Segal, "African Studies in Brazil," *Africa Today,* 15 (15), August/September 1969, p. 9.

[9] *Latin America* (London), August 8, 1969, p. 251.

recipients of United States aid, has in turn sent agricultural experts to Latin America as well as to many of the African states.[10]

2. *Aid: The Nonhemispheric Countries and the United States*

Although Canada and the nonhemispheric countries have played an increasingly important political and economic role in Latin America since the early fifties, they have been decidedly less active than the United States in the field of economic assistance to Latin America. Even in the peak years of 1960–1962, Europe's contribution to Latin America's net external financing was only 26 percent. It fell, with some oscillations, to 16 percent in 1966.[11] It is not surprising, therefore, that Latin America's political leaders have sometimes complained of a European tendency to view development funds for Latin America as primarily a United States responsibility.

The amount of aid to Latin America attributed to the nonhemispheric countries depends considerably on the treatment accorded the French contribution.[12] OECD figures show France to be the

[10] Melvin Gurtov, "Recent Developments on Formosa," *The China Quarterly,* July–September 1967, pp. 70–71; and *The New York Times,* June 29, 1966.

[11] Alliance for Progress, *Weekly Newsletter,* June 16, 1969, p. 2.

[12] The Development Assistance Committee (DAC) of the Organization for Economic Cooperation and Development (OECD) publishes annually financial flow data by donors and by recipients, but it apparently no longer makes available a threefold breakdown by donor, by recipient country, by type of aid. For our purposes the threefold breakdown for 1960–1965 is more useful than less detailed data for more recent years. Table 10.1 gives Latin American official bilateral aid transactions for 1960–1965 by donor, by recipient country, and by type.

It should be kept in mind that the last years have seen a decline in United States aid although Latin America has suffered less from this than some other regions. United States foreign aid appropriations have fallen from a high point of $6–7 billion during the first years of President Eisenhower's administration to about $1.6 billion of which $1.3 billion is for economic assistance. In fiscal 1968 Alliance for Progress aid was $524 million, about the same as the annual average for 1960–1965 (see Table 10.1). However, the estimated outlay for 1970 was only $461 million, and the fiscal 1972 budget request for Latin American bilateral programs was down to $405 million. The defeat in the Senate, in late 1971, of a $2.9 billion authorization bill for economic and military assistance presaged further reductions in Alliance for Progress loans and grants and some forms of technical and multilateral assistance. For a summary of United States aid to

TABLE 0.1

Official Development Assistance to Latin America, 1960–1965 by Type, by Donor Country

(in millions of U.S. dollars)

	Canada	France Depts.[a]	France L.A.[b]	Germany	Italy	Japan	United Kingdom	United States	Others	Total
Grant-like Flows Net										
Latin America								683.2		683.2
World Total				9.6				7,064.2	1.7	7,075.5
Net Official Grants										
Latin America	14.6	366.1	20.2	33.4	1.3	2.1	116.7	1,084.4	42.5	1,681.2
World Total	306.3	366.1	3,823.6	753.1	163.9	436.8	1,284.9	8,156.7	831.8	16,123.1
Gross Official Lending										
Latin America	106.6	104.1	67.3	275.8	249.2	57.5	86.2	2,087.3	66.5	3,100.5
World Total	152.8	104.1	730.0	1,678.8	642.7	337.7	1,133.6	5,511.9	377.4	10,668.9
Amortization on Official Lending										
Latin America	−17.1	−24.1	−10.5	−152.8	−216.2	−45.3	−45.3	−778.5	−9.4	−1,299.1
World Total	−26.6	−24.1	−204.4	−451.1	−410.4	−68.9	−214.7	−1,395.1	−65.5	−2,860.8
Net Official Lending										
Latin America	89.5	80.0	56.8	123.0	33.1	12.2	41.0	1,308.8	57.1	1,815.8
World Total	126.1		681.0	1,399.9	290.4	279.5	1,068.9	4,231.8	341.5	8,419.1
Total Official Net Bilateral Flows										
Latin America	104.1	446.1	77.0	156.4	34.4	14.2	157.7	3,076.5	99.5	4,165.3
World Total	432.4		4,870.7	2,162.5	454.3	716.3	2,353.7	19,452.6	1,175.0	31,617.6

[a] French Overseas Departments in America: Guadeloupe, Guiana, and Martinique.

[b] Latin America exclusive of French Overseas Departments.

Grant-like Flows Net: Loans repayable in recipients' currencies and transfer of resources through sales for recipients' currencies.

Net Official Grants: Gifts in money or in kind for which no repayment is required. Includes grants for technical cooperation, reparations, and indemnification payments.

Gross Official Lending: Loans by governments and official agencies in currencies other than that of the recipient country, with maturities over one year, repayment required in convertible currencies or in kind.

Amortization: Contractual repayments on loans and disinvestments of such assets.

Net Official Lending: Gross official lending minus amortization; does not take account of interest payments.

Sources: OECD, *Geographical Distribution of Financial Flows to Less-Developed Countries 1960–64*; OECD, *ibid. 1965*.

major nonhemispheric donor to the Americas. But 85 percent of French aid to the Western hemisphere goes to the Caribbean departments of Martinique and Guadeloupe, which are integral parts of France.[13] United Kingdom and Dutch aid in the Caribbean are less bothersome from a definitional standpoint since the territories involved have mostly become independent or associated states; and less critical from a quantitative standpoint since smaller amounts are involved than in the case of France.

Another variation in reporting practices adds to the difficulty of estimating aid. OECD states that "domestic and overseas administrative costs of aid programmes are, in principle . . . excluded." [14] France, however, counts as aid administrative and related costs that do not involve transfers to the recipient countries. These administrative disbursements were estimated to be about one billion francs for 1966,[15] that is, approximately 15 percent of French total aid and about 25 percent of official aid.

Interstate comparisons benefit from the reduction of the various types of aid to a single dimension measuring the cost or sacrifice each country imposes on itself. Pincus has proposed "to define aid as the present value of aid disbursements minus the present value of repayment, discounted at an appropriate rate of interest reflecting domestic opportunity cost of public capital." [16] Thus of the $1.7 billion of external financing received by Chile from the United States between 1961 and 1967, about $500 million to $700 million can be considered as outright aid, depending on what discount

---

Latin America during the decade of the Alliance for Progress, see *Development Assistance to Latin America 1961–1970,* House of Representatives, Committee on Foreign Affairs, April 14, 1971.

[13] The problems presented by French aid statistics are of interest not only from the standpoint of their effect on tabulations of Latin American aid, but also for the light they throw on the process of establishing a good aid image.

In Table 10.1 two columns have been provided for France, one for her own territories and one for Latin America proper.

[14] OECD, *Geographical Distribution of Financial Flows to Less-Developed Countries,* 1965, Paris, p. viii.

[15] *Le Monde,* March 16, 1966. French aid statistics also appear to include short term credits, a practice not approved of by OECD.

[16] John Pincus, *Economic Aid and International Cost Sharing,* Baltimore, 1965, p. 115.

rate is viewed as appropriate.[17] This criterion of financial sacrifice changes little the relative contributions of the larger aid-giving countries with the exception of France, whose position is improved. Taking account of the problems posed by French aid figures discussed above, it seems that greater refinement in measurement does not increase and may decrease the share of Europe, Canada, and Japan in aid, especially to Latin America, relative to that of the United States.

When donor countries were ranked on the basis of the amount of aid given relative to their per capita national income, the United States ranked only tenth among the 16 DAC countries (1967).[18] Nonetheless in 1960–1965 the United States provided about 60 percent of net official bilateral world aid and about 85 percent of net official aid to Central and South America (or 74 percent if French, British, Canadian, and Dutch aid to the Caribbean is included). When President Nixon sent his message on aid to the United States Congress early in 1971, he pointed out that because of increases in aid provided by other countries, the United States was at that time providing less than half of international development assistance. Indeed, provisional figures indicate that by 1970 United States aid had declined to about 43 percent of official aid, 36 percent of private aid (investments and credits), and 40 percent of the total aid of the non-Communist world.

3. *Types of Aid*

GRANTS. A United States team of researchers conducting a public opinion poll asked its respondents whether "the United States should give economic help to poorer countries, even if those countries can't pay for it?" [19] This strange question seems to imply a definition of aid that conforms with Latin American contentions that they pay for most of the economic assistance they receive. This results from joining together under a single notion governmental (bilateral and multilateral) aid on the one hand, and on the other hand, private transfers (investment, trade credits) which in the

[17] Victor E. Tokman, "An Evaluation of Foreign Aid: The Chilean Case," *Bulletin of Oxford University Institute of Economics and Statistics,* 31 (3), August 1969, p. 92.

[18] OECD, *Economic Assistance 1968 Review,* Table II.4.

[19] Goran Ohlin, *Foreign Aid Policies Reconsidered,* OECD, Paris, 1966, p. 60.

nature of the case have to be paid for.[20] If one views economic aid as being bilateral and multilateral official aid, the impression diminishes that economic aid is made up largely of transactions that lead to the indebtedness of the less-developed countries. In 1960–1965 the Latin republics received from all donors $2.4 billion in outright grants and grant-like flows out of a total official net bilateral flow of approximately $4.2 billion. Thus, 57 percent of official net bilateral aid to Latin America (and 48 percent of official bilateral and multilateral aid) was composed of grants and grant-like disbursements.[21]

Unfortunately for Latin America, the countries that give the largest proportion of their bilateral aid in the form of grants— France and a number of the smaller donors [22]—give very little aid to the Latin republics. The United States (1960–1965) gave 78 percent of its net official bilateral aid in the form of grants and grant-like transfers but Latin America was less a beneficiary of this than other areas. Only 57 percent of United States aid to Latin America was in the form of grants and grant-like transfers. Nonetheless, United States aid so dominates the Latin American picture that during these six years Canada and the nonhemispheric powers accounted for less than 10 percent of the outright grant aid received by the Central and South American republics (Table 10.1).

The future of grant aid for Latin America is not bright. In the

[20] Sometimes these confusions serve the ends of political rhetoric. Those who wish to emphasize how little aid Latin America receives exclude private transfers from aid statistics. When, however, they want to emphasize that aid is mostly paid for, they include private transfers.

[21] The proportion of grant and grant-like aid is increased by including the grant-element-in-loans. When the grant-element-in-loans (due to terms more favorable than on private financial markets) is added to grants themselves, about 75 percent of all world net official bilateral aid becomes grant aid. The proportion, however, varies considerably from country to country: Italy, 31 percent; Japan, 58 percent; Germany, 59 percent; Canada, 74 percent; United States, 79 percent; France, 82 percent; with some of the smaller countries approaching or attaining 100 percent. OECD, *Development Assistance 1968 Review,* Paris, 1968, p. 62.

[22] Caution is required in interpreting the excellent showing of some countries in OECD's statistical tabulations. These show that 100 percent of Switzerland's official aid commitments are in the form of grants. But almost all (about 97 percent) of Switzerland's aid is in the form of private transfers. Swiss official grants were $2.6 million in 1966 and $3.9 million in 1967, far less than that of any other DAC country. OECD, *ibid.,* p. 62 and pp. 258–261.

four years 1964–1967 grants and grant-like aid as a percent of total official world net aid declined steadily from 66 to 61 to 59 to 53 percent.[23] By 1967 some 80 percent of United States assistance to Latin America was loaned and not granted, a much higher ratio of loans to grants than characterizes United States aid to other parts of the world.[24] However, by 1969 the share of grant aid in total United States aid to Latin America increased.

TECHNICAL ASSISTANCE. Technical assistance or cooperation, not being a reimbursable expenditure, is part of grant aid. Since, however, it generally provides for the physical presence of the nationals of one country in another country, it is distinctly different from disbursements of a purely financial character. In 1967 technical assistance personnel of the donor nations, mostly serving abroad, numbered over 111,000 of whom 30,000 were from the United States. This exporting of technical personnel to the less-developed countries is supplemented by assistance to some 80,000 students and trainees of the less-developed countries, the great majority of whom go to the donor countries for their training.[25] These 200,000 persons living abroad constitute a major nontourist, noncommercial, nonmilitary foreign presence throughout the world.

Although Latin America received one-fifth of world expenditures for bilateral technical assistance (1965), it received only about one-tenth of technical assistance personnel, that is, somewhat less than 10,000 persons of whom close to 2,600 were in Central America and almost 1,600 in Brazil.[26] In Africa, technical assistance was one-third of bilateral aid, but in Latin America, only about one-quarter.[27]

VOLUNTEER SERVICES. Technical assistance personnel are supplemented in the case of the United States and a number of other

[23] Based on data in OECD, *ibid.*, pp. 262–263.

[24] United States Department of State, *Bulletin*, December 25, 1967; and OECD, *ibid.*, pp. 260–261.

[25] OECD, *ibid.*, pp. 276–277. Technical assistance personnel comprises teachers and educational administrators, operational personnel, advisors, and volunteers (for example, Peace Corps).

[26] OECD, *Technical Assistance and the Needs of Developing Countries*, Paris, 1968, p. 46.

[27] *Ibid.*, p. 44, and OECD, *Development Assistance 1968 Review*, Paris, 1968, pp. 260–261. About 20 percent of multilateral disbursements are also spent on technical assistance.

countries by various government and privately subsidized volunteer organizations such as the United States Peace Corps.

The German Development Service (Deutscher Entwicklungs-dienst), the British Volunteer Service Overseas, the Canadian University Service Overseas (CUSO), the Papal Volunteers for Latin America (PAVLA), and the Catholic Coordinating Committee for the Sending of Technicians (CCCST) are the principal organizations that, together with the United States Peace Corps and several Latin American volunteer groups, serve in Latin America.

In 1968 the British Volunteer Program had approximately 1,550 persons serving in it with a projected increase to about 2,000 for 1969.[28] However, partly as a result of political disturbances in Asia and Africa, the number of volunteers in November 1969 was only 1,655.[29] The British volunteers, unlike the United States Peace Corps, do little community work. In Peru, for example, they have been teachers and their number (14) contrasts with a yearly average of several hundred American Peace Corps members in that country. More than half (62 percent in 1967) of the British volunteers serve in Africa. Central and South America together receive only 8 percent and the Caribbean an additional 8 percent.[30]

The Canadian University Service Overseas and the German Development Service numbered less than the British volunteers in 1967 but because they served in fewer countries than the British, their number in some countries was greater. Thus the CUSO had only about 90 volunteers in Latin America (1968) but 47 of these were in Peru and 29 in Colombia providing a substantial representation in these two countries.[31]

The German Development Service, with over 1000 volunteers in 1967 and which, together with other German groups, provided in 1970 about 2,600 volunteers in 28 countries, is distinguished from the British, Canadian, and United States groups by being composed of somewhat older persons with a high level of professional skill.

[28] Central Office of Information, *Economic Aid: A Brief Survey,* London, 1968, p. 12.

[29] *The New York Times,* April 5, 1970.

[30] Coordinating Committee for International Voluntary Service (CCIVS), UNESCO, *Bulletin,* VI (4), April 1968, p. 2. The British program unites four organizations of which the Volunteer Service Overseas is by far the largest. The latter, organized in 1958, antedates the United States Peace Corps.

[31] CCIVS, UNESCO, *Bulletin,* VI (10), October 1968, p. 1.

168

The German members are sent as teams and provide professional service, especially vocational training. Being full-fledged engineers, architects, economists, and technicians of various types, their services are sometimes more highly prized than are those of the United States Peace Corps. About 25 percent of the German volunteers serve in South America, with a major concentration (83 in 1968) in Bolivia, where they reinforce a substantial German presence.[32] The German Protestant Organization (Dienst in Übersee) and the Catholic Organization (Arbeitsgemeinschaft für Entwicklungshilfe) add another 1,000 volunteers to the German contribution.

The Japan Overseas Cooperation Volunteers, who numbered a little less than 200 in 1967,[33] work largely in Southeast Asia, where the volunteers have faced considerable difficulties in areas formerly overrun by Japanese troops during World War II. Like the German Development Service the Japanese corps emphasizes the need for technical skills among its volunteers.

The French Volunteer Service derives from the Administrative Corps in Algeria during the Algerian War. French youths are allowed to substitute technical assistance for their 18 months of military service, and in 1968 approximately 6,000 were availing themselves of a two-year period of technical service, mostly in Africa. Italian volunteers to the Italian Coordinating Committee on Volunteer Service (CCVS) may also replace military service by overseas work, but this privilege is restricted to 100 such volunteers.[34]

The Communist International Youth Service of Solidarity and Friendship draws volunteers from Russia and East Europe who serve primarily in Africa and Southeast Asia. Cuba is the only Latin American country that receives these volunteers. Although the head office is in Budapest, the organization is said to be run by the World Confederation of Democratic Youth from Moscow.[35]

Some nations have urged the United Nations to set up an international service, an initiative that in 1968 led the Economic and Social Council of the United Nations to ask Secretary-General U Thant to establish an international volunteer corps. A year later the General Assembly approved the organization of a United Na-

[32] CCIVS, UNESCO, *Bulletin,* VI (6), June 1968, p. 1.
[33] *The New York Times,* November 5, 1967.
[34] CCIVS, UNESCO, *Bulletin,* VI (11), November 1968, p. 2.
[35] *Time,* December 1, 1967, p. 30.

tions volunteer service by a vote of 91–0 with the Soviet bloc abstaining.[36] Some religious organizations already constitute a form of international volunteer service. The Catholic CCST, established in 1964, draws its volunteers from Italy, Germany, Belgium, Austria, and other countries and has over 350 volunteers in Latin America, Brazil, and Bolivia accounting for over 60 percent of them. The Papal Volunteers antedate most of the national volunteer services and in 1969 had about 200 volunteers in Central and South America and the Caribbean.[37]

The United States Peace Corps grew rapidly from 750 volunteers in 1961 to 6,500 in 1963 and to 15,500 in 1966 in 58 countries. From this high point it declined to about 8,000 in 1971. Nonetheless, the Peace Corps, with over 3,500 volunteers (1969) in Latin America alone, far outnumbers the other national volunteer corps. Despite its dispersion, it has been able to place a large number of volunteers in individual Latin American countries, for example, almost 600 in each of Colombia and Brazil and 200 in Peru (1968). Numbers sometimes change rapidly. The Peace Corps in Chile dropped from almost 500 volunteers in 1966 to 200 in 1969 and to about 90 in 1970.[38] In 1971, however, President Allende asked for an increase in Chile's Peace Corps contingent, although not for community development work. Nonetheless, in January 1972, the Peace Corps was still down to 26 members (in forestry and other technical fields). Unlike Chile, Panama and Bolivia had, in 1971, requested the withdrawal of all Peace Corps personnel.

The United States Peace Corps originally sought specialists but changed its policy and largely recruited college students with little specialized training. More than half of the Peace Corps volunteers in Latin America at one time worked in community development activities, although the Peace Corps world proportion in this field was only one-quarter.[39] The director of the Peace Corps has

[36] *The New York Times,* August 10, 1969, and December 8, 1970.

[37] CCIVS, UNESCO, *Bulletin,* VI (5), May 1968, p. 1, and *Bulletin,* VII (2), February 1969, p. 3.

[38] In early 1969 Peace Corps volunteers and trainees in Latin America and the Caribbean numbered 3,554 distributed as follows: Colombia 599, Brazil 499, Venezuela 281, Bolivia 278, Ecuador 262, Chile 223, Peru 198, Dominican Republic 153, Honduras 152, Eastern Caribbean 145, Panama 137, Jamaica 117, Guatemala 112, El Salvador 101, Costa Rica 91, Paraguay 74, Guyana 44, Nicaragua 43, British Honduras 40, Uruguay 5.

[39] CCIVS, UNESCO, *Bulletin,* VII (5), May 1969, p. 3.

acknowledged a drop in requests for United States volunteers because foreign countries seek specialists and not young college students. As a result, in 1969–1970 the Peace Corps added over 100 union craftsmen and almost 400 experienced farmers and vocational education specialists to its ranks.[40] By late 1970 some 60 percent of new recruits were older, skilled persons.

The organizations for voluntary service by youth now have as collaborators several organizations that provide volunteer service by retired business executives. Established in 1965, the United States International Executive Service Corps operates in Latin America, Southeast Europe, Africa, and Asia. By the end of 1970, more than 900 volunteers had worked in Latin America, largely advising business enterprises.[41] The success of the Corps is, perhaps, indicated by the organization of Canadian and Japanese counterparts; Germany, Britain, and Australia are organizing similar groups.[42] VITA (Volunteers for International Technical Assistance) uses some 6,000 engineers and other technically trained professionals to provide advice on technical problems to the less-developed countries.

BILATERAL AND MULTILATERAL LOANS. About three-fourths of net bilateral official lending to the Latin republics (1960–1965) came from the United States. Of the remaining 25 percent almost half came from West Germany and Canada.[43] During these years the mean maturity of loans rose from 18 to 28 years and the mean interest rate dropped from 4.7 percent to 3.5 percent.[44]

The industrial countries as a group give approximately 10 percent of their official assistance through multilateral agencies.[45] Of the major industrial countries, France (1967) utilized the international agencies least in the disbursement of its official aid, the

[40] Joseph H. Blatchford, "The Peace Corps: Making it in the Seventies," *Foreign Affairs*, 49 (1), October 1970, pp. 126 and 133.

[41] *Visión Letter*, March 31, 1971, pp. 3–4.

[42] Alliance for Progress, *Weekly Newsletter*, August 18, 1969, p. 2.

[43] Italy rivaled West Germany in the gross amount loaned, but the rate of amortization on its loans to Latin America was so high in the period that its net lending was quite small. See Table 10.1.

[44] Goran Ohlin, *op. cit.*, p. 67.

[45] Only the Scandinavian countries—Denmark, Norway, and Sweden—gave more through the international agencies than bilaterally, although Belgium, Canada, and the Netherlands also have a higher ratio of multilateral to bilateral aid than do the larger industrial countries. *Ibid.*, pp. 302–303.

171

result of a policy the continuation of which was announced by Michel Debré at New Delhi in 1968.[46] The United States has taken a favorable view of multilateral aid but the proportion such aid represents of United States official aid (8 percent in 1967) was not much larger than that of France (7 percent). The United Kingdom, Japan, Germany, and Italy ranged from 11 percent to 17 percent.

A "secret" meeting in London of 21 countries in early 1970 indicated greater willingness on the part of the industrial nations to increase World Bank subscriptions to provide soft loans. The same year saw World Bank credits to Latin America exceed for the first time those allocated by the United States Agency for International Development (AID). At the same time, discussions between the United States and the Latin republics have envisaged a sizable increase in the lending capacity of the Inter-American Development Bank.[47] These developments suggest for the near future a substantial increase in the ratio of multilateral to bilateral loans, an increase already under way at the end of the decade.[48]

Latin America received (1960–1965) a larger part, about 16 percent, of its net official aid through the international agencies than did other world regions. Consequently, although Latin America received only 13 percent of all official bilateral aid, it received 24 percent of the multilateral aid contributed by the industrial countries.[49] Most of this aid was received through the World Bank and

[46] *Le Monde,* February 2, 1968. Nonetheless, France is contributing multilateral aid more freely than in earlier years. It rejected, however, the view of interim President Alain Poher, following the retirement of de Gaulle, that "bilateral aid is dangerous in principle." *Le Monde,* May 28, 1969.

[47] *The New York Times,* March 10, 1970. The meeting proposed an increase of funds for this purpose from $400 million to $1 billion. The United States share was to increase from $160 million to $400 million. This move toward expanded multilateral aid is consistent with the recommendation of the Peterson Report to President Nixon. *The New York Times,* March 9, 1970. World Bank and Inter-American Development Bank loans together were in 1971 about three times greater than AID loans. Department of State, *Bulletin,* September 27, 1971, p. 338.

[48] OAS, CIAP, *United States Cooperation with Latin America within the Framework of the Alliance for Progress.* OAS/Official Records/Series H/XIII, CIAP/438, January 8, 1971, p. IV-4. Germany, after the United States, the largest provider of Latin American development aid, pledged in 1971 to channel at least 20 percent of her aid through multilateral agencies. Alliance for Progress, *Weekly Newsletter,* August 2, 1971, p. 1.

[49] Calculated from data in OECD, *The Flow of Financial Resources 1961–65,* Paris, 1967, p. 238.

the United Nations Development Program, the net flow from the Inter-American Development Bank being negative in the years 1960–1965.[50] In 1964–1967 the United States accounted for almost 40 percent of the net contributions to all multilateral agencies.[51] In the last two years of this period Canada became the third largest net contributor, being surpassed only by the United States and Great Britain.

PRIVATE AND PUBLIC DISBURSEMENTS. Of financial flows to the less-developed countries in 1967, $7 billion was from governmental sources and $4.3 billion from the private sectors.[52] For most of the donor countries private net flows (1967) were about 30–50 percent of total flows to the Third World. Canada's transfers, however, were very largely public, only 16 percent being private flows. Switzerland, on the other hand, with 97 percent of its transfers from the private sector, gave virtually no public assistance.[53]

Approximately three-fourths of private flows is made up of investments [54] and one-fourth of trade credits.[55] At the beginning of the decade Latin America received the largest share of the export credits accorded by the industrial countries, some 60 percent in 1960 and 1961. By the middle of the decade, this had dropped drastically to about 4 percent, in part due to inflationary pressures in Latin America and to the increased caution induced in the exporting countries by repeated Latin American requests for refinancing of debts.[56]

[50] OECD, *Geographical Distribution of Financial Flows to Less-Developed Countries 1960–64,* and *ibid.,* 1965.

[51] OECD, *Development Assistance 1968 Review,* Paris, 1968, p. 78.

[52] *Ibid.,* pp. 302–303.

[53] Switzerland is distinguished among the Western countries by the fact that relative to its GNP its private sector provides the biggest flow of funds and its public sector the smallest. In 1969, Switzerland announced that it did not plan to increase its governmental assistance and, indeed, would rely increasingly on trade credits. *Neue Zürcher Zeitung,* June 24, 1969, p. 35.

[54] For data on nonhemispheric and United States investments in Latin America, see Chapter 3.2.

[55] OECD, *Development Assistance 1968 Review,* Paris, 1968, Table 16, line 15. The percentage that trade credit constitutes of total private flows varies greatly among countries. In 1967 the percentages were: Japan, 82; Germany, 59; Great Britain, 39; France, 28; Italy, 6; United States, 3.

[56] OECD, *Les moyens financiers mis à la disposition des pays moins développés 1961–65,* Paris, 1967, p. 176.

An official aid component enters into these private financial transfers in the form of measures taken by governments to encourage and facilitate private transfers through intergovernmental accords providing for the protection of private investments, through insurance against certain classes of investment and credit losses, through tax benefits to encourage investment in less-developed countries, and through information services and other assistance to private traders and investors.

Mention should at least be made of private noncommercial aid to Latin America. In most of the Western European countries church and other private groups contribute substantial amounts although these are modest compared with official aid. In Germany the Catholic and Evangelical churches contribute annually about 110 million marks ($30 million) for development aid.[57] In the United States voluntary agencies contributed about $65 million in 1966 for Latin American assistance alone, that is, well over 10 percent of United States net official aid to the region.[58] French private aid to the Third World has been estimated as less than 0.5 percent of French official aid.[59]

MILITARY ASSISTANCE. United States military assistance programs (MAP) to the Latin American states have taken the form of grant matériel, credit-assisted sales of military equipment, military training, and military missions.

In the 10 years 1956–1965 published figures showed that grant and credit assistance to Latin America amounted to a little over $800 million [60] as compared with almost $6,300 million in United States official economic assistance in the same period. Grant matériel assistance alone, from 1956 to 1967, was $523 million, approximately 10 percent of United States worldwide military grant assistance.[61] According to the published data, grant military aid to

---

[57] *Entwicklung und Zusammenarbeit* (Bonn), April 1970, p. 11. The churches also expend an additional 60 million marks provided by the government.

[58] Alliance for Progress, *Weekly Newsletter,* May 15, 1967, p. 2.

[59] *Le Monde,* March 19, 1968.

[60] About three-quarters of this went to five countries: Brazil, $242 million; Peru, $103 million; Venezuela, $93 million; Chile, $91 million; Colombia, $75 million. *United States Congressional Record–Senate,* April 14, 1967, p. S5119.

[61] Stephen P. Gibert, "Soviet-American Military Aid Competition in the Third World," *Orbis,* 13 (4), Winter 1970, p. 1121.

Latin America remained fairly stable during the decade 1956–1965, reached a high point in 1966 ($81 million), and then, under attack, declined to $21 million in the request for fiscal 1970 and to $16 million for fiscal 1971.[62]

President Johnson in his 1966 message to Congress on foreign aid announced his intention of substituting credit sales for grant aid wherever this was possible, but Congress in 1968 terminated the Department of Defense's authority to guarantee Export–Import Bank credits to the less-developed countries and to operate its revolving fund by which repayments had been used to finance new sales.[63] With the termination of these credit facilities European, especially French, sales of military equipment in Latin America increased, although other factors also contributed (see Chapter 12.3 and 12.8). Congress later authorized credit sales but imposed a $75 million ceiling on them.

Military assistance in the form of military missions stationed in Latin American countries became virtually a United States monopoly during and after World War II. However, the sale, or impending sale, of military equipment by Western European countries sometimes leads to the presence of European military missions in the purchasing countries. The United States military mission presence in Latin America, like grant matériel and credit sales, declined sharply from 800 in 1969 to 458 toward the end of 1970.[64] The planned reduction of military mission personnel was hastened when the Peruvian and Ecuadorian governments expelled their 70-man and 30-man missions following conflicts with Peru over her purchase of supersonic military aircraft and her treatment of the International Petroleum Corporation case, and with Ecuador over her seizure of United States fishing boats.

Between 1950 and 1969 about 28,000 Latin American officers and enlisted men received training by United States Army and Air Force schools in the Canal Zone.[65] A disproportionately large

[62] The accuracy of published military assistance data, affecting largely areas other than Latin America, was challenged by Senator Proxmire in 1971. See *The New York Times,* January 5, 1971, January 7, 1971, and May 4, 1971.

[63] Harold M. Hochman and C. Tait Ratcliffe, "Grant Aid or Credit Sales: A Dilemma of Military Assistance Planning," *Journal of Developing Areas,* 4 (4), July 1970, pp. 461–463.

[64] United States Department of State, *Bulletin,* August 4, 1969, p. 100, and *The New York Times,* November 1, 1970.

[65] United States Department of Defense, *Military Assistance and Foreign*

number of these trainees came from the smaller Central and South American countries (Nicaragua, Costa Rica, Panama, Ecuador, Bolivia). Latin American personnel are also trained in the United States at, among others, Fort Leavenworth, Fort Benning, and the Army Special Warfare Center at Fort Bragg. Between 1950 and 1969, 22,500 Latin American military personnel were brought to the United States and are often included among the number of Latin Americans receiving military training.[66] In fact, a large number of these Latin American military men who came to the United States under MAP training programs received orientation tours "more in the nature of guided vacations than actual training courses." The number who received "guided vacations," that is, goodwill trips, rather than military training, is difficult to establish, but in the case of Brazil it was approximately 85 percent.[67] Like the other elements of MAP, training programs have been cut back by congressional action.

After World War II Western Europe (France, Britain, Italy, Spain, West Germany, and Belgium) resumed its reception of Latin American officers for training in its military academies and schools but on a scale well below that provided by the United States. Thus, from the end of the war to 1965 Italy received only 175 Latin American officers in its military training centers.[68]

4. Political Uses

Most donor countries avow certain objectives pursued through their aid programs other than the economic development of the less-developed countries. This candor runs the risk of masking such humanitarian impulses as do exist in assistance activities. Government officials and aid administrators, however, find it expedient, when speaking to their own parliaments, to justify aid disbursements in terms of national self-benefit. There is substantial

---

Military Sales Fact Book, March 1970, p. 17. See also, Williard F. Barber and C. Neale Ronning, *Internal Security and Military Power: Counterinsurgency and Civic Action in Latin America,* Columbus, Ohio, 1966, p. 145 and pp. 162–163.

[66] United States Department of Defense, *op. cit.,* p. 17.

[67] House Subcommittee on National Security Policy, Committee on Foreign Affairs, *Reports of the Special Study Mission to Latin America on Military Assistance Training,* 1970, p. 7.

[68] Fabio Luca Cavazza, *Italy and Latin America,* The Rand Corporation, Santa Monica, RM-5400-RC, November 1967, p. 62.

176

public moral concern in support of aid for the less-developed countries in the smaller countries of Europe, but when, for example, the Swiss minister of economics wanted to justify foreign aid before the Foreign Affairs Commission, he emphasized its economic advantages: The developing countries take one-fifth of Swiss exports.[69] Similarly, United States government officials and aid administrators, in their anxiety not to seem overindulgent to the less fortunate, have a tendency, in statements directed to Congress and to some sectors of the public, to sound like those critics who stress the material benefits that the United States receives from its aid programs. Motives are, of course, generally mixed and the desire for self-benefits or the minimization of sacrifice is not entirely incompatible with more generous impulses. President Nixon's proposal "to create separate organizational arrangements for each component of our assistance effort: security assistance, humanitarian assistance, and development assistance" [70] distinguishes three motives in United States aid programs, but it is, of course, highly oversimplified to suppose that each of these three programs springs from a single motive or has a single objective.

A principal political concern behind development assistance programs stems from the conviction that great disparities between the per capita income of the less-developed and the more-developed nations is a threat to the peace and tranquility of the modern world. "The lesson of history is that a community of independent and prosperous nations is the best long-term guarantee of a secure America in a peaceful world. This is the goal of the foreign aid program." [71] "United States assistance is essential . . . to achieve . . . a world order of peace and justice." [72]

[69] *The New York Times,* September 20, 1967.

[70] Humanitarian programs are those that provide relief from natural disasters, help with child care and maternal welfare, and respond to the needs of international refugees and migrants. "Foreign Assistance for the Seventies," Message from President Nixon to the Congress, United States Department of State, *Bulletin,* October 5, 1970, pp. 369, 371–372.

[71] President Johnson on signing the Foreign Assistance Act of 1967.

[72] President Nixon's message to Congress in support of the Foreign Aid Program for fiscal 1970, United States Department of State, *Bulletin,* June 16, 1969, p. 515. Fear of violent upheavals in the underdeveloped two-thirds of the world was a principal motive given by a presidential advisory group to President-elect Nixon in justifying foreign aid programs. *The New York Times,* January 10, 1969.

177

These statements reflect, in the case of the United States, a governmental (and to some extent public) conviction that economic assistance to the less-developed countries is needed to ward off political turbulence and revolutionary currents that might jeopardize international order, and more specifically, long-term United States security interests. The cold war, the fear of communism, and the Cuban revolution gave these motives for development assistance more of an ideological cast at the beginning of the sixties than they appear to have retained today when upheavals of a more nationalistic character are also in question. That ideological motives, for example the inculcation of free enterprise and capitalist virtues, did not completely control United States assistance programs even in the more frankly cold war period is evident from the fact that United States aid administration tended to encourage central economic planning by the recipient countries. Administrative requirements dominated doctrinal positions.

Examined on a country-by-country basis, the political objectives of United States aid take on a more specific and immediate character than simply warding off communism or revolution. "From the first program loan in April 1962, a primary objective has been political stability and maintenance of Colombia's democratic political institutions through support of the succession of National Front governments." [73] The AID (United States Agency for International Development) mission in Brazil was considerably reduced in size during the last months of the Goulart government but increased, after the military coup of 1964 and during the presidency of Castelo Branco, from 260 to 470. [74] Standards for a $100 million economic development loan to Brazil were, according to the General Accounting Office, relaxed in 1968 because of "overriding United States political considerations." [75] Thus, warding off revolution naturally leads to the support of particular party or governmental alternatives, a support that may not rely simply on a long-term effort to raise the GNP but may employ aid programs as instruments for more immediate and specific political and economic effects.

The very existence of an aid program, by providing an available instrument, stimulates its utilization for political and economic

[73] United States Senate, 91st Congress, 1st Session, Document 91–17, *Survey of the Alliance for Progress*, p. 669.

[74] *The New York Times*, November 26, 1967.

[75] *The New York Times*, April 26, 1971.

ends not envisaged in the original development of the program. The Pelly Amendment to the Fishermen's Protective Act attempted to use economic assistance as leverage to protect United States fishing vessels against seizure in international waters (see Chapter 1.2). The Foreign Assistance Act also directed the president to consider similar action. The Hickenlooper Amendment of the Foreign Assistance Act made mandatory the suspension of economic assistance and sugar quotas to any country nationalizing United States property without appropriate compensation (see Chapter 4.6). Both the Food for Peace Act and the Foreign Assistance Act include restrictions aimed at countries that trade with Cuba.[76] The Conte–Long Amendment of the Foreign Assistance Appropriations Act of 1967 directed the President "to withhold [with some exceptions] economic assistance in any amount equivalent to the amount spent by any underdeveloped country for the purchase of sophisticated weapons systems. . . ." The Symington Amendment had similar objectives.[77]

Congress and private interests have shown greater enthusiasm for these uses of the aid program than has the Executive. A punitive ban on military credit sales was invoked only once against Peru and twice against Ecuador; the first ban was ended six months later. The Hickenlooper Amendment has never been invoked against a Latin American government although economic assistance to Peru was reduced as a result of the military coup of 1962, the Peruvian purchase of Mirage aircraft from France, and the IPC case.

Economic assistance programs generate concern in the donor country with how the aid is used and therefore with the recipient country's performance level, and thus create interventionist interests that did not previously exist and that are supported by the bargaining power of aid. In Title IX of the United States Foreign Assistance Act of 1966, the Congress imposed on the Agency for International Development the additional objective of ". . . assuring maximum participation in the task of economic development

---

[76] *United States Congressional Record—House,* September 20, 1967, p. H.12232.

[77] For more details on these various enactments, see *Aircraft Sales in Latin America,* Hearings, Subcommittee on Inter-American Affairs, House, 91st Congress, 2d Session, 1970, pp. 26–27; *U.S. Relations with Peru,* Hearings, Senate, Committee on Foreign Relations, 1969, p. 63; Harold M. Hochman and C. Tait Ratcliffe, *op. cit.,* p. 463.

on the part of the people of the developing country, through the encouragement of democratic private and local governmental institutions." [78] This desire to shape Latin American institutional life would not have been so keenly felt had there been no aid program in the first place. Similarly, United States military aid strengthens United States impulses to oversee and influence Latin American military administration. Thus it is just as accurate to say that United States aid has led to attempts to influence Latin America as to assert that it was developed for such ends.

Most uses of aid for political ends have a more serious purpose than was involved in the temporary withholding by the United States of a $14 million aid program for Panama in 1968 after the seizure of power by a National Guard junta. This had more the character of a bow to conscience and public opinion than of a serious attempt to control Panamanian political behavior.[79] Nonetheless, such cases are important because they show that whereas trade would not be deemed subject to review following a coup, development assistance sometimes is. Being a moral and gratuitous act, aid links the donor and recipient in a moral relationship that leads the donor to pass judgment on the recipient. A tutelary posture of moral rectitude has not been unusual in the United States–Latin American aid relationship and it may well have played a larger and more damaging role in intercontinental relations than the frank employment of aid as a counter in international bargaining.

The increased substitution of multilateral for bilateral aid may reduce the intervention capabilities of donor countries in the affairs of recipients, especially in instances where the donor provides only a modest share of the contributions to the multilateral agency. The United States, however, contributes so heavily to multilateral agencies (41 percent of the world total in 1967) and its formal and informal veto powers are so great that its influence would hardly be eliminated although, very probably, qualified. When the IPC case led to some expectations that multilateral aid to Peru might be

[78] United States Public Law 89–583, 89th Congress, H.R. 15750, September 19, 1966, Title IX, Section 281.

[79] The discontinuation of economic assistance to Haiti seems to have been motivated both by the repressive character of the Duvalier regime and by the failure of Haiti to pay its debts. In 1970 both the International Monetary Fund and the Inter-American Development Bank agreed to review Haiti's capital requirements.

affected, General Angel Valdivia stated, perhaps intending that the statement should increase the probability of the event, that World Bank credits and loans would not be withheld because "the United States government is not in a position to interfere with decisions of this great international organization." Indeed the Inter-American Development Bank, which is much more influenced by the United States and which is said never to have made a loan to which the United States objected, approved in November 1970 a loan to Peru of $23.3 million for irrigation and agricultural development on the favorable terms of 25 years at 2¼ percent interest. It is not impossible, however, that Third World countries will find that the bureaucracies of multilateral agencies may be more insistent on adherence to certain economic practices than the bureaucracies that administer national aid programs and have greater incentives to take into account criteria other than economic efficiency.[80]

Of the nonhemispheric countries Germany has, next to the United States, probably been most conscious of the potential bearing of aid on the conflict with communism and the Soviet Union, although German aid officials have emphasized that "even if there were no communism we would be giving help—and just as much. . . ."[81] Germany's conflict with communism entered in other than ideological fashion in her Hallstein Doctrine forbidding the provision of aid to governments recognizing East Germany. How difficult it is to give economic aid without political conditions is evident from the address of Foreign Minister Heinrich von Brentano to the Bundestag in 1961: "I have already emphasized that we are committed to give help without political conditions. Naturally this does not mean that we do not keep in view the political behavior and development of the countries that seek aid. Our interest in countries . . . in which we observe . . . similar judgments of world political events, is greater than in other countries that take

---

[80] On the foregoing questions see David A. Baldwin, "Foreign Aid, Intervention and Influence," *World Politics,* XXI (3), April 1969, p. 442; IADB news release, November 5, 1970; *Latin America* (London), December 20, 1968, p. 405. See Chapter 13.6 for a further discussion of United States use of aid for political purposes.

[81] Walter Scheel, "Der Deutsche Beitrage zur Entwicklungshilfe," in Hans-Adolf Jacobsen, *Deutschland und die Welt: zur Aussenpolitik der Bundesrepublik 1949–1963,* Munich, 1964, p. 72.

an opposite way. For this reason it is our task to observe pains-takingly the influence of the East bloc on these countries. . . ." [82] In Latin America Germany's objective of preventing the recognition of East Germany was supported by United States instrumentalities as well as by those Germany was able to bring to bear, and thus the practical significance of the latter in Latin America is not easy to evaluate. In any event, Latin America has so far been free of incidents such as occurred when West Germany's aid to Ceylon, Tanzania, and Egypt was affected by their relations with East Germany.[83]

France has viewed aid as enabling her to pursue more effectively her goal of cultural prestige and influence. According to the Jean-neney Report [84] French aid is related to France's desire to spread "a culture whose goal is the universal. . . . France wishes, more than any other country, to broadcast far and wide its language and its culture." The working papers underlying the Jeanneney Report make clearer that in the case of Latin America this means reorient-ing it toward Europe or, more specifically, toward France. A French aid "offensive" in Latin America would reduce Latin American de-pendence on the United States.[85] Unfortunately, French aid to Latin America never developed the proportions of an "offensive" and Latin American political leaders have noted on occasion that France provides little material assistance with its gifts of culture. Vasco Leitão, the retiring Brazilian minister for foreign affairs, was per-haps indulging in a little irony and reproach when he said that Brazilian relations with France were important "above all in the area in which France has the most to give us, that is to say, in the

---

[82] *Bulletin des Presse- und Informationsamtes der Bundesregierung,* Bonn, No. 85, May 6, 1961, p. 809.

[83] See I. M. D. Little and J. M. Clifford, *International Aid,* Chicago, 1966, p. 44; and Goran Ohlin, *op. cit.,* pp. 39–44. See Chapter 12.2 for further discussion of West German attempts to prevent recognition of East Germany.

[84] This is the basic document in the development of French aid policies. It has been reissued in English, somewhat abridged, by the Overseas De-velopment Institute of London, 1964. A major review of French aid policy was completed in 1971 and may supplant some of the guidelines of the Jeanneney Report. *Le Monde,* September 22, 1971.

[85] Goran Ohlin, *op. cit.,* pp. 30–31.

area of culture." [86] And former President Rómulo Betancourt of Venezuela expressed a more explicit disappointment when he said: "It seems that Europe is more interested in its former African colonies than in Latin America." [87] Since French aid has been limited, its utilization for political purposes in Latin America has been equally restrained.[88]

The Soviet Union's aid program in Latin America is small.[89] Latin America's share (Cuba excluded) of Soviet bloc aid offers to the Third World during 1954–1965 was only 5.4 percent.[90] The limited amount of Soviet aid has, however, not prevented its occasional employment for political purposes. Whereas the United States and other Western powers tend to establish programs that involve future commitments, the Soviet Union often operates in the West by individual offers at strategic moments and places. On the day that the United States ambassador visited President Arturo Costa e Silva to inform him officially that Washington was reducing its military aid program, the Soviet ambassador appeared in

[86] *Le Monde*, December 22, 1965, The Japanese ambassador to France in 1967 expressed a similar sentiment when he remarked that he could not be as enthusiastic in matters of trade with France as he was for cultural exchange. *Le Monde*, October 25, 1967.

[87] *Economist para América Latina*, February 23, 1968, p. 10.

[88] See, however, de Gaulle's behavior toward Brazil during the "Lobster War" (Chapter 11.3) and French pressure on Cuba (Chapter 4.6).

[89] L. Stepanov, "One Percent: The Problem of Economic Aid," *The Annals of the American Academy of Political and Social Science*, Vol. 386, November 1969, gave no encouragement to Latin America or other non-socialist countries to expect sizable increases in Soviet economic assistance. "There could be no greater absurdity than to impose on the socialist countries the obligation to an equal degree with imperialism to compensate the developing countries for damage caused them [by the capitalist countries]." Nonetheless the opportunities developing for the Soviets in South America due to increased diplomatic recognition and their favorable relations with Chile and Peru are almost inevitably forcing them into undertakings which they probably did not anticipate a few years ago.

[90] Stephen Clissold, "The Soviet Union and Latin America," in Claudio Véliz (ed.), *Latin America and the Caribbean*, New York, 1968, p. 450. Africa's share was 18 percent, Asia's 40.5 percent, and the Middle East's 36 percent. Half of Soviet bloc offers were from the Soviet Union. See also W. Raymond Duncan, 'Soviet Policy in Latin America since Khrushchev," *Orbis*, 15 (2), Summer 1971, p. 650.

order to offer Brazil credits for a subway and bridge for Rio de Janeiro.[91] Similarly, when Uruguay threatened to break diplomatic relations after the Havana Tricontinental Conference, the Soviets offered Uruguay a $30 million trade pact.[92] The Soviets sometimes play the role of buyer of last resort in emergencies when political conflicts or other difficulties have affected a country's normal markets. They are thus able to give trade transactions the character of economic assistance.[93] This is all the more necessary for the Soviets since they do not, unlike the West, normally provide aid in the form of either grants or outright loans. The Soviet provision of trade credits (repayable in commodities) is, then, aid in the sense that Western trade credits add to the flow of reimbursable financial resources. The aid component proper depends on the conditions under which these credits must be reimbursed and the facility that the credits provide for obtaining needed commodities and services at competitive prices.

Even the resources of a small country, judiciously employed, have, as in the case of Israel, permitted an aid program (see Chapter 8) with substantial political value, one that also provides a further illustration of the relation between aid programs and international conflicts. The Israeli program, largely shaped in the light of the Israeli–Arab conflict, has been given by its director a substantial part of the credit for African and Latin American votes favorable to Israel in the United Nations debates following the Six Day War in 1967.[94] Israel's aid program has also indirectly

[91] *The New York Times,* February 24, 1968.

[92] The Soviet regard for the sensitivities of Uruguay, where the Soviet Union has one of its largest and most important missions in Latin America, is perhaps also indicated by its very compliant and apologetic treatment of a Uruguayan protest over a violation of territorial waters by a Soviet ship. *Le Monde,* March 10–11, 1968.

[93] Goran Ohlin, *op. cit.,* p. 53. See, also, Chapter 11.3 below for further discussion of Soviet aid.

[94] *The New York Times,* August 28, 1968. Israel has had an assistance program even in a Moslem country, Iran, whose government has overridden Arab objections by simply refusing to acknowledge the Israeli presence. Israel has also provided an agricultural program for India even though the two countries do not have diplomatic relations. India, however, continues to vote pro-Arab. In its dispute with Pakistan thirteen Arab votes are more important than one Israeli vote. William Korey, "India and Israel," *New Leader,* July 17, 1967, p. 8.

184

served to keep Israel in touch with Latin American Jewry, which has provided some investment, but more importantly immigrants, to Israel.[95] South Africa, also faced, like Israel, with regional isolation, has looked across the South Atlantic for support, and to its diplomatic offensive has added certain aid measures, especially scholarships for Latin American students and agricultural experts for Argentina and Brazil.[96]

It is apparent from the cases of Italy and Japan that major industrial countries can carry on substantial relations with the Latin republics without a corresponding degree of governmental economic assistance, especially of grant aid. In 1967 Latin America received only 9 percent of Japan's total overseas assistance program and most of this was apparently in the form of export credits.[97] President Saragat's important 1965 trip to Latin America was successful from the Italian standpoint although the president's specific offers of aid were very limited indeed.[98] Other factors are involved in the size of nonhemispheric aid to Latin America; nonetheless, the limited contribution of Italy and Japan, the somewhat greater contribution of France and the United Kingdom, the still larger German program, and finally the sizable United States aid contribution seem to correspond to a similar succession of increasingly important political interests and objectives in the Latin hemisphere. The Israeli contribution, sizable in relation to national resources, also corresponds to the gravity of the political and security issues that have prompted its technical assistance programs.

5. Patron-Client Relations

The political significance of development aid sometimes reveals itself in its geographical distribution. A number of the industrial

[95] Latin American Jews have migrated to Israel at a rate 14 times greater than those of the United States and Canada. Moisés Kitrón, "La ALIA latinoamericana en Israel," in Abraham Monk and José Isaacson (eds.), *Comunidades judías de Latinoamérica*, Buenos Aires, 1968, p. 144. In 1970 the United States became for the first time the leading source of immigration to Israel. *The New York Times*, October 18, 1970. The World Jewish Congress estimates the Jewish population of Latin America at 831,000, with about 500,000 in Argentina, 150,000 in Brazil, 54,000 in Uruguay, and 45,000 in Mexico. *Latin America* (London), February 5, 1971, p. 47.

[96] *Le Monde*, December 29, 1967.

[97] *Bank of London and South America Review*, 3 (36), December 1969, p. 733.

[98] *Latin American Times*, September 21, 1965.

countries have developed patron–client relations with less-developed countries, especially in those cases where the less-developed country is a former colony of the industrial country. No country seems to be too small or too poor to be a patron. New Zealand is the major source of foreign aid to Western Samoa, which became independent from New Zealand in 1962. India, a major recipient of economic assistance, has provided aid to Ceylon, Nepal, Tanzania, and Indonesia.

The tendency to concentrate aid in areas where previous political relations, generally of a territorial character, existed has been unfortunate for Latin America. The Latin republics, unlike the new states of Africa and Asia, have been independent for a century and a half, and in any case their former colonial masters, Portugal and Spain, have hardly been in a position to assume a patron role. Great Britain, France, and Holland still have territorial interests in the Western Hemisphere but these are in the Caribbean, and by draining much of the British, French, and Dutch aid to the West they have reduced the amount of aid available to the Central and South American republics. The Commonwealth in 1961–1968 received 89 percent of Great Britain's aid, leaving 11 percent for the rest of the world.[99] Britain's aid to Jamaica is just about the same as it is to Chile, and British aid to Peru a little less than that which Guyana receives.[100] Similarly, of France's total net official bilateral aid in 1960–1965, 18 percent went to French territories, 40 percent to countries north of the Sahara, that is, mostly former French colonies, 35 percent to countries south of the Sahara, and only 1.2 percent to Latin America and 6 percent to other countries.[101] Obviously, the large component to underdeveloped French territories and to former colonies left little over for Latin America. In the Americas 85 percent of French official aid (1960–1965) went to its own departments and territories and only 15 percent to Latin America proper (see Table 10.1). Although France has in recent years disbursed

[99] Based on data in *Britain: An Official Handbook,* 1965, p. 439, and Central Office of Information, *Economic Aid: A Brief Survey,* London, 1968, p. 3.

[100] *Economist para América Latina,* January 26, 1968, p. 14.

[101] Calculated from data in OECD, *Les moyens financiers mis à la disposition des pays moins développés 1961–65,* Paris, 1967, p. 269. A more recent estimate is that one-quarter to one-third of all French official aid goes to underdeveloped regions of the Republic. André Philip, "Pour le Tiers-monde,"*Le Monde,* May 18–19, 1969.

its aid more widely, it still plans to concentrate about 50 percent of its aid in Africa.[102]

Even Canada, although a Western Hemisphere country, has had through its Commonwealth membership and its interest in francophone Africa aid objectives that competed very strongly, especially in earlier years, with Latin American aid interests. It was not until 1964 that Canadian aid to Latin America, as distinct from the Caribbean Commonwealth countries, began to play an appreciable role in Canada's development assistance program.[103]

Countries like Germany, Italy, and Japan, which lost their colonial possessions earlier, are less obligated by past colonial or political relations. Past associations and events do, nonetheless, exercise some effect. Italy still has economic involvements in Somalia and sends reparation payments to Yugoslavia and Ethiopia.[104] Similarly, Japan has its former "dependencies" in Asia arising from military conquest, and both Japan and Germany make substantial reparation payments, which cut into the funds available for aid to Latin America. Nonetheless, with fewer commitments than France and Great Britain, Germany has been freer to shift its aid to Latin America as it became somewhat disillusioned with aid to Africa, especially to the Arab countries.

Israel's aid, motivated like Germany's by sharp international conflicts, is equally catholic in its distribution, although it went through some geographic shifts, beginning with a concentration in Asia, spreading in 1957 to Africa and then in 1962 to Latin America. As in the case of Germany and Canada, Latin America became a recipient of substantial Israeli aid only after programs in other areas had been developed.

---

[102] *Le Monde,* February 12, 1969.

[103] *External Affairs* (Ottawa), XIX (7), July 1967, p. 287; and XXI (4), April 1969, p. 151. For Canada's aid involvement in the francophone countries, see also *Le Monde,* February 15 and April 2, 1968. In 1970, 80 percent of Canada's aid went to the Commonwealth, *The Economist,* January 9, 1971, p. 57.

[104] Reparation payments are counted as part of official bilateral aid in OECD tabulations. In 1960–1965 German, Japanese, and Italian reparations accounted for 19 percent, 53 percent, and 13 percent respectively of the total bilateral net official aid of these countries. OECD, *Geographical Distribution of Financial Flows to Less-Developed Countries 1960–64,* and *ibid., 1965;* and John White, *Japanese Aid,* Overseas Development Institute, London, 1964, pp. 21–22.

United States interests as well as the size of its program have dictated a geographically dispersed program.[105] Although the United States views Latin America as having a special relationship with it, this does not mean, as it has meant in the case of Britain and the Commonwealth or of France and the francophone countries, that Latin America receives the largest share of United States aid. It only means that Latin America receives most of its aid from the United States. Even so, Latin America's one-third minority share of United States aid gives it a share of world aid roughly proportionate to its population.

6. *Public Opinion*

Domestic opinion on economic assistance affairs has in most countries generally supported government programs, but not by a very great margin. Even this margin, except possibly in some of the smaller European countries, is suspect; when respondents are given a choice of governmental activities to support, their enthusiasm for aid diminishes. In addition, what is called "public opinion" is often an artificially induced and uninformed judgment supported by little spontaneous interest. A recent United States study is said to show strong public support for aid programs, but at the same time, most Americans have no idea what the programs cost.[106] In a 1969 poll taken in the United States for *Life* magazine, 69 percent of the respondents nominated foreign aid as their prime candidate for federal spending cuts.[107]

In German polls taken between 1962 and 1966, 40–50 percent of respondents said that aid was a good idea, 36–40 percent that it was not a good idea, and about 12–18 percent had no opinions. Poll results in France are similar, although in the period 1962–1964 the French showed an increased preference for aid to Africa south

[105] United States aid is well dispersed from an intercontinental standpoint but is more concentrated within regions. Fifteen countries account for 84 percent (1968) of AID assistance, six of which are Latin American republics: Brazil, $193 million; Colombia, $77 million; Chile, $58 million; Dominican Republic, $43 million; Nicaragua, $25 million; Panama, $20 million. Alliance for Progress, *Weekly Newsletter*, October 14, 1968, p. 2.

[106] Alliance for Progress, *Weekly Newsletter*, August 11, 1969, p. 2.

[107] *Time*, March 23, 1970, p. 16. On public support for aid programs, see E. K. Hamilton, *Toward Public Confidence in Foreign Aid*, Washington, D.C., 1970, and I. Rauta, *Aid and Overseas Development: A Survey of Public Attitudes, Opinions and Knowledge*, HMSO, London, 1971.

188

of the Sahara and a decreasing support for aid to the former French colonies. A Canadian poll showed more people in favor of reducing aid than increasing it, although in a sample of political leaders almost three-quarters were in favor of increased aid. This Canadian result is consistent with a tendency in recent years, even in countries with a majority public vote in favor of aid, toward decreasing support.[108]

It has been said by sources "close" to President Nixon that the president was prepared to ask Congress for an increase in aid in 1971 over the $1.5 billion level, but that he would first require evidence of a strong "grass roots" support for a larger United States contribution.[109] It is doubtful that such support can be demonstrated. Premier Sato, also concerned with political repercussions following an increase of Japanese aid to $1.8 billion in 1970, appealed to the Japanese electorate "to show warm understanding." [110]

In Europe most organized public activity, at least of a readily visible character, is in favor of increased aid. In May 1971, under the auspices of the Food and Agricultural Organization (FAO), an international march involving some 650 parades in 50 countries was organized to stimulate opinion of youth in favor of aid to the Third World. In Rome, more than 100,000 youths marched some 16 miles to the Vatican, where they were addressed by Pope Paul VI.[111]

In Holland public pressure in favor of aid led the government to announce that beginning in 1971 one percent of national revenues would be devoted to development assistance. This did not satisfy some supporters of aid who introduced legislation proposing a higher percentage. Similar legislation has been proposed in the Scandinavian countries.[112]

In Great Britain the Labour party and government were attacked for failing to honor pledges to increase aid, in fact, for reducing it.[113] Public pressure for increased aid received a gesture of support when a thousand Oxford undergraduates pledged to devote part

---

[108] Goran Ohlin, *op. cit.*, pp. 55–63.

[109] *The New York Times,* March 5, 1970.

[110] *Ibid.,* June 5, 1971.

[111] *Le Monde,* May 11, 1971.

[112] *Ibid.,* October 22–23, 1967, and May 18–19, 1969.

[113] See, for example, *Manchester Guardian Weekly,* November 2, 1967, p. 14.

of their incomes for the rest of their lives to aid developing countries.[114] An aid goal of one percent of GNP has been promoted by a national "sign-in" organized by British churches. Nonetheless, this activity represents a minority interest.[115]

In France a number of organizations concerned with development assistance to the Third World called on the government to increase, rather than to decrease aid and have taken steps to organize a national association.[116] The retirement of President de Gaulle and the two election campaigns in the spring of 1969 provided an opportunity for the ventilation of aid questions. Despite pressure from those in favor of increased aid, Pompidou's prudent attitude toward aid suggested a judgment that political support was not widespread, although he did not adopt so negative an attitude as those who, believing that charity begins at home, resurrected the slogan *"La Corrèze avant le Zambèze"* (*La Corrèze,* a French department, before Zambesia). Interest in aid to the Third World among French youth has been supported by Operation W, which educates and mobilizes French youth between the ages of 14 and 20 with respect to problems of Third World poverty.

These political pressures in Europe stemming from the spectacle of Third World poverty seem to show less preoccupation with Latin America than with Africa and Asia, which apparently suggest images of want more compelling than those of the South American continent. This is not surprising since, in fact, all 19 countries listed by the United Nations as being the least-developed countries of the world are in Africa or Asia.

7. *Economic Uses*

The former Canadian secretary for external affairs, Paul Martin, has pointed out that "immediate" commercial benefits are not a desirable goal of an aid program, implying presumably that such aims are unobjectionable provided they are sufficiently long-range.[117] A

[114] *The New York Times,* February 20, 1969.

[115] Reg Prentice, M.P., "More Priority for Overseas Aid," *International Affairs,* 46 (1), January 1970, p. 4.

[116] *Le Monde,* August 7, 1968, and February 12, 1969.

[117] *External Affairs* (Ottawa), XIX (7), July 1967, pp. 293–294. The motives for Canadian aid are, however, "partly philanthropic and mainly political. . . . There might well be instances in which Canada must make sure that her aid . . . serves its political purpose, rather than insist on its being used in the best effort toward economic development [of the Third

190

leading figure in French–Latin American economic relations, on the other hand, believes that commercial aims in the giving of aid are not only to be expected, but that "the contrary would be abnormal."[118] Most governments have, indeed, found it impractical, politically and economically, to maintain aid programs without demonstrating some economic compensations therefrom. The Canadian Export Credit Insurance Act provides Latin American importers with better credit terms than the unassisted Canadian exporter could offer, but the act was, as Mr. Martin pointed out, designed primarily to serve the exporter and not the recipient. In addition, Canadian bilateral aid is "by economic necessity rather than by conviction" tied to purchases in Canada. Some Canadian contributions to the Inter-American Development Bank have also been restricted to the procurement in Canada of goods and services with at least an 80 percent Canadian content.[119]

An official French journal has spoken of French technical cooperation in Brazil as "an important ace for penetrating this market,"[120] but France's aid to Latin America in the form of credits and loans has probably produced more construction contracts and other commercial successes than has her technical assistance, which is not large enough to have affected substantially France's trade position in Latin America. French relations with the Brazilian military establishment, although much reduced since the days of its important military mission (1919–1939), permitted in the postwar years some sales of military equipment.[121] But France's major successes in this area, especially her Mirage sales, have come more recently and appear to owe more to United States insistence on telling Latin American governments what military equipment they should and should not have than to French technical assistance.

A German minister of economic cooperation has also acknowl-

World]." S. G. Triantis, "Canada's Interest in Foreign Aid," *World Politics,* 24 (1), October 1971, p. 18.

[118] André Fines, "La France et l'Amérique Latine, relations commerciales, concours technique," *Revue Juridique et Politique,* 18 (3), July–September 1964, p. 445.

[119] *External Affairs* (Ottawa), XIX (6), June 1967, p. 208, and XIX (7), July 1967, pp. 293–294.

[120] *Moniteur officiel du commerce international,* September 16, 1964, p. 64.

[121] Jean-Paul Palewski, "Le Brésil et la France," *Revue Juridique et Politique,* 18 (3), July–September 1964, p. 413.

edged the role of development aid, especially credits, as a means of opening markets for German industry, particularly in countries where trade was formerly more or less nonexistent. The German volunteer service organization has been viewed as providing German industry with language capabilities that otherwise might not be in adequate supply.[122] Although the minister for economic co-operation was able to say that in 1964 Germany was the only major country not tying aid, he forecast that the German balance-of-payment would not permit this situation to continue.[123] In fact, by 1965, 80 percent of German capital assistance was already being spent on German goods and services and about 20 percent of funds provided to the less-developed countries by the World Bank were being spent in Germany, although Germany's share in contributions to the World Bank was below this figure.[124] In 1967 Germany, together with Great Britain and Italy, was in the middle range of industrial countries with respect to the proportion of its aid disbursements tied to purchases in the home market.

Unlike Germany with its strong political motives for an aid program, Japan, the other major defeated power of World War II, has been motivated principally by the economic rather than the political consequences of its defeat. Although eager to show the West its willingness to share responsibilities and while not indifferent to the possible uses of aid as an instrument of political influence in Southeast Asia and the Pacific region, Japan's aid program has been largely intended to support its drive to increase exports.[125] Similarly, Great Britain's aid program in the West, where it has not been primarily concerned with its Caribbean territories, has been related more to a desire to reestablish its commercial position in South America than to its political problems in Argentina, Venezuela, and Guatemala.

The interest of the United States State Department and of the administration generally in development aid to Latin America has been its presumed long and short term political utility. This has not

---

[122] *Le Monde,* August 3, 1967; and *The Economist,* April 9, 1967, pp. 130–131.

[123] Walter Scheel, *op. cit.,* p. 73.

[124] John White, *German Aid,* Overseas Development Institute, London, 1965, p. 208.

[125] John White, *Japanese Aid,* Overseas Development Institute, London, 1964, pp. 9–15.

excluded an interest in ensuring that United States aid funds are used by the Latin republics to buy United States products and services, but these benefits have been pursued mainly in order to encourage Congressional and public support for aid. When an Alliance for Progress announcement was headed "Aid Funds Spur U.S. Commodity Sales," [126] this was more a reflection of AID anxiety to gain support than it was evidence of a primary interest in employing aid for United States commercial benefits. Nonetheless, the need to take account of domestic pressures substantially affected aid policy, especially with respect to the requirement that the recipients use donor funds for purchases in the United States. When this practice began in 1960 only 41 percent of AID assistance was used to buy United States commodities, but by 1968 this figure had risen to 98 percent. This represented not only a shift in United States aid policy, but by influencing other donor countries, contributed to the extension of the practice. Canada and Japan, however, which together with the United States have been distinguished by a high level of tied aid, appear to have had independent motives.

Some forms of United States tied aid have largely been a response to domestic pressures: Export-Import Bank credits ($1.4 billion in 1968) as aid to American exporters and Public Law 480 agricultural commodities sold for dollars ($1.1 billion in 1968) as support for the agricultural sector.[127] But the tying of commodity aid and of technical assistance aid generally imposed little or no cost on the recipient.[128] A Pakistan study showed that tying imposed a 12 percent increase in procurement costs [129] and an UNCTAD Secretariat paper concluded that the use of tied loans and credits increases costs for the recipient by about 10–20 percent. OECD's 1968 review, however, points out that such computations assume worldwide competitive bidding, a condition that simply does not apply. Some countries that tie much of their aid, for example Japan and Germany, provide a very wide range of procurement alternatives so that much of tied funds can be spent for goods competitive

[126] Alliance for Progress, *Weekly Newsletter,* April 28, 1969, p. 1.

[127] Alliance for Progress, *Weekly Newsletter,* July 28, 1969, p. 2.

[128] See I. M. D. Little and J. M. Clifford, *op. cit.,* pp. 166–167 and pp. 174–175.

[129] Mahbub ul Haq, "Tied Credits—A Quantitative Analysis," in John H. Adler (ed.), *Capital Movements and Economic Development,* New York, 1967, p. 331.

with world markets. The OECD review concludes that added costs of tying do not apply to more than one-quarter to one-third of official aid flows.[130]

Although the United States initiated the practice of tying aid, it also supported the drive to free aid from these restrictions. President Nixon's Executive Order of November 1, 1969, permitted AID program loans to Latin America to be expended in Latin America in those cases where Latin American suppliers could quote a price lower than the United States market price. A year later a further loosening of tying requirements was introduced. Still later in 1970 the Development Assistance Committee of OECD was given a mandate to draw up a draft agreement for the consideration of the industrial countries to promote the untying of aid by all countries. The campaign for untying aid, supported in OECD by the United States, met opposition from Canada, France, and Japan. Formerly criticized for the practice of tying aid, the United States has now been criticized, especially in France, for seeking to end this practice. Its strong position in the Latin American market permits the United States, it is said, to untie aid without negative results for its own trade.[131]

Aid can also be collectively or multilaterally tied. Countries contributing to the Inter-American Development Bank (IDB), especially the United States, have objected to the practice of Latin American countries utilizing IDB loans to buy commodities or to finance services from industrial countries that do not contribute to IDB loan capabilities. As a result of a 1968 policy change, industrial countries are not eligible to receive orders from the Latin republics based on IDB loans unless they have contributed to IDB's financial resources.[132]

---

[130] OECD, *Development Assistance 1968 Review,* Paris, 1968, pp. 67–69. This is similar to Canadian arguments that competitive bidding by Canadian exporters and the broad range of Canadian goods and services available eliminate much of the disadvantages of tied aid. See *External Affairs* (Ottawa), XIX (7), July 1967, pp. 291–292.

[131] See *Commerce Today,* 6 (2), November 2, 1970; and *The New York Times,* September 16, 1970.

[132] Countries not members of the IDB, but eligible to receive orders because of contributions, were: Belgium, United Kingdom, Canada, Germany, Italy, Japan, Luxembourg, and Switzerland. The new regulation excluded France, Australia, Austria, New Zealand, Norway, South Africa, and Sweden. France subsequently authorized IDB to borrow on the French market, thus making France eligible to receive orders financed by IDB credits.

11. Diplomacy

1. *Visits*

WHO are the international jet set? Statesmen and high government officials seem to qualify as well as any for this denomination. Reviewing the year 1967 a political–military analyst finds the multitude of international political visits to be one of its more notable features:

> It seems that technological developments, especially the jet plane, have led politicians and statesmen, who used to be relatively sedentary people, into a hectic round of activity. In any case it is increasingly a modern international style at least to expedite, if not to settle, interstate questions, formerly dealt with through diplomatic channels, by quick visits of ministers, chiefs of government and heads of state. This is not always to the benefit of the questions involved. It seems, rather as if the widespread uneasiness, nervousness, and indeed irritation in interstate relations is month by month increased by this restlessness. The chronicle of the past year contains hundreds of such hasty meetings at so-called high and highest levels. . . .[1]

This observation has particular relevance for the relations of the nonhemispheric powers to Latin America. Beginning in 1964, the year of de Gaulle's visit to Mexico and South America, there occurred in Latin America a great influx of royal personages, presi-

---

[1] Alexander L. Ratcliffe, "Die militär-politsche Lage am Jahresende," *Wehrkunde,* XVI (12), December 1967, p. 617.

dents, prime ministers, ministers of foreign affairs, and heads of other prestigious ministries. This invasion reached its peak in 1965 and 1966 and then fell off in 1967 and 1968. Despite all the preceding visits and the existence of a substantial diplomatic network in Latin America, the state secretary of the German Foreign Office emphasized at the beginning of 1969 that the political dialogue between Latin America and Germany "will in the course of the year be pursued on the one hand through the visits of Latin American presidents and foreign ministers . . . and through the trips of German cabinet members and other high officials on the other hand." [2]

During the peak years of 1964–1966 the roster of visiting royalty included representatives of most of the reigning families of the world: Queen Juliana of the Netherlands, Prince Philip of Great Britain (1962, 1964, and 1966), Emperor Haile Selassie of Ethiopia, King Baudouin and Queen Fabiola of Belgium, Princess Margrethe of Denmark, the Shah and Empress of Iran, Prince Jean and Princess Charlotte of Luxembourg, Crown Prince Akhito and Princess Michiko of Japan, King Olaf of Norway, and Prince Bertil of Sweden.

Among the presidents who visited one or more Latin American countries in these years were Lyndon Johnson, Charles de Gaulle, Luebke of the Federal Republic of Germany, Senghor of Senegal, Kaunda of Zambia and Yameogo of Upper Volta,[3] Saragat of Italy, Archbishop Makarios of Cyprus, Shazar of Israel, and in addition, Secretary-General of the United Nations U Thant.

The roster of first ministers, ministers of foreign affairs and of economic affairs, and heads of other major ministries is still longer. To these visitors must, of course, also be added a great host of lesser officials, parliamentary delegations, and a variety of other missions with official status.

Although quantitatively less impressive than some of the earlier years, 1968 saw among others the visit of Pope Paul VI to Bogotá, the first visit of a British monarch, Queen Elizabeth (with Prince Philip), to Latin America, and the visit of Mrs. Indira Ghandi.

Brazil, Chile, and Argentina were well in the lead, during the

---

[2] Speech before the Ibero Club, University of Bonn, *Bulletin des Presse- und Informationsamtes der Bundersregierung,* Bonn, No. 11, January 29, 1969, pp. 93–94.

[3] President Yameogo's visit to Brazil was an unofficial trip made before his overthrow by the Army in January 1966.

peak years, in the number of distinguished visitors received, Chile's high-ranking position in this respect being a tribute to the prestige of the recently elected (1964) President Frei and his very evident interest in increasing contact with the nonhemispheric world. Peru, Mexico, and Uruguay received only about half as many distinguished visitors as did the ABC countries, and Colombia and Ecuador received still fewer.

The visits of royalty and to a considerable extent those of other chiefs of state and even of heads of government were often ceremonial in character. In many cases, including some visits of a highly ceremonial nature, substantive diplomatic interests were indicated by the presence of a large retinue of ministers, officials, and technicians prepared to discuss or even conclude various political, economic, and cultural accords. King Olaf of Norway's three-nation visit to Latin America coincided with the arrival of a 20-man Norwegian mission in Rio de Janeiro stimulated by Brazil's new shipping policy. The visit of Princess Margrethe of Denmark to every South American capital except Asunción and La Paz preceded the visit of the Danish minister of foreign affairs and a delegation of trade experts. President Saragat was accompanied on his trip not only by Foreign Minister Fanfani but by 15 government officials.

The emphasis given to state visits derives doubtless from the desire, through homage to the hosts, to augment the latter's prestige and to provide an acceptable form of flattery in order to support the state interests in pursuit of which the visits are undertaken. It is not by any means, however, only the prestige of the Latin American hosts that is at stake in these visits. Certainly the trips of General de Gaulle and President Saragat, perhaps the two most ambitious and publicized political visits of these past years, seem to have been intended just as much to augment the prestige of the visitors back home. The reports in the world and home press of these two visits tended to emphasize the triumphal receptions accorded the visitors rather than the tributes that the latter paid to their Latin American hosts. President Saragat's trip, which followed that of General de Gaulle, was reported in terms of a box score that compared the size and enthusiasm of the crowds receiving him with those that received General de Gaulle.[4]

[4] For Italian accounts of President Saragat's trip, see the major Italian newspapers for the period September 10 to September 25, 1965. Typical headlines: "Delirante entusiasmo in Brasile per il generoso discorso di

The diplomacy of the state visit is not without its risks. The visitors only too often disappointed their hosts by their failure to provide or even promise what was wished or hoped for. Latin Americans did not hesitate to compare the relative size of aid or favors bestowed by their visitors and to express their disappointment. The panache of the early visits may have indeed misled the Latin American political leaders of 1964–1966 to expect more than they received. During the past several years they have reduced their expectations from visiting statesmen.

Even the best planned visits run the danger of embarrassing contretemps. General de Gaulle's distribution of decorations to his Latin American hosts ran into an unanticipated reaction in Ecuador when the failure of all members of the military triumvirate to receive a decoration of equal splendor led to the return of the decorations to France. Prince Philip's 1966 visit to Buenos Aires seems to have provoked one of a continuing series of "attacks" by Argentinian nationalists on the Falkland (Malvinas) Islands. The visit of President Nasser's representatives to Argentina and Brazil in 1967 coincided with a UAR statement in Chile intended to make the Chileans happy by drawing a parallel between the UAR's sovereignty claim over the Gulf of Aqaba and Chile's claims in the Beagle Channel. This taking of sides in a highly sensitive area of Chilean–Argentinian relations reached Buenos Aires, where the UAR representative had to smooth over a situation full of asperities. Although events of this sort rarely seem to provoke serious crises in interstate relations (partly because the relations involved are not very close in the first place), they nonetheless lend point to the contention that political visiting may easily provoke "an irritation in interstate relations."

The disorders and embarrassments that occurred during Vice President Nixon's visit of 1958 and especially Governor Rockefeller's mission of 1969 were not, like the foregoing incidents, the accidental or superficial misfortunes of political voyages where not everything is controllable by protocol officers; they were, on the contrary, the more or less predictable ingredients of a volatile political brew moved from the diplomatic back burner to the public relations front burner.

Saragat," *La Stampa* (Turin), September 12, 1965. "Caloroso benvenuto a Saragat della populazione di Buenos Aires," *Corriere della Sera* (Milan), September 16, 1965.

2. Representation

The importance that the foreign powers attach to diplomatic action in Central and South America is reflected not only by the frequency of political visits but also by the size and character of their diplomatic missions to these countries. In 1914 of 14 Latin American countries [5] none was in the first (top) quintile of countries ranked by number of diplomatic missions received, and three—Dominican Republic, Honduras, and Nicaragua—were in the fifth (lowest) quintile. In 1940 a substantial change is recorded. Four countries—Argentina, Brazil, Chile, and Mexico—now rank in the top quintile and no Central or South American country is in the lowest quintile.[6] Two decades later (1963–1964) the situation is not greatly changed although the data for 1963–1964 are not quite comparable with those for the earlier years. The number of missions and diplomats received during these years are shown in Table 11.1. In order to provide some points of comparison with Latin American countries, the number received by the top ten countries is also shown. No Latin American country is among these top ten although Brazil had ranked ninth in 1922.[7]

Geographical size, population size, trade, and foreign investment levels do not by themselves account for all variations in the number of missions and diplomats received. Notable is Uruguay's 41 missions with over 200 diplomats (outranking Colombia, Peru, and Venezuela) and Panama's 42 missions (Table 11.1). The former benefited from a sizable East bloc representation and the latter from the diplomatic and consular requirements stemming from maritime traffic through the Canal.

The proportion of their diplomats that the various countries send to Latin America is highly variable. The United States posts almost 1 diplomat in 3 to Latin America, Italy 1 in 4, Japan 1 in 5, the United Kingdom and the Federal Republic of Germany 1 in 6,

[5] Argentina, Bolivia, Brazil, Chile, Colombia, Costa Rica, Dominican Republic, Ecuador, Guatemala, Honduras, Mexico, Nicaragua, Peru, and Venezuela.

[6] Based on Table 5 of J. David Singer and Melvin Small, "The Composition and Status Ordering of the International System: 1815–1940," *World Politics,* XVIII (2), January 1966, pp. 278–279.

[7] Chadwick F. Alger and Steven J. Brams, "Patterns of Representation in National Capitals and Inter-governmental Organizations," *World Politics,* XIX (4), July 1967, p. 652.

TABLE 11.1

Number of Diplomatic Missions and Diplomats Received by
Specified Countries, 1963–1964

South America	Missions	Diplomats	Central America	Missions	Diplomats
Argentina	65 [a]	[b]	Costa Rica	24	88
Bolivia	[b]	[b]	El Salvador	29	104
Brazil	56	431	Guatemala	27	108
Chile	45	214	Honduras	19	75
Colombia	37	162	Mexico	47	315
Ecuador	34	122	Nicaragua	20	51
Paraguay	21	95	Panama	42	172
Peru	37	203			
Uruguay	41	206			
Venezuela	34	174			

Top Ten Nations	Missions	Diplomats
United States	107	1408
France	98	716
United Kingdom	96	1305
Germany (Fed. Rep.)	94	778
Italy	85	707
Belgium	75	473
UAR	73	559
Japan	70	494
Soviet Union	69	732
India	66	530

[a] Alger and Brams (see below) do not give data for Argentina and Bolivia. The entry (65) for Argentina is for 1970 and is taken from the diplomatic correspondent of *La Nación* (Buenos Aires), February 15, 1970. (This number is 69 if accredited ambassadors not resident in Buenos Aires are included.) Since this number is for a time six to seven years later than the Alger-Bram data for the other countries, it probably inflates Argentina's position relative to that of Brazil and other Latin American countries.

[b] Not available.

Source: From Tables 3 and 4 of Chadwick F. Alger and Steven J. Brams, "Patterns of Representation in National Capitals and Inter-governmental Organizations," *World Politics*, XIX (4), July 1967, p. 652. See also note a.

and France 1 in 10.[8] These numbers match, very roughly, the economic, political, or migrant involvement of these six countries in Latin America.

The growth of the United States presence in Latin America after

[8] Based on Table 11.2 of this study in conjunction with Table II of Alger and Brams, *op. cit.,* p. 651.

World War II is reflected by the doubling of United States diplomatic personnel in Latin America in the 15-year period 1951–
1965 (Table 11.2). In 1951 United States representation was
about equal to the combined representation of the other five countries shown in Table 11.2, but by 1965 United States representation was more than 50 percent greater than the combined representation of these countries. In the early and mid-sixties about one
out of every three diplomats in Latin America came from the United
States.

In terms of the impression made on the host countries, the

TABLE 11.2

NUMBER OF DIPLOMATIC PERSONNEL [a] IN LATIN AMERICAN COUNTRIES [b]

	1951		1960s	
	In Embassies	In Consular Offices	In Embassies	In Consular Offices
France [c]	92	7	91	5
Germany [d]	—	—	99	23
Italy [e]	47	0	100	26
Japan [f]	54	10	109	22
United Kingdom [g]	157	111	159	87
United States [h]	383	104	777	189

[a] The definition of diplomatic personnel varies somewhat from country to
country. Nonetheless the numbers in the Embassy columns provide a useful basis
for comparison. Personnel attached to the consulate general in capital cities are
included under "Embassy." "Honorary Consuls" and similar categories are not
included. The consular column attempts to include only career diplomatic-
consular personnel of the country being represented. However it was not always
possible to make this distinction with confidence and the consular columns should
be treated with some reserve.

[b] Includes all Central and South American republics and the following Caribbean
countries: Dominican Republic, Haiti, and Cuba.

[c] Columns 3 and 4 are for 1966.

[d] Columns 3 and 4 are for 1969.

[e] Columns 3 and 4 are for 1963.

[f] Columns 1 and 2 are for 1957; columns 3 and 4 are for 1969.

[g] Columns 3 and 4 are for 1966.

[h] Columns 3 and 4 are for 1965.

SOURCES: R. E. Hefter (ed.), *The World Diplomatic Directory 1951*, London.
Annuaire général de l'administration Française, Paris, 1966. Consular Service
of the Federal Republic of Germany. Ministero degli Affari Esteri, *Annuario
Diplomatico della Repubblica Italiana*, 1963, Rome. Consulate General of Japan,
New York City. *The Foreign Office List and Diplomatic and Consular Yearbook
for 1965*, West Norwood, England. *The Diplomatic Service List 1966*, HMSO,
London. United States Department of State, *Foreign Service List, October 1965;
Diplomatic List February 1966*.

United States diplomatic presence seems much larger than even its sizable number suggests. Diplomatic personnel account for only about one-third of the population of United States embassies. The other two-thirds are from the Department of Defense, the CIA, USIA, and AID. In Latin America there were 832 AID personnel, 198 USIA personnel (1965), and 869 military assistance advisory group personnel (1967).[9] To citizens of the host countries these persons are not only part of the United States official presence— they are members of the embassies and hence United States foreign officers.[10]

The large United States diplomatic representation relative to that of the European countries is not simply a function of the size of the United States economic and political stake in Latin America or its penchant for overadministration abroad. Much of it results simply from the closeness of some Latin American countries, the considerable tourist traffic, and the amount of temporary and permanent movement between Latin America and the United States. All of this requires a substantial amount of more or less routine embassy and consular activity. The European countries send their largest missions to Brazil and Argentina, but the United States sends its largest embassy and consular group to Mexico.[11]

Soviet male accredited diplomatic personnel in Latin America doubled from approximately 150 in 1960 to about 300 at the end of the decade.[12] The number has grown since. Thus, Bolivia alone was reported in 1971 to have more than 90 accredited representatives.[13] Unlike United States embassies which employ many local

[9] The military assistance advisory groups do not include the smaller number of military attachés. The Congress first authorized military and naval attachés in a law of 1888 and the first attaché in Latin America was appointed to Mexico in 1894. Early in the new century the overall limit of ten attachés set by Congress was removed and more attachés were sent abroad, especially to Latin America. Alfred Vagts, *The Military Attaché,* Princeton, New Jersey, 1967, p. 33.

[10] John F. Campbell, " 'What is to be Done?' Gigantism in Washington," *Foreign Affairs,* 49 (1), October 1970, p. 95. See also Chapter 5, note 78, and note 27 below.

[11] Based on the detailed country tabulations from which Table 11.2 is derived.

[12] *The New York Times,* December 7, 1970.

[13] *Ibid.,* July 8, 1971.

persons, the Soviets bring their own service personnel with them. A substantial proportion of Soviet staffs is assumed to be personnel engaged in intelligence or at least in other than routine diplomatic activities. When Uruguay began diplomatic relations with the Soviets after World War II, they sent 3 Uruguayans to Moscow and received in return 47 Russians in Montevideo.

The doubling of Italian representation between 1951 and 1966 is not simply the effect of Italian postwar trade and investment interest in Latin America; it is in large measure due to the liquidation of diplomatic relations during World War II and the limited reconstruction of an Italian diplomatic service by 1951. By 1957 Japan had had substantial opportunity to reestablish its overseas foreign service and the doubling of Japanese representation in Latin America between 1957 and 1966 shown in Table 11.2 is evidence of the greatly increased economic activity of Japan in Latin America in recent years. In 1970, Japan had full embassy and consular operations in more Latin American republics (18) than any other country except the United States.

Where there has been no major postwar expansion of Latin American activity or no resumption of broken relations, foreign diplomatic representation in Latin America appears to have been more or less static. This is suggested by the French and British data of Table 11.2 and by data for Sweden, Belgium, and Holland. In 1951 these three countries had 104 embassy personnel in Latin America and a decade later, in 1962–1963, only 107.[14]

Foreign currency and economy problems [15] have in some cases restricted the growth or even led to a reduction in diplomatic personnel which cannot, therefore, necessarily be imputed to a lack of interest in Latin America. The closing by Canada of three of

[14] Compiled from *Sveriges Statskalander 1964,* Uppsala and Stockholm; *Who's Who in Belgium and Luxumburg,* Brussels, 1962; and *Who's Who in The Netherlands 1962/63,* Amsterdam.

[15] The accrediting of an ambassador to a Latin American country does not, of course, necessarily involve significantly increased representational expenses since the accredited ambassador may be one who is already stationed in and remains resident in another capital. Even major powers adopt this practice vis-à-vis a number of small countries. For small countries multiple accreditation is a virtual necessity. Iceland's first ambassador to Cuba was already ambassador to the United States, Canada, Brazil, Argentina, and Mexico.

its Latin American diplomatic missions [16]—Uruguay, Dominican Republic, and Ecuador—while sending a large and high-level visiting mission to Latin America (see Chapter 4.3) was partly motivated by economy but also apparently by a preference for visits over regular diplomatic channels.

Tendencies to depreciate the value of professional diplomatic personnel add to the loss of influence occasioned by the frequent arrival of officials from the home capital. The important role given to Governor Rockefeller's 1969 mission to Latin America was apparently not pleasing to United States diplomatic personnel in Latin America. Canadian diplomatic personnel have also noted their prime minister's tendency to rely on his own aides rather than on the diplomatic service. "I feel," said Prime Minister Trudeau in a television interview, "the whole concept of diplomacy today is a little bit outmoded. I believe much of it goes back to the early days of the telegraph when you needed a dispatch to know what was happening in a country, whereas now you can read it in a good newspaper." [17] By contrast, some French senators have pointed out that successful as General de Gaulle's trip to Latin America was, it was pointless as long as French representation in Latin America was inadequate to exploit it. [18]

3. *Style*

The foreign powers differ in the degree to which they feel able or willing to shape the course of events in the subcontinent. Speaking of intricate and intractable problems of Argentinian finances, Lord Salisbury in 1891 laid down a principle that continued to be important for British behavior in Latin America: "Her Majesty's Government [is not] in the least degree disposed to encroach on the functions of Providence." And 20 years later, Sir Edward Grey,

---

[16] Canadian embassies in the principal South American countries date only from World War II, Argentina and Brazil from 1941, and Chile from 1942. The three embassies closed by Canada had been opened in 1952, 1954, and 1960. Department of External Affairs (Ottawa), *Canadian Representation Abroad and Representatives of other Countries in Canada 1965* and *Canadian Almanac and Directory 1965*.

[17] *The New York Times*, March 8, 1970.

[18] *Le Monde*, November 24, 1966. French diplomats were said, at the time, to be paid 30–40 percent less than diplomats of other great powers. France was also said to spend only about 25 percent of what Germany was spending on its diplomatic representation.

at the Imperial conference of 1911, affirmed that the duties of British diplomats did not entail taking a hand in the politics of South America. On the contrary, Britain would "keep clear of all entanglements in the politics which are often very complicated, of the Central and South American republics with each other. . . ." [19] Nor was it British statesmen alone who were sensitive to the difficulties of understanding Latin American politics. A British historian, thoroughly versed in Spanish American history could, nonetheless, write in 1910: "The European student of this history seems to be reading a language whose grammar he does not know; political action moves on an unfamiliar plane; and in the catalogue of names and events it is hard to unravel motives or results. Even the political vocabulary is here used with a strange sense." [20] These statements did not reflect a willingness of Great Britain to forego intervention where British subjects and their claims were involved, but they do reflect British awareness of the risks of meddling in domestic and interstate relations in Latin America where no strong reasons to the contrary existed. This attitude was even easier to pursue after World War II, when the British presence in Latin America had been considerably reduced.

The United States has been less hesitant to tamper with the complicated gears of Latin American political and economic life. A comparison of one aspect of British and United States styles in Latin America is implicitly contained in an exchange between Walt W. Rostow, former counsellor and chairman of the Policy Planning Council of the United States Department of State, and Sir George Bolton, chairman of the Bank of London and South America. Pressed by Mr. Rostow as to whether British business interests in Latin America might not be assisted by British support for the Alliance for Progress, Sir George Bolton replied:

> I have had a fair amount to do with the Alliance for Progress and Mr. Rostow is an excellent advocate. My personal view is that Washington has made a mistake in imposing on potential beneficiaries standards of behavior both political and economic

[19] D. C. N. Platt, "British Diplomacy in Latin America Since the Emancipation," *Inter-American Economic Affairs,* 21 (3), Winter 1967, pp. 23 and 35.

[20] F. A. Kirkpatrick, "The Establishment of Independence in Spanish America," in *The Restoration, Cambridge Modern History,* Vol. X, New York, 1911, pp. 301–302.

which, while they might be acceptable in North America or the United Kingdom, are not necessarily acceptable to Latin American countries. I would not be in favor of this country formally joining the Alliance for Progress because I think we would then become involved in the political friction resulting from the imposition of such conditions and standards of behavior.[21]

The British concern with the political side effects of "imposing . . . standards of behavior" has not been shared to the same extent by United States leaders. Partly this seems to be due to the greater weight given in the United States to technical objectives and their means as compared with political considerations. Needless to say this applies largely to action abroad. North Americans are generally alert to the complexities of domestic political contexts and tread with circumspection, often too much so. Abroad, however, bereft of the rich political and social context normally available to them in the United States, United States administrators and officials often lose a sense of political delicacy. Even where they possess it they are sometimes encouraged to ignore it since they believe that the United States position (as donor, buyer, big power, technically advanced) permits them to do so. Alienation from the culture of the host country serves to dull sensitivities still further. The excessive optimism of professional and bureaucratic groups about what they can accomplish in the areas of their expertise is probably not without some responsibility for their willingness and that of political leaders to take political risks that could only be justified, if at all, by a high expectation of technical success. In many instances, however, technical and even diplomatic personnel are not aware of the political risks involved.

The disregard by the United States of Lord Salisbury's injunction not to encroach on the functions of Providence has led it into a tutelary relation with the Latin American states in almost all sectors of life. In technical affairs, in education, in economic planning and policy, in military procurement and organization, and in social and political organizations as well, United States officials and private organizations have often assumed or tried to

[21] The Hispanic and Luso-Brazilian Councils and the Western Hemisphere Exports Council, *Latin America: Prospect and Challenge,* Report of Conference at the Guildhall, London, March 10–11, 1964, p. 55.

assume leadership or guidance functions that could scarcely fail in the long run to irritate and to aggravate relations. This tutelary spirit is so deeply ingrained that in discussing Latin America, government officials and congressmen, military men and other professional experts and advisers seem unaware that they often use language appropriate only to a guardian discussing his ward. A witness at a government hearing pertinently reminded his auditors that some of the people of Latin America "deeply resent our sitting here presuming to plan their futures for them." [22]

It is possible, of course, to see in this tutelary relation only motives of political power and economic domination. However, the tutelary, patronizing relation has been as strong and as persistent as it has been because in many of its manifestations it has been supported by social reformistic motives, by a desire to rationalize (foreign) administration, and by the technical zeal of professional groups, civilian and military, official and private. How deeply ingrained the tutelary attitude toward Latin America is, is indicated by the fact that some of the severest critics of the United States role in Latin America are themselves excellent examples of the tutelary, managerial attitude toward Latin America. Dissatisfied with the operations of the Agency for International Development, they supported Title IX of the United States Foreign Assistance Act of 1966 which specified that AID, that is, the United States government, should assure "maximum participation in the task of economic development on the part of the people of the developing country, through the encouragement of democratic private and local governmental institutions." [23] Similarly they urged the United States not to sell (as well as not to give) weapons, or some classes of weapons, to Latin American countries. But Latin Americans are not necessarily pleased to learn that the United States government has undertaken to shape their institutions for them simply because some proponents of this effort have the most benign intentions; nor were, for example, most Peruvians less irritated by United States refusals to sell jet military aircraft to Peru because these refusals were sup-

---

[22] Testimony of Professor John J. Johnson, *Survey of the Alliance for Progress,* Hearings before the Subcommittee on American Republics Affairs, Committee on Foreign Relations, United States Senate, 90th Congress, 2d Session, Washington, 1968, p. 69.

[23] United States Public Law 89–853, 89th Congress, H.R. 15750, September 19, 1966, Title IX, Section 281.

ported by those who deplore United States interventions in Latin America or who deplore military governments and military expenditures.[24] Interventions by the CIA and the United States military in Latin American political life, the subject of heated controversy, for obvious reasons often based on unsatisfactorily documented data, have attracted much more attention than the more prosaic day-to-day tutelary interventions. Nevertheless, the latter probably have done more damage to United States–Latin American relations than the former.

During the last half of 1969, in relation to both Latin America and Vietnam, President Nixon acknowledged these American tendencies to assume a managerial and tutelary posture. In his foreign policy report to Congress in February 1970, the president, quoting an earlier statement, pointed out that "We Americans are a do-it-yourself people—an impatient people. Instead of teaching someone else to do a job, we like to do it ourselves. This trait has been carried over into our foreign policy." He recognized that the United States "directive and tutorial style clashed with the growing self-assertiveness and nationalism of the other Western Hemisphere nations." [25] It thus appears that a long-standing Latin American judgment of United States political style and one expressed by some United States specialists in Latin American affairs has penetrated executive consciousness.[26]

The tutelary style has tended to reinforce United States tendencies to think of and deal with Latin America as a whole. In analysis it is

[24] Congressional hearings provide excellent illustrations of United States intervention in Latin American domestic affairs being recommended by persons who presume themselves to be anti-interventionist. See, for example, *Survey of the Alliance for Progress,* Committee on Foreign Relations, United States Senate, 91st Congress, 1st Session, 1969, Document No. 91–17, p. 324, and *United States Relations with Peru,* Committee on Foreign Relations, United States Senate, 91st Congress, 1st Session, 1969, p. 33.

[25] "United States Foreign Policy for the 1970s: A New Strategy for Peace," Message from the President of the United States, 91st Congress, 2d Session, House Document No. 91–258. Note that this passage lamenting a United States "directive and tutorial style" implicitly assumes that while the United States should avoid doing the job for others, it is desirable to teach them how to do it. It is not easy to discard the tutorial role.

[26] And administrative consciousness. An AID administrator has noted: "We cannot tell them [Latin American countries] how to run their business. They must make their own decisions. . . ." *The New York Times,* February 25, 1970.

often pardonable, and in some contexts justified, to speak broadly of 'Latin America.' Diplomacy, however, unlike analysis, involves the interests and emotions of foreign governments and peoples. To deal with them as if they were provinces of a single country may be convenient but does not necessarily answer to their sense of individuality and to their special interests; and even less so as the countries of Latin America become more differentiated in political tendency and form blocs among themselves. The common complaint that the United States has treated Latin America *en bloc* ought not, however, to be pushed too far since the Latin American states themselves, in a desire to multiply their forces, often combine to pursue those interests which at least a majority of them share.

The tutelary style has its roots in various aspects of American life and of United States relations to other countries, and an increased awareness of it may not suffice to alter substantially the United States political style in Central and South America. A change in numbers is more easily effected than a change in style. In 1967, beginning with the large United States official presence in Brazil,[27] reductions in the numbers of United States officials in Latin America were instituted. Secretaries of state have, however, not always pressed strongly for their reduction because the State Department receives a useful supplement of $120 million annually for administrative support costs for nondepartmental personnel.[28] A spokesman in the United States embassy in Brazil pointed out that "We are not concerned with numbers alone. What concerns us is that the United States is exercising too direct a role here over too broad a spectrum. We have taken what might be called the Mother Hen approach. . . ."[29]

Although much of this tutelary style could have been avoided, it was not always easy to do so and avoidance will continue to be difficult in the future. It is not easy and may not even be desirable to make sizable grants and soft loans without some degree of

[27] In June 1967, the United States diplomatic and related personnel in Brazil were: embassy, 350; USAID, 568; military, 314; USIS, 206; Peace Corps, 661; plus 864 non-United States employees and various USAID contract personnel. *United States Congressional Record—House,* June 21, 1967, p. H7736.

[28] John F. Campbell, *op. cit.,* p. 95.

[29] *Los Angeles Times,* November 12, 1967.

control that may amount to guidance, if not outright interference,[30] in the affairs of the receiving countries. This is especially the case when groups in the donor country whose support is necessary for the programs are inclined to specify conditions under which the funds are to be employed. Congressmen feel not only entitled to express their preferences but required by their duties to do so. Thus a representative expressed his astonishment, after a visit to Brazil, that Congress "annually grant[s] blanket authority to assist foreign social welfare programs without even specifying the order of priority among the myriad social needs."[31] Besides, not all tutelary activity is initiated by the United States or is reluctantly received. In some fields, Latin American administrators and political and professional groups look to the United States and other countries for guidance, instruction, and supervision.

In addition, the economic, political, and military weight of the United States in the world at large, and in Latin America more specifically, provokes resentments, suspicions, and interpretations which though frequently justified are also often exaggerated and exacerbated by these forms of predominance. Prior to World War I and even prior to World War II some of this resentment in Latin America was channeled toward Great Britain.

Finally, it must be recognized that the lot of the earnest politician is a hard one and if he scrupulously avoids all appearances of improper intervention he may find himself accused of unfeeling indifference. When Governor Rockefeller, in his 1969 Latin American tour, was questioned in Uruguay on whether the United States would back democratic regimes in Latin America the governor implied the impropriety of the president of the United States seeking to decide which Latin American regimes were to be viewed as democratic.[32] However, when the governor met with Brazilian students he informed them that he had raised issues of press censorship, student arrests, and political and academic freedom in Brazil with President Costa e Silva.[33] He thus hoped, no doubt, to please those younger Brazilians not quick enough to appreciate some of the implications of such an intervention. In any case, circumspection

[30] See Chapter 10.4 for some discussion of how United States economic assistance tends to provoke United States intervention.

[31] *United States Congressional Record—House,* June 21, 1967, p. H7741.

[32] *Los Angeles Times,* June 29, 1969.

[33] *The New York Times,* June 19, 1969.

in these matters hardly suffices if sensitivity and tact are lacking. President Nixon's statement in a public address, shortly before the visits of Governor Rockefeller to Latin America, that the system of higher education in Latin America generally "is one of the most inferior in the world" was not well received south of the Río Bravo.[34]

The new look, in 1970, in United States economic assistance prescribed that the United States "talk less and listen more." This represented some appreciation of the offensiveness of the United States tutelary style. In fact, however, there were reasons equally urgent for the United States to "talk less and listen more." Issues between the United States and Latin America only too often generated conferences and speeches whose rhetoric was in excess of subsequent action and was a poor substitute for silence, private discussions, or blunt rejections. The compulsion to issue statements is in part a response to the voracious appetites of government press officers and the press corps, who sometimes are the primary stimulus for and the first consumers of government rhetoric.[35] The increasing use by governments of public relations specialists seems part of a larger trend in the Western world to believe that problems can be talked into disappearing. Political leaders, increasingly dependent as they are on communication specialists for election purposes, are in danger of acquiring from this experience a misplaced idea of the relation of communications to the solution of social problems.

[34] This criticism by the president was made before the United States Chamber of Commerce in the course of observations on student outbreaks in the United States. See *The New York Times,* April 29, 1969, for the text of the president's speech and the issue of May 1, 1969, for some Latin American reactions.

[35] It has not been uncommon for technical specialists to attempt to fulfill a political function. "All too often the civil servant as a politician turns a cause that is good in every sense into a 'weak' cause, through technically 'weak' pleading. . . . To an outstanding degree, politics today is in fact conducted in public by means of the spoken or written word. To weigh the effect of the word properly falls within the range of the lawyer's tasks; but not at all into that of the civil servant. The latter is no demagogue, nor is it his purpose to be one. If he nevertheless tries to become a demagogue, he usually becomes a very poor one." Max Weber, "Politics as a Vocation," in *From Max Weber: Essays in Sociology,"* edited by H. H. Gerth and C. Wright Mills, New York, 1946, p. 95.

211

That rhetoric plays the large role that it does in interstate relations, despite the obvious merits of silence, suggests that it performs functions of some importance and has causes not readily subject to control. Indeed, in the United States and other countries with highly competitive party politics, issuing statements and proposing programs are important to political leaders who find it politically useful and personally reassuring to keep saying and doing things of apparent significance.

Words, it is well known, are useful instruments for concealing both thought and the absence of thought. However, political leaders and diplomats often speak simply because, more than most, they are bound by ritual requirements. In 1970 the OAS held "an incredible record number of 111 meetings and conferences." [36] The delivery of public statements, even when their sincerity is doubted by most parties and when they have a high coefficient of vacuity, serves in international meetings to gloss over the uncomfortable awareness of many of the participants that they have little that is useful to say to each other, and least of all, in public. Speeches contribute an air of civility to occasions in which the frustrations of the participants might otherwise erupt into an embarrassing display of emotion.

The gift of speech sometimes puts interstate relations at the mercy of minor clashes which usually produce, however, only a temporary coolness unless the incident is itself the product of an underlying tension. Spanish ambassadors in Latin America have lived up to their nation's reputation for pride. A Spanish ambassador affronted at a Nicaraguan prize-awarding ceremony by references to Spain's conquest of Peru is alleged to have made insulting remarks to a Nicaraguan cabinet minister. The Spanish ambassador to Cuba, finding his country affronted by Castro in a radio address, hastened to the studio (confident, no doubt, that the length of a Castro speech afforded him time to do this) and sought to wrest the microphone from Castro's hands. Castro, in his turn, accused a French diplomat of having told dirty stories during an official reception. In 1967, charges in Ecuador alleged that United States technical assistance engineers received a $350 per month subsidy for each child, which Ecuador had to pay. The United States ambassador had the indelicacy to point out during the course of a talk in Quito that the living expenses of American engineers, which

[36] *Visión Letter,* May 12, 1971, p. 4.

Ecuador had agreed to pay, were in fact $300 per month for single men, $350 for married men, and involved no extra payment for children at all. This earned the ambassador a notice to leave the country within 48 hours. Evidently diplomatic ritual cannot entirely safeguard interstate relations from the vagaries of personal emotion.

Germany (with Italy), like the United States, has sought to help in the development of party and trade union democratic institutions, but her involvement in Latin American guidance has been so limited that she can hardly be classified as following American precepts. Germany has shown a desire to avoid identification with the United States tutelary and managerial style by stressing that the members of the German Development Service do not serve as advisers but as colleagues.[37] The German emphasis on professional competence rather than on youthful idealism, as in the United States Peace Corps, adds to the contrast in national styles. As a further defense against a managerial and interventionist image Germany, although maintaining a close watch on the use of her aid funds, avoided placing permanent aid missions in the field and preferred to conduct the administration of her programs largely from Bonn and Frankfurt by continuing negotiations with representatives of the recipient governments.[38] The United States, on the contrary, has put people in the field, believing that contact and supervision would produce not irritation but efficiency. Of AID's 13,700 employees (1971), 10,500 were overseas and 3,200 in Washington. The new winds of United States policy in Latin America may change this. A presidential task force on foreign aid has recommended the reorganization of the United States apparatus for economic assistance with greater emphasis on multilateral arrangements, with the expectation that ". . . the United States Government would need fewer advisers and other personnel abroad. It could assume a supporting rather than a directing role in international development."[39]

[37] *The New York Times,* December 13, 1965.

[38] John White, *German Aid,* Overseas Development Institute, London, 1965, p. 65.

[39] *The New York Times,* March 9, 1970. This lowered profile has been interpreted by Latin American political leaders as a concealed revocation of United States promises of economic assistance. *Visión,* May 22, 1971, p. 24.

Soviet aid activities also showed, originally, a contrast in styles with the United States. Indeed it appears that it was the capitalist United States and not the Communist Soviet Union that showed some concern for planning in the field of economic aid, although much of this was simply writing project proposals. The Soviets subsequently became more inquisitive before committing themselves to major aid projects, and Communist China then took over the role of providing aid with few questions asked.[40] In part, of course, a no-questions-asked attitude derives from a primary interest in an immediate political effect without regard to long-term economic consequences.

During part of the postwar period, the Soviets in Latin America were largely reduced to the cultivation of mass opinion, to the support of the Communist parties of the region, and in general to attacks on most of the established regimes of the area. Soviet success later in establishing diplomatic and trade relations with Latin America, although marking a shift in the Soviet position in Latin America, did not mean a complete abandonment of programs of mass appeal hostile to the governments that had recognized the Soviet Union, an abandonment that would have been little consistent with her political style. Thus the resumption of diplomatic relations between Colombia and the Soviet Union on January 19, 1968, after a 20-year lapse, did not deter the Soviet short-wave propaganda service, less than two weeks later, from charging in a Quechua language broadcast the murder of hundreds of Indians in Colombia.[41] Nor did Soviet interest in expanding and consolidating diplomatic relations prevent, three years later, activities that

[40] I. M. D. Little and J. M. Clifford, *International Aid,* Chicago, 1966, pp. 28–30. Lucien Pye, writing in 1961, does not seem to agree with Little and Clifford and attributes to the Soviets a constant need for control in their aid activities. He also points out American optimism with respect to possibilities of rapid change due to aid as compared with Soviet convictions that change occurs only as a result of very great efforts. See Lucien Pye, "The Political Impulses and Fantasies Behind Foreign Aid," in *The New Look in Foreign Aid,* Proceedings of the Academy of Political Science, New York, XXVII (2), January 1962, pp. 104–105.

[41] On the Bolshevik belief that "It pays to be rude," see Nathan Leites, *A Study of Bolshevism,* New York, 1953, pp. 34–42. Western political leaders, on the other hand, seem to have an over-optimistic view of the value of politeness in making the rudeness of others go away.

led to the expulsion of Soviet diplomats from Mexico and Ecuador for interference in domestic affairs.[42]

The increased Soviet interest in Latin America has been supported by a greater flexibility both in Soviet doctrine for Latin American revolution and economic development (see Chapter 8) and in Soviet economic arrangements with the Latin American states. Trade accords signed in August 1970 between Bolivia and the Soviet Union provide for Soviet payment in dollars for Bolivian minerals, an important departure from the barter deals preferred by the Soviets. Two months later a Soviet bank, The Foreign Commerce Bank of the USSR, for the first time joined a syndicate of Western banks to provide a loan of $19.5 million to Centrais Electricas of São Paulo. By virtue of this loan the Soviets will provide Centrais Electricas with heavy hydro-electric equipment.[43] In Peru, the Soviet trial purchase of $178,000 worth of cotton was, according to Soviet officials, a cash sale. In addition, all transactions under the two year Peruvian–Soviet trade treaty of February 1969 are to be in freely convertible currencies.[44]

While the Soviets have tended in Latin America to move from a concern with masses to a concern with governments, United States action has shown an increasing interest in moving from governmental to mass "targets." This appears in the development of USIA activities, the concern with measuring public opinion abroad, the interest in encouraging and supporting civic action by Latin American military establishments, and the organization of the Peace Corps, and in related activities intended to reach various working class and professional sectors of the Latin American populations.

---

[42] The involvement of the Soviet Union in facilitating the transfer of Mexican students at Lumumba University in Moscow to North Korea via East Berlin to train for revolutionary action in Mexico came as a shock to Latin America and had an air of mystery about it, precisely because the current Soviet line discounted the value of guerrilla warfare in Latin America and emphasized "correct" diplomatic and trade relations. It has been alleged that the subsequent uproar in Mexico was cultivated by the government for its own ends, but this, if so, apparently does not question the reality of the events that the Mexican government exploited. The dismissal of three Soviet diplomats in Ecuador was due to their apparent involvement in the preparation of a local strike.

[43] *Le Monde,* August 19, 1970, and October 4–5, 1970.

[44] Alliance for Progress, *Weekly Newsletter,* October 26, 1970, p. 3.

Italy seems to rely in Latin America on the exploitation of personal relations and strong sentiments of mutual regard and sympathy. She seems little disposed to preach to others how they should manage their affairs except in those instances where technical advice is asked. Some Italian officials engaged in service in Latin America believe that they have a greater sensitivity to their environment than do most other foreigners, that this permits more subtle behavior and renders them more *simpático* to Latin Americans. For these reasons, as well as those expressed by Sir George Bolton, they hesitate to be too closely associated with the United States in Latin America. Similarly, Italian fascists in Brazil, more astute than the Nazis in their relations with Brazilians, avoided close contact with the inept Nazis in order not to prejudice their own chances of success.[45]

Japan, even more than Italy, has maintained a discrete official presence in Latin America, while its business, industrial, and financial executives have become a notable part of the scene in all the airports of the region. The Japanese policy for its Overseas Cooperation Volunteers in Southeast Asia expresses much of the restraint and perference for a low silhouette that has characterized Japanese behavior in Latin America as well. Although the Japanese emphasize technical skill much more than does the United States Peace Corps, the Japanese volunteers are taught that despite their high technical abilities "they should not be the leading actors in dealing with the people they are aiding but only the supporting cast." [46] Japanese behavior in Latin America accords with that observed in the Pacific and in Southeast Asia where "Japanese businessmen have preferred to keep their heads down at the slightest sign of trouble." [47]

Among the nonhemispheric countries only France, in the postwar world, under de Gaulle, assumed the right to be the spiritual schoolmaster of the less fortunately endowed nations. But the exercise of this leadership was from so lofty a level that in some areas, especially Latin America, it involved little practical tutelage.[48] In 1964

[45] Alton Frye, *Nazi Germany and the American Hemisphere, 1933–1943,* New Haven, 1967, p. 103.

[46] Director of Training, Japan Overseas Cooperation Volunteers, *The New York Times,* November 5, 1967.

[47] *The Economist,* November 21, 1970, p. 66.

[48] See Alfred Grosser, "La politique extérieure affectée," *Le Monde,* June 19, 1968.

Latin American diplomats, viewing de Gaulle's forthcoming Mexican and Latin American visits, commonly expressed the view that they would be able to establish economic relations with France on a more businesslike basis than with the United States. France, they presumed, would want a *quid pro quo* but was unlikely to make aid conditional on this or that economic reform.[49] As it turned out, Latin American expectations of French aid were severely disappointed, but Latin American judgments of French as opposed to United States political styles were, nonetheless, probably sound.

The personal style of General de Gaulle called for a very firm counteroffensive to any challenge or seeming challenge to France's dignity or rights. Few heads of state would have permitted themselves the ironic tone of the General's replies to those West Coast Latin American governments that expressed their opposition to French nuclear tests in the Pacific. The General's style produced, in the case of the "Lobster War" with Brazil (see Chapter 1.2), a sharper conflict than did similar and more frequent fishing conflicts on the West Coast involving the United States. On two occasions France sent gunboats to protect French lobster fishermen off the Brazilian coast. On the second occasion Brazil sent a cruiser and an aircraft carrier, with crews on war pay, to search for the French destroyer *Tartu,* which thereupon retired to France. This led General de Gaulle to review Brazil's economic indebtedness to France and to refuse to receive a Brazilian emissary sent to smooth over matters. In the end, this prolonged incident did not prevent General de Gaulle from including Brazil in the itinerary of his South American trip.[50]

In the pursuit of political influence in Latin America some countries attempt a long-term more or less continuous buildup of goodwill, leverage, and influence, while others rely on *ad hoc* attempts to develop influence when contingencies occur for which little or no prior diplomatic or other preparation has been made. The long-term attempt to build up influence may require or seem

[49] *The Evening Star* (Washington, D.C.), February 17, 1964.

[50] For the exchange of letters between President João Goulart and General de Gaulle normalizing French–Brazilian relations, see *Revista Brasileira de Política Internacional,* VII (25), March 1964, pp. 116–118. For a brief account of the "Lobster War" (by a political opponent of de Gaulle), see Paul Reynaud, *The Foreign Policy of Charles de Gaulle,* New York, 1964, pp. 118–120.

to require an investment that only big powers can make. No country except perhaps the Soviet Union could afford the diplomatic, economic, and military investment that the United States has made in Latin America. Certainly West Germany, France, the United Kingdom, and Italy, through their aid, cultural, and political activities pursue long-term programs of establishing themselves more firmly in the Latin American world, but the costs that they are willing or able to bear in the process are generally modest,[51] partly, of course, because they are proportioned to more modest objectives.

For the smaller (and, in some cases, less foresightful) countries, long-term investments in the pursuit of influence are less feasible and an impending or immediate crisis tends to produce hasty *ad hoc* action. The contrast between long-term programs for the development of influence and *ad hoc* attempts to gain friendship at critical moments is not, however, always a difference between the big powers and the smaller, poorer countries. The contrast can be illustrated from among the smaller powers themselves, and especially by the struggle of Israel and the Arab countries for political support in Latin America. In the early sixties Israel began to provide substantial and much appreciated technical aid to Latin America and followed this up in 1965 and 1966 with considerable diplomatic activity.[52] The Arab countries, on the other hand, do not seem to have anticipated the desirability or the feasibility of a substantial effort in Latin America as the crisis of 1967 loomed, although the UAR had signed, in 1964 and 1965, some limited cultural accords (see Chapter 9.7). In late 1966 King Hussein presented Venezuela with four camels, but President Nasser did not get around to sending a special emissary to Argentina and Brazil until June 1, 1967, the day the six-day war broke out. A Syrian nine-man goodwill mission, also to Brazil and Argentina, did not arrive until the war was over.

Like Israel, South Africa also sought to develop a long-term program to meet its needs for political and economic support in Latin America (see Chapter 10.4).

---

[51] This, of course, does not mean that payoffs are proportionate to the amount of effort invested.

[52] In 1965 and 1966 President Shazar of Israel, Prime Minister Levi Eshkol, Deputy Prime Minister Abba Eban, Undersecretary Gideon Raphael, a number of heads of ministries, as well as several technical missions, visited Latin America.

The Greek–Turkish conflict in Cyprus illustrates, on the other hand, a crisis that precipitated a *post facto* search by both parties for political support in Latin America, although the probable anticipation of new and later crises gave this search for political support a forward-looking character as well. Following the Cyprus crisis of 1964, a two-man Turkish mission visited Venezuela, Uruguay, Ecuador, Peru, Colombia, Costa Rica, Argentina, and Brazil. This was followed by the appointment in February 1965 of an ambassador to Peru. This diplomatic activity by Turkey stimulated rival action by President Archbishop Makarios of Cyprus who, accompanied by his foreign minister, visited a number of Latin American countries in 1966.

Such *ad hoc* missions sometimes have a character of "too little" as well as "too late." Conscious of the self-seeking nature of gestures made only at the point when help is badly needed, countries courting Latin American support sometimes offer material inducements. In the case of the smaller countries these inducements may be small and uncertain, and in some instances seem to lend an air of the ridiculous to missions otherwise not without dignity. In Argentina, in Brazil, in Ecuador, and in Venezuela the Turkish mission to Latin America felt constrained in its press conferences to make vague references to the possibility of increasing Turkey's trade with Latin America. This was not lost on President Archbishop Makarios, who on his arrival in Bogotá alluded, in his press conference, to the future of trade between Cyprus and Colombia, more specifically to the possibility that Cyprus might buy Colombian coffee, and held out hope that Cyprus might open an embassy in Bogotá. A game that has a serious meaning, although not a different moral status, when played by a power able and sometimes willing to pay the piper, is perhaps pathetic when these conditions are not fulfilled. In Chile Archbishop Makarios was not received by President Frei, who had a bad cold.

The long-term, anticipatory buildup of influence and the *ad hoc*, *post facto* attempt to deal with a crisis are not mutually exclusive strategies. Thus the United States and most of the larger powers have had from time to time to improvise hasty measures if only for the simple reason that the long-term cultural, military, economic development and political programs have not succeeded in forestalling crises and contretemps. These situations have led to actions sometimes little consistent with either the aims or the tactics of

219

the longer-term programs. Some of these crises were unavoidable, the world not being either a very predictable or a very manageable structure. In some instances, however, especially in the case of the United States, programs intended to provide greater predictability and influence produced or facilitated the crises that then led to hasty corrective, or sometimes exacerbative, action.

Part III

RESULTS AND INTERPRETATIONS

12. Results

How well have the foreign powers achieved their objectives in Latin America in the postwar world?

Rigorous answers to this question cannot be given. The "objectives" of the foreign powers in Latin America differ in public and private groups, and in different segments of government and the government bureaucracy; they vary from administration to administration as well as in the course of a single administration. A head of government or his foreign minister may not have a clearly fixed objective in mind. And if he does, he may not take the pains to reveal it to others. Further, where clarity of intent exists objectives will usually be pursued in particular countries of Central and South America and not in "Latin America." Nor are data usually available for generating accurate and meaningful measures of foreign national achievements in Latin America except in some limited areas of economic rivalry.

These limitations acknowledged, we still hope to provide from our inquiry some answers, *grosso modo,* to the question posed above.

1. *Japan*

In the quarter century following World War II, Japan and the Federal Republic of Germany appear to have achieved, or to be achieving, their objectives in Latin America more fully than the other powers, and this despite the inevitable competition that each provides for the other.

Japan developed in Latin America new raw material sources important to her economy and retained there, principally in Brazil, her main emigration outlet. Both of these became increasingly important as replacements for raw material sources and emigrant outlets lost in the Far East by World War II. In 1938 Japan had obtained less than 4 percent of her imports from Latin America. This grew to 7–8 percent in the sixties.[1] Although Latin America has become an important provisioner, Japan has tried to avoid excessive dependence on this, as on any other single region.

Dependence on foreign raw materials imposes heavy requirements on foreign trade to pay for these imports. Japan has had notable success in increasing her share of the Latin American market. Before World War II, in 1938, Japan provided only 2 percent of Latin American imports. By 1948, after the war, this had dropped to 1 percent. But by 1960 Japan had increased its share to 4 percent and by 1968 to 6 percent (Table 3.1). No other industrial nation has had so large a rate of increase.

Japan's exports to Latin America, and probably her imports as well, will very likely grow further as a result of her active investment policy. Japan is the fourth largest investor in Latin America after the United States, Great Britain, and West Germany and may soon surpass Britain. Today only 19 percent of Japan's overseas investments are in Southeast Asia as compared with 28 percent in Latin America.[2] Japanese traders have feared the eventual consequences of the Central American Common Market (CACM) and of the Latin American Free Trade Area (LAFTA) on their own aspirations toward economic expansion in Latin America, but these concerns are being relieved by an investment policy, which in the last years has sometimes led half of Japan's total direct investment, and rarely less than a third, to be placed in Latin America.[3] The stability of this policy, however, remains as yet to be tested in the new Latin American environment of increasingly stringent controls over foreign investment and foreign enterprises. The con-

[1] IMF, *Direction of Trade,* various years. In 1948 when Japanese imports were still at a very low level and before active trading relationships had been reestablished with other countries, about 13 percent of Japan's imports came from Latin America.

[2] Penelope Roper, *Investment in Latin America,* The Economist Intelligence Unit, London, 1970, p. 10; and Chapter 3.2.

[3] Nobuo Ito, "Japan's Trade Relations with Latin America," *The Inter-American Scene,* 2 (4), Fall 1970, p. 10.

tinuation of this policy is no doubt important to those Latin American countries anxious about the possible defection of United States and European investors. Peru especially looks for continued investment from its second largest customer.

Japanese postwar migration to Latin America continued to fulfill Japan's need for a population outlet (Chapter 5.1), especially in a period when so many Japanese had to leave formerly conquered territories. In the last few years, however, Japan has had little excess population and her limited emigration to Brazil has served largely to facilitate her trade, investment, and procurement objectives in Latin America (Chapter 5.2).

Japan has not had to pursue political objectives in Latin America other than to maintain the conditions favorable to trade, investment, and migration, and this has required primarily a policy of discretion, of "sticking-to-business," and of avoiding alienation of any significant sector of Latin American opinion or political power.[4]

On the whole, Japan has succeeded admirably in avoiding serious frictions that might have jeopardized her successes in Latin America. In 1965 she, like several other countries, had to face a minor campaign in several Latin American countries, notably Peru, Colombia, and Brazil, by anti-Communist, anti-Castro deputies, and by some trade union groups, intended to make her desist from trade with Cuba.[5] Japan has also had a small share in the series of conflicts with Latin American countries over offshore fishing (Chapter 1.2). In Central America Japanese textiles became (in 1965) a source of contention between Guatemala and Costa Rica when the Central American Association of Textile Industries alleged that Japan threatened to monopolize the Central American market. None of these incidents has led to anything approaching a crisis in the relations between Japan and the Latin republics.

Achievement must be judged not only by the gains made relative

[4] Following the coup that replaced President Illia with General Onganía and that led to violence at the universities, Argentina sent a special envoy to Great Britain, France, West Germany, and the United States. This envoy was supposed to visit Japan as well, but he reportedly had to call off the trip because he was unable to arrange for audiences with Emperor Hirohito and Prime Minister Sato. This, if exact, seems a rather unusual Japanese reaction to internal Latin American political developments.

[5] In 1965 Japan was the second largest buyer of Cuban sugar (7.8 percent of Cuban production as compared with Russia's 46.2 percent). Jean Lamore, *Cuba*, Paris, 1970, p. 107.

to objectives pursued, but also by the costs sustained in achieving them. Japanese achievements in Latin America are all the more striking just because Japan's costs have been modest. Her support in recent years for the migration to Brazil of skilled personnel needed at home was a low-cost activity. Her willingness to make investments and seek overseas contracts of low profitability for the sake of expansion and not clearly calculable long-term future benefits has imposed greater costs. But on the other hand, Japan has spent very little on aid to Latin America (see Table 10.1) and even her trade credits have often been short-term rather than long-term. Japan carries on only a very limited cultural program in Latin America [6] and her trade fairs and delegations of businessmen and officials impose only modest costs that have a very direct return in trade and investment. No other industrial nation can show in Latin America so much gained at so little cost.

2. Germany

Germany's postwar interests in Latin America, like those of Japan, stemmed in part from the substantial number of her nationals, and descendants of nationals, in Latin America, and the migration thereto after World War II (Chapter 5.1). Her principal objectives, however, were to reestablish her economic position in Latin America and to affirm her right to speak for all Germans, that is, to prevent the recognition of East Germany. In addition, the exposed position of West Berlin vis-à-vis the Soviet Union made the Federal Republic more sensitive than other Western European powers to political currents in Latin America that might affect her security.

Germany's objectives in Latin America have, then, been more far-reaching than those of Japan. She has had major political as well as economic goals, and their achievement has depended not only on the Latin American republics but also on the behavior of third nations (the Soviet bloc on the one hand and the United States on the other) capable of undermining or supporting her own actions in Latin America.

[6] The Japanese appear to have as much pride in their cultural accomplishments as the French, but they have made relatively little effort to exploit this for economic and political purposes, partly because they feel that Japanese culture is too alien to the West and, perhaps, because the distinctive features of Japanese culture are viewed as private Japanese accomplishments and not intended for "export."

226

Germany has not fully recovered her prewar trade position in Latin America but she has made substantial progress toward this end. In 1938 Germany had provided about 18 percent of Latin America's imports and today provides about 10 percent. Her share increased from a negligible amount in 1948 to 3.4 percent in 1950, to 7.4 percent in 1955, and to about 9–10 percent in the sixties. Although this is less than her prewar share, Germany has regained her prewar rank as the second largest provisioner of Latin America.

Germany, with $890 million [6a] of private direct investments, is close to rivaling Great Britain as the second largest foreign investor in Latin America (Chapter 3.2) and if present trends continue she may (together with Japan) surpass Britain, an achievement that would very likely also forecast a further increase in the German share of the Central and South American markets. Of course, if Britain's investments in the British West Indies, including the Bahamas and Bermuda, are added to her Central and South American investments, she still has a substantial lead over the Federal Republic.

Unlike Japan, Germany now depends less than before the war on imports from Latin America and this has prevented her from having as large deficits in her trade balance with Latin America as Japan and the other major European countries.

In the political sphere the Federal Republic attained in the fifties and sixties her objective of forestalling recognition of East Germany by the Central and South American states. The Cuban revolution, however, gave East Germany diplomatic recognition in a Caribbean country. It was alleged in 1962 in Brazil that a Brazilian–East German "Protocol of Conversation" dealing with commercial matters carried a juridical implication of recognition, but this was denied in the Brazilian Senate by the minister of foreign affairs.[7] Nothing came of this sortie on behalf of East Germany.

West Germany has tended by her own recent actions to devalue the importance to her of the Hallstein Doctrine, by which she broke diplomatic relations with countries that recognized East Germany. Bonn's decision in 1967 to renew diplomatic relations with Rumania and in 1968 with Yugoslavia marked a partial abandonment

[6a] T. Graydon Upton, address to International Conference on Latin American Investment Policy Models, Hamburg, Germany, October 13, 1971, p. 4.

[7] *Revista Brasileira de Política Internacional,* V (18), June 1962, pp. 85–86.

227

of the Hallstein Doctrine. The conversations in 1970 between Chancellor Willy Brandt of the Federal Republic and Premier Willi Stoph of East Germany depreciated the doctrine further, although West Germany has not indicated that recognition of East Germany by friendly powers is in any way acceptable to her. After the Social Democrats replaced the Christian Democrats in power in West Germany (1969), some Latin American countries began to consider recognition of East Germany. It was, however, President Allende of Chile who finally recognized East Germany in March 1971. Although regretting the recognition and stating that she would not institute reprisals, West Germany made clear, nonetheless, that Chilean recognition of East Germany constituted a burden on West German–Chilean relations.[8]

German diplomatic and economic activities in Latin America have not been as trouble-free as those of Japan. Nazi emigrants created problems for German diplomacy (Chapter 5.3) and from time to time complicated her endeavor to present an image of a new Germany politically and morally sound as well as capable of performing the German economic miracle. The Mannesmann case [9] led to a short period of tension between Brazil and Germany but was settled in 1966. Leaving aside continuing embarrassments from the Nazi past, there have been no enduring, systematic sources of tension between Germany and the Latin republics. Problems have been episodic with only temporary effects on relations, effects that do not appear to have altered the level or rate of German progress in Latin America. Germany has, however, spent far more than Japan on economic assistance (Table 10.1) and on cultural diplomacy (Chapter 9.2) in pursuit of her political and economic objectives.

3. *France*

Compared with Japan and West Germany, the postwar performance of France in Latin America has fallen short of achieving the objectives and fulfilling the expectations signaled by General de Gaulle's Mexican and South American trips.

[8] *Le Monde,* April 24, 1971. Until its recognition by Chile, East Germany had had in Latin America only a commercial mission in Mexico, and Chamber of Commerce representatives in Brazil, Chile, and Ecuador.

[9] Notes issued to Brazilians by a Mannesmann executive in Brazil were rejected by the company as not being a company responsibility. Vigorous reaction by the Brazilian government led to a $13 million settlement.

France had not, prior to World War II, been a major trading partner of Latin America, although like most of the European industrial countries Latin America was more important to her prior to than after World War II. France has sought to increase her exports to the Latin American markets but has not succeeded, except in occasional years, in attaining even her pre-World War II share, although she has not fallen much below it. Most of the years following General de Gaulle's trips have not, in this respect, differed materially from those that preceded them.[10]

In France there is a clear awareness of the failure of French aspirations in Latin America to be realized. Recalling the high hopes inspired by General de Gaulle's two trips of 1964, a French observer used the occasion of the General's death in late 1970 to summarize the outcome for France:

> The level of cultural and economic exchanges was not materially modified by a trip which was supposed to launch collaboration between France . . . and the countries of Latin America at all levels. Many errors, many oversights and negligences have been committed. The bankers and businessmen who rushed to Latin America in the wake of the president were not all up to the stature of the great gaullist designs. . . .
>
> It is only to the extent that economic cooperation has had a political meaning that it has really produced any effects. Contributing to break the embargo imposed by the United States, France, with $55 million worth of exports in 1969, has become the leading western provisioner of Cuba.[11]

France has had, nonetheless, some notable successes in winning capital construction contracts (Chapter 3.3). French investments

[10] Based on IMF, *Direction of Trade,* various years. France's share of the Latin American market has, both prior to and after World War II, mostly varied between 3 and 4 percent. On her success in military matériel exports see below. The substantial increase in exports to Latin America (30 percent) in 1970 may represent a fluctuation of no great long-term importance or the beginning of a long-hoped-for upward trend.

[11] Marcel Niedergang in *Le Monde,* November 12, 1970. France's $55 million worth of exports to Cuba in 1969 compares with about $14 million in 1959.

in Latin America (Chapter 3.2) have been erratic, generally low in most years with an occasional major increment.[12]

In the political sphere, de Gaulle's interest in reducing the influence of the United States and the Soviet Union [13] did not succeed, in the long run, in achieving an increased status for France in Latin America. French prestige and influence [14] did gain perceptibly from General de Gaulle's state visits, from his hostility toward and independence of the United States, and from the sale of Mirages (see below), but this gain was not sustained. Indeed, the decline after 1964–1965 was no doubt all the greater because of the disappointment of Latin expectations. The limited nature of French aid and trade, the privileged trading position given by France in the EEC to Latin America's competitors in Africa and the Antilles, France's continuation of nuclear tests in the Pacific over Latin American protests, culminating in her enforced cancellation of part of her 1971 test series under Peru's threat to break diplomatic relations, her failure to sign even Protocol II of the Treaty of Tlatelolco (Chapter 2.3), her fishing conflict with Brazil (resumed after de Gaulle's visit), her differences with Cuba, her conflict in 1967 with Argentina over the admission of Argentinian beef in the

[12] After a series of years, 1960–1966, in which estimates of French net investments in Latin America ranged between $2 and $10 million per year, France had a net investment of $60 million in 1967. Penelope Roper, *op. cit.,* p. 8.

[13] Competition between Soviet and French influence in Cuba came to light in the trial of Aníbal Escalante, former secretary of the Partido Socialista Popular. Exiled by Castro to the Soviet Union in 1962, Escalante was allowed to return to Cuba as a private citizen but was put on trial in 1968 for passing documents and information to the Soviet Union. In the trial, Escalante was charged with opposing French influence for fear it would diminish that of the Soviet Union. In a document sent to Moscow, Escalante alleged that Cuban leaders were moving closer to France in order to separate Havana from the Soviet Union, and that "the new attitude of de Gaulle . . . has provoked in our country a current that pushes us politically closer to France." *Le Monde,* February 1, 1968.

[14] One of the more mysterious aspects of international affairs is the pursuit of prestige, an ill-defined commodity whose role in international affairs has not been adequately investigated. Generally, prestige is assumed to increase influence and indeed this appears to have been a basic principle of de Gaulle's diplomacy. No doubt it can lead to influence, but France's well-deserved prestige was apparently not associated with other attributes that would have enabled her to obtain a greater return from it.

230

Common Market,[15] her war in Algeria, which at the time alienated some sectors of Latin American governmental and public opinion,[16] and her attitude in the United Nations toward Israel, which was not well received in some Latin American diplomatic circles,[17] all provided points of friction with a number of Latin American states. In addition, official France offended left-wing sentiment in Latin America, especially among youth, when the May 1968 student revolt was crushed.[18] Latin American nationalists and leftists are, however, not insensitive to the support they receive from French intellectuals.[19]

France's problems in Latin America have, then, been more numerous and serious than those of Japan, West Germany, and Italy. It is unlikely, however, that Latin American popular reaction to France has been as critical as has been Latin governmental reaction.

Despite her difficulties in Latin America, France has had notable successes in an area of marked United States interest and advantage—military sales and military relations. France has not re-

[15] In 1967 (six months before the foot-and-mouth outbreak of 1967) French pressure led the EEC to limit concessions made earlier to Argentinian beef. Argentinian cattlemen called for sharp reprisals against France. According to French sources, France's Société Sofrelec lost its consulting contract for studies for the Chocon hydroelectric complex to an English consulting firm. See *Primera Plana* (Buenos Aires), July 4–10, July 7–17, 1967; and *Le Monde*, December 3–4, 1967.

[16] Jean-Paul Palewski, "Le Chili et nous," *Revue Juridique et Politique*, 18 (3), July–September 1964, p. 380.

[17] *Le Monde*, November 12–13, 1967.

[18] The French ambassador to Argentina who was briefly interrupted, in July 1968, by anti-imperialist slogans shouted at him while presenting prizes to young Argentinian painters, was, no doubt, being subjected to a novel experience. See *Le Monde*, July 19, 1968.

[19] The mutual esteem of French and Latin American leftists is, perhaps, sustained by a not-too-close contact. Carlos Quijano, director of the important left-wing weekly *Marcha* (Montevideo), complained to a French leftist guest that when in France he had been surprised at the "légèreté" with which French intellectuals of the left spoke of Latin America. The French leftist, on the other hand, in talking with Quijano, was made uneasy by the latter's sympathy for the politics of General de Gaulle. Jacques Arnault, *Journal de Voyage en Amérique Latine*, Vol. I, Paris, 1969, p. 126. The breach in 1971 between French intellectuals and Castro over the case of Heberto Padilla (Chapter 9.1) is, in the light of these differences, less surprising.

231

covered the position she once held in the military mission field in Peru and Brazil (Chapter 2.2), but she has increased her contacts with Latin American military establishments along with her Mirage and tank sales. In the first half of 1969 Brazil received visits from a French air matériel mission, a 40-man engineering mission from the Centre des hautes études de l'armement and a mission from the Institut des hautes études de la défense nationale.[20] Colombia's Mirage purchase was followed by technical assistance agreements for the training in France of Colombian air force pilots and mechanics by French air force personnel.[21]

France's sales of Mirages to Peru, Brazil, Argentina, and Colombia and of tanks to Argentina and Ecuador [22] have not only enabled her to replace some United States products and reduce United States influence. These and other military sales in Latin America have been important for France's foreign commerce and trade balance: In 1970 French sales of $1.3 billion of military equipment were 8 percent of her world export trade.

France's broader interest in reducing Latin American dependence on the United States has also been gratified. A decline in the political fortunes of the United States in Latin America and the increased Latin American interest in nonhemispheric contacts were entirely in accord with French governmental desires. They were also in part a result of French (and other) action, since a Latin American interest in nonhemispheric relations was dependent in part on welcoming signals from abroad.

4. *United Kingdom*

If France's postwar position in Latin America showed no very

[20] *Le Monde,* May 11–12, 1969.

[21] *Le Monde,* December 22 and December 26, 1970.

[22] Between 1968 and 1970 France sold to Peru 12 Mirage-5's and several Alouette helicopters; to Argentina 14 Mirage III's and a number of Alouette and WG-13 helicopters; to Brazil 16 Mirage III's, 7 Fouga-Magister jet trainers and several Paris liaison aircraft; and to Colombia 16 Mirage-5's. France has also sold AMX-13 tanks to Argentina and to Ecuador, armored cars to Ecuador's police for use against guerrillas, and 155 mm artillery to Argentina. Argentina's 14 Mirage III's were said to have cost her $49 million and Brazil's 16 Mirage-5's about $40 million. Venezuela reportedly ordered 15 Mirages in 1971. *Interavia,* XXV, August 1970, p. 983; *Le Monde,* September-December 1970, various issues.

striking change from its prewar status, that of Great Britain, on the contrary, showed a marked decline. The possibility of such a decline was, of course, all the greater because Great Britain, as compared with France, had so much more to lose in the region from the economic and political effects of World War II and the years that followed.

These years did not present Britain with grave crises in the Caribbean, but the dissolution of imperial power in India, Southeast Asia, the Middle East, and Africa prepared the way, together with Britain's unwillingness or inability to assume avoidable economic burden, for a partial withdrawal from the Caribbean. The failure of the Federation of the Indies and the East Caribbean Federation (Chapter 1.1) left the road open for each territory to follow its own penchant.

British governments showed no great enthusiasm for strong measures to maintain British rule or influence in the Western Hemisphere and certainly did not look for this policy of renunciation to produce the political aggravations that in fact occurred from sovereignty claims in Central and South America by Guatemala, Venezuela, and Argentina (Chapter 1.1), and in the Antarctic by Chile and Argentina (Chapter 1.3). However, in the total perspective of British concerns in Europe and elsewhere these aggravations have been minor. Britain's conflict with Argentina over the Falkland Islands did not prevent Argentina from expressing gratitude to the British tribunal that served in 1966 in the Encuentro River arbitration. A year later she accepted a British court of arbitration to settle a dispute in the Lapalena area and, still later, British mediation of her eighty-year-old conflict with Chile over two islands in the Beagle Channel.[23]

Apart from minor political problems created by territorial issues, Britain has for the most part succeeded in maintaining satisfactory relations with the Latin republics. The British ban on Argentinian and Uruguayan beef and lamb following an outbreak of foot-and-mouth disease, and subsequent limitations on imports after the ban was raised, caused in late 1967 and early 1968 severe tensions with Argentina similar to those France had experienced six months

[23] *The New York Times,* July 28, 1967; and *Marcha* (Montevideo), July 30, 1971, p. 6.

earlier. Great Britain has also suffered from some Latin American animus because of Commonwealth preferential trading. On the whole, however, France and the privileged trading positions in the EEC of the francophone African countries drew Latin American ire much more than did the United Kingdom and the Commonwealth.

It was in the economic—and not the political—sphere that the impact of World War II and its aftermath was, for Great Britain, harshest. From a 14 percent share of the Latin American market in 1938, the United Kingdom sank to a 9 percent share in the immediate postwar years; then as Japanese and West German penetration of the market increased, its share gradually drifted downward and stabilized at about 5 percent throughout the sixties. This made Britain the fourth ranking country after the United States, Germany, and Japan, compared with its prewar third place rank.

The United Kingdom, like most industrial countries, continued to buy more from Latin America than it sold. In 1965–1967 it was running annual visible trade deficits of about $350 million and in 1968–1969 deficits of about $250 million. Like France, Britain showed a substantial gain (about 14 percent) in 1970 in her trade with Latin America, reducing her trade deficit to about $73 million. These trade deficits were in part offset by surpluses from dividends, interest, shipping, insurance, and earnings from financial services. Britain's sales of military equipment, especially naval vessels, to Latin America, although less publicized than France's sales of her Mirage, have been substantial and should continue to have a favorable effect on British trade balances. The six British frigates ordered by Brazil, delivery of which is to begin in 1974, represent by themselves a $240 million order.

Britain's losses in the Latin American market were not the result of British trading interests elsewhere. The British government, at least, had sought, especially from 1965 on, to improve its trading position, but with only a slight show of success until 1970.

Britain still holds second place in Latin American foreign investments. Despite restrictions on investment abroad the United Kingdom still manages to provide substantial funds for investment, much of it, like France, from the reinvestment of profits (see Table 3.4). However, the approximately 4 billion in 1914 dollars of foreign investments in Latin America had sunk in the late sixties to perhaps 1.5 billion of current dollars.

5. *Italy and Spain*

Compared with Japan and West Germany, Italy and Spain have hardly achieved great successes in Latin America in the postwar years. But on the other hand, relative to their prewar positions in the region and relative to the objectives they have pursued in the postwar years, they have done better than have France and Great Britain.

As in the case of Japan and West Germany, Latin America continued to serve as a major postwar outlet for Italian and Spanish emigration, at least until the early sixties when Switzerland, France, and Germany began to offer more rewarding opportunities for emigrants (Chapter 5.1).

In the economic sphere, Spain and Italy more than held their own in Latin America, which has been for both of them an important economic region. In this respect Spain and Italy differ from the larger Western industrial countries, whose trade is increasingly among themselves. Considering the size of its economy, Italy's $600 million worth of imports from Latin America is impressive when compared with the United Kingdom's and Japan's $800 million or even Germany's $1,100 million.

Both Spain and Italy have increased their share of the Latin American market. Spain's share is only a modest 2 percent but has, nonetheless, more than doubled since 1948 (see Table 3.1). Her trade with Cuba was, during much of the sixties, larger than that of any other European country. Spain continued, however, to run a sizable negative trade balance with South America (with the exception of Chile) and regretted her exclusion from the Latin American Free Trade Association (LAFTA).[24] Italy's increase has been slight but she ranks nonetheless as the fifth trading partner of Latin America after the United States, Germany, Japan, and Britain, and in Argentina is a major economic power. Italy's investment position, especially in Argentina, is strong, and in 1960–1965 she ranked third in new investments in Latin America, very close to second-place Germany which, however, in 1966 began to outstrip her.[25] She has had some notable successes in winning capital

---

[24] *ABC* (Madrid), March 18, 1971. Although Spain's imports from Latin America exceed exports by about 50 percent, this is a smaller imbalance than in her other markets, where imports in 1970 exceeded exports by about 100 percent.

[25] Penelope Roper, *op. cit.,* p. 8.

construction contracts and also in the sale of military matériel, having sold 24 Macchi jet trainers to Argentina in 1968 [26] and 112 more to Brazil in 1970.[27]

In the political sphere Italy has established satisfactory positions, on the whole, in Latin America. While more or less resigned to the dominant presence of the United States, the Italian and Spanish governments could not accept with equanimity the possibility of a major increase in French influence.[28] That this did not in the long run occur was a satisfaction to both official Italy and Spain but owed more to the failure of France to maintain the impetus of its 1964 initiatives than to Italian or Spanish countermeasures (e.g., the Saragat–Fanfani visit).

Like Japan, Italy has been free of severe tensions with the Latin American states and the vicissitudes of its prewar and postwar political developments have little complicated its recent diplomacy in Latin America. Latin America illustrates as well as any region an Italian contention that no policy is the best foreign policy and that this has won Italy only friends. The Instituto Italo-Latino-americano may, at some auspicious future moment, serve a more ambitious Italian posture in Latin America (Chapter 9.5).

Unlike Italy, Spain's problem in Latin America was precisely to overcome political disabilities—those that stemmed from the sixteenth century as well as from 1936. These became increasingly severe after the failure of the Perón Madrid–Buenos Aires axis. Despite these handicaps Spain was able, in the mid-sixties—as the Civil War years and her Falange-dominated policies receded some-what into the background—to develop satisfactory relations with most of the Latin republics. They, together with the Arab countries, were largely responsible for Spain's successes in the votes of the 22nd and 23rd General Assemblies on Gibraltar as they had been earlier in assuring her entry into the United Nations. And if Spain has not succeeded in establishing full diplomatic relations with

[26] Alain Joxe and Cecilia Cadena, "Armamentismo dependiente: caso latinoamericano," *Estudios Internacionales* (Santiago de Chile), IV (14), July–September 1970, p. 73. This paper contains a valuable appendix (pp. 71–81) summarizing Argentinian, Brazilian, Chilean, and Peruvian military purchases between 1965 and May 1970.

[27] *The New York Times,* May 31, 1970.

[28] The Spanish were troubled not only by President de Gaulle's triumphal tour of Latin America, but also by that of President Saragat and Chancellor Erhardt.

Mexico, she has at least a commercial attaché in Mexico which permits an official connection between the two governments. These political successes were interrupted, probably only temporarily, in August 1971 when Cuba withdrew most of its Embassy personnel from Madrid following sharp disagreements between the two countries during discussions of a commercial accord. Although Spain has not achieved in Latin America the ambitions and the role some Spanish circles feel her historical and cultural ties entitle her to, at least she has largely overcome the reserve that still marked her relations with Latin America a decade ago.

6. *The Smaller Countries*

Of the smaller countries, among which, with apologies, we include Canada,[29] it is only the latter that has shown a substantial (relative) gain in exports to Latin America. From a trivial share of the Latin American market in 1938, Canada in 1968 reached approximately the same level as France or that of the Scandinavian countries taken together, that is, about 3 percent. Her share of world trade is greater than this. This "small" country had in 1969 a 5 percent share of the world market, that is, a share as large as Latin America's and greater than that of Africa or Southeast Asia.[30] Among the smaller countries, only the Middle East oil-exporting states (Kuwait, Saudi Arabia) have shown a similar increase.

The Dutch and Scandinavian shares have remained on the whole unchanged over the years. Switzerland has had a slight gain in its export trade with the Latin republics and Belgium a substantial decline. In the prewar and early postwar years Portugal's exports to and imports from Latin America were a substantial part of her trade. Since then Latin America has played a declining role in the Portuguese economy. A 1966 commercial accord with Brazil increased trade between the two countries but even with this assistance Portugal's exports to Brazil were, in 1969, only a little more than 1 percent of her export trade.

[29] The term "smaller country" seems to be reserved for large countries with small populations, small countries with large populations, small countries with small populations, and sometimes countries of any size that mostly mind their own business in world affairs.

[30] Department of External Affairs (Ottawa), Jean-Luc Pepin, *Canada's Trade with Developing Countries,* 1970, p. 3.

The failure of the smaller countries (Canada excepted) to play a larger role in the Latin American market has not been due to indifference or to more attractive trading opportunities elsewhere.[31] Most of these countries have exhibited an eagerness to protect or increase their sales in Latin America. Some, notably Sweden, Switzerland, and Holland, have investments in Central and South America that have been as or more important to them than their trade.

Few of these countries have political objectives in Latin America independent of their trade and investment interests. Diplomacy is largely a means of paving the way for economic transactions or smoothing over frictions arising from economic rivalry, as in the case of Scandinavian conflict with Latin American, especially Brazilian, shipping policy and shipping interests.

There is, however, a second set of smaller countries whose objectives in Latin America have been very largely political—Israel, the Arab states, South Africa, Portugal, Cyprus, Greece, and Turkey. Earlier, Israel and Portugal were from time to time rewarded for their efforts to mobilize support (Chapter 4.1), but their successes in the last sessions of the Assembly and Security Council have been few and achieved only with great difficulty.

7. The Soviet Union

Soviet political objectives in Latin America have varied, according to the ambitions and doctrines of different periods, from an early concern to develop Communist parties able to overthrow and wrest power from the bourgeoisie, to popular front tactics to enable these parties to increase their influence in government or within political alliances, or to enable them simply to support Latin American nationalism and thus encourage the Latin republics to decrease their contacts with and dependence on the United States.[32]

The Soviet Union was unsuccessful in the pursuit of its aim of overthrowing bourgeois governments. Attempts to overthrow the government in El Salvador (1932) and Brazil (1935) failed. The postwar period also opened inauspiciously for Soviet political

---

[31] Some have been able to make gains only in Cuba. Thus, Swedish imports from and exports to Cuba increased more than threefold in the years 1959–1964.

[32] Herbert S. Dinerstein, *Soviet Policy in Latin America*, The Rand Corporation, Santa Monica, RM-4957-PR, May 1966, pp. 2–3.

238

interests with the breaking by Chile (1947), Brazil (1947), and Colombia (1948) of diplomatic relations with the Soviet Union. In Chile, Communist influence was further reduced by the outlawing of the Communist party. In Guatemala Communist influence in government circles ended with the fall of Arbenz (1954). Between 1947 and 1952, the estimated membership of Latin American Communist parties dropped from about 376,000 to about 198,000.[32a] Given the cold war atmosphere following the Soviet blockade of West Berlin, the limited flexibility of Soviet doctrine and policy prior to the death of Stalin, and the relative disinterest of the Soviet Union in Latin America, these defeats probably altered little its opportunities to influence the official circles of the Latin republics or to increase its sometimes uncertain control over the Communist parties of the region.

The Cuban revolution and Castro's declaration of Marxist–Leninist loyalty in December 1961 finally gave the Soviet Union an enormous success, even though it transpired in a manner little conformable to Soviet theory and expectations and brought with it economic and political costs. Latin American coolness toward Soviet attempts to establish a military base in the Latin American region, the missile crisis of 1962, Castro's independence, and the resentments induced by Castro-inspired interventions in Latin America added up to substantial political costs. The gains were nonetheless considerable. For a Communist government, more or less dependent on Soviet goodwill, to control one of the wealthiest republics of Latin America,[33] one located in the Caribbean, which more than Central and South America has been viewed as an area of major strategic importance to the United States, was well beyond Soviet expectations or even hopes in the post-Stalin period.

Despite, and perhaps in part because of, the steady growth of Latin American nationalism, similar Communist successes in the

[32a] Rollie E. Poppino, *International Communism in Latin America: A History of the Movement, 1917–1963*, New York, 1964, Appendix II. Communist Party membership in Latin America has, except for Cuba, changed little since the early fifties. It has been estimated at about 200,000 for 1960 and about 180,000 for 1969 (exclusive of Cuba's 12,000 members in 1960 and 120,000 in 1969). W. Raymond Duncan, "Soviet Policy in Latin America since Khrushchev," *Orbis*, 15 (2), Summer 1971, p. 656.

[33] Cuba, before Castro, ranked only behind Uruguay and Venezuela in income per capita. Latin American Center, University of California, Los Angeles, *Statistical Abstract of Latin America 1961*, p. 33.

sixties did not occur. Guerrilla outbreaks in Peru, Venezuela, Guatemala, Colombia, and Bolivia were eliminated or largely contained. But Soviet prestige was not much involved in these defeats which brought more into question Cuba, left nationalist, and Maoist doctrine and strategy, than the cautious formulations of Soviet theoreticians and strategists.[34] This restraint enabled the Soviets to benefit more readily in the late sixties from a Latin American interest in shifting its political and economic relations away from the United States to Europe, Japan, and other areas. The moderation of Soviet pretensions in Latin America, its growing appreciation of Latin American realities,[35] the changes in official doctrine, with the replacement of the Soviets by the Chinese[36] as the

[34] Luis Corvalán, general secretary of the Chilean Communist party, now finds words like "revolution" too indelicate to use: "It is possible that in some countries the popular democratic forces will also come to power by means of elections. But it is obvious that in many other Latin American countries these forces will most likely gain power *by other means*" [emphasis added]. *Digest of the Soviet Press,* May 18, 1971, p. 38. Luis Carlos Prestes, secretary of the Brazilian Communist party, like Chile's a Soviet-line party, has published an article in a French Communist review condemning urban guerrilla tactics in Brazil. *Latin America* (London), January 8, 1971, p. 16. On recent Soviet policy in Latin America, see W. Raymond Duncan, *op. cit.,* pp. 643–669.

[35] The Latin American Institute of the USSR was founded in 1961. For earlier Soviet studies of Latin America and the work of the institute, see J. Gregory Oswald, "Contemporary Soviet Research in Latin America," *Latin American Research Review,* Vol. 1, Spring 1966, pp. 1–26. See also V. V. Volsky, "The Study of Latin America in the USSR," *Latin American Research Review,* 3 (1), pp. 77–87. Russell H. Bartley, "A Decade of Soviet Scholarship in Brazilian History: 1958–1968," *The Hispanic American Historical Review,* L (3), August 1970, pp. 445–466, also briefly describes Soviet research interests in Latin America as well as reviewing in greater detail their work on Brazil. *Soviet Image of Contemporary Latin America, A Documentary History, 1960–1968,* Austin (Texas) and London, 1970, provides translated excerpts from recent Soviet writings on Latin America. Martin H. Sable, *Latin American Studies in the Non-Western World and Eastern Europe,* Scarecrow Press, Metuchen, New Jersey, 1971, provides a valuable bibliography.

[36] For Chinese involvement in Latin America see Cecil Johnson, *Communist China and Latin America 1959–1967,* New York, 1970, and additional literature cited therein. Peking's interest in opening a dialogue with the United States and the West risks undermining China's "we are not a big power" posture as well as its desire to be spokesman for the Third World.

240

most radical revolutionaries, facilitated a rapprochement which has led to the resumption or initiation of Soviet diplomatic relations with the Latin republics. These successes were capped in 1970 by the election of a Marxist, Salvador Allende, to the presidency of Chile in an alliance with the Communist party of Chile. This event was all the more important to the Soviet Union because the prospects of armed revolutionary successes were not promising in Latin America and also because the electoral victory of a Marxist in Latin America provided justification of Soviet doctrine and policy over the more violent doctrines of radical left nationalist revolutionaries, especially since the Chilean Communist party is an orthodox adherent of the Soviet political line. The success of an electoral alliance that included the Chilean Communist party led the Soviet Union to encourage other Latin American Communist parties to follow the Chilean example. Primarily this has meant preparations for the November 1971 election in Uruguay where the Communist party is the largest of fifteen groups united in the *Frente Amplio,* the August 1972 election in Ecuador, the December 1973 election in Venezuela, and the April 1974 election in Colombia.[36a]

The Soviet Union now has diplomatic relations with all South American countries and with Mexico and Costa Rica in Central America. These relations will facilitate Soviet economic interests in the region if, as is likely, the expansion of economic activities is of interest to the Soviets for other than political reasons.[37] As the Soviet Union becomes increasingly a consumer society its import requirements are likely to become larger and more diversified. Although self-sufficient in many raw materials and foodstuffs, there are some Latin American products that it does not produce or produces in insufficient quantities, such as wool, rawhides, coffee,

[36a] *The Economist Foreign Report,* August 5, 1971.

[37] The USSR has made clear her interest in trade and economic collaboration with the industrial capitalist countries. See, for example, Ministry of Foreign Trade (Moscow), *Foreign Trade,* No. 5, 1971, pp. 6–7. How important, economically, trade with the Third World is for her is more difficult to say, although Western experts increasingly believe that Soviet aid policies have economic as well as political motives. Karel Holbik, *The United States, The Soviet Union, and the Third World,* Hamburg, 1968, p. 26. In any event, the Soviet Union has begun direct cargo service between Leningrad, Hamburg, the Low Countries, La Guaira, Guayaquil, Callao, and Chilean ports as far south as Valparaiso. *Latin America* (London), August 6, 1971, p. 251.

cacao, vegetable oils, and bananas.[38] Nonetheless whatever ambitions the Soviets may have had in the development of trade have hardly been fulfilled. The favorable East bloc trade balance with Latin America (including Cuba) that existed prior to Castro became thereafter a negative balance as Soviet bloc sales declined without a corresponding decrease in imports. After reaching a low point in 1961–1962, Soviet bloc total trade recovered and surpassed earlier figures, but is still trivial compared with the trade of Latin America's principal trading partners (Chapter 3.1). The Soviet Union reported a 23 percent increase in trade with Latin America between 1968 and 1969, almost entirely accounted for by increased imports from, not exports to, Latin America, but a year later, between 1969 and 1970, a 33 percent drop.[39] Nonetheless it is apparent that if the Soviets are able and willing to provide quality goods at competitive prices, a criterion that the Soviet bloc has not always met in its Latin American exports,[40] they at least have more receptive trading partners there than previously existed.

8. *The United States*

The United States has had, in the postwar period, broader interests and more ambitious objectives in Latin America than the nonhemispheric powers. It stood, therefore, both to gain and lose heavily in the pursuit of its goals.

Compared with the early postwar years, the present United States position in Latin America appears one of substantial deterioration. In part this is due to the inflation of its economic and political status in the region occasioned by the more or less enforced withdrawal and exclusion of allied and enemy nations from Latin

---

[38] N. Gladkov in *Ercilla* (Santiago de Chile), October 28–November 3, 1970.

[39] Ministry of Foreign Trade (Moscow), *Foreign Trade,* No. 6, 1970, p. 55, and *ibid.,* No. 5, 1971, p. 58. Soviet exports to the Latin republics in 1968 and 1969 were 20.3 and 22.6 million rubles respectively. Imports for the same two years were 74.2 and 93.9 million rubles. These figures are exclusive of Cuba, with which total trade declined from 812 million to 770 million rubles.

[40] Soviet Volga passenger cars, Soviet trolleybuses, and Gaz-69 jeeps sold to Colombia are said to have performed poorly. Still, these imports permitted Colombia an increase in her coffee exports to the Soviet Union. Alliance for Progress, *Weekly Newsletter,* February 2, 1970, p. 3.

America during World War II and the early postwar years of recuperation. The almost inevitable return—economically and politically—of the allied and enemy nations to Latin America as recuperation progressed and normalcy was reestablished could hardly have failed to affect adversely these newly won United States positions in the region.

These transitions are clearest in the field of trade. The United States share of the Latin American market rose from a little under 40 percent in the last prewar year (1938) to almost 60 percent ten years later in 1948, and then gradually declined until 1962 to somewhat over 40 percent as Germany, Japan, Italy, and other powers began to recover or enlarge their prewar commercial position (see Table 3.1). Despite the postwar decline the United States share is still approximately what it was prior to World War II, that is, about 40 percent.

The large United States share of the Latin American import market has not meant during the sixties a large trade balance in favor of the United States. From 1961 to 1969 the average annual balance was about $160 million in favor of the United States, not very sizable for a total annual trade of $8 billion. This surplus disappears and becomes a United States trade deficit with Latin America if one takes into account that some $200 million annually of Venezuelan oil is recorded as coming from the Netherlands Antilles because the oil is refined there before reaching the United States.[41] In 1970, however, the United States marked up a $900 million trade surplus with Latin America and followed this with about a $500 million surplus in the first half of 1971,[41a] despite United States trade difficulties during that year in other world regions.

Despite these recent favorable trade balances with Latin America, signs are multiplying that a decline in the United States share of the Latin American market may be setting in. Data for 1968–1970 show declines in United States shares in several South American countries, including Argentina, Brazil, Chile, Colombia, and Peru. However, the stability of these trends is uncertain since 1970–1971 figures (incomplete) show a good recovery of United

[41] John R. Petty, "The U.S.–Latin American Trade and Payments Relationships," *Inter-American Economic Affairs*, 24 (2), Autumn 1970, p. 88.
[41a] *Commerce Today*, March 8, 1971, p. 35.

States market shares, with gains in the important Brazilian, Mexican, Argentinian, and Peruvian markets.[42]

Data on import growth in individual Latin American markets in the five-year period 1964–1969 compared with United States exports to these markets in the same time period show that the United States lost ground relative to other exporters in Bolivia, Brazil, Ecuador, Paraguay, Peru, Uruguay, Venezuela, the Dominican Republic, Panama, and in all of the Central American Common Market countries (CACM). The United States just about held its own or lost only a little ground in Argentina and Mexico and gained ground in only three countries, Chile, Colombia, and Guyana. The EEC countries, on the other hand, gained ground in eight Latin American countries, including substantial gains in the important Brazilian and Mexican markets.[43] The decline in the United States share of the Latin American market, however, largely disappears if attention is confined to manufactured exports. The United States share for the 19 Latin American republics declined only 1 percent between 1962–1964 and 1968 and it increased 9 percent in the Guianas and the Caribbean islands.[44]

The trend, if any, being established by recent figures will not be fully evident for several years. Even then, however, their significance for the United States position in the Latin market will not be clear without taking into account at least two other factors.

[42] *Commerce Today,* October 18, 1971, pp. 34–35. Declines in market shares are generally accompanied by a rising absolute level of United States exports, although not in Colombia and Peru, where during the twelve months ending mid-1970 absolute declines occurred. See *ibid.,* various issues, but especially October 19, 1970, p. 38, and January 25, 1971, pp. 40–41. The United States share of world exports declined steadily from 16.4 percent in 1960 to 13.8 percent in 1970; and its share of manufactures from 23.8 percent in 1962–1964 to about 20.5 percent in 1970. Incomplete data suggest a small upturn in 1971. *Ibid.,* December 14, 1970, pp. 8–9, and September 6, 1971, p. 37.

[43] *Business International,* December 11, 1970, p. 397. The United States (relative) decline in all the CACM countries was largely due to the increased trade among the CACM countries themselves. The EEC share also declined in all these countries, although not as much as that of the United States.

[44] *Commerce Today,* December 28, 1970, pp. 12–13. "Manufactured exports cover chemicals, machinery, transport equipment, and other manufactures (principally metals, textiles and various nondurable consumer goods) and exclude processed food, fats and oils, mineral fuel products, firearms of war and ammunition."

First, the United States share of the market is, in a broader definition, not simply the goods exported from the 50 states, but also the goods sold to Latin America by United States enterprises in Latin America,[45] in Canada, and in Western Europe. Second, a decline in the United States share of the Latin American (or world) export market has to be interpreted in light of the relatively small role that international trade plays in its GNP, about 4 percent compared with the 10–35 percent for the principal industrial nations [46] whose economic well-being depends more largely on their export position.

The postwar return of European and Japanese enterprise to Latin America deprived United States firms of some important capital construction projects (Chapter 3.1), but in the field of private direct investment the demand and opportunities for capital in Latin America were so great and so varied that flows from the United States and other capital-exporting countries were only modestly inhibited by each other and much more by the attractions of other regions and, from time to time, by the political and economic conditions prevailing in Latin America, especially by expropriations and the fear of expropriations.

For particular United States enterprises and economic sectors substantial amounts of capital have been expropriated. Oil, other extractive industries, and utilities have been principally affected, although losses in Cuba covered, of course, a much wider range of enterprises. The loss of United States properties in Cuba with a

[45] In 1966 United States manufacturing (nonextractive) affiliates in Latin America had $5.9 billion in local sales, that is, about $1.5 billion more than United States exports to Latin America for the year. These manufacturing affiliates accounted for 37 percent of Latin American total manufactures and 41 percent of the region's exports of manufactured goods. Penelope Roper, *op. cit.*, pp. 17, 20–21.

[46] In 1968–1969 exports as a percent of GNP were: Japan 10, France 11, Italy 14, Britain 16, West Germany 19, the Netherlands 35, and Belgium 40. IMF, *International Financial Statistics,* XXIII (12), December 1970. Although United States exports are only 4 percent of her GNP, the latter is so large (in 1966, 46.5 percent of the non-Communist world GNP) that her exports equaled nonetheless almost 17 percent of the total exports of the non-Communist world. S. H. Roback and Kenneth Simmonds, "International Business—How Big Is It?" *Columbia Journal of World Business,* V (3), May–June 1970, p. 12. For this reason even a modest United States trade deficit can create difficulties for the United States balance of payments.

book value of slightly under $1 billion represented 12 percent of United States direct investment in Latin America in 1959.[47] One estimate of expropriations over the decade since Cuba is that it is "certainly less than one-tenth of net new investment," which, having been taken by the speaker as having an annual average of $700 million, places this estimate of expropriations at under $700 million for the decade.[48]

The United States Department of Commerce knows of no official estimates of expropriations and forced sales for the region.[49] In the absence of data, an analysis[50] of cases cited in *The New York Times* from January 1, 1960 to December 31, 1969, disclosed expropriations in Latin America during the decade of the sixties somewhere between $3.27 billion and $1.80 billion. Subtracting $1.15 billion for Cuba, other Latin American expropriations fall between $2.12 billion and $0.65 billion. The upper figure represents the presumed gross value of the property expropriated and the minimum figure represents property losses sustained on the assumption that all promises of compensation have been or will be fulfilled. Excluding Cuban losses, the estimated annual average expropriation rate falls somewhere between $212 million and $64.5 million. Since the average level of United States private direct investment in Latin America in the 1960s was $10.3 billion, the expropriation rate fell between 3 percent and 0.6 percent of the investment level.[51]

[47] Leland L. Johnson, "U.S. Business Interests in Cuba and the Rise of Castro," *World Politics*, XVII (3), April 1965, p. 422. The United States Foreign Claims Settlement Commission has received and docketed 1,143 claims by United States corporations asserting losses in Cuba in excess of $2.8 billion. Over 7,000 individual United States citizens have filed claims totaling $490 million. Foreign Claims Settlement Commission of the United States, *Annual Report,* 1969, p. 14.

[48] William D. Rogers, former president, Center for Inter-American Relations, in *Foreign Investment in Latin America: Past Policies and Future Trends,* published by Virginia Journal of International Law, 1970, p. 80.

[49] Personal communication, April 6, 1971.

[50] The following summary is based on Gregory A. Carter, *A Brief Review of Expropriation of United States-Owned Property in Latin America in the 1960s,* Ms, April 1971. In the text, "expropriation" refers to transfers of United States-owned property whether due to nationalization or forced sale. The non-Cuban expropriations represent 16 cases of which 4 were in Chile, 3 in Peru, 2 in Brazil, and 1 each in Argentina, Bolivia, Colombia, Ecuador, Guatemala, Mexico, and Venezuela.

[51] Gregory A. Carter, *op. cit.,* p. iii. Carter's lower bound corresponds closely with the estimate of William D. Rogers cited above.

The true valuation of properties expropriated, and more especially, of compensation paid, are generally confidential and it is difficult to provide more exact estimates. However, inspection of individual cases suggests that the true figure is probably well above $64.5 million per year.

For companies whose properties have been nationalized, the financial consequences depend largely on the profit rate, on the proportion of profits returned to the United States in preceding years, and on the length of time over which operations have continued. Thus, the enforced sale to Chile of Anaconda, which had operated profitably over a long period, contrasts with Bolivia's nationalization of Gulf Oil soon after it went into full operation on a 40-year concession agreement following an investment of $140 million.[52] Profit rates of nationalized companies can generally be assumed to be substantially above the rates reported in official studies. Petroleum affiliates, and during the period of high copper prices, the copper companies, had earning ratios well over 20 percent. For the decade of the sixties, returns on manufacturing investments were said to be approximately 12 percent both in developed and in less-developed countries.[53] However, a study of United States companies showed that the median corporation manager felt that an expected annual return on investment of 20 percent (before taxes) was needed to undertake operations in Latin America, a profit rate identical with that expected by the sample for foreign investments in other areas as well. Nineteen percent of managers said they expected profit rates of less than 15 percent, and 11 percent expected profit rates between 25 and 34 percent.[54]

The multinational corporation has been viewed as having a

[52] Bolivia agreed to pay $78.5 million to Gulf over a 20-year period, without interest, starting in 1973. Bolivia's French consultants had recommended $100 million. *Latin America* (London), September 18, 1970, p. 298.

[53] United States Department of Commerce, *Survey of Current Business,* 50 (10), October 1970, p. 32.

[54] Guy B. Meeker, "Fade-Out Joint Venture: Can It Work for Latin America?," *Inter-American Economic Affairs,* 24 (4), Spring 1971, p. 37. The interesting figures provided by this study should be treated with caution. The investigator sent questionnaires to 340 United States companies and received replies only from 90 (26 percent). On the specific question of the annual expected profit rate, only 70 of these 90 respondents replied. One is probably entitled to assume that the average anticipated or required profit rate would be increased if adequate answers were available from those who failed to reply to this question.

special advantage in forestalling expropriations, since a state may hesitate to alienate simultaneously several of the important capital-exporting countries and will be less able to play one country off against another.[55] A premium is placed on irregular means of protecting or promoting corporation interests because, powerful as the international and multinational [56] corporations may be, in legal actions against a state they are "weaker than Andorra." [57] They themselves have no standing before the International Court of Justice. Only a government can press a claim before the Court on their behalf, and when corporations are multinational, difficulties arise with respect to representation of claims.[58] In the case of national corporations, governments can attempt to intervene to obtain a settlement through espousal (government-to-government negotiations), by international arbitration or through the International Court. Thus, representation of private corporations by the state,

[55] It is probably for these reasons that Latin Americans have turned down a World Bank proposal for an international investment insurance agency that would have operated with an international arbitration board. In sensitive industrial sectors, multinational ownership is not likely to prevent state intervention, although it may lead to an above-average settlement. A Chilean copper refinery was placed under state control although Fiat of Italy owned one-quarter, United States interests another quarter, and British and Chilean nationals the remainder. *Le Monde,* September 19–20, 1971.

[56] The term "multinational corporation" is used here for corporations that derive their capital and management from more than one country. An "international corporation" is one that operates in several countries but is a national corporation with respect to management and ownership. In practice, however, these distinctions may be difficult to make. The term "transnational" is also used for both types of companies. For a listing of the subsidiaries and associate companies in Latin America (and elsewhere) of United States parent companies, see the invaluable *Who Owns Whom: International Subsidiaries of U.S. Companies 1970,* London, 1970.

[57] Virginia Journal of International Law, *op. cit.,* p. 16.

[58] Important in this area is the Barcelona Traction Light and Power Company case instituted before the International Court of Justice in 1962. "When a corporation is incorporated in Canada, operates primarily in Spain, and is owned primarily by Belgian interests, which states have standing to allege violations of international law by Spain harmful to the corporation?" For the answer, a review of the case and its impact on international law, see *Georgia Journal of International Comparative Law,* 1 (1), Fall 1970, pp. 179–187. That corporations (or their governments) find recourse to the IJC unsatisfactory is indicated by the absence of any further cases in 1970 on the IJC docket after the Barcelona Traction case was completed in February 1970.

sometimes viewed as an unwarranted support of private interests, is in some cases inherent in international law.

Most corporations prefer to use their own resources and those of private financial allies to carry on direct negotiations with foreign governments, although this does not by any means exclude appealing to their own government to utilize its means of leverage on their behalf.[59] Corporation financial transactions often exceed those of the governments with which they may be in conflict. General Motors sales of over $24 billion exceed the gross national product of all except the first 14 nations of the world. Its sales are greater than Argentina's GNP and four times greater than that of Colombia. General Motors, of course, is exceptional even among the giant corporations, but Standard Oil of New Jersey, Ford, Royal Dutch Shell, and others have sales exceeding the GNP of countries like Egypt, Chile, Peru, and Israel.[60] The importance of these larger corporations on the international financial and industrial scene is reflected in the fact that more than 80 percent of United States foreign direct investment is accounted for by 200 companies.[61]

The multinational corporations create problems not only in the legal and political sphere, but also for the analyst. International economic competition is still in considerable part a zero-sum game in which the gains of one nation in foreign commerce are the loss of some other nation. The multinational corporation, however, makes the attribution of income more difficult, although this is far from being a new problem and already exists wherever portfolio funds cross national boundaries. Names long associated with particular countries often turn out to have a different national ownership. The Bank of London and South America (BOLSA), a famous name in Great Britain and South America, is owned in part (25 percent) by the Mellon Bank of Pittsburgh. In Colombia, Land Rovers are assembled from components provided by a Spanish company, the Yugoslav Zastava car turns out to be a Fiat, while the Nissan is produced by Renault and the Simca by Chrysler.[62]

[59] Gulf Oil apparently asked the United States government, without success, to invoke the Hickenlooper Amendment in retaliation for the Bolivian expropriation. *The New York Times*, October 31, 1969.

[60] A similar situation can occur with state enterprises. The Bolivian state mining enterprise COMIBOL has a bigger budget than the state itself.

[61] United States Department of State, *Bulletin*, May 24, 1971, p. 670.

[62] *The New York Times*, January 25, 1971. As the result of a merger in late 1971, BOLSA is more properly called Lloyds and Bolsa International

The United States government also sustains financial losses from the nationalization of United States companies. These losses take the form of reduced tax income, tax write-offs of corporation losses, and possible losses on government insurance against expropriation. As of March 1, 1971, the Overseas Private Investment Corporation (OPIC), an agency of the United States government created in 1969, that insures against various investment risks, had paid only one claim ($320,000) in Latin America.[63] OPIC's investment insurance program (taken over from AID) involves about 3,500 coverages totalling $7.3 billion. As of December 31, 1969, United States corporations had paid $90.1 million in premiums and had received $3.5 million in payments. The latter, however, do not yet "reflect the vastly increased exposure and the losses to be expected on nearly $5 billion of insurance written in the last three years." The low rate of losses paid is largely due to the fact that "as a matter of policy, oil exploration, concession agreements and investments in subsurface assets are not insured." [64] Nationalization in Chile will drastically change OPIC's favorable ratio of premiums received to payments made. International Telephone and Telegraph has already filed a claim with OPIC for ITT property "virtually expropriated" by the Chilean government. ITT claims an investment of $153 million, two-thirds of which is covered by OPIC.[64a]

Government losses are also political. In the international sphere confiscations have signaled and dramatized the loss of United States influence, a loss only very partially mitigated by nationalizations affecting the property of other countries as well. Political losses occur also in the domestic field. The influential industrial interests

---

Bank Limited, "with additional support" from the Mellon National Bank and Trust Company of Pittsburgh. *The Economist,* October 16, 1971, pp. 94–95.

[63] Personal communication, March 1, 1971. This claim was for an expropriation in Haiti.

[64] OPIC, *An Introduction to the Overseas Private Investment Corporation,* November 1970, pp. 3–4. About $2.3 billion of United States investment in Latin America were insured against political risks between 1961 and the first half of fiscal 1971. The two most active periods were 1968 ($734 million) and the first half of 1970 ($415 million). United States House of Representatives, Committee on Foreign Affairs, *Development Assistance to Latin America 1961–1970,* April 14, 1971, p. 19.

[64a] *The New York Times,* September 16, 1971, and Alliance for Progress, *Weekly Newsletter,* November 1, 1971, p. 2.

affected, as well as congressional and some popular resentment, embarrass the United States government and require it to demonstrate a willingness and ability to satisfy domestic interests and opinions while at the same time it tries to prevent its long-term political objectives in Latin America from being compromised by these pressures.

Expropriation, or the threat of expropriation, have affected principally petroleum, mining and utilities.[64b] However a very large part of foreign investment is affected by increasing requirements for local control. This has met with some resistance from United States investors. Still, "Mexicanization," the requirement that most classes of foreign enterprises in Mexico be held 51 percent by local capital, did not discourage United States and other foreign capital from undertakings in Mexico, an indication that political stability and an expanding economy can overcome the hesitation of foreign entrepreneurs to relinquish control. In December 1970, the Andean countries, Colombia, Peru, Chile, Bolivia, and Ecuador agreed to a common regime for the control of foreign capital: All new foreign companies are to be owned 51 percent by local capital and all profits over 14 percent on invested capital must be reinvested. No foreign investments are to be allowed in utilities, transport, communications (advertising, radio, television, newspapers, magazines), and banking. Existing foreign enterprises must sell at least 51 percent of their captial to national investors within 15 years (20 years in Bolivia and Ecuador). Advantages of free trade arrangements among the five member states are reserved exclusively to national companies, joint ventures, and foreign corporations that agree to convert to a national or joint status.[65]

[64b] Mining, petroleum, and utilities represent a declining share of United States Latin American investment. From 1960 to 1969 the net book value of all United States direct investment in Latin America grew at an average annual rate of 5.7 percent while manufacturing investment grew at the rate of 12.4 percent. Sixty-nine percent of United States manufacturing investment is now concentrated in Argentina, Mexico, and Brazil. T. Graydon Upton, *op. cit.*, p. 4.

[65] In exchange, foreign enterprises are not to be expropriated without proper compensation and are guaranteed access to foreign exchange for the remission of profits and the liquidation of investments. Peru may require local participation sooner than 15 years. Colombia and Ecuador, more fearful about the effects of the pact on the flow of foreign investment, forced Chile, Peru, and Bolivia to weaken some of the conditions originally

Argentina also decided to take the path of "Argentinization" but reversed part of its policy of economic nationalism in order to re-encourage foreign investors. Nationalist groups in Argentina, however, pursued their own program of "Argentinization" by bombing Chrysler, Phillips Electric, Fiat, and Swift de la Plata.[66]

Despite increased control over foreign capital and uncertain political conditions, the book value of United States investments in Latin America continued to grow at the end of the decade, as did total earnings (see Table 3.3). Following a period of greatly increased preference for Canada and Western Europe, United States capital in 1968 and 1969 began to show a renewed interest in Latin America. Two enforced sales in Chile, an enforced utility sale in Peru, and the International Petroleum Corporation case in that country, did not prevent investments in the Latin republics from increasing in 1969 by $600 million.[67] In 1971, Occidental Petroleum signed a 35-year contract with Peru involving a seven-year exploration program and an investment of $50 million. However, the full effects of President Allende's program in Chile, of the Andean Pact, "Argentinization," and of new controls over banking and oil in Venezuela remain to be seen. The Overseas Private Investment Corporation reported in 1971 that they were receiving only three new applications for investment insurance per month, as compared with 22 per month in 1968.[68] The United States Department of Commerce anticipated a small decline in 1971 in plant and equipment expenditure by United States affiliates in Latin America as compared with accelerating expenditures in all other parts of the world.[69] The Council of the Americas, an or-

planned for the pact. Thus foreign capital was excluded from fewer fields than had originally been envisaged. The pact took effect on June 30, 1971. Since then further inroads have been made in the intent of the pact, including a decision of the Colombian supreme court that the pact's treatment of foreign capital is unconstitutional.

[66] *The New York Times,* May 31, 1971.

[67] *International Commerce,* October 5, 1970, p. 19.

[68] *Visión Letter,* June 23, 1971. The foregoing figures refer to all of OPIC's applications, but since Latin American investments comprise more than half of their insurance business, it reflects resistance to Latin American (as well as possibly other) investment.

[69] Senator Jacob Javits, Address to the American Chamber of Commerce of Mexico, April 14, 1971. See also Department of Commerce, *Survey of Current Business,* September 1971, pp. 27–28. These trends do not, of course, exclude rapidly increasing investment in some areas of Latin America, such as Mexico and Brazil.

ganization of 202 United States firms representing 85 percent of United States private investment in Latin America, claimed in early 1971 that 84 investment projects in the Andean countries had been deferred because of the Andean Pact. It is difficult to know how firm these investment commitments would have been had there been no Andean Pact, but it appears likely that a number of United States corporations will hesitate to accept joint ventures until sufficient experience under the Andean Pact has accumulated. The political climate of the West Coast South American nations will need to inspire the same confidence that made joint ventures in Mexico acceptable. United States net investment outflows still reflect the effect of recent Peruvian, Chilean, and Venezuelan investment policy. Although the total book value of United States Latin American investments increased in 1969, United States net investment outflows in that year dropped sharply as a result of decreased flows to Peru, Chile, and Venezuela.[70]

Although United States trade and investment face difficulties in Latin America, it has been in the political rather than in the economic sphere that the United States has suffered its most important setbacks. The Alliance for Progress, despite a substantial financial and technical effort, did not generally provide the hoped for political stability, attachment to democratic principles, cordial political relations, and rejection of left or Communist ideologies and political ties.[71] Nor did the Alliance produce the purely economic development gains that some hoped for. To be sure Latin America's "gross domestic product increased at a rate of 5 percent

[70] United States House of Representatives, Committee on Foreign Affairs, *op. cit.,* p. 18.

[71] One major case study of the effectiveness of the Alliance concludes that although economic objectives were not achieved, the "maintenance of Colombia's democratic political institutions through support of the succession of National Front governments . . . has been accomplished." This may be so, but it can hardly be established that the National Front governments of Colombia would have ceased to exist without the Alliance for Progress. See *Survey of the Alliance for Progress,* Subcommittee on American Republics Affairs, Committee on Foreign Relations, United States Senate, 91st Congress, 1st Session, Document 91–17, April 29, 1969, p. 669. Hereafter cited as *Survey of the Alliance for Progress.* For an attempt to determine quantitative relations between aid and political change in Latin America, see Charles Wolf, Jr., *The Political Effects of Economic Programs: Some Indications from Latin America,* The Rand Corporation, Santa Monica, RM-3901-ISA, February 1964.

for the decade as a whole. Although this rate, which went even higher during 1968 and 1969, reaching a level of 5.7 percent, can with good reason be described as inadequate, it does fulfill the goal established for developing countries, and exceeds the rate recorded by nations that are today highly industrialized at the same stage in their economic development." [72] On a per capita basis the result is less encouraging in most countries and even less so when the distribution of income in Latin America is taken into account.[73] In addition, the servicing of Latin America's past debts and new loans had already by the middle of the decade risen to about one-sixth of Latin American export earnings,[74] and in more recent years, to about one-half of United States aid expenditures.[75]

[72] Felipe Herrera, president of the Inter-American Development Bank, October 5, 1970, IADB press release. Despite a sizable literature on the Alliance for Progress, rigorous evaluations of United States aid to Latin America in terms of purely economic development goals are rare, no doubt because they are so difficult to make. Official reviews of the Alliance are generally favorable to it. A useful guide to these is provided by Willard L. Thorp, "Foreign Aid: A Report on the Reports," *Foreign Affairs*, April 1970, pp. 561–572. Quantitative studies are less encouraging. See, for example, Wendell C. Gordon, "Has Foreign Aid Been Overstated? International Aid and Development," *Inter-American Economic Affairs*, 21 (4), Spring 1968, p. 16.

[73] The annual rate of growth of Latin American per capita product between 1960 and 1967 was 1.7 percent. This is less than the annual per capita growth rate (2.0 percent) in the decade (1950–1960) preceding the Alliance for Progress. On a per capita basis the best gains (1960–1967) were made by Panama, 5.2 percent; Nicaragua, 4.1 percent; Guatemala, 3.0 percent; Peru, 3 percent; El Salvador, 2.9 percent; Bolivia, 2.9 percent; Mexico, 2.8 percent; Chile, 2.4 percent. Brazil and Argentina had per capita growth rates of 1.3 and 1.1 percent respectively, and Uruguay a decline of 1.1 percent. ECLA, *Economic Survey of Latin America 1968*, New York, 1970, p. 10. These national growth rates should be treated with great caution. National income figures and other data from many of the less-developed countries are highly unreliable. See Laurence Whitehead, "Basic Data in Poor Countries: The Bolivian Case," *Bulletin Oxford University Institute of Economics and Statistics*, 31 (3), August 1969, pp. 205–227, particularly pp. 222–225. On income distribution in Latin America, see United Nations, *Economic Survey of Latin America 1969*, New York, 1970, pp. 364–417.

[74] The debt service-export ratio was about one-fifth in Argentina, Brazil, and Chile. *Survey of the Alliance for Progress*, p. 142.

[75] Debt service payments declined, however, in 1969 to $2.2 billion as compared with $2.3 billion in 1968. Service payments on external debts as a percent of exports declined in all the major exporting countries. These per-

254

The role of the United States as a creditor is frequently over-estimated. Thus, of the $1.3 billion of foreign debts that Argentina is due to pay between May and December 1972 (and which no doubt will have to be refinanced), only $285 million is owed to the United States, less than is owed to Italy and a little less than is owed to West Germany. Similarly, the Peruvian $1.1 billion short-term debt was in 1971 mostly owed to West Germany, other European countries, and Japan rather than to the United States, and a little more than half of Chile's foreign public debt of $2.3 billion was owed to countries other than the United States.[76]

United States military assistance (matériel, training grants, and credit facilities) succeeded during a part of the postwar period in winning both military sales and a position of influence with the Latin American military and with governments interested in keeping their military happy. United States predominance in the sale of matériel to Latin America has, however, been smaller and less enduring than is commonly supposed. Perón, eager to free Argentina from dependence on United States arms, turned to Britain which, between 1945 and 1955, delivered 255 military jet aircraft to Latin America compared with only 32 by the United States. In the following decade, 1955–1965, the situation was reversed and the United States delivered 299 planes against 108 by Great Britain and 80 by France.[77] Nonetheless, in 1965, of 458 jet planes in

---

cents were in 1969: Argentina, 23.9; Mexico, 22.4; Uruguay, 18.8; Brazil, 17.9; Chile, 15.9; Peru, 13.8; Colombia, 11.2; Venezuela, 2.0. According to the World Bank, total Latin American debts on December 31, 1969, were $17.6 billion, of which $6.7 billion were official bilateral debts, $4.2 billion multilateral, and $6.7 billion private.

[76] *Latin America* (London), June 18, 1971, p. 195 and *The New York Times,* July 12, 1971. Economic development loans are now old enough so that repayments to the aid-giving countries are substantial. Thus, the United Kingdom at the end of the decade received repayments on earlier aid loans that were a little less than one-third of her current aid. Reg Prentice, M.P., "More Priority for Overseas Aid," *International Relations* (London), 46 (1), January 1970, p. 1.

[77] *Survey of the Alliance for Progress,* p. 127. Given the secrecy that sometimes surrounds the purchase of military equipment, it is generally wise to treat published figures on these matters with some reserve. Nonetheless, they are generally adequate for establishing the relative role played by the United States and the European nations in the provision of matériel to Latin America.

operation in Latin America less than half (220) were of United States origin.[78] Europe also competed vigorously with the United States in the provision of naval vessels. Between 1945 and 1965 the United States delivered 37 vessels, Great Britain 16, and other nations 12.[79]

United States military sales between 1962 and 1968 (of over $250 million exceeded those of Europe, but in 1967 Congress imposed restrictions on military credit assistance [80] and introduced legislation intended to discourage Latin American countries from buying "sophisticated" weapons (supersonic planes). The years 1967–1969 saw a complete reversal of Latin American buying patterns, with indignant Latin republics buying almost $200 million worth of armaments from Europe, more than double the amount spent in the United States. Britain, France, Canada, Italy, West Germany, and Spain sold nearly $1 billion worth of military goods to Latin America (1965–1970); Britain and France alone, in the two years 1969–1971, are estimated to have made sales of $600 million.[81]

The decline in United States military training assistance and military mission personnel, and the increased European military contact with Latin American military establishments, marked a deterioration in United States relations more significant than the loss of credit sales. Nonetheless, looking back at the sixties, the United States government and military could view the defeat and containment of guerrilla forces by Latin American military estab-

[78] Alain Joxe and Cecilia Cadena, *op. cit.,* p. 35.

[79] Most of these vessels were destroyers and destroyer escorts. *Survey of the Alliance for Progress,* p. 126. In 1965, of 79 Latin American naval vessels 44 were of United States origin, 22 from Great Britain, 6 from Italy, 5 from Canada, and 2 from Sweden. Alain Joxe and Cecilia Cadena, *op. cit.,* p. 35.

[80] United States aircraft firms normally require a 10–15 percent down payment and complete repayment in 5–7 years. Private commercial credit not guaranteed by the United States government costs between 11 and 12 percent, and if guaranteed by the government about 10 percent. British and French aircraft firms require down payments of 6–15 percent with the remainder to be paid over 8–10 years at an interest rate ranging from 5 to 8 percent. *Aircraft Sales in Latin America,* Subcommittee on Inter-American Affairs, Committee on Foreign Affairs, House, 91st Congress, 2d Session, April 29 and 30, 1970, p. 24.

[81] Statement of United States Secretary of Defense Melvin R. Laird, *The New York Times,* June 28, 1971.

lishments as in part due to United States military assistance programs, although, to be sure, how large a contribution these programs made to the attainment of these results is hardly clear.[82]

Although the United States derived some benefits from its economic and military assistance programs, many of them failed to endure. Ten years after the Alliance for Progress was initiated, the Soviet and Communist Chinese [83] presences were on the increase throughout Latin America. Chile had a Marxist president and a cabinet with several Communist members, although it is arguable that without the Alliance for Progress more such instances might have occurred. Relations with the Peruvian and Bolivian military-led governments were cool, although Peru's economic difficulties appeared to modify her attitudes a little and the overthrow of General José Torres in Bolivia promised at least a momentary respite from Bolivian hostility. The conflict over the 200-mile marine territorial and fishing limit had not been resolved, and in 1971 Ecuador was seizing United States tuna boats more vigorously than ever before. The United States attempt to isolate Cuba imposed substantial costs on both Cuba and the Soviet Union but succeeded only partially, and early in the new decade was facing further failure. Soviet naval incursions in the Caribbean raised once more the threat of foreign nuclear power in the hemisphere. The nuclear policies of Brazil and Argentina were little in accord with United States (and Soviet) preferences. Most South American countries were pursuing policies with respect to armaments, foreign

[82] For additional evaluations of the success of United States military assistance programs, see *Survey of the Alliance for Progress,* pp. 305–309.

[83] Chile's recognition of Communist China and the latter's resumption of relations with Cuba at an ambassadorial level mark what appear to be an increased Chinese interest in Latin America, an interest that like that of the Soviet Union may lead China to temper somewhat her attitude toward armed struggle in the Latin republics. Peking has been willing to reproduce articles from the regular Communist party presses of Brazil, Peru, and Bolivia in the *People's Daily* (Peking), has accorded little attention to the small Chinese-line parties, and, while paying attention to Latin American students, shows no fondness for revolutionary groups made up of intellectuals (instead of peasants). The *People's Daily* (November 20, 1970) has made a particular point of supporting Latin American legislation on the 200-mile limit for territorial waters. Communist China also donated $100,000 for relief work to Peru following the earthquake of 1970. *Latin America* (London), January 8, 1971, pp. 9–10.

investments, trade, and relations with Communist and other non-hemispheric powers that imposed increasing stresses on United States relations with them. Nongovernmental and opposition political groups—even those of a conservative persuasion—were often not more favorably disposed to the United States than those in power. Just as the successes of Japan in Latin America are magnified by the small costs it sustained in achieving them, so the failures of United States policy are deepened by the considerable costs incurred.

Virtual unanimity reigns with respect to the decline of United States prestige and influence in Latin America, a unanimity that helps, no doubt, to ensure that the judgment will prove correct. And yet despite the abuse of the United States in Latin American political and intellectual circles, United States standing as a scientific and military power is now apparently greater in South America than that of the Soviet Union and, it appears, it displaced the Soviet Union during the course of the decade.[84] Again, although Uruguayans condemned United States action in Vietnam, a 1968 poll by the Uruguayan Institute of Public Opinion showed that the present-day countrymen of José Enrique Rodó [85] esteem the North American Calibans about as highly as they do Frenchmen and Britons.[86]

The United States is also the country recognized in Latin America as providing by far the best opportunities. In this matter attitude surveys are clearly borne out by the widespread interest in Latin America in learning English (Chapter 9.10) and by emigration statistics.[87] In considering the United States standing in Latin

[84] From Gallup polls taken in 1959 and 1969. *The New York Times,* January 22, 1970.

[85] José Enrique Rodó (1871–1917) was the Uruguayan author of *Ariel* (1900), a work that achieved popularity through its comparison of the spiritual qualities of Latin Ariels with the gross materialism of North American Calibans.

[86] The percent of respondents having a very good or good opinion of the United States was 63, of France 63, of Great Britain 68, of Russia 20. Those with a bad or very bad opinion of the United States were 7 percent, of France 1 percent, of Great Britain 1 percent, of Russia 33 percent. EMNID, *Informationen* (Bielefeld), No. 10, 1968, p. A8.

[87] A Gallup poll taken in early 1971 in Uruguay and Brazil showed that of those Uruguayans and Brazilians interested in emigration (17 and 32 percent respectively), the United States was the country of emigration most frequently chosen. *The New York Times,* March 21, 1971.

America one must recognize that Latin Americans have had a long-standing love–hate relation with the United States and that the apparent decline in the latter's prestige is certainly not new and perhaps is no deeper than at other stages of Latin American– United States relations.[88]

Finally, some United States failures in Latin America are tempered by the recognition that they are often failures relative to United States governmental evaluations. This does not mean that in fact they necessarily affect the United States negatively or at least to the degree presumed in some government and private circles. One might suppose that this would be the more readily recognized since recent United States administrations have not shown a major preoccupation with Latin American policy or Latin American affairs. Thus the political failures have occurred in a region whose importance for the United States is by no means self-evident.[89]

[88] United States governments have generally been concerned to promote affection for the United States among foreigners, although it has sometimes managed to undo what United States citizens by themselves are often able to accomplish. Canada's secretary of state for external affairs, Mitchell Sharp, has pointed out the dangers of basing foreign policy on such impulses: "To be liked and to be regarded as good fellows are not ends in themselves; they are a reflection of but not a substitute for policy." Department of External Affairs (Ottawa), Press Release No. 70/15, October 1970, p. 4.

[89] The widespread view that Latin America is or will shortly become a region of great importance to the Western world has been noted above ("Latin American Potential," Chapter 4.2). David Bronheim believes "that there is very little in Latin America that vitally affects the United States national interest." He points out that three groups stress the contrary view: one, Latin American Marxists and intellectuals who "are determined to persist in their belief that the strength of the United States is directly connected with its exploitation of Latin America"; two, the United States business community with investments in Latin America; three, government and private circles with long-standing connections in and affection for Latin America and whose emphasis on the vital importance of Latin America for the United States has largely a sentimental origin. David Bronheim, "Relations Between the United States and Latin America," *International Affairs* (London), 46 (3), July 1970, p. 505. For a statement emphasizing the disinterest of United States political leaders in Latin America, see an interview with Professor John Plank, formerly of the United States State Department, in *Panorama* (Buenos Aires), September 28, 1971, p. 55. See also *Washington Post*, September 9, 1971.

13. Interpretations

OUR analysis has already suggested a number of explanations for the various successes, difficulties, and failures that the foreign powers encountered in Latin America. It remains to add some observations of a broader character suggested, but not necessarily demonstrated, by these experiences in interstate relations.

1. *Hubris* [1]

Societies are highly resistant to conscious attempts to control their direction and rate of change. Changes may indeed be effected but they are not often of the magnitude or the character intended. The attempt of the United States in the sixties to reshape the Latin societies, to alter their rate of development, and to oppose changes of which it disapproved, discounted the intractability of societies, especially to outside control. This disregard stemmed, in part, from a failure to recognize that these ambitious objectives required modifications in important properties of the societies that could not be effected simply by influencing foreign governments.

Soviet attempts in earlier years to achieve revolutionary overthrows of Latin American governments and to institute Communist social orders, and Nazi Germany's efforts in the thirties to shape some parts of Latin America in its own image were also overreaching attempts to change societies, although Soviet expectations of

---

[1] By *hubris* the Greeks denominated a presumption so great that it verged on impiety. Ambition is commendable but punishable when it reflects a boundless self-assurance.

success were probably on the whole very modest.[2] The Nazis and the Soviets organized or supported political parties within the societies to perform the desired transformation, although outside direction and resources counted heavily. United States political intervention was on a narrower scale. Opposition to political movements provided a less effective basis for mass action and political influence than did the promotion of movements for radical social change by the left and by the right. The instruments by which the United States sought to effect change scarcely provided the leverage needed to achieve effects of the magnitude aimed at.

The three countries that pursued these ambitious transformations had several things in common. All three were major powers. All were motivated by actual or potential conflicts in the international arena, that is, by national security considerations, a motive sufficiently vital to induce the pursuit of far-reaching objectives. And all three had claims to represent the future evolution of mankind, although the "American way of life" was, to be sure, not as sharply delineated, except by example, as its two competitors.

2. *The Managers*

The temptation of the United States government to undertake a task in Latin America beyond its competence and resources was strengthened by its confidence in the relevance and quality of its technical and managerial skills. Technical personnel—economists and other social scientists, educationists, military men, communications specialists, among others—were representatives of a generation with an exaggerated sense of their understanding of the social environment and of the transforming power of their skills, a confidence easier to sustain given their limited comprehension in many cases of the political and social processes characteristic of the various Latin states. It seemed not to be appreciated in government and some professional circles that the skills that made the Apollo mission a reasonable undertaking were not indicative of the availability of knowledge relevant for economic and political "engineering" in Latin America. A more advanced state of knowledge in these areas would not have altered the situation greatly, since an essential

---

[2] France momentarily in the mid-sixties, under de Gaulle, also seemed about to pursue an ambitious objective in Latin America which, however, was permitted to lapse—very likely because France's resources did not correspond to the scope of her ambitions.

difference between physical and social engineering is not their relative state of knowledge but the nature of the materials worked on, a difference sometimes ignored. The "hostile" environment of outer space was in fact neutral and indifferent, characteristics that scarcely describe the Latin American or any other social environment. Had the planners and managers of the Alliance for Progress developed their designs a few years later when the United States government and people were finding it difficult to control problems in their own country—inflation, unemployment, disaffection, violence, addiction, racial conflict—they might conceivably have been more sensitive to the intractability of social systems. As it was, the greater confidence of the early sixties did nothing to restrain their pursuit of ambitious objectives in societies whose governments, peoples, and social mechanisms they understood and controlled even less than their own.[3]

Confidence in technical and managerial skills implied that success depended on the adequacy of the resources for putting these skills to work. The apparent plenitude of the resources made available to the Alliance for Progress was thus an assurance of success. Large sums provided confidence through the imposing nature of large numbers and their ability to inhibit the contemplation of failure.

The effects of professional self-confidence were intensified by professional vested interests which, in their turn, were reinforced by the magnitude of United States activities in Latin America and other Third World countries. An important sector of professional opportunities became associated with these activities. At the same time the increased demand for professional personnel increased the risk of a reduced level of competence. Thus day-to-day United States policy and action in Latin America were increasingly dispersed into the hands of persons whose professional training and experience failed to provide them with the political understanding that was essential in almost all spheres of action in Latin America.[4]

---

[3] By contrast, German inexperience in Third World affairs so undermined the confidence of German officials that during the early years of the German aid program a French or British visitor to Bonn was welcomed as an expert "for no better reason than the status of his country as a former colonial power." John White, *German Aid*, London, 1965, p. 63.

[4] Project Camelot—a $6 million study designed by a university group for the Department of the Army to study revolutionary currents and their control, and which led to a minor political disaster for the United States in

The required political understanding was not always one specific to Latin America, useful as that would have been. In many instances a greater general sensitivity to the role of political and social forces in societies would have preserved technical practitioners from applying "models" that ignored factors of overriding importance.

The Department of State 1970 plan for reform suggests that the authority and prestige of specialists and managers has now invaded its corridors. The department "has relied too long on the 'generalist' and has been slow to recruit and develop officers in the wide range of special aptitudes, skills, and knowledge which the new diplomacy requires." What the new diplomacy requires is "a new breed of diplomat-managers, just as able as the best of the old school, but equipped with up-to-date techniques and backed by a Department organized on modern management principles." [5] These "up-to-date techniques" have, in fact, not demonstrated their superior relevance for the tasks of United States foreign policy. Characteristically, reform has focused less on substantive issues than on improving management skills and devising procedures for the study of issues, devising procedures being, no doubt, a more congenial object of attention than the issues themselves.

3. *Contradictions*

The larger a power, the more far-reaching and numerous will be its objectives in Latin America. The more numerous these objectives and the means put at their disposal, the greater is the probability that they will lead to contradictory and self-defeating lines of action. These contradictions occur both among the multiple means used to support a single program devoted to a single goal, and also among distinct major objectives and the various instrumentalities

---

1965 in Latin America, especially in Chile—illustrates several of the problems: (1) two professional groups, military and social scientists, (2) with skills largely irrelevant to and inadequate for the particular task undertaken, (3) an ill-conceived operation made more attractive by the professional opportunities afforded by a sizable amount of money, (4) a political ineptness not forestalled by a diplomatic service not informed of the action being taken. A brief account of the Camelot affair and some of the issues raised by it can be found in Kalman H. Silvert, *The Conflict Society: Reaction and Revolution in Latin America*, New York, 1966 (revised edition), Chap. 9, "American Academic Ethics and Social Research Abroad."

[5] *Diplomacy for the 70s*, United States Department of State publication 8551, Washington, D.C., 1970, pp. 4–5.

by which they are pursued. One premise of the Alliance for Progress was "the simultaneous compatibility of all objectives: economic growth, social equity, political stability, constitutional democracy, promotion of United States private economic interests, and protection of the United States national security." [6]

United States efforts to help Latin American military establishments to be more effective forces in internal security missions provide a characteristic example of actions at cross purposes within a single program. Effectiveness meant being politically as well as technically effective, since a military force alienated from the population or important sectors of it could be as ineffective as a poorly trained one. However, the training and advisory relations between the United States and several of the Latin militaries led to such a close identification of the Latin American military with the United States that it weakened the position of the military vis-à-vis their own people and often was a source of embarrassment to them. [7] Thus the pursuit of technical efficiency sometimes reduced political effectiveness. In order to increase the latter the United States provided support for civic action programs to improve the image of the Latin American military establishments. But this United States support for a long-standing program of Latin origin compromised its success by once again introducing an alien presence.

Civil programs were even more susceptible to self-defeating contradictions, being more numerous and involving much larger funds and more personnel. Economic aid intended both to buy political support for United States policies and to promote economic development often could not pursue one objective without injury to the other. As they were administered, almost all programs involved a large amount of United States intervention and paternalism;

[6] Abraham F. Lowenthal, "Alliance Rhetoric for Latin American Reality," *Foreign Affairs,* April 1970, pp. 499–500.

[7] General Maldonado (Colombia) illustrates the sensitivity of some Latin American military men to their dependence or alleged dependence on the United States: "As for the so-called American advisors, personally I haven't met any in four years of campaigning. . . . Between you and me, we really don't need the Americans. On the contrary, officers of other Latin American countries come to us to take courses in our anti-guerrilla school." *Le Monde,* February 25, 1967. For a balanced discussion of the relation between United States assistance and Colombian anti-guerrilla operations and doctrine, see Richard L. Maullin, *Soldiers, Guerrillas and Politics in Colombia,* R-630-ARPA, Rand Corporation, Santa Monica, November 1970.

264

consequently, they conflicted with the aim of building up influence and goodwill by provoking a persistent aggravation of relations.

The pursuit of contradictory objectives and programs that involve offsetting consequences occurs in the behavior of other countries as well. From 1919 when Mikhail Borodin arrived in Mexico, began to organize Communist activity, and held conversations with President Venustiano Carranza, until 1971 when, during a period of greatly increased Soviet diplomatic activity in Latin America, Mexico and Ecuador ordered Soviet diplomats out of the country, Soviet action in Latin America (as elsewhere) has been distinguished by persistent attempts to cultivate diplomatic relations while at the same time using local Communist parties and Soviet intelligence, trade, and diplomatic personnel in antigovernment acts. This dual line of action led to repeated breaches of relations with Latin American governments,[8] although tolerance by some governments for Soviet political interventions has at times seemed greater than that accorded to other governments. The Soviets appear to benefit in Latin America, as elsewhere, from a view that propaganda and subversion are so ingrained a feature of Soviet behavior that it would be petulant to expect Soviet officials to observe the same degree of discretion and restraint required of others. Nonetheless, the Soviet Union suffered a number of defeats in Latin America as a result of her simultaneous pursuit of these objectives. An examination of these cases suggests that a more subtle behavior might have enabled the Soviets to carry off both lines of their policy with even greater success.

Conflicting or offsetting programs and objectives occur not only among a foreign power's activities in Latin America but between its Latin American activities and its actions in other parts of the world. The more powerful a country, the more extensive are its relations and activities in various parts of the world. This diversity and multiplicity of relations almost inevitably result in activities that conflict with objectives pursued in Latin America. Thus United Kingdom objectives vis-à-vis the Commonwealth, and French ob-

[8] For examples of the foregoing, see the Introduction (pp. 1–65) to Stephen Clissold (ed.), *Soviet Relations with Latin America, 1918–1968: A Documentary Survey*, New York and London, 1970. Also useful are J. Gregory Oswald and Arthur J. Strover (eds.), *The Soviet Union and Latin America*, New York, 1970, and J. Gregory Oswald, *Soviet Image of Latin America: A Documentary History 1960–1968*, Austin, Texas, 1970.

jectives vis-à-vis the francophone countries of the EEC, undercut British and French objectives in Latin America. Indeed the numerous conflicts with Latin America occasioned by French action in other parts of the world (see Chapter 12.3) illustrate very well that even a power whose political and economic relations with Latin America are not very close can still find its foreign relations around the world a source of embarrassment to its relatively limited goals in Latin America. Similarly, Germany's pursuit in 1970 of a rapprochement with Eastern Europe made more difficult her attempt to prevent the recognition of East Germany by Latin American and other Third World countries.[9] Germany's relatively close alignment with United States foreign policy has also made her politically suspect to Chile's far left. Thus both West Germany's recent relations with the Soviet bloc and her past and present relations with the United States have made her position in the new Chile more difficult.

Soviet, East German, and UAR attempts to cultivate Latin American governments were undercut by their participation in the Havana Tricontinental Congress. Soviet attempts (in support of East Germany) to exclude West Germany from United Nations deliberations on economic aid irritated Latin American and other Third World countries which are appreciative of West German aid. Soviet support for a 12-mile territorial sea limit will confront it in 1973 (at the projected conference on International Law of the Sea in Geneva) with a choice of modifying its position or antagonizing a number of Latin American countries that claim a 200-mile limit. The Soviet ambassador to Ecuador has already run into difficulties. Following a news conference, he was accused in Ecuador of doing "diplomatic pirouettes." [10]

As Japan begins to play a larger role in world affairs, it, too, no doubt will begin to suffer from the incompatibilities that plague other major powers. In the past decade, however, Japan's limited

[9] Prior to Chile's recognition of East Germany, Carlos Altamirano, secretary general of Chile's Partido Socialista, pointed out: "We have seen that the Federal Republic has begun to resolve its basic problems with the USSR. If Federal Germany comes to an understanding with the USSR, with Poland, and recognizes the Oder-Neisse line, and initiates conversations with the Democratic German Republic, I do not see how she can take reprisals against our country [for recognizing East Germany]." Joaquin Andrade, "Chile, el enfrentamiento inevitable," *Punto Final, Documentos* (Santiago de Chile), Supplement to Issue 120, December 22, 1970.

[10] *The New York Times,* March 28, 1971.

266

role in world political affairs has largely protected it from these difficulties.

Conflicts or incompatibilities within single programs of modest size aimed at a single objective are largely avoidable. The pursuit of activities in one part of the globe that are dysfunctional for relations in other parts is, however, another matter. The foreign powers in Latin America cannot possibly avoid all these incompatibilities but can only try to minimize the damage that they entail.

4. *The Home Front*

The activities of foreign governments and private groups in Latin America are affected by their home fronts, which may be more or less advantageous for the competitive struggle in Latin America in which they are engaged. In part, the home front represents for each government a set of domestic priorities and objectives that may, like its various worldwide activities, conflict with its aims in Central and South America. This is evident enough when tariffs or budgetary issues conflict with trade and aid policy. But conflict occurs also in numerous areas where it is least anticipated. Thus United States antipollution measures have complicated relations with Venezuela whose oil has a high sulphur content, and marijuana consumption in the United States created problems in United States–Mexican relations. West German domestic taxes on coffee consumption antagonized the Latin coffee-producing countries, which resented a German mode of raising tax monies that reduced its consumption of coffee.

The divergence of interests and policies among the various branches and agencies of government, among private groups, and between government and private groups, affect the success of their respective aims in Latin America. In the United States, conflicts between the Administration and Congress set some limits generally on the ability of either to attain its full objective, but even if one of the two concedes to the other, the initial domestic dissension often has had in the meantime unfavorable repercussions in Latin America and on the attainment of objectives. Congressional protectionism has repeatedly clashed with Administration desires for fewer trade restrictions and has produced at times a paralysis of trade policy and at other times an apparent oscillation of intention that unnerves Latin American officials and businessmen equally. The unanimous adoption by the Latin American countries in the

267

February 1970 Caracas meeting of the Inter-American Economic and Social Council of a resolution requiring that the United States pay compensation to the Latin republics for any damages to them resulting from future violations of a United States "stand still" commitment, that is, a commitment not to impose any new restrictions on trade with Latin America, was a disregard (perhaps intentional) of the realities of United States governmental structure. No United States representative could have put his signature to such a resolution, but the Latin American countries nonetheless included the clause in the final resolution, making a concession to reality by placing it within brackets to show that this portion was not acceptable to the United States.[11] Responsibility for these Latin American attitudes partly rested on imprudent statements reflecting Executive or Administration hopes and intentions that did not make clear the uncertainties of Congressional action. Accustomed to a strong presidential or executive regime in their own countries, some Latin Americans are led to accord still greater weight to such statements than is intended by United States spokesmen.

The United States position in Latin America is equally affected by government dissension over an issue almost as important to Latin America as trade, namely, economic and military aid. The United States Congress became in the late sixties increasingly impatient with United States aid commitments to Latin America. It forced reductions in bilateral economic aid, supported cuts in military assistance, and opposed the sale of military jet planes. United States military observers had a more accurate appreciation of the futility of United States attempts (both by Congress and by the Administration) to prevent South American military establishments from acquiring advanced weapons. United States concern with the effect of military purchases on economic development and on a possible arms race led, predictably enough, to Latin American purchases of European equipment. At the same time, it incurred Latin American ill-will, thus producing a setback for both United States political and economic objectives.[12]

---

[11] *The New York Times,* February 7, 1970.

[12] Even in direct discussion of these matters some congressmen have seemed unwilling to accept the possibility that United States action might lead to even greater military expenditures by Latin American countries because of their purchase of expensive European equipment. For the Peruvian case, see the testimony and statement of Luigi Einaudi in *United*

Leaving aside the considerable effect on Latin American governments and private groups of a greater or lesser amount of aid and of a more or less liberal trade policy, conflicts between the Executive and Congress affect Latin American–United States relations by increasing uncertainty on both sides and providing a longer period of aggravated attention than a decision, taken without a long buildup of prior publicity, would produce. This is a disadvantage that centrally managed and *dirigiste* states, whose decision processes are less open to observation, largely avoid. That Soviet credits can be committed quickly and dramatically, without long prior debate as in the United States, facilitates their political effectiveness which is, perhaps, only gradually dissipated by the lag in actual expenditures.

Conflicts within the Executive itself are generally less visible but account, nonetheless, for some of the difficulties of governmental action in foreign areas. When French executive responsibility for the underdeveloped countries was decentralized, French ambassadors in Third World countries, but more particularly in Africa, were embarrassed by having to deal with three different and competitive services, the Foreign Affairs Ministry, the Secretary of State for Technical Cooperation, and the Secretary-General for African Affairs.

In the United States the White House has sometimes been more responsive to Congress than to the State Department on issues important to Latin America. Different departments of the govern-

---

States Relations with Peru, Hearings before the Subcommittee on Western Hemisphere Affairs, Committee on Foreign Relations, United States Senate, April 14–17, 1969, Washington, D.C., 1969, pp. 1–51.

An additional concern, that United States arms sales caused military takeovers, ignored that military coups are not civil wars; that Latin American military establishments have more than enough weapons to mount a coup irrespective of military assistance; and that military coups in Latin America have a long history antedating United States military assistance. A recent attempt to study Latin American military coups is Egil Fossum, "Factors Influencing the Occurrence of Military Coups d'Etat in Latin America," *Journal of Peace Research* (Oslo), No. 3, 1967, pp. 228–251. This investigator apparently did not consider it worthwhile including military aid among his eleven variables. In 1971 a report of a Foreign Affairs subcommittee of the U.S. House of Representatives concluded that "there is no convincing evidence that MAP (Military Assistance Program) training has encouraged military takeovers of governmental power in recipient countries." *Washington Post,* April 5, 1971.

ment also acquire reputations for being more or less "understanding" of the position of foreign governments. The State Department almost inevitably attaches greater value to "good relations" than do government departments that have more concern for private or other government interests. Characteristically, a Japanese minister negotiating a curb on Japanese textile exports to the United States thought that the State Department might take a softer stand on the dispute than had the Commerce Department.[13] When the United States Export-Import Bank refused to grant Chile credits to buy three Boeing planes until Chile made clear its plan of compensation for nationalized copper properties (see Chapter 4.6), President Salvador Allende regretted the decision but found that "it would be more regrettable if it had been prompted by the State Department." [13a]

In the West German ministries Latin American and most other country-oriented interests are represented at a lower level of the government hierarchies than in the United States, France, and Great Britain. This reduces conflicts within the government between Latin American policies and policies concerned with other regions, but this advantage is offset by a neglect of opportunities for action in Latin America to which a Latin American office would be more alert.[14]

Western governments rarely enjoy a relationship of perfect amity with their business communities. The diversity of interests within each of the latter hinders, in any case, government policies toward Latin America from satisfying all sectors of their business worlds. Disagreements between government and business on purely economic issues in Latin America are frequent, but the most characteristic source of disagreement affecting government policy is the conflict between government political aims and business commercial aims. Thus Administration political motives for supporting and

[13] *The New York Times,* June 21, 1970.

[13a] *Latin America* (London), August 20, 1971, p. 1.

[14] Albrecht von Gleich, *Germany and Latin America,* The Rand Corporation, Santa Monica, RM-5523-RC, 1968, pp. 28–29. Because the entry of German specialists on Latin America into government positions of responsibility is hindered by the limited amount of country-oriented activity in the ministries, fewer Germans find Latin American affairs an attractive field of specialization.

270

aiding Central and South American common market and free trade zones clashed with United States business fears that such developments threatened United States commercial interests.[15]

Election speeches and other forms of United States political debate are meant for domestic audiences but sometimes have repercussions abroad not anticipated by their authors. Congressional hearings and other settings in which representatives and senators express their views are often treated in Latin America as conveying Administration or predominant United States opinion. Nongovernmental expressions of opinion play a similar role. A Washington *Post* editorial in 1967 attacking the Peruvian government for its intention to acquire jet aircraft resulted in a sharp reaction in government and political circles in Lima and made more certain the action to which the *Post* objected. If diplomacy errs sometimes on the side of excessive delicacy, the "plain man" also errs in supposing that "plain speaking" is necessarily the way to get things done.

This diversity of United States voices is often exploited in Latin America in order to characterize the United States in whatever way is convenient for the speaker. Former President Lleras Restrepo of Colombia, in an address to his countrymen, pointed out, probably with little effect, that "In speaking of the United States, people personify the country as if it were one person. . . . But we must abandon this idea and convince ourselves that our relations with the United States have to do with a very complex country. . . ."[16]

Western European governments have also found that legislators and journalists can aggravate relations, but their more limited relations with Latin America have led to fewer incidents of this sort.[17] This relative immunity is further enhanced by a restraint practiced by most European countries that contrasts sharply with United States private, but especially government, practices of making public considerable information on government and private operations.

[15] See *Hearings*, Senate Joint Resolution 53, Committee on Foreign Relations, 90th Congress, 1st Session, 1967, particularly pp. 26–29.

[16] *The New York Times*, July 4, 1969.

[17] Of course, even a controlled press and a government newspaper may commit indiscretions. Castro had to castigate *Granma* for revealing prematurely that Cuba was preparing to buy 120,000 tons of fertilizer from France. "A new idiocy . . . that risks collapsing the negotiations." *Le Monde,* February 28, 1967.

Partly due to a self-protective discretion and partly, perhaps, to lack of funds for statistical reporting, the scope of European private enterprise in Latin America is not always easy to determine. The visibility of United States companies and their disinterest for the most part in protective coloration, together with government publication of detailed data on United States investments, income, profits, and transfers of funds, contrasts with European discretion and nondisclosure on these matters. United States disclosures are, notes a British observer, "laudable, but expose them to criticism avoided by other countries," for example, Italy, whose discreet business enterprises in Latin America are more extensive than ordinary observation is likely to reveal.[18]

5. *Responses to Failure*

Difficulties and failures may suggest to both the political and managerial temperaments not certain limitations imposed by the nature of the social–political reality, but rather failure along remediable dimensions. Not the principal goals nor the basic understanding of the situation but rather the means employed are subjected to review.

This response is partly due to the long-term character of important commitments like a ten-year Alliance for Progress. Initial difficulties can be disregarded in an enterprise whose success depends on a long-term effort, and even later disappointments are tolerable in the light of expectations of ultimate success. In the meantime, the effort mobilized has become sufficiently imposing in manpower, domestic political import, acquired domestic interests, and foreign habituation to become less subject to radical surgery. The multiplicity of special programs and the lack of clear definition of what success with respect to them mean, make it easier to defer the day of reckoning or to make reckonings that promise success. Instrumentalities originally intended to promote some more or less clearly acknowledged end take on a life of their own and generate a set of purely internal program goals.

[18] Penelope Roper, *Investment in Latin America,* The Economist Intelligence Unit, London, 1970, p. 9. The large amount of detailed data on foreign investment published by the United States government is by no means free from error, more especially with respect to profit rates (see Chapter 12.8), but provides a more adequate basis for analysis than the data released by European governments.

272

In the early stages of ambitious programs, program leaders are prone to meet failing expectations by broadening the attack through the introduction of additional instruments, programs, and resources. This increases, rather than decreases, the probability of failure since it introduces more elements of incompatibility, multiplies the previously existing errors and difficulties which were left unchanged, and increases the frictions resulting from an overly prominent foreign presence.

The supposition that difficulties can be resolved by administrative changes also marks the history of many long-term programs. Planned changes in the administration of economic and military aid for Latin America and various study reports indicate a persistent belief that modifications of the managerial process will provide greater success.[19] A new emphasis on a "low profile," that is, on avoiding a tutelary and interventionist posture, marked progress, mostly because it was a change that went beyond organizational alterations.[20]

Just as in early stages of a program persons with political commitments and vested interests find greater merit and hope in it than a more detached view might suggest, so, too, political attacks on a faltering or moribund program often exaggerate its degree of failure. Criticism of the Alliance for Progress easily neglects the genuine successes, particularly in local environments, in the provision of educational facilities, water supply, transportation and communication, and industrial and agricultural equipment. That so many individual successes could not add up to an overall political-economic success or counter the equally prominent failures and frictions, is a measure of the difficulty of the undertaking.

---

[19] Dean Acheson exaggerates, very usefully, an important point that the managers often do not care to acknowledge. "Good men can run the worst kind of organization and poor men can't run the best." *Los Angeles Times*, December 13, 1970. The Administration, however, believes that a new "U.S. International Development Corporation and a U.S. International Development Institute to replace the Agency for International Development . . . [will] enable us to reform our bilateral development assistance program to meet the changed conditions of the 1970s," although it is not at all clear that these changes will solve any of the major problems of the Alliance. President Nixon's Aid Message to Congress, 1971.

[20] The new-found attachment to a "low profile" appeared to be somewhat shaken by the election of Salvador Allende in 1970 as president of Chile.

273

Some observers are impressed less by the failure of the United States to achieve its goals than they are by ill-effects suffered by Latin America from United States policy. Thus Senator J. William Fulbright, in a Senate subcommittee meeting, affirmed: "I have reached the conclusion that because of fear and obsession with the possibility of communist influence, we have, for all practical purposes, brought social change and progress toward democratic processes [in Latin America] to a standstill." [21] Senator Fulbright is surely correct in emphasizing the negative effect of cold war preoccupations on United States policy in Latin America, but he grossly flatters United States influence in supposing that the course of the subcontinent's political and social evolution in recent years has been determined by United States conduct. The resistance, by no means total, of Latin American political institutions, attitudes, and practices to change is determined much more by characteristics of a social structure shaped over several centuries than by recent United States policy.[22]

The ultimate failure of a policy or the enforced cancellation of a program does not in itself demonstrate the unwisdom of having undertaken it in the first place or deny a greater or lesser value to it during some interim period. Thus Chile's recognition of East Germany does not demonstrate that West Germany's two-decade campaign in Latin America to prevent East Germany's recognition did not serve useful political purposes for the Federal Republic during the period of its success.

[21] *Survey of the Alliance for Progress,* Subcommittee on American Republic Affairs of Senate Committee on Foreign Relations, 91st Congress, 1st Session, Document No. 91–17, April 19, 1969, p. 312.

[22] See Section 8 below, Latin America. A growing literature emphasizes Latin American dependence on external markets as a source of her underdevelopment. This need not conflict with a due appreciation of Latin American social and political structures as a principal source of present-day difficulties of her economic development. For an analysis of Latin American underdevelopment that gives weight both to Latin America's relations to external markets and to the social and political structure shaped thereby in the colonial period, see Keith Griffin, *Underdevelopment in Spanish America: An Interpretation,* London, 1969, especially Chapter 7. For other discussions of the dependency theme see *The American Economic Review,* 60 (2), May 1970, pp. 225–246, and Susanne Bodenheimer, "Dependency and Imperialism: The Roots of Latin American Underdevelopment," *Politics and Society,* 1 (3), May 1971, pp. 327–357. A very useful addition to this literature is Joseph Hodara, "La dependencia de la dependencia," *Aportes* (Paris), No. 21, July 1971, pp. 6–15.

Many failures to resolve issues of international political life imply that for one or more of the parties involved any resolution or settlement was bound to be more disagreeable than the continuation of conflict. The high tolerance of governments for unsettled issues or for temporary *ad hoc* settlements that settle nothing seem also to be based on the hope, not entirely unjustified, that the sheer passage of time will somehow solve their problems.[23] Long-standing territorial differences in Antarctica and the Falklands illustrate instances where all the parties prefer an unresolved status to the disagreeableness of attempting to force a settlement. The United States government has preferred 15 years of conflict with South American countries over territorial waters and fishing rights to any solution or compromise that it seems to think is available to it.

The benefit of an early confrontation of a problem is seen in the case of France's 1946 incorporation of her Caribbean possessions into a constitutional status more in accord with postwar aspirations in colonial areas. Great Britain, on the other hand, delayed action in the Caribbean until political arrangements for the British Caribbean islands became more difficult to effect. It is true that France now faces movements for increased autonomy in the Antilles but this only proves that political life continues and that the resolution of a problem does not guarantee perpetual concord.

6. *Leverage*

Despite the conspicuous use of force in the world, most government foreign objectives that conflict with the interests of other nations are pursued through the exercise of various forms of leverage to which such terms as bargaining, threats, coercion, and reprisals are applied. With the exception of "bargaining," these terms have harsh connotations and even "bargaining" readily takes on a pejorative significance if the behavior referred to does not conform to a relatively narrow range of commonly accepted practices.

The foreign powers are assumed to have a much greater ability to impose and resist demands than the Latin American states, a situation thought to characterize generally the relations of the industrial nations with the suppliers of raw materials, or the advanced nations with the Third World, and to apply particularly to the

---

[23] "When you are threatened with anything that displeases you, try to put it off as long as you can. For we see every hour that time brings events which may free you from your problems." Francesco Guicciardini (1492–1540), *Ricordi,* First Series, No. 76.

United States in its relations with Latin America. Yet in the political sphere, the last several years have seen an unquestionable deterioration of the United States ability to influence Latin American behavior (see Chapter 12.8). How is this to be explained?

(1) The existence of apparently potent instruments of leverage does not guarantee their employment. The Hickenlooper, Conte–Long, Symington and Pelly Amendments, forged by Congress to affect Latin American decisions, have not been employed, and the ban on military credit was used only twice and with obvious reluctance.

(2) The target of these amendments was not only Latin America but the United States Executive, which in congressional views was lax in using military and economic assistance to protect United States investments and tuna boats and in discouraging Latin American purchase of expensive "sophisticated" weapons. Slowdowns in aid and in investment decisions substituted in part for failure to invoke these punitive amendments, but the former probably had less deterrent effect than an automatic application of the latter.

(3) The principal constraint on Latin American action vis-à-vis the United States was its interest in United States trade, investment, and aid. However, beginning especially with President Frei's campaign in 1964 to increase trade and financing with Europe, a number of Latin American countries sought to diversify their trade and investment funds. Although this succeeded only partially, the direction of movement and the increased political–economic contacts with nations other than the United States, including the Soviet bloc, gave Latin American governments a greater freedom and willingness to risk United States governmental and private displeasure.[24]

(4) Latin American and other Third World pressure for trade concessions at UNCTAD I and II put the industrial nations on the defensive. The United States was active at UNCTAD and in OECD in supporting Latin American trade positions, while at the same

[24] The United States is still the largest single importer of coffee, the world's second largest export commodity (after petroleum). But in 1964–1969 Colombia sold more than half of its coffee to countries other than the United States as compared with only one-third five years earlier. Commodity as well as market diversification has occurred. In the early sixties Brazil earned more than half its export earnings from coffee as compared with only one-third in 1970.

276

time defending its own tariff policy against Latin American attacks. This defensive posture does not mean that the United States did not have potentially powerful trade instruments for obtaining political concessions, but Latin American disregard in the last several years of some of the most cherished aims of United States policy clearly suggests that these trade instruments have not been forcefully employed or else that their leverage is far less than is presumed, perhaps due to the factors discussed in point (9) below. United States payments to Latin American sugar suppliers of a preferential price well above the world market price probably affects the behavior of some Latin American governments, especially as the expiration of current quotas approaches and new quotas are to be set.[25] Similarly, it seems unlikely that the Mexican government, faced with large and persistent negative balances, is indifferent to the fact that almost one-half of its foreign exchange earnings comes from the $1 billion earned by tourism, mostly from the United States.[26] Evidently such facts are likely to lead to self-imposed constraints whether or not the United States government or people show any disposition at a given moment to make use of them.

(5) The Latin American republics are often aided by foreign businessmen and their organizations whose own interests depend on promoting those of Latin American governments and business groups. Besides, the Latin republics are not without a few sources of leverage of their own. Their votes in the United Nations have been important both to the United States and to other nations. United States reprisals for inadequately compensated property seizures had to face the possibility of counterreprisals in the form of additional confiscations. The freedom of action of the United

[25] About 85 percent of Latin America's $450 million of sugar exports go to the United States, where they earn about $200 million above world market prices. Competition for quotas is one area in which Latin American countries have competed as well as combined with each other in dealing with the United States. This subsidy to Latin America supports a price level for United States domestic sugar suppliers higher than they would receive under free market conditions. H.R. 8866, 1971, reduced Latin American sugar quotas from 3.0 million to 2.6 million tons. Alliance for Progress, *Weekly Newsletter,* June 14, 1971, p. 1.

[26] In fact, these foreign exchange earnings are more likely to be endangered by United States investments in Mexican tourist facilities than by United States government or consumer pressure.

277

States government was further limited by its concern with communist penetration of Latin America. This required United States Administrations to avoid endangering Western Hemisphere governmental solidarity vis-à-vis Cuba, radical nationalists, and Soviet and Chinese influence. In effect, this was an incitement to Latin American blackmail of the United States. A Latin American diplomat remarked, referring to Mr. Nixon's disregard of Latin America: "Everything happens as if Mr. Nixon were saying to us, 'Threaten me and I will help you.' " [27]

(6) The concern of some United States constituencies to compensate Latin states whose less affluent condition and whose past relations with the United States were accepted in varying degrees as a charge on Western conscience, also moderated the United States bargaining posture.

(7) One advantage that the United States is thought to have, namely, its unity in the face of Latin American multiplicity, may be illusory. From a bargaining standpoint divergences within a country can sometimes be just as weakening as multiplicity on the other side of the bargaining table. On most issues of major importance to the Latin American economies it has been just as easy or easier to get unity in Central and South America than to get unity among various United States private and public sectors. The recent development of Latin American blocs may, however, change this. In the meantime, to influence the behavior of over 20 different states is, perhaps, more difficult than influencing the behavior of a single state even though it be a "giant."

(8) The hesitations of Executive action in some instances probably served United States government objectives badly. Congressman Pelly points out the consequences of a too-early removal of pressure:

> In 1969, when everything else had failed, I introduced a bill to cut off the importation of fish or fish products into the United States from any country that illegally seizes U.S. fishing boats. This bill would have had a decided economic

[27] *Le Monde,* May 14, 1971. Paraguayans, aggravated by the threatened loss of their first sugar quota during the process of revision of the United States Sugar Act of 1971, have also remarked, referring to their own record of siding with the United States on most issues, that apparently a country will do better if it occasionally sacks the United States Embassy and burns a few United States flags. *Los Angeles Times,* August 22, 1971.

effect upon these Latin American countries, and the day of the hearing on the bill, they agreed to begin negotiations.

This probably is a tale out of school, but our own State Department came to me and asked if I would withhold the bill and if the Chairman of the committee would cancel the hearing. They said an agreement had been arrived at that negotiations would begin in neutral Argentina. Well, I was delighted, if not skeptical, and of course the negotiations never got any place.[28]

It is unlikely that any of the Latin American West Coast states would, in 1969, have withdrawn their claim to exclusive fishing rights in the 200-mile zone. But the United States "diplomatic" response tolerated the continuation of a conflict (revived again in 1971) that a more resolute action might have ended by forcing a compromise. It is not at all clear that a lesser tension over a greater time is to be preferred to a greater tension over a shorter time.

(9) Great-power attempts to exercise influence should not be equated with the actual exercise of influence.[29] In evaluating United States or other great-power instruments of influence it is easy to overlook that while they may be able to exercise considerable leverage over the interests of some elements within the Latin republics, they do not necessarily affect the interests of those who are in power at a given time or those who are able to exercise pressure on those who are in power. Thus the leverage may in fact be less than one supposes. Criticism of and opposition to the United States is often a major political asset or issue in Latin American domestic politics. The use by the United States of trade, investment, and aid to induce policies favored by it may be ineffec-

[28] Congressman Thomas M. Pelly, Remarks to AFL–CIO Maritime Trade Department Luncheon, Washington, D.C., March 31, 1971.

[29] Newspaper headlines often suggest a United States leverage that subsequent events disprove. "U.S. Warns Chile Her Plan to Take Over Copper Holdings Could Hurt Relations," *The New York Times,* February 3, 1971. "Venezuela Given a Trade Warning: U.S. Hints Reprisal if Curbs on Investors Continue," *The New York Times,* February 22, 1971. A United States Treasury Department "get tough" policy against Chile in mid-1971 (Chapter 4.6) and President Nixon's threat in early 1972 to invoke the Hickenlooper Amendment against uncompensated expropriations have yet to demonstrate more positive results than the State Department's "soft line."

279

tive if these policies and the United States presence enter into Latin domestic power struggles. Getting into and staying in power is, for some sectors of the political class, more important than the interests threatened by United States reprisals. Nor is opposition to the United States simply a tool on the Latin domestic political scene. It is often a widely held political value and reduces the ability of proferred benefits or threats to influence Latin American decisions. And even if these benefits or threats do exercise leverage at a given moment, the labile character of Latin politics often means that a position of influence may be lost overnight.

10) Since conspicuous failures of United States influence in the last several years have coincided with reductions of economic and military assistance, it is possible to argue that the former are largely the product of the latter. The preceding paragraphs suggest, however, that the size of resources employed did not determine the results attained.

As an instrument of leverage, economic and military aid—the strategy of benevolence or, if one prefers, of bribery—has the defect, especially in the case of long-term programs, of not readily providing for termination. Indeed it becomes increasingly difficult to cut off aid as the recipient habituates himself to its receipt and views what was once a grant as a debt that is owed him.[30] Consequently, what seems like a good policy in the short run and what appears as a small expenditure in the near term becomes a bad policy and an expensive one in the long run. In Bolivia the United States consulate and the residence of the United States ambassador were bombed by leftist groups when AID insisted that Boliva pay its agreed contribution of 10–15 percent to a project.[31]

When in the spring of 1971 the United States suspended military assistance sales to Ecuador following her renewed seizure of United

[30] This is not always the case. United States economic aid to Taiwan, one of the more successful United States aid programs, was terminated by mutual agreement.

[31] Selden Rodman, *South America of the Poets,* New York, 1970, pp. 77–78. This incident illustrates two other points. First, AID insisted on holding up the project pending the receipt of the Bolivian share because it feared that otherwise Congress might reduce its appropriations. Secondly, the incident illustrates United States managerial and technical over-ambitiousness. "We're so enthusiastic about what we're helping them accomplish, we may have caused them to over-extend themselves." *Ibid.*

States tuna boats, Ecuador charged the United States with economic coercion and violation of Article 19 of the OAS Charter, thus making clear that assistance freely given creates for the recipient a legal claim to its continuation. In effect, what was presumed to provide the United States with leverage over Ecuador, the latter attempted to convert into leverage over the United States. The United States undersecretary of state pointed out: "In no way can assistance of any kind be considered as obligatory, timeless and changeless. . . . The existence of assistance, or its acceptance, cannot be automatic and irrevocable." [32]

If "to have received from one to whom we think ourselves equal, greater benefits than there is hope to Requite, disposeth to counterfeit love, but really secret hatred," [33] how much more likely this is when those benefits are cut off after habituation to their receipt.

European and Japanese attempts to influence the Latin American states were, with the exception of the Soviet Union [34] and, perhaps, of West Germany, largely in the interests of trade and investment and did not involve the continuous tensions provoked by large-scale aid operations and by the political and national security concerns of the United States. International commerce and foreign investment, however, are not simply individual private transactions. Trade and investment are affairs of state, and bargaining in the ordinary sense of communicating prices and specifications may be accompanied by government threats and counterthreats.

The Latin states have not shown themselves unduly intimidated by the fact that a number of the European powers and Japan buy more from them than they do from the European powers. Certainly they are aware of the import of this but it has not inhibited momentary indulgences of national honor. Argentina took reprisals against Great Britain and France because of a British embargo on and French barriers to Argentinian meat (see Chapter 12.3 and

[32] Department of State, Press Release No. 24, February 1, 1971.

[33] Hobbes, *Leviathan,* Chapter 11.

[34] The Soviets had some difficulty in keeping Castro in line, and after Castro arrested Aníbal Escalante in November 1967, the Soviets failed to ship enough oil to meet Cuban needs. In an attempt to resist Soviet pressure, Castro introduced fuel rationing early in 1968, but his endorsement of the Soviet invasion of Czechoslovakia in August of that year represented, finally, his capitulation. The reestablishment of Cuban relations with a number of Latin American states may enable Castro to resist Soviet pressure a little more effectively.

281

12.4). But where political passions have not been aroused, caution and discretion ("buy from those who buy from you") are more likely to be operative. Argentina's award in 1967 of a $6 million contract to an Italian consortium, over United States bidders, to build a satellite communication system linking Argentina with the COMSAT system, was believed due to the bargaining power of Italy's very large 1967 negative trade balance with Argentina and the United States large positive balance during the same year.[35] France, however, apparently anxious not to disturb her military sales in Latin America or her prospects for the sale of the supersonic Concorde which was about to make its first flight to South America, succumbed to Latin American, especially Peruvian, pressure when she cancelled part of her 1971 nuclear test series (Chapter 12.3).

Nonhemispheric investments and loans in Latin America are, like those of the United States, hostages to Latin America, and especially so since some of the nonhemispheric powers have a higher proportion of their overseas investments in Latin America than does the United States. Germany lost investments in two world wars and German businessmen are thought to be more sensitive to possible expropriations than most, but similar considerations apply to Japan and Italy.[36] Latin America also possesses hostages of a more traditional character. Thus the large Japanese population in Brazil would make aggressive Japanese behavior vis-à-vis Brazil very awkward. This applies also to other national groups, especially those who have retained their original nationality and a conspicuous national identity.

7. Economics and Politics

The countries that principally pursued commercial objectives in Latin America more largely and more readily achieved their aims than countries with far-reaching political goals. The United States, too, was more successful in the pursuit of its economic than its political interests. Greater success in the economic than in the political field is not surprising. Much of economic activity is decentralized because it is carried on by private sectors. Responsibilities and talents are dispersed, and success, taken over many enterprises, is not dependent on one agency or policy. The single-

[35] *The New York Times*, February 23, 1967.
[36] John White, *op. cit.*, pp. 140–141.

minded pursuit of profit provides a clearer criterion of success than is generally available for guiding political action. But more important, economic activities are cooperative as well as competitive. Those who wish to sell are aided by those who wish to buy. The exporter of capital has a partner, reluctant or not, in the importer of capital. Economic ambitions may be thwarted by factors internal and external to the marketplace, but they rarely have to face the difficulties encountered by political programs that revolve about emotional and controversial issues in which national and party interests are at stake.

Although the contrast between private, decentralized economic activity and centralized political activity still holds, developments, many of which are already quite old, are increasingly blurring distinctions. The participation of individual enterprisers abroad in national programs of economic action was already noted by the Federal Trade Commission in 1916: "Competition in Latin America is not individual but national. . . . Each country . . . pools its commercial and financial forces, and with the support of its government moves into foreign markets united. The individual manufacturer becomes of secondary importance. . . . If American interests are to succeed, they must develop a like solidarity. . . ." [37]

The organization by government of the industrialists and merchants of a nation into a force to conquer [38] a foreign market finds its symbol and concrete manifestation in the trade fair. But more important has been government credit facilities for overseas sales. As competition has sharpened, the length of the period for which government credits are made available seems to have become almost as important as the price or quality of the commodity. Japan especially has had to conform to this competitive requirement by providing more long-term credit.

Government intervention in international trade competition was

[37] Federal Trade Commission, *Report on Trade and Tariffs in Brazil, Uruguay, Argentina, Chile, Bolivia, and Peru,* Washington, 1916, cited by J. F. Normano, *The Struggle for South America,* London, 1931, pp. 69–70.

[38] Discussions of commerce very easily fall into military language. Markets are "attacked," "penetrated," "laid seige to." Competitors "confront each other" and "defend hard-earned positions." Export requires a "concerted offensive" and the development of a "general strategy of exportation." Even benevolent activities are described in military language. Maurice Couve de Murville affirmed some years ago that France was about "to launch a very important offensive of financial aid to Latin America."

further stimulated by aid programs. The requirement that United States, German, and Canadian official financial aid to Latin America be spent in the donor countries probably bolstered their export positions in the region. In 1962–1964 about 10–12 percent of United States exports to Latin America were aid financed. Unfortunately it has not been established to what extent these aid-financed exports would have been supplied by other countries had financing not been tied.[39]

Trade with the Third World has become increasingly dependent on the ability or willingness of governments to encourage foreign investments that help to circumvent the effect of Third World tariff barriers. Besides, a country's own foreign subsidiaries are receptive customers. England has had, for the most part, to turn down Latin American requests for more development capital, but Foreign Minister Michael Stewart was aware that some investments must be made "if only to prevent the United Kingdom from being progressively squeezed out of these markets."[40] This consideration was all the more compelling since the ability of investments to generate trade is much greater in Third World markets than in those of the advanced industrial countries. United Kingdom manufacturing investments in Nigeria generated United Kingdom exports of £39 per £100 invested against only £1 of exports to £100 invested in the United States, where local suppliers are available to fill requirements.[41]

It is not possible to determine with accuracy from available data the extent to which the varying trade successes in Latin America of the different industrial nations have depended upon the different supporting programs of their governments. It is evident, however, that today private enterprisers cannot hope to make the most of their foreign trade potentials unless they have much the same facilities that are provided by the governments of competitor nations.

Private business has increasingly been displaced, even in the older capitalist societies, by state enterprises. In Latin America a large part of economic activity not only falls under the control of

[39] See Ruth Logue, "Aid-Financed Exports: Problems of Concept, Measurement and Interpretation," especially pp. 4–5, 8, 14, *Inter-American Economic Affairs*, 21 (3), Winter 1967. See also Chapter 10.7 above.

[40] *Manchester Guardian Weekly*, November 4, 1965, p. 4.

[41] *The Banker* (London), No. 515, January 1969, p. 35.

government policy and supervision but is operated by government businesses. About 35 percent of economic activity in Latin America is estimated to be under government control.[42] Celso Furtado estimates Brazilian government participation in the economy to have increased from 4 to 25 percent during the postwar period.[43] A 1970 estimate of the capital value of Brazil's largest enterprises attributes 45 percent to state enterprises, 35 percent to foreign enterprises, and 20 percent to Brazilian private enterprises.[44] Of Brazil's 34 largest nonforeign firms in 1968, 15 were public enterprises.[45] In Argentina the public sector was estimated to account for 28 percent of the national product in the mid-sixties. Public sector investments rose from 11 percent (1900–1929) to 34 percent (1929–1950) and were estimated at 20 percent in 1965.[46] Of the 50 largest businesses in Argentina, state enterprises accounted for 34 percent of sales, Argentine private enterprise for 15 percent, North American for 22 percent, and European for 29 percent.[47]

[42] *Statistical Abstract of Latin America 1967*, Latin American Center, University of California, Los Angeles, 1968, p. 24.

[43] Celso Furtado, "De l'oligarchie à l'Etat militaire," *Les Temps Modernes*, 23 (257), October 1967, p. 583.

[44] *Visão*, August 29, 1970, p. 302.

[45] Silas Cerqueira, "Sur la crise brésilienne," *Revue Française de Science Politique*, XVIII (1), February 1968, p. 26. Brazil's development bank, which was intended to aid private industry, made, in the period 1952–1964, the great bulk of its allocations to the public sector. Nathaniel H. Leff, *Economic Policymaking and Development in Brazil 1947–1964*, New York, 1968, p. 40. Between 1947 and 1960 Brazil's public sector contribution to the formation of fixed capital rose from 16 to 38 percent with the private contribution falling from 84 to 54 percent and the mixed private and public sector rising from 0 percent in 1947 to 8 percent in 1960. Fernando Henrique Cardoso, "Hégémonie Bourgeoise et indépendance économique: Racines Structurales de la crise politique Brésilienne," *Les Temps Modernes*, 23 (257), October 1967, p. 669.

[46] Marcos Kaplan, "El Estado empresario en la Argentina, *El Trimestre Económico*, 36 (1), January–March 1969, p. 87.

[47] Guillermo Martorell, *Las Inversiones Extranjeras en la Argentina*, Buenos Aires, 1969, p. 124. The proportion of GNP consumed by government shows major Latin American countries mostly in the same range as the principal Western nations (15–19 percent). The figures for Latin American countries are: Argentina 16 percent, Brazil 14 percent, Chile 10 percent, Colombia 7 percent, Peru 11 percent, Venezuela 15 percent. Charles W. Anderson, "Political Factors in Latin American Economic Development," *Journal of International Affairs*, 20 (2), 1966, pp. 240–241.

Public expenditures as a percent of total domestic product was (1966) 30 percent or more in Brazil, Chile, and Uruguay, and 25–30 percent in Argentina, Bolivia, Colombia, Costa Rica, Ecuador, Mexico, Panama, and Peru.[48]

That economic transactions revolve around government institutions both as makers of policy but also as enterprisers themselves, may provide an impetus for the Latin states to increase economic relations with those nonhemispheric countries that have *dirigiste* economies and which themselves operate major economic enterprises. When the Colombian government awarded the French government enterprise, Renault, a contract to build and operate an auto assembly plant, a Colombian government official observed that Renault's status as a government firm helped it to win the contract over the nine other bidders.[49] The other firm awarded a contract for assembling vehicles was also a state enterprise, Mexico's Diesel Nacional.

The flexibility of a European state enterprise and the competitive advantage thus conferred in Latin America is illustrated by the reaction of United States bidders—General Motors, Ford, Chrysler, American Motors—for the Colombia auto assembly plant. They viewed as "nonsensical" the condition that the successful bidder must buy and market Colombian products to a value equal to that of the automobile components imported into the country. Under this provision Renault bought in Colombia and marketed between 1969 and 1970 $3 million worth of Colombian coffee, meat, tobacco, cotton, and rice.[50]

Political preferences and motives express themselves more readily through state enterprises than in the decisions of private entrepreneurs, even though the latter may be under political pressures. For this reason some European businessmen expect that the Chilean state concerns will turn increasingly to Europe and away from the

[48] This compares with about 30–40 percent in Western Europe and 30 percent in Canada and the United States. United Nations, *Economic Survey of Latin America 1968*, New York, 1970, p. 101.

[49] *The New York Times*, August 12, 1969. Italy has benefited, not only from the prominence of its state enterprises, but also from its not too close identification with the Atlantic Alliance. For a discussion of the political aspects of international commerce and, more especially, of Fiat's international successes, see Louis Turner, *Invisible Empires: Multinational Corporations and the Modern World*, New York, 1971, pp. 124–129.

[50] *The New York Times*, August 20, 1970.

United States.[51] In his speech on the eighth anniversary of his regime, Castro pointed out to Europe that it had much to gain from revolutions in Latin America since these would affect only United States monopolies. It seems that with the advent of President Salvador Allende some European enterprisers and governments now share this either as a hope or as an expectation. The Chilean far left believes that "the blond German capitalists" will try to replace the United States, but holds the view that the resulting West German economic advances will be a renewed form of North American influence concealed in a West German industrial presence.[52] Of course, state enterprises may discriminate against all foreign businesses, as in Argentina where "Argentinization" requires that orders placed by state enterprises be filled if possible by Argentine concerns.

Political considerations in economic transactions should not obscure the contrary phenomenon, that is, the disregard of what seem to be important political preferences for the sake of economic gains. This, of course, is the relationship usually stressed by various maxims concerning the ability of money to erase moral ties. Although Cuba gave facilities to anti-Franco Spaniards and was a Communist state, Cuban–Spanish trade flourished to the advantage of both countries. Similarly, the Soviets apparently found it easier to do business with General Castelo Branco than with João Goulart, although it was not clear that economic gain was their principal aim.

Political control over the economies of Latin America, enhanced by state enterprises and central planning, endows domestic political power with greatly increased value and importance. For the same reason it renders access to and influence with the holders of political power of great importance both for all sectors of the national population and for foreign enterprises. Good personal relations between officials of foreign private corporations and Latin American government agencies become increasingly important, and France and Italy, whose representatives, both private and governmental, are well esteemed in official Latin American circles appear to benefit from these relations. Still, these excellent personal relations do not prevent government intervention in the marketplace from making disagreements a political as well as an economic or

[51] *The Times* (London), December 21, 1970.
[52] *Punto Final* (Santiago de Chile), November 24, 1970, pp. 16–17.

market matter. Disagreements between governments or between governments and private corporations are likely to have more serious repercussions than disagreements between private buyers and sellers.

8. *Latin America*

Latin American economic institutions and practices were not the only features of Latin American societies that affected the foreign powers differently. For those few powers, especially the United States and the Soviet Union, for whom Latin America was not only a marketplace but an arena for the pursuit of broader objectives, their successes and failures were bound to be sensitive to the social structures of the Latin republics.

Most countries of Latin America share with other less-developed nations a characteristic that places a great strain on the policies and programs of any country that, like the United States, aspires to a high level of influence over them and their development. In the industrialized societies the institutions and organs of society have generally developed a certain insulation from each other, a partial autonomy that permits analysis and action with respect to one or another of them to proceed without taking the entire society into account. Thus to plot the probable economic course of a Western European state and to attempt to guide it in a given direction does not require equal attention to the demographic structure, the state of race relations, the retirement policy for state employees, the world price of coffee, political moods, rural migrations to the capital, the productivity of large-scale versus small-scale agriculture, the economic views and political ambitions of the military, and so on. But in Latin America (and underdeveloped countries generally) the neglect of any one sector or aspect of the society risks grossly misunderstanding the course of events, compromises programs of action, and—unfortunately for economic planning— may make the virtually impossible seem feasible.

A central feature of Latin American life is (in the terminology of medical pathology) the political hypertrophy of society, that is, the hyperpenetration of the political into most organs, functions, and spheres of life.[53] Consequently, all that is most problematic in

[53] For an interpretation of Latin America in terms of the nondifferentiation of diverse spheres and the penetration of the political into all aspects of life ("political metastasis"), see Roger Vekeman SJ, "Analyse psychosociale de la situation pré-révolutionnaire," Jean-Louis Segundo SJ, "Diag-

Latin American society comes to focus in the political sphere. Economic, juridical, religious, cultural, educational, military, social, and personal affairs are all too often resolved through administrative and political organs and persons, that is, by attaining at one level or another access to and the support of power and influence. Thus political power becomes the basic currency of the society. This characteristic of Latin American life has given increased importance to the inside track, knowing the ropes, and hence to the role of the middleman or fixer.[54] It has been remarked that the Latin American passion for politics is not, as is sometimes alleged, a matter of temperament; it is the passion for acquisition, advancement, and survival.[55]

The hyperpoliticization of Latin societies drains the attention and efforts of important sectors of the society and focuses them on the political arena or on political means of resolving problems. The struggle for power, or for access to its holders, expresses the most varied interests, conflicts, and aspiration, and the exercise of power becomes equivalent to the total "administration" of the society, and in some cases, the paralysis of it. In such a situation those who are dispossessed of power or have no access to it (among both the poor and the rich) have little alternative—if they do not withdraw into passivity—except to find in a continuous manipulation of political activities and persons, or in alterations, sometimes violent, of the political regime and of the political structure, or in evasions of laws and norms, their means of personal and group salvation.[56]

---

nostic politique de l'Amérique latine," and Jacques Chonchol (now Chile's minister of agriculture), "Facteurs d'accélération révolutionnaire," in *L'Amérique latine en devenir,* Centre Catholique des Intellectuels Français, Paris, 1963.

[54] It also increases the importance to the foreign businessman of migrants from his own country since they have connections and experience that the foreign businessman has not yet acquired.

[55] Jean-Louis Segundo, *op. cit.,* p. 70. European impatience in the nineteenth century with the spectacle of Latin American political life deprived the young Latin republics of the sympathy of even those who might most have been expected to support them. Engels, writing to Marx, noted that "In America we have witnessed the conquest of Mexico, and are happy about it. . . . It is in the interests of its own development that henceforth Mexico should be placed under the tutelage of the United States." Luis E. Aguilar (ed.), *Marxism in Latin America,* New York, 1968, pp. 66–67.

[56] That this process is so pronounced in the less-developed societies does not preclude its presence in advanced industrial societies. What we may, in

In the Western European industrial nations, a higher degree of national and racial homogeneity and of access to education made it easier to forge, both by reform and by revolution, political institutions and attitudes that progressively enabled the dispossessed and underprivileged to share more fully in the increasing wealth of society and to defend themselves against excessive exploitation. In much of Latin America the existence of great differences in race, culture, and language [57] resulting from conquest and slavery led not only to sharp differences in income, education, and class but made thereby more feasible the use of political instruments for the exploitation and suppression of the many by the few. This produced a moral state in which plunder and venality became important means for the advancement of one's own material well-being. An inadequate expansion of productivity and wealth exacerbates this state of affairs. When expectations rise but the growth of material wealth is slow, individual or class gains in income will more readily occur at the expense of others. Under such circumstances, an equilibrium of sharing, if one exists, is likely to be disrupted by either the poor or the rich. Plunder and corruption, present in varying degrees in most societies, are increased by a lack of confidence in the future and a fear of political change. Some members of the middle and wealthy classes and of the foreign business community, not being able to foresee the future clearly, or in some cases believing that they foresee it only too well, view economic activity as a means of making large profits in the shortest time and getting much of it out of the country.[58] These views and

fact, be observing today in the Western world is the intensification of this process of hyperpoliticization. Obviously, "hyperpoliticization" does not here mean "taking an interest" in politics and "performing one's civic duties."

[57] Paraguay is unique in its high bilingual level. In the mid-sixteenth century the Spanish conquerors had become so habituated to Guarani that on the arrival of a group of Spanish women in Asunción, they found difficulty in "speaking in Spanish to real ladies dressed in the manner God expected." Joan Rubin, "Language and Education in Paraguay," in J. A. Fishman, et al. (eds.), *Language Problems of Developing Nations*, New York, 1968, pp. 477–478.

[58] The export of capital by Latin Americans is a subject of speculation but available evidence indicates it is very large indeed. Latin American private funds that are of record in the United States alone amounted to $7.7 billion in December 1969 (as compared with United States direct investment and other private assets of $20.4 billion in Latin America).

this behavior create or accelerate the conditions that are feared and intensify the behavior induced by them. This has had consequences for economic development that were not exactly amenable to alteration by programs instituted from the outside and that barely took into account the social and political context into which they were fitted and which they were intended to affect.[59]

United States planners and administrators of the Alliance for Progress might have done well to confront their early enthusiasm with the case of Argentina. Argentina, one of the least representative of the Latin American states by reason of its relatively high per capita income, its European ethnic composition, its 90 percent literacy rate, its population increase roughly the same as Canada and the United States, was, after World War I, one of the six or seven richest countries in the world.[60] In the period 1925–1934, Argentina's mean income per person was almost 75 percent that of the United States, and yet in 1958 it had fallen to 15 percent of the United States figure.[61] The failure of a country so favorably endowed as Argentina to maintain its economic rank in the world might have been a warning signal that Latin America posed special

---

Survey of Current Business, 50 (10), October 1970, p. 23. A New York bank director affirms that Latin American funds in his bank exceed the total loans made by the bank to the countries from which these funds come. *Le Monde,* May 16–17, 1971. A minister of the Frei government estimated that in the period just prior to mid-October 1970, that is, before Salvador Allende took office (November 4, 1970), about 14,000 persons and assets of about $100 million left Chile. *Cuadernos Americanos* (Mexico), XXX (2), March–April 1971, p. 15.

[59] Naturally the foregoing broad-brush interpretation of an entire continent and its history can at best resemble reality only in the manner in which a caricature resembles its subject.

[60] *The Economist,* Latin American Economic Survey, Supplement, September 25, 1965.

[61] The mean income per person for both countries in relative numbers was:

	1925–1934	1940	1949	1953	1958
United States	100	100	100	100	100
Argentina	73	57	38	23	15

Review of River Plate (Buenos Aires), September 13, 1960, cited by Gustavo Lagos, "L'intégration de l'Amérique latine et son influence sur le système international," *Tiers Monde,* 6 (23), July–September 1965, p. 744.

problems of economic development whose secure diagnosis was very important, if not indispensable, for United States policy.[62]

If basic features of Latin American society and of its relations with the industrial nations made United States development objectives unrealistic and its development strategy in Latin America misplaced, so, too, other peripheral aspects of Latin American society, some of which are perhaps expressions of a deeper malaise, contributed to the same result. Of the three parties involved in the Alliance for Progress plan for the provision of capital to Latin America—Latin America, United States private enterprise, and the United States government—only the United States government fulfilled its commitment.[63] Problems of internal and external financing were aggravated by the use of short-term loans to finance long-term investments, the productivity of which in many cases was questionable. Responsibility for this seems to rest both on Latin American governments and on the permissive attitudes of lenders whose interests were sometimes more political than economic. In addition, internal reforms promised by Latin American countries were generally allowed, after the receipt of aid, to lapse or to be used to benefit those in power.[64]

---

[62] World Bank figures on per capita national product for 1968 placed Argentina as the 29th ranking country. A few of the countries that now outrank Argentina (Israel, East Germany, Ireland, Trinidad–Tobago, Libya) did not exist as independent states during the period when Argentina was among the first ten countries of the world. But even subtracting these, Argentina's rank has still fallen sharply. A completely satisfying account of this decline is not yet available, but see James R. Scobie, "Buenos Aires of 1910: The Paris of South America that Did Not Take Off," *Inter-American Economic Affairs,* 11 (2), Autumn 1968.

[63] *Foreign Investment in Latin America: Past Policies and Future Trends,* Report of a Regional Meeting of the American Society of International Law, published by the Virginia Journal of International Law, 1970, pp. 69–70. That Latin America did not provide as much development capital as had been anticipated does not mean, as seems sometimes to be assumed, that the bulk of Latin American capital was provided from external sources. Although the figures vary from country to country and year to year, Latin America provided during the 1960s 93 percent of the capital investments in the region. This, of course, does not mean that it would not have benefited greatly from the funds sent abroad both by Latin Americans and by United States industry in Latin America.

[64] Eduardo Frei Montalva, "The Alliance that Lost Its Way," *Foreign Affairs,* April 1967, p. 443.

Population growth in Latin American countries, Argentina and Uruguay excepted, imposes great strains on gross national product increments, and although United States analysts were well aware of the problem this created for increasing material welfare, initial Alliance for Progress expectations apparently did not face the question whether, given Latin American resistance, birth rates could or would be reduced.[65] Latin America has been largely deprived of an opportunity to relieve population pressure and inadequate employment by sending large numbers of workers abroad. Italian workers with limited opportunities for employment in southern Italy were able to follow Italian capital and benefit from the enlarged work opportunities provided by Western European prosperity. But with the exception of Puerto Rico, Cuba, and Mexico, and former immigrants who returned to Europe, Latin American rural and urban workers could not or in any case did not follow Latin American capital to the United States and Europe.[66]

An understandable preoccupation with the United States in

[65] To religious, military, mercantilist, and nationalist motives for Latin American resistance to population control must now be added the revolutionary's acceptance of the human consequences of population growth for the sake of a presumed later and larger good. Fernando Szyszlo, one of Peru's foremost painters, expresses the matter as follows: "We recognize that the larger the population the greater the pressure for revolution. When I was born, the population of South America was less than the population of the United States. Now it is greater, and by the year 2000 it may be two or three times as great. You don't fear Cuba or North Vietnam, but you do fear China, don't you? Just because China's population is so huge. If 30, or even 100 million were wiped out by nuclear weapons, it wouldn't hurt China at all; she'd still keep attacking. . . . Internally, it's the same: the greater the population, the more irresistible the pressure for social change." Selden Rodman, *op. cit.*, pp. 61–62.

[66] A substantial migratory movement occurs among the Latin American countries (see Chapter 5) but this does very little to ease the continent-wide problem. On the contrary, in the political sphere it produces interstate tensions. Nor is the increasing use of joint ventures in which Latin American capital holds 51 percent control likely to provide a substantial increase in managerial and professional jobs. According to a report by the Inter-American Council for Education, Science and Culture of OAS, about 92 percent of the 40,000 managerial jobs and 97 percent of 100,000 technical and professional jobs in United States firms in Latin America are said to be held by Latin Americans.

Latin America provided easy opportunities for both the left and the right to neglect other relevant aspects of their situation. Anti-Americanism was exploited by right-wing and conservative groups in order to deflect attention from themselves. This often represented a genuine hostility, especially by the large landed proprietors, who found among some Alliance for Progress strategists an enthusiasm for their liquidation and who, in reprisal, were just as willing as the political left to threaten United State investments. Nor were Latin American businessmen, government officials, and administrators immune to emotions stemming both from administrative harassment by Alliance for Progress overseers and from the latter's insistence on a tax structure and other reforms that would have touched them too closely. Despite the new benefits that they received from the Alliance for Progress, the urban business and official class sought to preserve, like the landowners, their established privileged positions, a struggle in which they received assistance from the political left through the latter's indiscriminate condemnation of the Alliance for Progress. Radical groups, largely composed of or led by middle and upper class persons, expressed a residual loyalty to their own classes by focusing much of their attack on the United States rather than on their own élites and on domestic institutions.

Although partly based on cultural differences, Latin American sensitivity to the United States is founded in the history of United States relations with Mexico, Haiti, Nicaragua, the Dominican Republic, Guatemala, Cuba, and Panama, and on conflicts of a more largely economic nature in all parts of the subcontinent. The sins of the fathers have been visited on the sons very fully in the case of the United States, partly, of course, because the sons are clearly viewed as guilty in their own right. Other nations, with perhaps the exception of Spain,[67] have been more successful than the United States in erasing the effects of the past. Latin America is largely indifferent to past Japanese and German militarism, with which it has had little direct experience. And it was possible for France in 1964, during the course of de Gaulle's visit, to return to Mexico, apparently without fear of opening old wounds, Mexican flags taken by the French in 1862 and displayed since then in the Invalides.

[67] See the discussion of Mexican–Spanish relations, Chapter 6.

Soviet efforts in Latin America through most of the postwar period suffered equally or more than those of the United States from an ignorance and disregard of Latin American realities. These realities were, nonetheless, such as to provide signal advantages to a country that claimed to represent egalitarian aspirations and expressed hostility toward countries, classes, and social institutions from which important groups in the Latin American populations were becoming increasingly alienated.[68] However, in the sixties, left groups of a more nationalist character and sometimes of Cuban inspiration mobilized political sentiments that were offended by the antinationalist overtones of Soviet ideology and by increasing Soviet preoccupation with intergovernmental relations.

Latin America's distance from the Soviet Union and relative proximity to the United States make the Soviet Union seem less dangerous to Latin America than the United States, although for some Latin American states the Soviet military presence in Cuba decreased this sense of security. Just as United States relations with some of the Eastern European Communist states benefit from the latter's uneasy proximity to the Soviet Union, so Soviet relations with Latin America benefit from the latter's proximity to the United States. Not even Cuba is likely to fear that the Brezhnev doctrine can be applied to it, at least not in the manner in which it was applied in Czechoslovakia.[69]

The relaxed attitude of many Latin American official and popular sectors toward the Soviet Union and their local Communist parties made United States conceptions of national security and alliance objectives difficult to appreciate and share. An alliance is not necessarily subject to stress because its members are of unequal power, but it almost always will be if the members have a very different stake or degree of involvement in its objectives. Latin American political classes did not so much feel themselves to be allies facing a common threat as they felt themselves objects of

[68] The solemn homage in the Chilean Chamber of Deputies and Senate in 1967 on the occasion of the 50th Anniversary of the October Revolution had no counterpart in Western Europe.

[69] Despite giant jet transport planes and nuclear powered naval vessels, territorial contiguity or close proximity is today an important condition for facilitating annexation or full political–military control of foreign territory. This contrasts with past Spanish, Portuguese, British, and French acquisitions in the sixteenth and seventeenth centuries of territories and populations thousands of miles from their homelands.

United States interference. That the United States has never had the experience of living with powerful neighbors did not help her to conduct these security relations with Latin America in a manner more consistent with their national pride and dignity.

9. *Unpredictability*

It is symbolic of the uncertainties that United States political policy faced in Latin America that two years after its inception, the Alliance for Progress was so rudely shaken by the assassination of its architect. Nor did President Kennedy foresee the enormous increase in the United States military commitment in Vietnam and the effect that this would have on the government's position and freedom of action in Latin America and other Third World countries. Evidently one's own actions may be as little predictable as those of others.

The sudden death of foreign political leaders has also on occasion destroyed expectations and positions of strength. The death of General Barrientos, president of Bolivia, in a plane crash altered virtually overnight the United States position in Bolivia. In the Third World, however, it is more frequently the labile character of domestic politics that suddenly removes political leaders. The overthrow of Ben Bella (Algeria), Nkrumah (Ghana), and Sukarno (Indonesia), was a particularly striking series of political changes that affected especially Soviet Third World positions. In Latin America both constitutional and unconstitutional changes of government have brought successes as well as setbacks for the United States government. The Brazilian coup of 1964 was a major gain for the United States government position in Brazil; but the less stern attitude toward the national discipline required for economic development and the less favorable disposition toward the United States of General Castelo Branco's successor, President Costa e Silva, altered once more the United States position in Brazil.

Political instability and uncertainties as to whether the political party in power will prevail at the next election [70] suggest to some governments the value of building up multiple positions of influence in a country, that is, in hedging one's bets. The exclusive support

---

[70] In Costa Rica in the 20 years following 1948 during which free elections continuously prevailed, no government was able, despite the advantage of being in power at election time, to elect its own presidential designee.

of one political party, especially if it has a strong ideological or political bent is disadvantageous if its stay in power is uncertain, unless, of course, other political groups are going to be hostile in any case. The strategy of hedging bets is not, however, without risks since governments in power are only too sensitive to the less than wholehearted endorsement and support given to them. A third strategy, to avoid taking sides in Latin American domestic politics, has been largely followed by Britain, France, and Japan. General de Gaulle's preference for conducting interstate relations without regard to ideological positions was successful, on the whole, in maintaining a flexibility that made him welcome in many parts of the world, if not in Ottawa and Washington. Germany and Italy, together with the United States, provided support for Christian Democracy in Latin America, but the United States was led by its large economic, military, and political programs of the sixties to support in addition a variety of political parties, personalities, and tendencies that were presumed sympathetic to and capable of collaborating in these programs. This flexibility stopped short of parties identified with Marxist views or Soviet sympathies. The allocation by the United States of $5.9 million to Chile in the fiscal 1972 military assistance program represented a first United States step in Latin America toward determining whether former distinctions need always be followed.

The rapid and often unpredictable changes to which Third World political and economic life are subject require a talent for adaptability and flexibility on the part of foreign governments and their private sectors. Both British and German observers have attributed some of the difficulties of their commerce with Latin America to the continued prominence of old commercial houses with long prewar experience in Latin America which have failed to adapt to postwar changes. Until the late sixties the Russians showed a similar rigidity during their political and economic offensive in the Third World, and even today substantial vestiges of this still handicap their new-found flexibility. These minor rigidities of behavior often reflect more far-reaching failures of adaptation. Persistent refusals by the United States to issue visas to various Communist and other left intellectuals seem to show neither an awareness of the changing character of Latin American and United States political environments nor a capability for assessing the relative assets and deficits of a policy easier to evaluate than most.

Dramatic and unpredictable events are sometimes alleged to produce sudden changes in political attitudes. United States and Cuban earthquake relief following the 1970 earthquake in Peru were said to have caused "two pronounced political shifts," [71] sudden improvements in United States–Peruvian relations, and a new Peruvian respect for Cuba. The absence of Soviet earthquake aid in June and the arrival later in July of only 21 of the 65 promised Soviet planes, followed by a Soviet announcement that the rest of the supplies would have to come by ship, apparently led to a drop in Soviet prestige in Peru. If "a sudden political shift" did indeed take place, it seems likely that the same labile moods which permitted this rapid change in prestige in one direction will permit equally rapid changes in the other direction. Events such as Sputnik and Apollo 11 seem to have somewhat more enduring effects because they are part of a continuing development that provides a supportive context for attitudes that otherwise would be at the mercy of the slightest current. [72]

Unpredictable changes abroad and unanticipated developments domestically combine to render long-term programs hazardous. Programs like the Alliance for Progress tend to assume, implicitly or explicitly, that the conditions that appear to make the initiation of the program desirable and feasible will continue throughout the period envisaged for it. In fact, of course, these conditions often alter drastically. For this reason, *ad hoc* actions aimed at certain immediate effects in immediate well-defined contexts have very real advantages.

Today, however, nothing seems so improvidential as a reliance on the inspiration or opportunity of the moment. This was not always the case. Statesmen and diplomats have long been inured to the advent of the unexpected. Political reporting and intelligence operations have always provided some protection against total sur-

[71] *The New York Times,* June 15, 1970.

[72] The fluctuating results of polls on some issues reflect not so much "changes in attitude" as the absence of attitude, that is, the disinterest of the respondents in formulating positions or views independently of the need to respond to an interviewer. For an attempt to assess the effects of Sputnik on Chilean public opinion, see Eduardo Hamuy, Danilo Salcedo, and Orlando Sepúlveda, *El primer satélite artificial: sus efectos en la opinión pública,* Santiago de Chile, 1958.

prise, but on the whole the unpredictability of the future was accepted as a normal feature and hazard of conducting interstate relations. In the contemporary world increasing stocks of information and continually improving means of storing and maintaining access to them, together with constantly refined techniques of analysis, have led government and business enterprises to develop planning and decision devices which try to take account of the conditions of uncertainty that face the enterprise and generate courses of action for some of the multiple directions that the future may follow. As these devices have become more widely accepted, managers of state affairs and state organizations have shown an increasing interest in them. Their availability seems to reduce the tolerance for uncertainty and the capacity for self-reliance.[73] Unfortunately, most political crisis planning is relatively ineffective because choices are usually highly sensitive to very specific elements of the context in which crises arise, elements which can hardly be known in advance. Contingency planning has considerable advance educational value, but government leaders and their advisers are for the most part dependent in specific crises on *ad hoc* decisions and not on responses devised in advance for hypothetical circumstances.

Most government decisions revolve not around sudden crises but around persistent problems and issues. For such problems *ad hoc* modes of response seem ineffective. Leaving aside whether it was a sensible objective for the United States to pursue, the aim of

[73] Probably the prestige of these developments as well as their possible utility increase their attraction. But perhaps another factor is that university curricula and the selection and self-selection of personnel in government political service increasingly lead to the recruitment of persons whose training includes quantitative studies and the methods of inquiry appropriate to them. This training is indispensable for those who wish to pursue scientific and academic careers and valuable for the government political analyst. Yet for the person who must interpret the political and social behavior of foreign groups and who does not have the possibility of passing several lifetimes in various societies, a reasonably deep study of comparative social and political history and related disciplines is essential and can better endow him with the ability to understand, live with, and respond effectively to the political behavior of others than can a correlation matrix. The matrix may be of the highest value for organizing empirical data and may inspire or test theoretical ideas of importance. But this does not justify the confusion that seems to have arisen between the aims and tools appropriate to a foreign office and to the classroom and laboratory.

raising the per capita national product of the Latin American countries would certainly seem to require some sort of long-term planning. But it is not self-evident that even such long-range objectives could not be handled by a series of *ad hoc* decisions taken at especially opportune moments. This would more particularly seem to be the case if one aim of the program is to be able to exercise leverage either on behalf of the program itself or for the benefit of other goals. The very existence of a long-term commitment reduces leverage. Soviet aid has shown the political benefits that can be derived from a largely *ad hoc,* rather than programmatic, mode of action.

A principal goal of government in the foreign area is to establish positions of influence in foreign countries. It might seem reasonably clear that the attempt to attain influence cannot be deferred until the moment the influence is needed.[74] Nonetheless an opposite position has some merit. Influence is an unstable commodity partly because leaders and governments change, and partly because other circumstances often lead to a rapid dissipation of influence after it has been acquired. For this reason it might indeed be sensible to attempt an *ad hoc* creation of influence by investing heavily, quickly, and abruptly over a short period rather than expending smaller amounts of effort and resources over a longer period.

The advantages of the long-term and the *ad hoc* modes of action can partly be combined by sequential decision-making which retains the outlines of a longer-term program while providing for substantial flexibility at each decision point as information accumulates and conditions change. Indeed, this flexibility should include the option of scrapping the entire program. In practice, of course, something of this nature does occur but a lot of flexibility is lost by much planning in advance and particularly by the *commitments* that such plans create. By announcing the Alliance for Progress as a ten-year program the United States government gave hostages to Latin America, to the United States public and business, and to its own aid bureaucracy.

10. *Dilemmas*

Much of the foregoing gives the impression that a better appreciation of one or another aspect of political life or a fuller or more

---

[74] See the discussion in Chapter 11.3 on this theme, especially with respect to the smaller powers.

intelligent use of one or another device would have turned policy failures into successes. Indeed when one reviews the almost endless books, including the present one, that reveal with such ease the errors of politicians, statesmen, and bureaucrats, it becomes difficult to understand how with so much intelligence and perspicuity about, it was possible for governments to behave so ineffectively.

May it not be that recognizing difficulties and errors (even in advance and not simply *post facto*) does not necessarily mean being able to circumvent or remove them? Criticism usually assumes that alternative lines of action would have provided acceptable solutions had statesmen been well enough informed or resourceful enough to choose them. Perhaps this is an overoptimistic view of the world. Perhaps with respect to some problems the truth is that the statesman's interventions have little chance of success no matter what he does. We resign ourselves, on occasion, to the extremes of nature, and we recognize, too, that we may find ourselves helpless in the face of some diseases. In the political sphere, however, we reject as intolerable, as subversive of human dignity, the notion that at times planning and action may be futile, at least in the sense that what we do has no more chance of success than many other lines of action (or inaction) that might be proposed.

Perhaps, too, the critic's view of political life overlooks that the existence of more effective lines of action does not preclude the existence of conditions that imposed the line of action that was in fact followed. The alternative lines of conduct that we prescribe *post facto* sometimes turn out, on closer inspection, to assume a state of the world, especially a quality of leadership,[75] that did not in fact exist.

Leaders who institute major programs often seem to do so as if they were going to be the sole administrators of them. Possessing in themselves the advantages of single-mindedness and of freedom from the constraints later to be imposed by an enormous collaborative (and competitive) effort, they judge the prospects of the program in this favorable light. Leaving aside cases where a certain amount of cynicism is involved, this produces a higher expectation

---

[75] Political leaders are often selected because of abilities relevant to getting into power and staying in power. These prime qualities of the politician may answer to the requirements of domestic politics, but they are often inadequate for responsibilities in foreign affairs.

of success than is justified. In fact, of course, the program is about to recruit several thousand persons and hundreds of committees [76] and organizations, and is about to set into motion a train of side or secondary effects, both domestic and foreign, that dominate the resulting picture more than do the intended effects of the program (see, for example, Chapter 10.1). These secondary effects are taken even less into advance account than are side effects in medical practice.

Fortunately, failures of major programs are not always as disastrous as they well might be. The grave contingencies that sometimes inspire such programs, and which the programs are intended to forestall, generally have a probability well below unity. It turns out, then, that we may invest enormous resources to meet contingencies which will not arise, or which when they arise may be evaluated less negatively than in anticipation. In some contexts where the feared events are uncertain and, if realized, not immediately disastrous, it might be just as sensible to put all the resources about to be devoted to forestalling them into productive use and to apply them and their accumulated "earnings" in massive amounts if and when the apprehended dangers take on a more tangible form. This requires, of course, that time ("lead time") for such action be available after the danger signals become very clear.

But perhaps a better way to avoid expensive failures might be not to seek more sophisticated plans of action but to pursue more modest aims. Modest aims, and decisions taken with the fullest provision for withdrawal or radical modification, might provide modest successes that in the long run could add up to greater benefits than are provided by "enterprises of great pith and moment" for which one is ill-prepared and ill-equipped.

---

[76] "If some six or eight sensible men be brought together to consult, they become so many fools." Guicciardini, *Ricordi,* Second Series, No. 112.

Index

Acheson, Dean, 273n
Adelman, Maurice, 132n
Adenauer, Konrad, 21
ad hoc decisions, 298-300
Adler, John H., 193n
advocacy of Latin American interests, 119-125. *See also under countries*
affinities, national, 104-118. *See also under countries*
Africa: 9, 79n; aid relations, 161, 167, 168, 186, 187; and Brazil, 28, 29, 68; contacts with Latin America, 106-109; trade, 119, 237; and United Nations, 56
Afro-Asian Conference, 108n
Afro-Asian and Latin American Solidarity Organization, 22
L'agence de coopération culturelle et technique des pays francophones, 134n
Agence France Presse, 156
Agency for International Development, *see* U.S. AID
Aguilar, Luis E., 289n
AID, *see* U.S. AID
aid: bilateral *versus* multilateral, 171-172; conflicting objectives, 263-265; economic uses of, 190-194; evaluation of, 253n, 254n; grants, 165-167; methods of calculating, 162, 164, 165, 187n; patron-client relations, 185-188; political uses of, 159, 160, 166n, 176-188, 253n, 298; private *versus* public, 173-174; public opinion on, 188-190; relative donor shares, 162-165; technical assistance,

167; termination of, 28n, 280-281; tying of, 122, 191-194 *passim;* volunteer services, 167-171. *See also* Alliance for Progress; leverage; United States, aid; U.S. AID; United States, military assistance; *and under countries*
Air France, 64
Akhito, Crown Prince of Japan, 196
Alanso, Isidoro, 101n
Alexander, Robert J., 94n
Alger, Chadwick F., 199n, 200n
Algeria, 29
Allende, Salvador: 21, 25, 67n, 273n, 286, 291n; attitude toward U.S. State Department, 270; election of, 241; recognition of East Germany, 228; and U.S. investments, 75, 252; and U.S. Peace Corps, 170
Alliance for Progress: 75, 160, 162n, 164n, 193, 296, 298; attacked by Latin American left, 294; British criticism of, 205-206; evaluation of, 253-254, 257, 262, 264, 272, 273, 288, 291-293, 300; and Israel, 130; proposed administrative reform, 273: *See also* United States, aid, *and* U.S. AID
Alliance Française, 134, 135, 138, 148, 157
Alsogaray, Álvaro C., 128
Altamirano, Carlos, 266n
Amadeo, Mario, 112n
América Latina, 114
American Motors, 286
Amérique Latine, 114

Anaconda, 247
Andean Pact, 251, 252, 253
Andrade, Joaquin, 266n
Angola, 28, 29, 161
Anguilla, 4
Antarctica, 16-17, 275
Antarctica Treaty, 17
Anti-Americanism, 294. *See also* prestige, public opinion
Antofagasta (Chili) and Bolivian Railway, 72
Apollo XI, 144n, 261, 298
APSA, 67
Aranales Catalán, Emilio, 56
Arbeitsgemeinschaft für Entwicklungshilfe, 169
Arbenz Guzmán, Jacobo, 239
arbitration and mediation, 5n, 6, 233
Arce, José, 6n
Ardao, Arturo, 114n
Argentina: 27, 49, 51n, 54n, 57, 68, 232, 236, 249; as aid recipient, 161; Atucha nuclear power plant, 48, 49; cultural activities of foreign powers in, 94n, 134, 138, 141, 145n, 151-155 *passim,* 157; diplomatic missions received, 199, 200, 202; economic decline, 291, 292n; and EEC, 120; foreign investment in, 42, 235, 251n; income growth per capita, 254n; Jewish population, 185; meat embargoes, 7, 233, 281; migrants, 80, 83, 87, 91, 97n; migration policy, 82, 84, 89; nuclear policy, 257; official visits to, 196, 218, 219; public sector, 285n; and South Africa, 28; state enterprises, 285; territorial issues, 4, 6, 7, 16; territorial waters, 12, 14; trade, 32, 33n, 38; and United Kingdom, 233
"Argentinization," 252, 287
Arinos, Afonso, 107
Armas Barea, Calixto A., 51n
Arnault, Jacques, 84n, 114n, 231n
Aruba, 3n
Associated Press, 156
Association internationale des parlementaires de la langue française, 133
Atahualpa, 109n
Atlantic Alliance, 19, 25, 286n
Atucha atomic power plant, 48, 49
Auslandsorganisation, 85
Australia, 16, 55n, 65, 89, 194n
Austria, 34n, 194n
autonomy and independence movements, 4-6, 8-9, 275

Baerresen, C. W., 35n
Bahama Islands, 4
Bailey, Norman A., 52n, 130n
Bailey, Samuel L., 82n, 86n, 97n
Balaguer, Joaquín, 156n
Baldwin, David A., 181n
Balous, Suzanne, 132n, 133n, 135n
bananas, 11, 120, 242
Bank of London and South America, *see* BOLSA
Bank of Tokyo, 72
banks, foreign, 39-40
Barbados, 4, 10, 31, 103n
Barber, Willard F., 176n
Barcelona Traction Light and Power Company, 248n
bargaining, 278, 281. *See also* leverage
Barghoorn, Frederick C., 146n
Barker, R. E., 154n
Barnes, Peter, 30n
Barrientos Ortuño, René, 296
Bartley, Russell H., 240n
Bastos de Ávila, Fernando, 82n
Bates, Margaret, 82n, 85n
Baudouin, King of the Belgians, 196
Bautista Alberdi, Juan, 82
Beagle Channel, 198, 233
Belaúnde Terry, Fernando, 104
Belgium: 176, 194n; aid, 171n; diplomatic representation, 200, 203; investments, 43, 64n; military training, 26; state visit, 196; trade, 34, 237, 245n
Belize, 5
Bell, Wendell, 107n
Ben Bella, Ahmed, 296
Benton, William, 155n
Bergeroux, N. J., 8n
Berne Union, 154
Bertil, Prince (Sweden), 196
Betancourt, Rómulo, 183
Black Panthers, 108
black power, 7n, 108
Blancpain, Marc, 113n
Bodenheimer, Susanne, 274n
Boix, Emile, 93n
Bolivia: 130n, 146, 148, 240, 249n, 257n, 280n, 286; aid, 169, 170, 176; and Andean Pact, 251; expropriations, 247n, 249n; income growth, 254; trade, 35n, 244; Soviet diplomatic mission, 202; and United States, 257
BOLSA, 205, 249
Bolton, Sir George, 57, 59, 205, 216
Bonaire, 3n

book exports, 151-155
Bormann, Martin, 100
Borodin, Mikhail, 265
Bouscaren, Anthony T., 79n
Bradford, Colin I., Jr., 61n
Brams, Steven J., 199n, 200n
Branco, Castelo, *see* Castelo Branco
Brandt, Willy, 228
Brazil: 48, 54n, 66, 68, 257; and
  Africa, 107; aid, 161, 170, 174n,
  176, 178, 182, 183, 188n, 191;
  coffee, 276n; coup of 1964, 296; cultural activities of foreign powers in,
  134-138 *passim*, 141, 145n, 147, 152,
  153, 157; diplomatic missions received, 199, 200, 202, 209n; fishing
  conflicts, 13, 16, 217; foreign investments in, 43, 44, 45, 251n; foreign
  languages in, 85; and Germany, 227;
  income growth, 254n; and India, 106;
  and Japan, 225, 226; Jewish population, 185n; "Lobster War," 217;
  migrants, 80, 81, 82, 85-90 *passim*;
  migrants as entrepreneurs, 91; military affairs, 26, 28-29, 176, 232, 234,
  236; nuclear policy, 31n, 257; official visits to, 196, 210, 218, 219;
  and Portugal, 28-29, 111n, 112-113,
  237; potential, 58n, 59; public sector, 285; and South Africa, 28; and
  Soviet Union, 238; territorial waters,
  12, 14, 16; trade, 32, 33n, 91n, 244
Brazilian Traction, Light and Power
  of Toronto, 43n
Brezhnev doctrine, 295
British Broadcasting Corporation, 140,
  147n
British Commonwealth, 10, 121, 234,
  265
British Conservative Party, 20
British Council, 138, 140-141, 148
British Guiana, 4, 5, 8. *See also*
  Guyana
British Honduras, 4, 6, 142n, 170n
British Labour Party, 20, 189
British Virgin Islands, 4
British Volunteer Service Overseas, 168
broadcast services, 140, 147, 149
Bronheim, David, 11n, 259n
Bryan-Chamorro Treaty, 12
Buchan, Alastair, 29n
Bulganin, Nicolai, 39, 146
business and government, 270

Caballero Calderón, Eduardo, 136n
Cabral, Pedro Alvares, 106
Cadena, Cecilia, 236n, 256

Caetano, Marcello, 29, 122
Caire, Guy, 96n
Camelot, *see* Project Camelot
Campbell, John F., 202n, 209n
Canada: 49, 58, 64n, 102, 134n, 286n;
  aid, 162, 163, 166n, 171, 173, 187,
  189, 190-191, 194; and Cuba, 61,
  73; diplomatic representation, 203-
  204; distance from Latin America,
  69; economic results, 237; fishing
  conflicts, 13; investments in Brazil,
  43, 44; military sales, 256; and OAS,
  60-62; objectives, 60, 62; trade, 32,
  34, 237; U.S. investments in, 46;
  volunteer services, 168, 171
Canadian Export Credit Insurance
  Act, 191
Canadian University Service Overseas
  (CUSO), 168
Cano, Sanin, 146
Cárdenas, Lázaro, 146
Caribbean: 10, 233; as aid recipient,
  164, 168; students abroad, 142;
  western security interests, 25, 239.
  See also under countries
Carlos Prestes, Luis, 240n
Carmichael, Stokely, 108, 109
Carranza, Venustiano, 265
Carter, Gregory A., 246n
Castelo Branco, Humberto, 115, 120,
  178, 287, 296
Castro, Fidel: 75, 212, 239n, 264n;
  appeal to Europe, 286; and black
  power, 108; and Escalante case,
  230n, 281n; and French intellectuals,
  136; and French properties, 72; inter-
  vention in Latin America, 23, 239;
  Latin American attitudes toward, 23;
  and Soviet Union, 23, 230n, 239, 242,
  281n; and U.S. policy in Latin
  America, 75. *See also* Cuba
Catholic church, 18, 101, 109n, 174
Catholic Coordinating Committee
  (CCST), 168, 170
Cavazza, Fabio Luca, 20n, 21n, 51n,
  70n, 97n, 113n, 126n, 143n, 176n
Central American Association of
  Textile Industries, 225
Central American Common Market
  (CACM), 224, 244
Centre des hautes études de l'armement,
  232
Cerqueira, Silas, 285n
Césaire, Aimé, 8
Ceylon, 74, 186
Chaplin, David, 102n

Charlotte, Grand Duchess of Luxembourg, 196
Charter of Algiers, 122
Chile: 48, 49, 68, 127, 135, 263n, 295n; aid, 164, 170, 174n, 188n, 297; Allende government, 241, 273n; Andean Pact, 251; Antarctic claim, 16, 17; and China, 67, 257n; and Christian Democratic Party, 21; cultural activities of foreign powers in, 145n, 151, 152, 153; diplomatic missions received, 199, 200; expropriations, 247, 252; far left and West Germany, 266, 286; foreign debt, 254n, 255; foreign investments in, 42, 253; income growth, 254n; official visits to, 196, 219; public sector, 285n, 286; recognition of East Germany, 227, 266n, 274, territorial waters, 12, 14; trade, 33n, 235, 244; U.S. policy and Allende government, 270, 279n
Chilean-French Mixed Commission, 113
China: 240-241n, 278; cultural diplomacy, 147; diplomatic representation, 257n; distance from Latin America, 67; early contacts with Mexico, 106; migrants, 102; political interests, 30, 257n
Chocon hydroelectric complex, 231n
Chonchol, Jacques, 289n
Christian Democracy, 20, 21, 128, 297
Chrysler, 249, 252, 286
CIA, 137, 202, 208
Cialdea, Basilio, 85n, 86n
civic action, 215, 264
Cleaver, Eldridge, 108
Clifford, Evans, 105n
Clifford, J. M., 182n, 193n, 214n
Climent, Juan Bautista, 99n
Clissold, Stephen, 54n, 98n, 183n, 265n
coercion, see leverage
COFACE, 39, 72
coffee, 219, 241, 267, 276n
Cohen, Stephen S., 127n
cold war, 20n, 52-53
Colli, Nestor S., 71n
Colombia: 19n, 54n, 65n, 232, 249; aid, 168, 170n, 174n, 188n, 253n; Andean Pact, 251; cultural activities of foreign powers in, 140, 145n, 150n, 152, 157; diplomatic missions received, 199, 200; guerrilla warfare, 240, 264n; foreign investment in, 42; and Japan, 225; political visits to, 196, 219; territorial issue,

12; territorial waters, 14; trade, 33n, 35n; public sector, 39, 249, 285n, 286
colonialism, 3, 4, 5-6, 7, 8-9, 19, 29, 55, 56
COMIBOL, 249n
Committee on Latin American Studies, 142
commodity stabilization, 121
Commonwealth Sugar Agreement, 10
communism, 20, 21-22, 53, 84, 260-261
communist bloc, 32, 33n, 37, 146n
Communist International Youth Service, 169
communist parties: European, 21-22; Latin American, 22, 214, 238-239, 239-240, 257n, 265, 295; Soviet relations with Latin American, 214, 238, 265
COMSAT, 282
Concorde, 67n, 282
Confalonieri, Carlo Cardinal, 109n
conflicting objectives, 263-267
Congo-Brazzaville, 28
Congress, see U.S. Congress
construction projects: 286; competition for, 47-50; effect on trade with Latin America, 48
Conservative Overseas Bureau, 20
Conte-Long Amendment, 179, 276
Cooperative Republic of Guyana, see Guyana
Cornblit, Oscar, 91n, 98n
Cornelius, William G., 18n
Cortês, Geraldo de Menezes, 82n, 85n, 86n
Cortés, Hernán, 109, 110n
Corvalán, Luis, 240n
Costa e Silva, Arturo, 136, 183, 210, 296
Costa Mendez, Nicanor, 66, 69, 122
Costa Rica: 14, 145n, 146, 147, 286; diplomatic missions received, 199n, 200; elections, 296n; and Japan, 225; military assistance received, 170n, 176
Council of the Americas, 252-253
credit incentives for trade, 24, 38, 39
Cuauhtémoc, 110n
Cuba: 11, 57, 61, 145n, 239n, 264; and Africa, 108; and black power, 108; cultural diplomacy, 136-137, 149n, 150n; embargo of, 24, 257; Aníbal Escalante case, 230n, 281n; expropriation, 72-73, 246; fishing conflicts, 13; and France, 64-65, 230n, 281n; and Jamaica, 103; and Japan, 225; migrants, 293; military presence in

Africa, 28; nuclear policy, 30, 31n; and OAS, 24; shipping to, 24n: and Soviet Union, 23, 169, 230n, 239, 281n, 295; and Spain, 103, 235, 237, 287; territorial waters, 14; trade, 24, 32, 64, 179, 225n, 235; U.S. intervention, 24, 27, 257, 294; U.S. investments in, 46; and U.S. Latin American policy, 75. *See also* Castro

Cuban missile crisis, 19
cultural accords, 135, 137, 147-148
cultural programs, 131-158. *See also country entries*
Curaçao, 3n, 9
Cyprus, 55, 68, 196, 219, 238

Davison, W. Phillips, 102n, 149n
Debré, Michael, 121, 172
debts: collection of, 71-72; repayment and servicing, 166, 254-255
de Gaulle, Charles: 8, 10, 50n, 119, 172n, 190, 217n, 230n, 231n, 261n; and French migration, 100n; on Latin American potential, 58; Latin American visit, 63, 66, 120, 196, 198, 204, 216-217, 228, 229, 236n, 294; political objective, 63, 230; political style, 22, 127, 183n, 217, 230n, 297
de Gobineau, Joseph, 114
de Jong, Petrus J. S., 10
de la Sauchère, Eléna, 151n
de la Vallée Poussin, Et., 90n
del Campo, Salustiano, 110n
Delgado, Julian, 43n
de Murville, Maurice Couve, 283n
Denmark, 65, 171n, 196, 197
dependency, 274n
de Prat Gay, Gastón, 19n, 56n
Deutscher Akademischer Austauschdienst, 139
Development Assistance Committee (DAC), 162n, 194
día de la Hispanidad, 111
día de la raza, 111
Dienst in Übersee, 169
Diesel Nacional, 286
Dinerstein, Herbert S., 128n, 238n
diplomacy: 13; styles of, 70-71, 204-220. *See also* tutelary style *and under countries*
diplomatic representation: 199-204, 238-239; depreciation of, 204; determinants of, 199, 203-204; growth of, 200-201. *See also under countries*
distance, effect on political relations, 66-69, 295

Dollot, Louis, 132n, 137n
Dominican Republic: 102, 145n, 244; aid, 170n, 188n; diplomatic missions received, 199, 204; territorial waters, 14; U.S. intervention, 25, 27, 294
double nationality, 111
Duncan, W. Raymond, 23n, 183n, 239n, 240n

East Caribbean Federation, 4, 233
East Germany, *see* German Democratic Republic
Eban, Abba, 218n
Echeverría, Luis, 59
economic planning, 127, 129, 178, 278, 287, 288
Economist para América Latina, 143
Ecuador: 130n, 145n, 232, 286; aid, 160, 175; Andean Pact, 251; Antarctic claim, 16; banana exports, 11, 120n; diplomatic missions received, 200, 204; fishing conflicts and territorial waters, 12, 13, 14, 16n, 266, 280-281; official visits, 196, 198, 219; Soviet diplomats expelled, 265, 266; trade, 244; U.S. military mission expelled, 26n, 175; U.S. relations, 170n, 175, 179, 257
EEC: 10n, 144; and Antilles trade, 9-10, 121n; and Argentinian beef, 230, 231n; and francophone countries, 230, 234, 269; and Latin American trade interests, 119-124
Egypt, *see* UAR
Einaudi, Luigi, 26n, 101n, 268n
Eisenhower, Dwight D., 162n
Elder, Robert E., 141n, 148n, 149n, 150n, 151n, 155n
Elizabeth, Queen, 196
El Salvador, 15, 200, 237, 254n
embargoes, 7, 24, 233, 257, 281-282
emigration, *see* migrants
emigration from Latin America, 258n
Encuentro River, 233
enforced sale, *see* expropriation
Engels, Friedrich, 289n
Enrique Rodó, José, 258
Epstein, Fritz T., 26n
Erhard, Ludwig, 63, 236n
Erickson, John, 25n
Escalante, Aníbal, 230n, 281n
Eshkol, Levi, 218n
Ethiopia, 107, 196
EUCD, 21
Europe: 11, 19-20, 23, 143, 202; challenge to United States, 62-66; gains in Latin American markets, 244; in-

Europe (Continued)
vestments, 40-43 *passim;* limited security interests, 27; military sales, 64, 175, 255-256; trade rivalry with U.S., 37. *See also under individual countries and* Latin America, foreign investments

"l'Europe tropicale," 121n

European Economic Community, *see* EEC

exchange programs, 139, 150-151

exports, *see* trade

expropriation, 72, 129, 246-252, 282. *See also under countries*

Fabiola, Queen, 196

Falange, 110, 151, 236

Falkland Islands, 4, 6, 7, 22, 198, 233, 275

Fanfani, Amintore, 19, 24, 55, 62n, 70, 119, 143, 197

Farah, Empress of Iran, 196

Federal Republic of Germany: 13, 20, 65, 66, 281; advocacy of Latin American interests, 122; aid, 160, 163, 166n, 171, 172, 176, 187, 194n, 262n; aid, economic uses, 173n, 192; aid, political uses, 181-182, 185; aid, public support, 188; book exports, 152-154 *passim;* and Chilean left, 266, 287; coffee taxes, 267; conflict with Brazil, 228n; construction projects, 47-49 *passim, 67;* as creditor, 255; cultural diplomacy, 137-140, 156; diplomatic problems, 228; diplomatic representation, 199, 200, 201; diplomatic style, 213, 218, 270; investments, 40-45 *passim, 47;* migrants, 83, 84, 85, 89, 226; migrants, economic benefits from, 92, 94; migrants, political effects, 97, 98, 100; military sales, 256; as a model, 127-128; objectives, 51, 52, 57, 226, 260, 266; official visits, 196; reparation payments, 187n; restitution of German property, 72; results, economic, 227; results, political, 227-228; trade, 32, 33, 34, 35n, 38, 40, 244n, 297; volunteer service, 168-169

Federal Trade Commission, 283

Federation of the Indies, 4, 233

Ferenczi, Imre, 80n

Fernandes, Florestan, 91n

Fiat, 248n, 249, 252, 286n

Fines, André, 92n, 191n

Finland, 65

Fisherman's Protective Act, 12, 13, 178

fishing conflicts, 12-13, 217, 275, 278-279, 280-281. *See also under countries*

Fishman, J. A., 290n

fishmeal, 11

Fleet, Michael, 101n

Food and Agriculture Organization (FAO), 189

Food for Peace, 179

foot-and-mouth disease, 7, 233

Ford, 249, 286

foreign-born, *see* migrants

Foreign Commerce Bank of the USSR, 215

foreign investments: 173; affected by migrants, 93-95; book value, European and U.S. shares, 40-41; flow, European and U.S. shares, 41, 42-47; return on, 247; statistical reporting, 271-272

Fortaleza, 13

Fossum, Egil, 269n

France: advocacy of Latin American interests, 120-121, 122, 123; and African states, 124; aid, 162, 163, 164, 165, 166, 169, 171, 172, 176, 185, 186; aid, economic uses, 173n, 191, 194n; aid, political uses, 182; aid, public support of, 190; book exports, 152-154 *passim;* conflict with Argentina, 230, 231n; conflict of objectives, 266; construction projects, 47-49 *passim;* cultural diplomacy, 131-137, 157; diplomatic representation, 200, 201, 203, 204; diplomatic style, 216-217; distance from Latin America, 67, 68; fishing disputes, 13, 16, 230; French left and Latin American left, 231; intra-governmental conflict, 269; investments, 40, 41, 43, 44, 46, 230n; *latinité,* 52, 113-114; "Lobster War," 13, 217; migrants, 83, 87; migrants, economic benefits from, 92; migrants, political benefits from, 99-100; military missions, 26, 191, 232; military sales, 27, 175, 191, 231-232, 255, 256, 282; as model, 127, 128; nuclear tests, 23, 230, 282; official visits, 195, 197, 198; political objectives, 52, 58, 63, 70, 261n; prestige, 258n; protection of nationals, 71, 72; relations with Cuba, 64n, 72, 229n, 230n; results, economic, 229, 231-232; results, political, 230-231, 232;

rocket base, 7, 29n; territorial questions, 3, 7, 8, 9, 16; trade, 32, 33, 34, 35n, 36, 39, 229, 245n; trade fairs, 39; and Treaty of Tlatelolco, 30; and U.S. pressure, 63-65. *See also* affinities; de Gaulle; language instruction
Franco, Francisco, 63, 103, 110
Free Democratic Party, 21
Freeman, Orville L., 58
Frei Montalva, Eduardo, 20n, 22n, 25n, 65, 127, 197, 219, 276, 292n
French Guiana, 7
French Polynesia, 7
French Volunteer Service, 169
Frente Amplio, 241
Friedrich Ebert Foundation, 21
Friedrich Naumann Foundation, 21
Frye, Alton, 85n, 97n, 216n
Fuentes, Carlos, 109
Fulbright, J. William, 274
Furtado, Celso, 284, 285n

gadna-nachal, 130
Galindo, Alberto, 90n
Galtung, Johan, 68n
García Lupo, Rogelio, 19n
García Robles, Alfonso, 30n
Garibaldi, Giuseppe, 115n
General Motors, 249, 286
geopolitics, 19
German Democratic Republic: 52, 266; cultural diplomacy, 140, 147, recognition of, 52, 137, 227-228, 261n
German Development Service, 168, 169, 213
"German miracle," 128
Germany, *see* Federal Republic of Germany
Gerth, H. H., 211n
Gewandt, Heinrich, 128n
Ghana, 29
Ghandi, Indira, 60, 106, 196
Gibert, Stephen P., 173n
Gibraltar, 52, 55, 236
Gibson, Carlos, 74n
GKN, 47n
Gladkov, N., 242n
Gleich, Albrecht von, *see* von Gleich
Glick, Edward B., 130n
Goethe Institute, 138, 139, 148
Goldman, Marshall I., 160n
Goldwater, Barry, 58
"golondrinas," 82n
Gómez Martínez, Fernando, 19n
Gonzalez, Gustavo R., 116n
Gordon, Wendell C., 254n

Goulart, João, 155, 178, 217n, 287
government enterprises, *see* state enterprises
Goytisolo, Juan, 99n
Grandjeat, Pierre, 89n, 90n
Granma, 271n
Great Britain, *see* United Kingdom
Great Corn Island, 12
Greece, 24, 55, 219, 238
Grey, Sir Edward, 204
Griffin, Keith, 274n
Grondona, Mariano, 117n
Grosser, Alfred, 22n, 216n
Guadeloupe, 7-8, 121n
Guantánamo, 11, 27
Guatemala: 18, 170n, 225, 239, 240; diplomatic missions received, 200; income growth, 254n; territorial claims, 4, 6, 7; territorial waters, 15; U.S. intervention, 27, 294
Guereña, Jacinto Luis, 99n
guerrilla warfare, *see* Latin America, internal security
Guevara, Ernesto (Ché), 23
Guicciardini, Francesco, 275n, 302n
Gulf of Aqaba, 198
Gulf of Fonseca, 12
Gulf Oil, 247, 249n
Gurtov, Melvin, 162n
Guyana: 142n, 146; and Africa, 108; aid received, 170n; black power, 109; and Caribbean Federation, 4; territorial conflict, 9; trade, 244

"H" Program, 63
Haile Selassie, Emperor, 107, 196
Haiti, 15, 145n, 180n, 250n, 294
Hallstein Docrtine, 181, 227, 266n
Halmos, Paul, 157n
Hamilton, Edward K., 188n
Hamm, Harry, 108n
Hamon, Leo, 63n
Hamuy, Eduardo, 298n
Han Guk University, 147
Hani, Susumu, 105
Hanke, Lewis, 110n
ul-Haq, Mahhub, 193n
Harbron, John D., 102n
Hasson, Joseph A., 20n
Havana Cultural Congress, 136
Havana Solidarity Conference, 140
Havana Tricontinental Conference, 184
Henrique Cardosa, Fernando, 285n
Herrera, Felipe, 254n
Hickenlooper Amendment, 73-74, 179, 249n, 276, 279n

Hirohito, Emperor of Japan, 225n
Hispanidad, 52, 111, 113
Hitachi, 47n
Hobbes, Thomas, 281n
Hochman, Harold M., 175n, 179n
Hodara, Joseph, 274n
Holbik, Karel, 39n, 241n
Holland, *see* Netherlands
Holmes, John W., 62n
Honduras, 11, 12, 15, 199, 200
Houston, John A., 55n, 56n
Houtart, François, 101n
Hovet, Thomas, Jr., 56n
Hudson, Richard, 30n
Humboldt Stiftung, 139
Hunt, James C., 42n, 46n, 121n
Hussein, King of Jordan, 218

"Ibero-American," 114
ICEM, 90
Iceland, 203n
IDB, *see* Inter-American Development Bank
ideological conflict, 20, 21-22
Illia, Arturo, 225n
IMF, 180n
immigration, *see* migrants
Imperial Conference of 1911, 205
imperialism, *see* colonialism
imports, *see* trade
Impreglio, 48
independence movements, *see* autonomy
India: 60, 65, 200; and aid, 161, 184n, 186; and Brazil, 106, 196; objectives, 59-60; state visit, 196
Indianos, 96
Indonesia, 186
influence, 279-280, 296-297, 299-300. *See also* bargaining; leverage
Informational Media Guaranty Program, 155
Ingrey, Norman A., 89n
Institut des hautes études de la défense nationale, 232
L'institut français d'Amérique latine, 134n
Institute of Latin American Studies (London), 142
Instituto Italo-Latinoamericano, 20n, 143, 236
Institutos de Cultura Hispánica, 145, 146
insurance: of investments, 174, 250, 252; for trade, 24, 38-39, 174, 191
Inter-American Defense Board, 27
Inter-American Development Bank (IDB), 62, 75, 172, 173, 180n, 181, 191, 194, 254n

Inter-American Economic and Social Council, 268
Inter-American Press Association, 156n
Inter-American Treaty of Reciprocal Assistance (Rio Pact), 27
Inter-American Tropical Tuna Commission Treaty, 13n
internal security, *see* Latin America, internal security
International Court of Justice, 16n, 24n, 248
International Geophysical Year, 17
International Petroleum Corporation (IPC), 74, 175, 179, 180, 252
International Solidarity Institute (ISI), 21
International Telephone and Telegraph (ITT), 250
International Visitors Program, 150
interventions, *see* U.S., interventions
intra-governmental conflicts, 267-272
investments, *see* foreign investments
Iran, 147, 196
Ireland, 65
Isaacson, José, 185n
Israel: 65, 238; aid, 56, 129n, 130, 184-185, 187, 218; and Argentina, 37; and France, 231; as model, 130; national security, 28, 56; official visits, 196, 218n; political style, 218
ItalConsult, 47n
Italian Coordinating Committee on Volunteers (CCVS), 169
Italy: 20, 21, 22, 65; advocacy of Latin American interests, 119, 120; affinities with Latin America, 104, 114; aid, 163, 166n, 169, 171, 172, 173n, 176, 185, 187, 189, 192, 194n; book exports, 152, 153, 154; construction projects, 47-49 *passim;* as creditor, 255; cultural diplomacy, 143-144, 157; diplomatic representation, 199, 200, 201, 203; diplomatic style, 70, 216; investments, 41, 43, 44, 45, 272; migrants, 82-87 *passim;* migrants, economic benefits from, 91, 92, 95, 96; migrants, political effects, 91n, 97; military sales, 236, 256; military training, 26; as model, 126-127; political objectives, 51, 55, 57, 62, 70; results, economic, 235; results, political, 236; state enterprises, 287n; state visits, 196, 197; trade, 32, 33, 34, 35n, 37, 235; "triangular policy," 19-20, 57n; volunteer services, 169, 171

310

Ito, Nobuo, 105n, 224n
Ivory Coast, 65

Jamaica, 4, 10, 15, 61n, 103, 107, 170n
James, Daniel, 60n
Japan: 23, 27, 225n, 266, 281; advocacy of Latin American interests, 123, 124; aid, 163, 166n, 172, 185, 189, 194n; aid, economic uses of, 173n, 192; construction projects, 47, 49; as creditor, 255; cultural diplomacy, 152, 153, 157, 226n; diplomatic representation, 199, 200, 201, 203; diplomatic style, 71, 216; distance from Latin America, 69; early contacts with Latin America, 104, 105; fishing conflicts, 13, 16; investments, 41, 43, 44, 45, 47, 224; migrants, 81, 83, 85, 86, 89, 90, 95n, 225, 226; migrants economic benefits from, 91, 93n, 94; migrants, political effects of, 97-98, 282; as model, 128, 128n; objectives, 60, 63; official visits, 196; and Panama Canal, 11, 69n; raw material shipping distance, 69; reparation payments, 187n; restitution of Japanese property, 70; results, economic, 224-225, 226; results, political, 225-226; sugar purchases from Cuba, 225n; trade, 32-36 *passim*, 38, 39, 224, 245n; volunteer service, 169
Japan Overseas Cooperation Volunteers, 169
Jean, Grand Duke of Luxembourg, 196
Jeanneney Report, 182
Jews, 184-185
Johannesburg, 68
Johnson, Cecil, 147n, 241n
Johnson, John J., 207n
Johnson, Leland L., 246n
Johnson, Lyndon B., 63, 175, 196
joint ventures, 253
Jordan, 218
Journal of Latin American Studies, 143
Joxe, Alain, 236n, 256n
Juan Carlos, Prince, 110
Juliana, Queen, 196

Kaplan, Marcos, 285n
Kaunda, Kenneth, 68, 196
Kelchner, Warren H., 52n
Kennedy, Edward M., 90
Kennedy, John F., 66n, 296
Kenny, Michael, 96n
Kenworthy, Eldon, 97n
Keohane, Robert Owen, 56n

Khrushchev, Nikita, 39, 146
Kiesinger, Kurt Georg, 10
Kirkpatrick, F. A., 67n, 205n
Kiser, Clyde C., 79n
Kitrón, Moisés, 185n
Kitzinger, Sheilah, 107n
Kojima, Kiyoshi, 45n
Konrad Adenauer Foundation, 21
Korean War, 19n
Korey, William, 184n
Krieger Vasena, Adelbert, 120
Krisher, B., 71n
Kuczynski, R., 79n
Kuwait, 7, 65, 237

Labelle, Yván, 101n
Lacerda, Carlos, 72
LAFTA, 224, 235
Lagos, Gustavo, 291
Laird, Melvin R., 256n
Lamore, Jean, 225n
language instruction: France, 131, 133-135, 138n; Germany, 138-139; United Kingdom, 141; United States, 149
Lapalena, 233
LaPalombara, J., 127n
LATIN, 156
Latin America: and Africa, 106-109, 119; debt servicing, 254n; dependency, 261n; domestic capital, 290n, 292n; exploitation, 289-291; foreign investments in, 40-47, 224, 227, 229-230, 234, 235, 238, 252-53; foreign nationals in, 80, 81-84, 87; hyperpolitization of, 288-289; income growth, 254n, interest in non-U.S. relations, 65-66; internal security, 23-24, 232n, 238-241 *passim*, 256, 264; leverage, 120, 277-278, 281-282; migration policy, 90; priesthood, 101-102; public sector, 37n, 129, 285n, 286; social structure, 288-291; trade balances, 34, 35n, 36, 37-38; trade, decline in, 34-35; trade diversification, 32, 33, 36-37; and United Nations, 54-57; and World War I and World War II, 51, 52. *See also subject and country entries*
"Latin America," 114, 209, 223
Latin American Free Trade Area, 224, 235
Latin American Institute of the USSR, 240n
Latin American potential, 36, 57-59, 259n

Latin American students abroad: 145n; in France, 136-136, 142n; in Germany, 139; in Great Britain, 142; in Italy, 143n; in Spain, 145n; in UAR, 147; in U.S., 150; in USSR, 146
latinidad, 52, 113-114
latinité, see latinidad
League of Nations, 51-52, 54, 145n
Leff, Nathaniel H., 285n
Legris, Michel, 7n
Leitão da Cunha, Vasco, 68, 182
Leites, Nathan, 214n
Leoni, Raúl, 5
leverage: 13, 15, 36, 37-38, 72-75, 120, 178-180, 249; failure of U.S. leverage, 63n, 275-281. *See also* bargaining; diplomacy; influence
Levi, Arrigo, 70n
Ley de Residencia, 84
Lipset, S. M., 91n
Little Corn Island, 12
Little, I. M. D., 182n, 193n, 214n
Lleras Restrepo, Carlos, 65, 117, 271
Llorens, Vicente, 99n
Lloyds and Bolsa International Bank Limited, 249n
"Lobster War," 13, 217
Lodge, George C., 75n
Logue, Ruth, 284n
long-term and short-term programs, 298-300
Lowenthal, Abraham F., 264n
"low profile," 273
Luebke, Heinrich, 196
Lyon, Margot, 21n

Makarios, Archbishop, 68, 196, 219
Maldonado, General, 264n
Malraux, André, 113, 114
Malvinas Islands, *see* Falkland Islands
managerial temperament: 261-263, 273n, 280, 299, 302; its responses to failure, 272-275. *See also* tutelary style
Mannesmann, 47n, 228
Mantaro Dam, 47-48, 49
MAP, *see* United States, military assistance
Marcha, 9, 231n
Margrethe, Princess (Denmark), 196, 197
Martí Bufill, Carlos, 91n, 96n
Martin, Paul, 58, 61n, 190, 191
Martínez Moreno, Raúl S., 6n
Martinique, 7, 121n
Martorell, Guillermo, 285n
Marx, Karl, 289n

Mathews, Roy A., 61n
Mau, James A., 107n
Maullin, Richard, 101n, 264n
Mazrui, Ali and Molly, 134n
mediation, *see* arbitration
Médici, Emílio G., 14
Meeker, Guy B., 247n
Meggers, Betty J., 105n
Mellon National Bank and Trust Company, 249n
"Mexicanization," 251
Mexico: 140, 185n, 267; aid, 161; and British Honduras, 6n; cultural activities of foreign powers in, 134n, 140, 141, 145n, 153, 157; diplomatic missions received, 199, 200, 202; early contacts with China and Japan, 105-106; and East Germany, 228n; fishing and territorial waters, 12, 13, 15; foreign investments in, 42, 251; and France, 294; income growth, 254n; joint ventures, 251; migrants, 80, 81, 293; public sector, 286; Soviet diplomats expelled, 265; and Spain, 3n, 98-99, 109-110, 145n, 236-237; state enterprises, 286; state visit, 196; students abroad, 145n, 156n; trade, 33n, 35n, 244, 277; and Treaty of Tlatelolco, 31; U.S. intervention, 289n, 294
Mexico-U.S. Fisheries Agreement, 13, 15
Meyriat, Jean, 46n, 66n, 67n, 87n, 121n
Michener, James A., 110n
Michiko, Princess, 196
migrants: descendents, 85-86; economic benefits from, 90-96, 289; effect on book imports, 152-153; flows, 86-90; foreign born, 80, 81; inter-American 293n; national origins, 83, 86-90; naturalization, 80, 81, 82-84; political effects of, 97-103; remittances, 95-96
military assistance, *see* United States, military assistance
military attachés, 202n
military coups and military sales, 268n
military forces, 9, 11, 25, 27n
military missions, 11, 26, 27, 101n, 175, 191, 232, 264n
military sales, *see* Europe *and under countries*
Military Sales Act, 13
military training, 175-176
Mills, C. Wright, 211n
Miró, Joan, 144
Mitsubishi, 47n

models for Latin America, 126-130
Mongolian spot, 105
Monk, Abraham, 185n
Monticelli, Giuseppe, 84n, 85n, 89n
Montserrat, 4
Mora, José A., 130n
Mora y Araujo, Manuel, 68n
Moreas, Octavio de, 85n
Moreira, Adriano, 99n, 112n
moshav, 130
motion picture exports, 157
Mozambique, 29, 161
Muller, Hilgard, 68, 69
multinational corporations, 247-249
Munro, Dana G., 74n

Nasser, Gamal Abdel, 198, 218
National Front governments (Colombia), 253n
nationalization, *see* expropriation
national security interests, 18-20, 22-29, 177-178, 261. *See also under countries*
nativism, 110
NATO, 19, 61
naval exercises, 27
Nazism, 18, 85, 97n, 100, 216, 260
Neiva, Artur Hehl, 79n, 82n, 89n
Nepal, 186
Neruda, Pablo, 146
Netherlands: 65, 243; advocacy of Latin American interests, 122, 124; aid, 164, 171n, 186, 189; and Cuba, 73; diplomatic representation, 203; investments, 42, 43, 44, 45, 238; territorial problems, 3, 5n, 8-9, 9-10; trade, 34, 35n, 237, 245n; and Treaty of Tlatelolco, 29
New Caledonia, 7, 64n
newspapers, *see* press
New Zealand, 16, 186, 194n
nickel, 64n
Niedergang, Marcel, 229n
Nigeria, 10n, 29, 284
Nixon, Richard M.: 10, 172n, 177, 279n; on hemispheric unity, 69, 117; Latin American criticism of, 278; Latin American trip, 1958, 198; on Latin American universities, 211; and U.S. aid, 165, 180, 189, 194, 273n; and U.S. intervention, 208
Nkrumah, Kwame, 296
Normano, J. F., 93n, 98n, 114n, 154n, 283n
Norway, 16, 171n, 194n, 196, 197
nuclear non-proliferation pact, 31
nuclear power plants, 48

nuclear tests, *see* France; Treaty of Tlatelolco

OAS: 18, 27, 65, 110, 144; and Barbados, 10; and Canada, 61-62; and Cuba, 24; and Ecuador, 281; and Israel, 130; and Jamaica, 10, 61n, 103; and Trinidad-Tobago, 10
Occidental Petroleum, 252
ODCA, 20
Oder-Neisse Line, 266n
OECD, 123, 164, 193-194, 276
Ohara, Yoshinori, 45n, 71n
Ohlin, Goran, 165n, 171n, 182n, 184n, 189n
oil, 7, 69, 74, 75, 179, 180, 237, 243, 245, 247, 249, 250, 251n, 252
Olaf, King of Norway 196, 197
Olinto, Antonio, 107n
Oliver, Covey T., 58
O'Mara, Richard, 17n
Onganía, Juan Carlos, 38, 259
OPANAL, 31
Operación España, 144
OPIC, *see* Overseas Private Investment Corporation
Organismo para la proscripción de las armas nucleares en la América Latina, 31
Organization of African Unity, 108
Organization of American States, *see* OAS
Organization for Economic Cooperation and Development, *see* OECD
Oswald, J. Gregory, 23n, 240n, 265n
Overseas Cooperation Volunteers, 216
Overseas Private Investment Corporation, 250, 252

Padellaro, Giuseppe, 143n
Padilla, Heberto, 137, 231n
Pahlevi, Mohammed Reza, Shah of Iran, 196
Pakistan, 184n, 193
Palacio, Léo, 100n
Palewski, Jean-Paul, 26n, 191n, 231n
Palmerston, Lord, 66
Panama: 11, 15, 49, 147, 254n, 286; aid, 170, 175, 180, 188n; diplomatic representation received, 199, 200; trade, 244
Panama Canal, 11, 69n
Panama Canal Zone, 11, 27, 30, 175
Pan-American Health Organization, 62
Papal Volunteers for Latin America (PAVLA), 168, 170

Paraguay: 54n, 142n, 170n; bilinguality, 290n; diplomatic missions received, 200; sugar quota, 278n; trade, 244
Parenti, G., 93n
Parkinson, Fred, 19n
Parry Committee, 62, 142
Partido Socialista Popular (Cuba), 229n
patron-client relations, 185-188
Paul VI, 189, 196
Peace Corps, *see* U.S. Peace Corps
Pelly Amendment, 13, 179, 276
Pelly, Thomas, M., 12n, 278, 279n
Pengel, Johan Adolf, 9
Pepin, Jean-Luc, 237n
Pérez Jiménez, Marcos, 79n
Pérez Ramirez, Gustavo, 101n
Perón, Juan Domingo, 236, 255
Peru: 69, 196, 219, 232, 240, 254n, 257, 286; aid, 168, 170, 174n; and Andean Pact, 251; conflicts with U.S., 170n, 175, 179, 180-181, 271; cultural activities of foreign powers in, 135, 141, 145n, 152, 153, 157; diplomatic missions received, 199, 200; earthquake relief, 298; foreign debt, 255; investments in, 42, 252-253; and Italy, 48, 49, 104; and Japan, 104-105, 225; Mantaro Dam, 47-48, 49; military missions in, 26; military training, 26; public sector, 285n; and Spain, 109; territorial waters, 12, 15; trade, 33n, 244
Pestieau, Carolyn, 59n
Peterson Report, 172n
Petras, James, 91n
Philip, André, 186n
Philip, Prince, Duke of Edinburgh, 196, 198
Phillips Electric, 252
Picasso, Pablo, 144
Pigasse, Jean-Paul, 36n
Pin, Emile, 101n
Pincus, John, 164
Pizarro, Francisco, 109
Plank, John, 259n
Platt, D. C. M., 62n, 66n, 70n, 205n
Plaza Lasso, Galo, 65, 160
Poher, Alain, 172n
Poland, 115
political hypertrophy, 288
political motives in economic decisions, 286-288
political rhetoric, 19, 57, 166n, 211-212, 271, 283n

Pompidou, Georges, 67n, 133, 158n, 190
Popov, V., 129n
Poppino, Rollie E., 239n
population control, 293n
population growth and aid, 293
population and revolution, 293n
Portugal: 65, 152, 153, 161, 186; and Brazil, 28-29, 111n, 112-113, 237; migrants, 79, 82, 83, 84, 85n, 89, 90, 91, 94, 95, 96; national security, 28; political objectives, 55; trade, 34n, 237
Prado, Manuel, 113
Prentice, Reg, 190n, 255n
press, 22, 142, 155-156, 271
prestige, 230, 258, 298. *See also* public opinion
profit rates, 247
Project Camelot, 262n
protection of nationals, 71-75. *See also* migrants
Proust, Marcel, 113
Proxmire, William, 175n
public opinion, 188-190, 258, 298. *See also* prestige
Puerto Rico, 11, 30, 293
Pujol, Alain, 100n
Pye, Lucien, 214n

Quadros, Jânio, 55, 107
Quechua, 214
Quipano, Carlos, 231n
Quita Sueño Bank, 12

Radio Havana, 149n
Radio Moscow, 140, 147, 149n
Radio Peking, 140, 147, 149n
Raphael, Gideon, 218n
Rastafarians, 107
Ratcliffe, Alexander L., 195n
Ratcliffe, C. Tait, 175n, 179n
Ratliff, William E., 147n
Rauta, I., 188n
remittances, 95-96
Renault, 49, 64, 249, 286
reparation payments, 187
restitution of confiscated property, 72-73
Reuters, 142, 156
reverse preferences, 121, 122, 124
Reynaud, Paul, 217n
Rhodesia, 55
Riemens, 145n
Rivers, Julian P. H., 111n
Roback, S. H., 245n
Robinson, David, R., 12n, 30n

Rockefeller, Nelson A., 117, 198, 204, 210
Rodman, Selden, 109n, 280n, 293n
Rodrigues, José Honorio, 96n, 107n, 151n
Rogers, William P., 30n
Rojas, Patricio, 160
Roncador Bay, 12
Ronning, C. Neale, 176n
Roper, Penelope, 41n, 50n, 94n, 224n, 230n, 235n, 245n, 272n
Rosas, Juan Manuel, 115n
Rostow, Walt W., 205
Rout, Leslie B., Jr., 5n
Royal Dutch Shell, 249
royalty, visits of, 195-196, 197
Rubin, Joan, 290n
Rubottom, R. Richard, Jr., 115n, 150n
Rumania, 50, 66
Rusk, Dean, 116

Saba, 3n
Sable, Martin H., 240n
St. Eustatius, 3n
St. Kitts-Nevis-Anguilla, 4
St. Maarten, 3n
St. Martin, 3n
St. Patrick's Battalion, 115
Sakura Maru, 39
Salcedo, Danilo, 298n
Salisbury, Robert Arthur Cecil, Earl of, 204, 207
Sánchez Vásquez, Adolpho, 136n
Sanders, Thomas G., 85n
Sanz de Santa María, Carlos, 160
São Paulo-Rio Grande Railway Company, 72
Saragat, Giuseppe: 104, 115, 119, 196; and Instituto Italo-Latinoamericano, 143; on Latin American potential, 57; Latin American visit, 102, 185, 197, 198, 236n; and "triangular policy," 19-20, 24, 143
Sato, Eisaku, 90, 189, 225n
Saudi Arabia, 237
Scandinavia: shipping conflict with Brazil, 238; trade, 237. See also under countries
Scelle, Georges, 52n
Scheel, Walter, 181n, 192n
Schlootz, Johannes, 140n
Schmitt, Peter A., 142n
scholarships, see Latin American students abroad
Schwartzman, Simon, 68n
Scobie, James R., 95n, 292n
Scott, Winfield, 115

Segal, Aaron, 10n, 11n, 55n, 161n
Segundo, Jean-Louis, 288n, 289n
selection of political personnel, 299n, 301n
Sender, Ramón S., 144
Senegal, 29, 68n
Senghor, Léopold Sédar, 68n, 196
Sepúlveda, Orlando, 298n
Serrana, 12
Serranilla Banks, 12
"the Seventy-Seven," 66, 122
Sharp, Mitchell, 60, 73, 259n
Shazar, Zalman, 196, 218n
Shearer, Hugh L., 10, 107
Shell Oil, 7
Siemens, 48, 67
Silvert, Kalman H., 263n
Simca, 249
Simmonds, Kenneth, 245n
Singer, J. David, 199n
Small, Melvin, 199n
Social Democrats (Germany), 21
social engineering, 261-262
Socialist Internationale, 20
Société Sofrelec, 231n
Solano López, Francisco, 142n
Solari, Aldo, 91n
Sollie, Finn, 17n
South Africa: 27, 238; aid, 185, 194n; distance from Latin America, 68, 69; national security, 28; political objectives, 55, 60, 218; and South Atlantic Treaty Organization, 28
South Atlantic Treaty Organization, 28
SOUTHCOM, 11
Southhampton, 67
South Korea, 19n, 147
sovereignty, see territorial issues; territorial waters
Soviet Union: 13, 16, 17, 23, 65, 281; aid, 169, 183-184, 269; aid, Soviet and U.S. styles compared, 213, 214n; and Argentine nuclear power plant, 48n; barter vs. hard currency payments, 215; cold war, 22, 26; conflict with Cuba, 281n; conflicts with Latin American states, 266; construction offers, 50; cultural diplomacy, 146-147, 155, 157; diplomatic representation, 25, 200, 202-203, 238-239, 241, 265; diplomatic style, 214-215, 265; distance from Latin America, 67, 295; ideological advantages, 295; intervention, 265; as model, 127, 128-129; and Nuclear Non-Proliferation Treaty, 31n; ob-

Soviet Union (Continued)
jectives, economic, 53, 241-242;
objectives, political, 53, 54n, 238,
260-261; prestige, 258n; results, economic, 241-242; results, political,
238-241; rivalry with France in
Cuba, 230n; trade, 32, 33n, 34, 241-
242; trade accords, 215; trade fairs,
39; and Treaty of Tlatelolco, 30, 31;
and 200-mile limit, 266
Spain: 6, 13, 27, 49, 66, 176, 186,
295; aid, 63; book exports, 151, 152,
153; conflicts with Latin America,
294; and Cuba, 103, 235, 237, 287;
cultural diplomacy, 144-146, 157;
diplomatic relations, 237; double
nationality, 111; and Gibraltar, 52,
55, 236; "H" program, 63; and
League of Nations, 145n; migrants,
79, 82, 83, 84, 87, 89, 99n, 101,
235; migrants, economic benefits
from, 91, 95, 96; migrants, political
effects of, 97, 98-99, 103; military
sales, 256; national security, 28; official visits, 236n; objectives, 52, 54-
55, 63; results, economic, 235; results, political, 236-237; tensions
with Mexico, 3n, 99, 109-110, 145n,
236-237; ties with Latin America,
110-112; trade, 32-38 passim, 65,
235; and United Nations, 149, 236
Spanish-Arabic Center, 148
Sputnik, 298
Stalin, Joseph, 239
Stalin Peace Prizes, 146
Standard Oil Company (New Jersey),
249
"stand still" commitment, 268
state enterprises, 249n, 284-287
Stepan, Alfred, 101n
Stepanov, Lev, 53n, 183n
Stewart, Michael, 25n, 284
Stoph, Willi, 228
strategic doctrine, 19
Strover, Anthony J., 23n, 265n
students, see Latin American students
abroad
styles of diplomacy, see diplomacy
Suaréz, Andrés, 73n
sugar, 10, 225n, 277, 278n
Sukarno, Achmed, 296
Surinam, 3, 5n, 8, 45
Swan Island, 11, 12n
Sweden: 47, 171n, 194n; advocacy of
Latin American interest, 119, 123n;
and Cuba, 238n; diplomatic repre-
sentation, 203; investments, 41, 238;

military sales, 27, 256n; official
visit, 196; shipping conflict with
Brazil, 123n; trade, 32, 34, 160, 238n
Swift de la Plata, 252
Switzerland: advocacy of Latin Ameri-
can interests, 124; aid, 166n, 173,
177, 194n; construction interest in
Latin America, 49; investments, 43,
44, 238; trade, 32, 34, 35, 237
Symington Amendment, 179, 276
Syria, 218
Szyszlo, Fernando, 293n

Tahiti, 68
Taiwan, 161, 280n
Tanzania, 186
tariffs, see reverse preferences; trade
preferences
Tartu, 217
TASS, 156
tax incentives, 39
technical personnel, see managerial
temperament
Tendler, Judith, 43n
territorial issues: 3-12, 16-17, 275; and
aid, 186-187. See also Antarctica;
fishing conflicts, territorial waters
territorial waters, 12-16, 184n, 266.
See also fishing conflicts
Third World: 135n, 139, 154; and
Canadian aid policy, 61; competition
within, 108, 121-122; Soviet views
of, 129; support of Spain in UN, 55;
trade preferences for, 122-124
Thorp, Willard L., 254n
tied aid, see aid
Tietze, Christopher, 82n
Tigner, James Lawrence, 60n
Tisserant, Eugene Cardinal, 109n
Tokman, Victor E., 165n
tolerance for unsettled issues, 275
Torres, José, 257
trade: between Latin America and industrial nations, 32-34; decline in
importance of Latin American trade,
33, 34, 35n; diversification of Latin
American trade relations, 32, 36,
276; export and import distributions,
33, 34, 245n; export campaigns of
industrial countries, 36, 38, 39; generated by aid and investment, 284;
and migrants, 91-93; nonhemispheric
competition with the U.S., 37, 38;
state control of, 282-288; trade balances of industrial countries, 33, 35,
37, 38, 282; trade incentives of in-

dustrial countries, 35, 36. *See also EEC and country entires*
trade fairs, 39
trade preferences, 121-122
translations published in Latin America, 153
Treaty for the Prohibition of Nuclear Weapons in Latin America, *see* Treaty of Tlatelolco
Treaty of Rio de Janeiro, 24n
Treaty of Rome, 120
Treaty of Tlatelolco, 23, 29-31, 230
Triangular Policy, 20, 24, 143
Tricontinental, 22
Tricontinental Congress, 266
Trinidad-Tobago, 4, 10, 15, 103n
Trudeau, Pierre, 60, 61, 204
Turkey, 28, 55, 219, 238
Turner, Louis, 286n
tutelary style, 180, 206-210, 273, 289n. *See also* managerial temperament; United States, diplomatic style

UAR: 55, 147-148, 238; *ad hoc* diplomacy, 218; and Brazil, 29; cultural diplomacy, 147n; diplomatic missions received, 200; national security, 28
UNCTAD I, 53, 121, 276
UNCTAD II, 53, 121, 122, 123, 126, 193, 276
UNESCO, 149
United Kingdom: 10, 72; advocacy of Latin American interest, 119, 121, 122; aid, 154, 163, 164, 171, 172, 173n, 189, 192; aid to Commonwealth, 186, 188; aid, volunteer services, 141, 168; book exports, 152, 153, 154; conflict of objectives, 265-266; construction projects, 47, 48, 49; cultural diplomacy, 140-143, 147n, 155, 157; debt repayments, 255n; diplomatic representation, 199, 200, 201, 203; diplomatic style, 70, 204-206, 218; distance from Latin America, 66-67; and EEC, 10; embargo of Argentine meat, 7, 233, 281; expropriation of property, 72; and Gibraltar, 52, 55; investments, 40-46 *passim,* 234; migrants, 83, 87, 92-93; military sales, 22, 234, 255, 256; military training, 26; official visits, 196, 198; political objectives, 52, 59-60, 62, 63, 70; prestige, 258n; results, economic, 231-232; results, political, 233-234; support of U.S., 25n; territorial questions, 3-7 *pas-*

sim, 16-17, 22, 198, 233, 275; trade, 32, 33, 34, 35n, 234, 245n, 297; trade fair, 39; and Treaty of Tlatelolco, 29, 30; and United Nations, 9, 55n
United Nations: 28, 98, 149, 190, 266; and Arab-Israeli conflict, 56, 184, 231; Brazil in UN peace forces, 29n; Brazilian support of Portugal, in, 29; and British Caribbean states, 9; international volunteer corps, 169; Latin America in Security Council, 54n; Latin American membership, 56; Latin American support of U.S. in, 18; regional blocs in, 56-57; solicitation of Latin American votes in, 53-56, 238, 277; and Spain, 54, 55, 236; Special Committee on Colonialism, 9, 55; and Treaty of Tlatelolco, 30, 31n
United Nations Conference on Trade and Development, *see* UNCTAD I; UNCTAD II
United Nations Development Program, 57, 173
United States: 6, 53, 286n; *ad hoc* political action, 219-220; advocacy of Latin American interests, 122-125; aid, 162-167 *passim,* 188n, 292; aid, economic uses of, 173n, 192-194, 283; aid, evaluations of, 253-254; aid, multilateral, 171-173; aid, political uses of, 177-181, 185; aid, public support for, 188; aid, Soviet and U.S. styles, 214; aid, tied, 193-194; aid, volunteer services, 170-171; conflicts, 11, 12, 175, 267; conflicts, fishing, 12, 13, 16, 257; as creditor, 255; cultural diplomacy, 147n, 148-151, 152, 154, 155, 157; diplomatic representation, 101n, 199-204 *passim,* 209n; diplomatic style, 75, 180, 205-211, 213-214, 219, 273, 279, 289n; and EEC, 122-124; embargo of Cuba, 24, 25, 246, 257; expropriation, 73-74, 245-253; influence and prestige, 23, 258, 259n, 275-276, 279-280; interventions, 18, 25, 27, 74-75, 179-181, 207-208, 210, 261, 264, 294; intragovernmental conflict, 73, 124, 179, 267-270, 276; investment, 40-43 *passim,* 245-253; investment, distribution, 42, 43n, 44, 46, 47, 251n; lack of affinities, 115-118; and League of Nations, 52; leverage, failure of, 275-281; and the managers, 261-263; migrants, 101; mili-

United States (Continued)
tary assistance, 26, 27, 174-176, 202, 247, 255-257; military missions, 26n, 101n, 175, 264n; military presence, 27; military sales, 13, 174-175, 255n, 256, 268; models for Latin America, 130; national security, 23, 25, 177-178, 295; official visits, 196, 198, 210; political objectives, 58, 74-75, 260-261, 264; political results, 253-259; pressure on nonhemispheric powers, 62-66; protection of nationals, 73-75; proximity to Latin America, 66-67, 68n, 69, 295; responses to failure, 272-273; territorial questions, 11-12, 17; trade, 32-37 *passim*, 243-245; and Treaty of Tlatelolco, 29-30, 31; tutelary style, 180, 206-210, 273, 289n; and United Nations, 55n; at UNCTAD, 122-123

U.S. AID: 208n, 250n, 280; administrative reform, 273n; mission personnel, 178, 202, 209n, 213; seeks public support, 193; and Title IX, 179, 207; untying loans, 194; and World Bank credits, 172. *See also* Alliance for Progress; United States, aid

U.S. Chamber of Commerce, 211n

U.S. Congress: 160; conflict with administration, 124, 179, 267-270, 276; and economic aid, 162, 179, 189, 268, 280n; and military assistance, 175, 268-269

U.S. Department of the Army, 262n

U.S. Department of Commerce, 246, 252, 270

U.S. Department of Defense, 175, 202

U.S. Export-Import Bank, 75, 175, 193, 270

U.S. Foreign Assistance Acts, 73, 179, 207

U.S. Foreign Claims Settlement Commission, 246n

U.S. Information Agency, 141, 148-149, 155, 202, 209n, 215

U.S. International Development Corporation, 273n

U.S. International Development Institute, 273n

U.S. International Executive Service Corps, 171

U.S.-Mexican War, 115

U.S. Peace Corps: 101, 168, 169, 215, 216; growth and distribution, 170, 209n; selection policy, 170, 213

U.S. Southern Command, 11

U.S. State Department: administration, 209, 263; and fishing conflicts, 13, 16, 279; "soft line," 75, 270, 279n

U.S. Sugar Act of 1971, 278n

U.S. Treasury Department, 279n

University of Costa Rica, 147

University of London, 142

unpredictability, 296-300

UPI, 156

Upper Volta, 196

Upton, T. Graydon, 227n, 251n

uranium, 23

Uruguay: 15, 27, 82n, 239n, 286; aid, 170n, 184; cultural activities of foreign powers in, 154; diplomatic representation received, 199, 200, 203, 204; income growth, 254n; Jewish population, 185n; official visits, 196, 219; public opinion on U.S., 258; Soviet relations, 184n, 203, 241

Uruguayan Institute of Public Opinion, 258

USIA, *see* U.S. Information Agency

U Thant, 169, 196

Vagts, Alfred, 202n

Valdés, Gabriel, 127

Valdivia, Angel, 181

Valencia, Guillermo León, 65

Valkenier, Elizabeth K., 129n

Vanoni Plan, 127

Vekeman, Roger, 288n

Véliz, Claudio, 19n, 42n, 46n, 54n, 66n, 98n, 121n, 183n

Venezuela: 13, 15, 218, 232n, 239n, 241, 267; cultural activities of foreign powers in, 135, 145n, 152, 153, 156n, 157; diplomatic missions received, 199, 200; and Guyana, 5; investments in, 42; migrants, 79n, 80, 81; public sector, 285n; trade, 35n, 244

Vernant, Jacques, 133n

Victoria-Minas Company, 72

Vietnam, 19n

Vincent, Jack E., 57n

Virgin Islands, 30

Visión, 66n

visits, official, 62, 65-66, 195-198. *See also under countries*

VOA, 140, 147n, 149

Volsky, V. V., 240n

Volunteers for International Technical Assistance (VITA), 171

von Brentano, Heinrich, 181

von Gleich, Albrecht, 20n, 44n, 51n, 97n, 100n, 138n, 140n, 156n, 270n

318

von Humboldt, Alexander, 139n

Wagatsuma, Hiroshi, 105n
Wakaisumi, Kei, 71n
Warner, Malcolm, 157n
Washington Post, 271
Weber, Max, 211n
Western Samoa, 186
West Germany, *see* Federal Republic of Germany
Whitaker, Arthur, 54n, 110n
White, John, 187n, 192n, 213n, 262n, 282n
Whitehead, Laurence, 254n
Willems, Emilio, 86n, 98n
Willemstad, 8
Wilson, Harold, 10, 25n
Wirth, John D., 59n
Wohlstetter, Albert, 69n
Wolf, Charles, Jr., 253n
Wood, Bryce, 74n

Wood, David, 25n, 27n
World Bank: and multilateral aid, 172, 181, 192; proposed investment insurance agency, 248n
World Confederation of Democratic Youth, 169
World Court of Justice, *see* International Court of Justice
World War I, 51, 52
World War II, 18, 19, 26, 29n, 52, 55, 70, 72, 110, 115
WUCD, 20

Yameogo, Maurice, 196
Ycaza Tigerino, Julio, 117n
Yepes, J. M., 111n

Zabola Ortiz, Miguel Angel, 19n
Zambia, 68, 196
Zavala, Silvio, 24n
Zinger, Harry, 129n

SELECTED LIST OF RAND BOOKS

Bellman, Richard E., and Stuart E. Dreyfus. *Applied Dynamic Programming.* Princeton University Press, Princeton, New Jersey, 1962.

Bretz, Rudy. *A Taxonomy of Communication Media.* Educational Technology Publications, Englewood Cliffs, New Jersey, 1971.

Dantzig, George B. *Linear Programming and Extensions.* Princeton University Press, Princeton, New Jersey, 1963.

Davies, Merton, and Bruce Murray. *The Space View: Photographic Exploration of the Planets.* Columbia University Press, New York, 1971.

Downs, Anthony. *Inside Bureaucracy.* Little Brown and Company, Boston, Massachusetts, 1967.

Dreyfus, Stuart. *Dynamic Programming and the Calculus of Variations.* Academic Press, Inc., New. York, 1965.

Fisher, G. *Cost Considerations in Systems Analysis.* American Elsevier Publishing Company, New York, 1970.

Goldhamer, Herbert, and Andrew W. Marshall. *Psychosis and Civilization.* The Free Press, Glencoe, Illinois, 1953.

Hammond, Paul Y., and Sidney S. Alexander (eds.). *Political Dynamics in the Middle East.* American Elsevier Publishing Company, New York, 1971.

Hirshleifer, Jack, James C. DeHaven, and Jerome W. Milliman. *Water Supply: Economics, Technology, and Policy.* The University of Chicago Press, Chicago, Illinois, 1960.

Hitch, Charles J., and Roland McKean. *The Economics of Defense in the Nuclear Age.* Harvard University Press, Cambridge, Massachusetts, 1960.

Horelick, Arnold L., and Myron Rush. *Strategic Power and Soviet Foreign Policy.* The University of Chicago Press, Chicago, Illinois, 1966.

Johnson, John J. (ed.). *The Role of the Military in Underdeveloped Countries.* Princeton University Press, Princeton, New Jersey, 1962.

Leites, Nathan. *A Study of Bolshevism.* The Free Press, Glencoe, Illinois, 1953.

Leites, Nathan. *On the Game of Politics in France*. Stanford University Press, Stanford, California, 1959.

Leites, Nathan, and C. Wolf. *Rebellion and Authority*. Markham Publishing Company, Chicago, Illinois, 1970.

Liu, Ta-Chung, and Kung-Chia Yeh. *The Economy of the Chinese Mainland: National Income and Economic Development, 1933–1959*. Princeton University Press, Princeton, New Jersey, 1965.

Nelson, Richard R., Merton J. Peck, and Edward D. Kalachek. *Technology, Economic Growth and Public Policy*. The Brookings Institution, Washington, D.C., 1967.

Nelson, Richard R., T. Paul Schultz, and Robert L. Slighton. *Structural Change in a Developing Economy: Colombia's Problems and Prospects*. Princeton University Press, Princeton, New Jersey, 1971.

Novick, David (ed.). *Program Budgeting: Program Analysis and the Federal Budget*. Harvard University Press, Cambridge, Massachusetts, 1965.

Pascal, Anthony. *Thinking About Cities: New Perspectives on Urban Problems*. Dickenson Publishing Company, Belmont, California, 1970.

Pincus, John A. *Economic Aid and International Cost Sharing*. The Johns Hopkins Press, Baltimore, Maryland, 1965.

Robinson, Thomas W. (ed.), et al. *The Cultural Revolution in China*. University of California Press, Berkeley, California, 1971.

Sharpe, William F. *The Economics of Computers*. Columbia University Press, New York, 1969.

Speier, Hans. *Divided Berlin: The Anatomy of Soviet Political Blackmail*. Frederick A. Praeger, Inc., New York, 1961.

Stepan, Alfred. *The Military in Politics: Changing Patterns in Brazil*. Princeton University Press, Princeton, New Jersey, 1971.

Wolf, Charles, Jr. *Foreign Aid: Theory and Practice in Southern Asia*. Princeton University Press, Princeton, New Jersey, 1960.

Wolfe, Thomas W. *Soviet Power and Europe, 1945–1970*. The Johns Hopkins Press, Baltimore, Maryland, 1970.

321